Second Edition **The**

EVERYDAY
Writer

Andrea A. Lunsford
STANFORD UNIVERSITY

with a section for multilingual writers by

Franklin E. Horowitz
TEACHERS COLLEGE
COLUMBIA UNIVERSITY

BEDFORD / ST. MARTIN'S
Boston ◆ New York

For Bedford/St. Martin's

Executive Editor: Marilyn Moller
Developmental Editor: Kristin Bowen
Senior Production Editor: Shuli Traub
Senior Production Supervisor: Dennis J. Conroy
Art Director/Cover Design: Lucy Krikorian
Text Design: Anna George
Copy Editor: Judith Lechner
Composition: Monotype Composition
Printing and Binding: Quebecor/Kingsport

President: Charles H. Christensen
Editorial Director: Joan E. Feinberg
Editor in Chief: Nancy Perry
Director of Marketing: Karen R. Melton
Director of Editing, Design, and Production: Marcia Cohen
Managing Editor: Erica T. Appel

Library of Congress Catalog Card Number: 00-103337

Manufactured in the United States of America.
6 5 4 3 2
f e d

For information, write: Bedford/St. Martin's, 75 Arlington Street, Boston, MA 02116   (617-399-4000)

ISBN: 0-312-39911-1 (plastic comb)
        0-312-39909-X (spiral)

Acknowledgments

Acknowledgments and copyrights appear at the back of the book.

The
EVERYDAY
Writer

Visit *The Everyday Writer* Web site for up-to-the-minute information on writing and research, with interactive exercises, FAQs about writing online, advice on the twenty most common errors, and annotated links to some great Web sites for writers.

join us at <**http://www.bedfordstmartins.com/lunsford/everyday_writer**>.

How to Use This Book

Our goal in *The Everyday Writer* is to provide a "short and sweet" writing reference you can use easily on your own—at work, in class, even on the run. Small enough to tuck into a backpack or briefcase, this text has been designed to help you find information quickly, efficiently, and with minimal effort.

Ways into the book

- The *quick access menu* inside the front cover gives a quick list of the book's contents. Once you find the general topic you are looking for on the Quick Access Menu, it will point you to the section of the book in which you'll find more specific information. Turn then to that tabbed section, and check the menu on the tabbed divider for the exact page.
- The *index* lists everything covered in the book. You can find information by looking up a topic ("articles," for example) or, if you're not sure what your topic is called, by looking up the word you need help with (*a* or *the*).
- A *brief contents* on the inside back cover lists chapters and headings in detail.
- *Boxed editing tips* at the beginning of most chapters will help you check your drafts with a critical eye and edit as need be.
- *FAQs* (frequently asked questions) *about errors* are covered in the first tabbed section, with brief explanations, hand-edited examples, and cross references to other places in the book where you'll find more detail.
- *Documentation models* are easy to find in two tabbed sections—one for MLA style and the other for APA, CBE, and Chicago styles.
- *Tips for multilingual writers* appear in a separate tabbed section and in boxes throughout the book. You can also find a list of the topics covered, including language-specific tips, on the tabbed divider for that section.
- *Revision symbols* are listed in the back of the book. If your instructor uses these symbols to mark your drafts, consult this list.
- A *glossary of usage* (Chapter 37) gives quick advice on commonly confused and misused words.

We hope that this book will prove to be an everyday reference—and that these reference features will lead you quickly and easily to whatever information you need.

IN MEMORIAM

As this book goes to press, teachers and scholars of rhetoric and writing across the country are mourning the loss of Robert Connors, who died in an accident on June 22. Friends from graduate school days, Bob and I conceived *The St. Martin's Handbook* in 1984, and through the years we worked on a number of different projects together. Although Bob had decided to step away from these textbooks in order to focus his energies on his historical studies, his wit and wisdom remain central to the origins of our work together. The world feels smaller, and much sadder, without him.

Like its predecessor, *The Everyday Writer*, Second Edition, rests on two simple insights. First, writing surrounds us: it's not something we do just in school or on the job but something that is as familiar and everyday as a pair of worn sneakers or the air we breathe. I want to acknowledge this "everydayness" of writing and encourage users of this book to see, as Steve Martin does, that writing is *something they do every day*. Second, all learning, including learning to write, grows out of what we already know and understand, linking our "everyday" knowledge to something new—whether that something new is a form of punctuation, a sentence pattern, a stylistic choice, or a method of research. Thus *The Everyday Writer* speaks to students in everyday language about how to use what they already know to expand their writing repertoires.

The first edition of *The Everyday Writer* aimed to enact these two principles by providing a quick and simple reference that writers can easily use on their own. The overwhelmingly positive response of students and teachers to the first edition shows it hit the mark. The second edition builds on this success by continuing to offer advice about everyday writing tasks *in* everyday language and to focus on the ways technologies are forming and transforming much of the writing that we do. But the new edition does more, offering expanded coverage of online writing, multimedia, and oral presentations, and new chapters on Web design, argument, and "writing to the world." So read on—and see how *The Everyday Writer*, Second Edition, will provide just the kind of reference text today's students need.

Highlights

Attention to everyday language *in* everyday language. Each chapter opens with a brief example showing everyday use of that chapter's subject. Everyday language pervades the book, giving students clear, straightforward answers they can understand, with examples from school, from the workplace, and from home.

FAQs on the most common errors.   A "crisis-control" center provides practical answers to the most frequently asked questions (FAQs) about writing, with questions gleaned from nationwide research into student writing patterns and teacher responses to the writing of first-year college students. This study identified mistakes in the grammar, syntax, and use of standard written English that writers are most likely to make as well as the larger rhetorical concerns readers are most likely to comment on. This tabbed section opens the book in brief, everyday language and provides hand-edited examples to help students recognize and edit for these problem areas.

Boxed editing tips.   Detailed editing tips, usually at the beginning of each chapter, help students work with their own writing. All handbooks provide rules, but *The Everyday Writer* goes the extra step by providing tips to help students apply the rules to their own drafts.

Unique coverage of language.   Chapter 34, a chapter on language variety, helps students "shift language gears," as they often need to do, among ethnic, regional, occupational, and standard varieties of English; Chapter 32, a chapter on writing to the world, helps students face the challenge of communicating across cultures.

A complete section for multilingual writers.   Written by Franklin E. Horowitz of Teachers College, Columbia University, this section covers grammatical and rhetorical issues of concern to multilingual writers, including ESL writers. Boxed tips throughout the book offer advice on topics where ESL writers need extra help. Whenever possible the advice is language-specific, with special tips for twenty languages.

Special attention to matters of style.   Brief style boxes help writers with the kinds of stylistic choices they must make as they move among various communities, fields, jobs, and disciplines. New technology style boxes offer special tips for writing online—from netiquette advice to format guidelines for readable email.

Help with many common everyday writing tasks.   Today's writing tasks are many and varied, and *The Everyday Writer* offers help with some of the most important ones: email (Chapter 59), professional and business writing (Chapter 59), oral presentations (Chapter 57), multimedia presentations (Chapter 58), and collaboratively produced projects (Chapter 5).

New to this edition

An appealing new, full-color design. A more colorful design makes this edition even easier to use by highlighting key reference and navigational features.

Expanded coverage of design and new media. A new tabbed section about online writing and design includes extensive and down-to-earth guidelines on document design (Chapter 15), on working with graphics in print or online, and on designing and authoring Web texts (Chapter 16).

Crucial new advice about writing online. New technologies continue to offer challenges as well as enormously exciting opportunities for writers. As a result, this new edition offers practical advice about composing online throughout. In particular, the FAQs about writing online (Chapter 14) gather together practical answers to questions many students ask about conducting research and writing online. New technology style boxes offer practical online style tips throughout. A complete directory to advice on writing online appears at the end of the book. Finally, this edition provides the most current guidelines on using, evaluating, citing, and documenting Internet sources in MLA, APA, CBE, and Chicago styles.

A unique chapter on writing to the world. Chapter 32 offers practical advice to help students communicate effectively across cultures. By showing students that what seem to be their own "normal" rhetorical ways are not universal, not the *only* ways, and by giving examples from many different nations and cultures, this new chapter aims to get students thinking about how they can best reach, understand, and learn from people across cultures.

A new argument chapter. Chapter 9 includes guidelines for critical thinking, instruction on the basics of classic methods for developing an argument, an introduction to the Toulmin model, and a full student essay.

A new almanac and Web directory. This writer's reference offers facts, URLs guiding students to useful Web sites, and other reference materials from across the disciplines: metric conversion tables, population statistics, common symbols and formulas, a list of Nobel Prize winners in literature, and more.

A wider array of ancillaries

The Everyday Writer Online (available on CD-ROM for Windows and Macintosh)

Instructor's Notes, Andrea A. Lunsford and Vic Mortimer

Exercises for The Everyday Writer, Lex Runciman and Carolyn Lengel

Exercises for Multilingual Writers, Maria McCormack

The Everyday Writer Web Site <http://www.bedfordstmartins.com/lunsford/everyday_writer>

Exercise Central <http://www.bedfordstmartins.com/lunsford>

The Bedford Bibliography for Teachers of Writing, Fifth Edition, Patricia Bizzell and Bruce Herzberg

The New St. Martin's Guide to Teaching Writing, Cheryl Glenn and Robert Connors

The St. Martin's Manual for Writing in the Disciplines, Richard Bullock

Acknowledgments

The Everyday Writer has benefited from much wisdom, advice, and help from others. Of ongoing significance is the extensive collaboration I have enjoyed with Francine Weinberg, whose legendary abilities to condense and clarify helped me write a *brief* handbook; Kristin Bowen, whose fine work is evident on every single page; Marilyn Moller, who continues to be an editor *par excellence* as well as a very good and enormously generous friend; Shuli Traub, whose patience and organizational skills have helped me meet very tight deadlines; Priya Ratneshwar, who gave her thoughtful assistance in many matters, great and small; John X. Kim, who helped with the new almanac; Karen Melton, whose imaginative marketing sense has helped the book, I hope, reach a very wide audience; Lucy Krikorian, to whom I owe the *Print* magazine award-winning cover design; and Anna George, to whom I owe the wonderful interior design. For this edition, I have also had the benefit of Nancy Perry's support and, for the first time, the astute insights of Joan Feinberg and Chuck Christensen, publishers unparalleled in my experience!

I am also grateful to the students in my first-year writing classes; to my students and colleagues at the Bread Loaf School of English, whose incisive questions about *The New St. Martin's Handbook* and *The Everyday Writer* prompted especially strong revisions; to Melissa Goldthwaite, Jennifer Cognard-Black, Nikki Hamai, and Tracie Telling, all of whom have searched for elusive quotations and innumerable examples with intelligence and good cheer; to Frank Horowitz for his continuing meticulous work on the chapters for multilingual writers; to Heather Murphy, whose PowerPoint presentation appears in Chapter 58; to Todd English and his students Annette Goubeaux, Jennifer Kwok, James Ma, Michelle Oxner, and Vivi Puteri, whose Web-based project appears in Chapter 16; and especially to Heather Ricker, who composed the argument essay featured in Chapter 9. The work of these student writers adds strength and depth to the book.

I have benefited mightily from a group of particularly astute and helpful reviewers, including Kim van Alkemande, Shippensburg University; Tom Amorose, Seattle Pacific University; John Baugh, Stanford University; John Beard, Coastal Carolina University; Diane Belcher, The Ohio State University; Kristin Berkey-Abbott, Trident Technical College; Elizabeth D. Bernadin, University of South Carolina, Columbia; Anne Bliss, University of Colorado, Boulder; Paula Bostic, Montgomery College, Rockville; Melissa Bregenzer, Danville Area Community College; Michal Brody, University of Texas, Austin; William J. Carpenter, University of Kansas; Paul Cohen, Southwest Texas State University; Peter Concannon, Santa Fe Community College; Gail Corso, Neumann College; Dan Cross, Belleville Area College; Jonathan S. Cullick, University of Minnesota; Marsha Curtis, University of Massachusetts; Adam Davis, Truman State University; Helen Deese, University of California, Riverside; Christy Desmet, University of Georgia; Amy Devitt, University of Kansas; Heather Diefenderfer, Western Washington University; Cynthia Earle, New Hampshire College; Lisa Esch, Trident Technical College; Marcia Farr, University of Illinois at Chicago; Helen Fox, University of Michigan; Keysha Gamor, Montgomery College, Rockville; Maricela Garcia, South Texas Community College; Lucinda Garthwaite, University of New Hampshire; E. Laurie George, University of Washington; Jonathan C. Glance, Mercer University; Steve Gottlieb, Quinnipiac College; Anam Govardhan, Western Connecticut State University; Shelley Grice, Jamestown Community College; Laura Gurak, University of Minnesota; Marcia Peoples Halio, University of Delaware; Susanmarie Harrington, Indiana University–Purdue University, Indianapolis; Mary Hart, Laramie County Community College; Freda Hauser, University of New Hampshire; Vicki Holmsten, San Juan College; Lauri Howard, Georgia State University; John Hyman, American University; John Jebb, University of Delaware; Joan Karbach, Tri-State University; Beth Lana, Abilene Christian University; Glenda Stewart Langley, New Mexico Institute of Mining and Technology; Jon A. Leydens, Colorado

.

xii *Preface*

School of Mines; Carolyn Lord, North Seattle Community College; Karen Lunsford, University of Illinois at Urbana–Champaign; Richard Marback, Wayne State University; Maria McCormack, Columbia University; Nancy McCoy, Danville Area Community College; Heather J. McDonald, Daytona Beach Community College; Tracey Mead, College of St. Catherine; Patricia R. Menhart, Broward Community College; Robert Mundhenk, Northampton County Community College; Susan Myers, Portland Community College; Joyce Neff, Old Dominion University; John Norman, The Ohio State University; James O'Neil, Edison Community College; Stephanie Pelowski, University of Kansas; Robbie Pinter, Belmont University; George L. Pullman, Georgia State University; Katharine C. Purcell, Trident Technical College; Donna Qualley, Western Washington University; Doug Reitinger, University of Wyoming; Alexandra Rowe, University of South Carolina, Columbia; Jeff Schonberg, Angelo State University; Nancy Shankle, Abilene Christian University; Dawn Skorczewski, Emerson College; Carol Smith, Fort Lewis College; Lolly Smith, Everett Community College; Michael Strysick, Davidson College; Rafael Tapia, St. Augustine College; Sharon Thomas, Michigan State University; Charles Thomson, Laramie County Community College; Deborah Vause, York College of Pennsylvania; Deborah Viles, University of Colorado, Boulder; Susan Lewis-Wallace, Northwestern State University; Irwin Weiser, Purdue University; Phyllis West, El Camino Community College; Roger West, Trident Technical College; Jane Williams, Texarkana College; and Ruth Winn, Texarkana College. My thanks to them all.

Andrea A. Lunsford

Think for a moment about how important errors have been in your life. Remember when you first learned cursive writing—and how hard it was to make those loops and how many times you had to erase and start over? Or remember learning to use new software—and all the missteps you made along the way? Such mistakes provide the kind of trial and error necessary to all learning.

So it is for all writers. Even the best writers make errors, leaving out a word or an essential comma, writing *its* instead of *it's*. The good news is that we can learn to edit our writing and to correct our errors. The first three chapters of *The Everyday Writer* provide answers to the most frequently asked questions (FAQs) about writing. These guidelines will help you recognize, understand, revise—and learn from—the most common errors.

1

Broad Content Issues

As a writer, you are in some ways like a band leader. You must orchestrate all the elements of your writing into a persuasive performance, assembling your ideas, words, and evidence into one coherent structure. Most readers in North America expect you to be their guide—to help them understand your meaning. To meet these expectations, you must pay careful attention to several broad content issues: whether your purpose is clear, who your audience is, which points need to be fully established, and so on. Instructors reading college essays most often comment on these five content issues: (1) use of supporting evidence, (2) use of sources, (3) achievement of purpose, (4) attention to audience, and (5) overall impression. Look at the examples of such questions and comments in this chapter to help you understand responses to content issues that readers have to your own writing.

1a   Check your use of supporting evidence.

Effective writing needs to accomplish two basic goals: to make a claim and to prove it. Readers expect that a piece of writing will make one or more points clearly and will support those points with ample evidence—good reasons, examples, or other details. When you use evidence effectively, you help readers understand your point, making abstract concepts concrete and offering proof that what you are saying is sensible and worthy of attention. (In fact, this issue of supporting evidence is the one that readers in our research asked students about *most often,* accounting for 56 percent of all the comments we analyzed.) When readers make statements such as the following ones, they are referring to or questioning your use of supporting evidence:

> This point is underdeveloped.
>
> The details here don't really help me see your point.
>
> I'm not convinced—what's your authority?
>
> The three reasons you offer are very persuasive.
>
> Good examples. Can you offer more?

For more discussion of the use of good reasons, examples and precedents, and citing authority, see 9d and 9f. Providing supporting details in paragraphs is covered in 7b.

1b   Check your use of sources.

One important kind of supporting evidence comes from source materials. To back up the points you are making, you need to choose possible sources, evaluate them, and decide when to quote, when to summarize, and when to paraphrase them. Using sources competently not only helps support your claim but also builds your credibility as a writer: you demonstrate that you understand what others have to say about a topic and that you are fully informed about these varying perspectives. When readers make comments such as the following ones, they are referring to or questioning your use of sources:

> Only two sources? You need at least several more.
>
> Who said this?
>
> One of the clearest paraphrases I've seen of this crucial passage.
>
> Your summary leaves out three of the writer's main points.
>
> Your summary is just repetition—it doesn't add anything new.
>
> This quotation beautifully sums up your argument.
>
> Why do you quote at such length here? Why not paraphrase?
>
> You cite only sources that support your claim—citing one or two with differing views would help show me you've considered other opinions.

For further discussion of choosing, reading, and evaluating sources, see 12a–d; for more on quoting, paraphrasing, and summarizing, see 12e. Incorporating source materials in your text is covered in 13c.

1c Check to see that you achieve your purpose.

The purposes for writing vary widely. You might, for example, write to ask for a job interview, to send condolences, to summarize information for a test, or to trace the causes of World War II for an essay. In academic or professional writing, you need to pay careful attention to what an assignment asks you to do, noting particularly any key terms in the assignment, such as *analyze, argue, define,* and *summarize.* Such words are important if you are to meet the requirements of the assignment, stay on the subject, and achieve your purpose. Readers' questions such as the following often reveal how well you have achieved your purpose:

Why are you telling us all this?

What is the issue here, and what is your stand on it?

Very efficient and thorough discussion! You explain the content very clearly and thus reveal your understanding of the article.

Why simply give a lot of plot summary here—it does little to analyze character development.

For guidelines on considering purposes, see 4b.

1d Check your attention to audience.

All writing is intended to be read, even if only by the writer. The most effective writers are sensitive to readers' backgrounds, values, and needs. They pay attention to their audience by taking the time to define terms readers may not know, providing necessary background information, and considering readers' perspectives on and feelings about a topic. Following are some typical reader comments on audience:

Careful you don't talk down to your readers.

You've left me behind here. I can't follow.

Your level of diction is perfect for relating to the board of trustees.

I'm really enjoying reading this!

Don't assume everyone shares your opinion about this issue.

For guidelines on considering your audience, see 4c and Chapter 33.

1e   Check for overall impression.

When friends, colleagues, or instructors read your writing, they often give you information about the overall impression it makes, perhaps noting how it is improving or how it needs to be improved. You will do well to note such responses carefully and to analyze them to determine your strengths and weaknesses as a writer. Setting up a conference with a writing tutor or your instructor is one way to explore these general responses. Readers tend to comment on their overall impressions at the very beginning or the very end of an essay, saying things like this:

> I was looking for more critical analysis from you, and I've found it!
>
> Much improved over your last essay.
>
> Your grasp of the material here is truly impressive.
>
> What happened here? I can't understand your point in this essay.
>
> Good job—you've convinced me!

For more specific ways of assessing the overall impression your writing creates, see 8a and 8b.

2

Organization and Presentation

The most important or brilliant ideas in the world will have little effect on an audience if they are difficult to recognize, read, or follow. Indeed, research confirms that readers depend on writers to organize and present their material in ways that aid understanding. In regard to organization and presentation, the instructors in our study most often asked questions about or commented on these features, in order of frequency: (1) overall organization, (2) sentence structure and style, (3) paragraph structure, (4) format, and (5) documentation.

2a   Check the overall organization.

Readers expect a writer to provide organizational patterns and signals that will help them follow what the writer is trying to say. Sometimes such organizational cues are simple. If you are giving directions, for example, you might give chronological cues (first you do A, then B, and so on), and if you are describing a place, you might give spatial cues (at the north end is A, in the center is B, and so on). But complex issues often call for complex organizational patterns. For example, you may need to signal readers that you are moving from one problem to several possible solutions or that you are moving through a series of comparisons and contrasts. Here are some common teacher comments concerning organizational features:

> I'm confused here—what does this point have to do with the one before it?
>
> Your most important point is buried here in the middle. Why not move it up front?
>
> Organization here is chronological rather than topical; as a result, you summarize but do not analyze.
>
> How did we get here? You need a transition.
>
> Very clear, logical essay. A joy to read.

For more discussion on writing out a plan, see 6c. For more on effective patterns of development, see 7c; and on using transitions to aid organization, see p. 50.

2b Check sentence structure and style.

Effective sentences form the links in a chain of writing, guiding readers' understanding each step along the way. If you have never taken a close look at how well your sentences serve to guide your readers, spend a little time examining them now. How long do your sentences tend to be? Do you use strings of short sentences? Do your sentences flow logically from one thought to another, or do you make the reader work to figure out the connections between them? Do your long sentences confuse the reader or wander off the topic? How do your sentences usually begin? How do you link them to one another? Following are some typical questions about and comments on sentences:

> The pacing of your sentences here really keeps me reading—excellent variation of length and type.
>
> Can you combine sentences to make the logical connection explicit here?
>
> Your use of questions helps clarify this complex issue.
>
> This is not effective word order for a closing sentence—I've forgotten your main point. Can you find a better sentence?
>
> These sentences all begin with nouns—the result is a kind of dull clip-clop, clip-clop.

Too many short, simple sentences here. This reads like a grocery list rather than an explanation of a complex issue.

This sentence goes on forever—how about dividing it up?

For a more detailed discussion of sentence types, see Chapter 24. Sentence conciseness is covered in Chapter 22, and sentence variety in Chapter 23.

2c   Check paragraph structure.

Paragraph structure can help readers follow the thread of thought in a piece of writing. You may tend to paragraph by feel, so to speak, without thinking very much about paragraph structure as you write. In fact, the best time to examine your paragraphs is generally *after* you have completed a draft. Here are some typical readers' questions and comments about paragraphs:

Why the one- and two-sentence paragraphs? Elaborate!

Your introductory paragraph immediately gets my attention and gives an overview of the essay—good!

I can't follow the information in this paragraph. Can you reorder it?

What is the main idea of this paragraph?

Very effective ordering of details in this paragraph.

This paragraph skips around two or three points. It has enough ideas for three paragraphs.

For guidelines on editing paragraphs, see p. 40. For more detailed information on paragraph development in general, see Chapter 7.

2d   Check format.

An attractive, easy-to-read format makes a reader's job pleasant and efficient. Therefore, you should pay close attention to the physical presentation of your materials and to the visual effect they create. Part of your job as a writer is to know what format is most appropriate for a particular task. In the research conducted for this book, readers made the following kinds of comments about format:

You need a title, one that gets across your meaning.

Why use this tiny single-spaced type? It is almost impossible to read.

Number pages—these were not in the right order.

Your headings helped me follow this report. Why not use subheadings?

For more discussion of format, see Chapter 15 on document design.

2e Check documentation.

Any writing that uses source materials requires careful documentation—in-text citations, endnotes, or footnotes; lists of works cited or bibliographies—to guide readers to your sources and let them know you have carried out accurate research. While very few writers carry documentation guidelines around in their heads, smart writers know which guidelines to use and where to find them. Here are some readers' questions and comments that focus on documentation:

I checked my copy of *Emma,* and this quotation's not on the page you list.

What are you paraphrasing here? Your introduction merely drops readers into the middle of things. *Introduce the material paraphrased.*

What are you summarizing here? Where do these ideas come from?

I can't tell where this quotation ends.

Keep in-text citations as simple as possible—see information in handbook.

Why aren't works listed in alphabetical order?

This is *not correct* MLA citation style. Check your book!

What is the date of this publication?

For information on MLA documentation, see Chapters 48–51. APA, CBE, and Chicago styles are covered in Chapters 52–55.

3
The Twenty Most Common Errors

Grammar, punctuation, and other sentence-level matters will seldom draw much attention unless they interfere with the meaning you're trying to get across. Because they can get in the way, however, they are important to your success as a writer.

What kinds of surface errors are you likely to find in your writing, and how will readers respond to them? Our study of college writing patterns revealed that spelling errors are by far the most common type of error, even with spell checkers, by a factor of more than three to one. (A list of the words most often misspelled can be found in Chapter 36.) Our study also showed that not all surface errors disturb readers, nor do instructors always mark all of them. Finally, not all surface errors are consistently viewed as errors. In fact, some of the patterns identified in our research are considered errors by some readers but stylistic options by others.

While many people think of correctness as absolute, based on hard and fast unchanging rules, instructors and students know better. We know that there are rules but that the rules change all the time. "Is it okay to use *I* in essays for this class?" asks one student. "My high school teacher wouldn't let us." "Will more than one comma error lower my grade?" asks another. Such questions show that rules clearly exist but that they are always shifting and thus need our ongoing attention.

Our research shows some of the shifts that have occurred in the last century alone. Some mechanical and grammatical questions that are of little or no concern today used to be perceived as extremely important. In the late nineteenth century, for instance, instructors at Harvard said that their students' most serious writing problem was the inability to distinguish between the proper uses of *shall* and *will.* Similarly, split infinitives represented a serious problem for many instructors of the 1950s. Nowadays, at least since the starship *Enterprise* set out "to boldly go" where no one has gone before, split infinitives seem to wrinkle fewer brows.

These examples of shifting standards do not mean that there is no such thing as correctness in writing—only that *correctness always depends on some context.* Correctness is not so much a question of absolute right or wrong as it is a question of the way the choices a writer makes are perceived by readers. As writers, we are all judged by the words we put on the page. We all want to be considered competent and careful, and writing errors work against that impression. The world judges us by our control of the conventions we have agreed to use, and we all know it. As Robert Frost once said of poetry, trying to write without honoring the conventions and agreed-upon rules is like playing tennis without a net.

A major goal of this book is to help you understand and control the surface conventions of academic and professional writing. Since you already know most of these rules, the most efficient way to proceed is to focus on those that are still unfamiliar or puzzling.

To aid you in this process, we have identified the twenty error patterns (other than misspelling) most common among U.S. college students and list them here in order of frequency. These twenty errors are likely to cause you the most trouble, so it is well worth your effort to check for them in your writing. Here are brief explanations and examples of each error pattern along with cross-references to other places in this book where you can find more detail and additional examples.

> **For Multilingual Writers:** *Language-Specific Tips*
>
> Is your first language Arabic? Chinese? Spanish? something else? See the directory for multilingual writers at the back of the book to find tips about predictable error patterns in seventeen different languages.

1   Missing comma after an introductory element

When a sentence opens with an introductory word, phrase, or clause, readers usually need a small pause between the introductory element and the main part of the sentence. Such a pause is most often signaled by a comma. Try to get into the habit of using a comma after every introductory element, be it a word, a phrase, or a clause. When the introductory element is very short, you don't always need a comma after it. But you're never wrong if you do use a comma after an introductory element, and sometimes the comma is necessary to prevent a misreading.

▶ Frankly, we were baffled by the committee's decision.

▶ In fact, the Philippines consists of more than eight thousand islands.

▶ To tell the truth, I have never liked the Mets.

▶ Determined to get the job done, we worked all weekend.

▶ Because of its isolation in a rural area surrounded by mountains, Crawford Notch doesn't get many visitors.

▶ Though I gave advice for revising, his draft only became worse.

    The comma is needed here to prevent a misreading; without the comma, we might read the clause as *Though I gave advice for revising his draft.*

▶ In German, nouns are always capitalized.
        ˄

This sentence would at first be misunderstood if it did not have a comma.
Readers would think the introductory phrase was *In German nouns* rather
than *In German.*

For guidelines on editing for commas after introductory elements, see
p. 314. For more on commas and introductory elements in general,
see 23b, 24l, and 38a.

2 Vague pronoun reference

A pronoun is a word such as *he, she, it, they, this, that, which,* and *who* that
replaces another word so that the word does not have to be repeated.
Pronouns should refer clearly to a specific word or words (called the
antecedent) elsewhere in the sentence or in a previous sentence so that
readers can be sure whom or what the pronoun refers to. There are two
common kinds of vague pronoun reference. The first occurs when there
is more than one word that the pronoun might refer to; the second occurs
when the reference is to a word that is implied but not explicitly stated.

POSSIBLE REFERENCE TO MORE THAN ONE WORD

▶ Transmitting radio signals by satellite is a way of overcoming the
                                                the airwaves
problem of scarce airwaves and limiting how ~~they~~ are used.
                                            ˄

What is being limited—the signals or the airwaves?

▶ Before Mary Grace physically and verbally assaulted Mrs. Turpin,
the latter
~~she~~ was a judgmental woman who created her own ranking system of
˄

people and used it to justify her self-proclaimed superiority.

Does *she* refer to Mary Grace or Mrs. Turpin? The editing removes any doubt.

REFERENCE IMPLIED BUT NOT STATED

▶ The troopers burned a refugee camp as a result of the earlier attack.
      destruction of the camp
This was the cause of the war.
˄

What does *this* refer to? The editing makes clear what caused the war.

a policy
▶ **Company policy prohibited smoking, ~~which~~ many employees resented.**
     ^

What does *which* refer to—the policy or smoking? The editing clarifies the sentence.

For guidelines on editing for clear pronoun reference, see p. 244. For more on pronoun reference, see 29g.

3 **Missing comma in a compound sentence**

A compound sentence is made up of two or more parts that could each stand alone as a sentence. When the parts are joined by *and, but, so, yet, or, nor,* or *for,* use a comma to indicate a pause between the two thoughts.

▶ **We wish dreamily upon a star, and then we look down to find**
                                 ^
ourselves standing in mud.

▶ **The words "I do" may sound simple, but they mean a life commitment.**
                                      ^

In very short sentences, the comma is optional if the sentence can be easily understood without it. But you'll never be wrong to use a comma, and sometimes a comma is necessary to prevent a misreading.

▶ **Meredith wore jeans, and her feet were bare.**
                         ^

Without the comma, readers might at first think that Meredith was wearing her feet.

For guidelines on editing for commas in compound sentences, see p. 314. For further discussion and examples, see 24h and 38b.

4 **Wrong word**

"Wrong word" errors can involve mixing up words that sound somewhat alike, using a word with the wrong shade of meaning, or using a word with a completely wrong meaning. Many wrong word errors are due to the improper use of homonyms—words that are pronounced alike but spelled differently, such as *their* and *there.*

▶ The Pacers played ~~there~~ *their* best, but that was not good enough.

▶ *Paradise Lost* contains many ~~illusions~~ *allusions* to classical mythology.

▶ He noticed the ~~stench~~ *fragrance* of roses as he entered the room.

Wrong shade of meaning: a *stench* is a disagreeable smell; a *fragrance* is a pleasing odor.

▶ Working at a computer all day often means being ~~sedate~~ *sedentary* for long periods of time.

Wrong meaning: *sedate* means "composed, dignified," and *sedentary* means "requiring much sitting."

For guidelines on editing for words, see p. 285. For information about choosing the right word for your meaning, see Chapter 35. For discussion of choosing respectful words, see Chapter 33.

5   Missing comma(s) with a nonrestrictive element

Use commas to set off any part of a sentence that tells more about a word in the sentence but that your reader does *not* need in order to understand the word or sentence. A nonrestrictive element is one that is not essential to the basic meaning of the sentence.

▶ Marina, who was the president of the club, was first to speak.

The reader does *not* need the clause *who was the president of the club* to know the basic meaning of the sentence: who was first to speak. As a nonrestrictive (or nonessential) element, the clause is set off by commas.

▶ Louis was forced to call a session of the Estates General, which had not met for 175 years.

The reader does *not* need the clause *which had not met for 175 years* to understand which assembly the sentence is talking about because the *Estates General* has already been named. This clause is *not* essential to the basic meaning of the sentence and should be set off by a comma.

▶ **Kristin's first doll, Malibu Barbie, is still her favorite.**
⌃   ⌃

The reader knows which doll is Kristin's favorite—her *first* one; *Malibu Barbie* is thus *not* essential to the meaning of the sentence and needs to be set off by commas.

For guidelines on editing for commas with nonrestrictive elements, see p. 314. For additional explanation, see 38c.

6   Wrong or missing verb ending

It is easy to forget the verb endings *-s* (or *-es*) and *-ed* (or *-d*) because they are not always pronounced clearly when spoken. In addition, some varieties of English do not use these endings in the same way as standard academic or professional English. Be on the lookout for these incorrect or omitted endings, and check carefully for them when you edit.

　　　　uses
▶ **Eliot ~~use~~ feline imagery throughout the poem.**
　　⌃

　　　　　　　　　　dropped
▶ **The United States ~~drop~~ two atomic bombs on Japan in 1945.**
　　　　　　　　⌃

For more on verb endings, see 25a and 25c. For subject-verb agreement, see Chapter 26.

7   Wrong or missing preposition

Many words in English are regularly used with a particular preposition to express a particular meaning. For example, throwing a ball *to* someone is different from throwing a ball *at* someone: the first ball is thrown to be caught; the second, to hurt someone. Using the wrong preposition in such expressions is a common error. Because many prepositions are short and are not stressed or pronounced clearly in speech, they are often left out accidentally in writing. Proofread carefully, and check a dictionary when you're not sure about the preposition to use.

　　　　　on　　　　　　*in*
▶ **We met ~~in~~ Union Street ~~at~~ San Francisco.**
　　⌃　　　　　　　⌃

In and *at* both show place, but use *on* with a street and *in* with a city.

> President Richard Nixon compared the United States ~~with~~ ^{*to*} a "pitiful, helpless giant."

Compare to means "regard as similar"; *compare with* means "to examine to find similarities or differences."

> Who called ^{*off*} the game yesterday?

Adding *off* makes clear that the game was canceled. To *call* a game can mean either to postpone it or announce it.

For guidelines on checking for prepositions, see p. 509. For additional information about choosing the correct preposition, see 24g.

8 Comma splice

A comma splice occurs when only a comma separates clauses that could each stand alone as a sentence. To correct a comma splice, you can insert a semicolon or period, add a word like *and* or *although* after the comma, or restructure the sentence.

> Westward migration had passed Wyoming by_; even the discovery of gold in nearby Montana failed to attract settlers.

> I was strongly attracted to her, ^{*for*} she had special qualities.

> I was strongly attracted to her, ^{*although*} she had no patience with children.

> ^{*Having*} ~~They always had~~ ham for Easter, ~~this~~ was a family tradition.

For guidelines on revising comma splices, see p. 254. For additional information about ways to avoid or revise comma splices, see Chapter 30.

9 Missing or misplaced possessive apostrophe

To make a noun possessive, you must add either an apostrophe and an -*s* (*Ed's book*) or an apostrophe alone (*the boys' gym*). Possessive personal pronouns, however, do *not* take apostrophes: *hers, his, its, ours, yours*.

> Overambitious parents can be very harmful to a ~~childs~~ *child's* well-being.

> Ron Guidry was once one of the ~~Yankee's~~ *Yankees'* most electrifying pitchers.

> Garnet Hill is pleased to announce ~~it's~~ *its* spring white sale.

For guidelines on editing for possessive apostrophes, see p. 332. For additional explanation, see 41a.

10 Unnecessary shift in tense

Verb tenses tell when actions take place: saying *Willie went to school* indicates a past action, whereas saying *he will go* indicates a future action. When you shift from one tense to another with no clear reason, you can confuse readers, who have to guess which tense is the right one.

> Joy laughs until she ~~cried~~ *cries* during *Seinfeld*.

> Lucy was watching the great blue heron take off. Then she ~~slips~~ *slipped* and ~~falls~~ *fell* into the swamp.

> Kathy is in charge of finance; she ~~will~~ always ~~keep~~ *keeps* her office locked.

For guidelines on editing unnecessary shifts in tense, see p. 181. For more on using verb tenses in sequences, see 25f.

11 Unnecessary shift in pronoun

An unnecessary pronoun shift occurs when a writer who has been using one kind of pronoun to refer to someone or something shifts to another pronoun for no apparent reason. The most common shift in pronoun is from *one* to *you* or *I*.

> When one first sees a painting by Georgia O'Keeffe, ~~you are~~ *one is* impressed by a sense of power and stillness.

> *we*
> If we had known about the ozone layer, ~~you~~ could have banned
> ^
> aerosol sprays long ago.

For guidelines on editing for confusing pronoun shifts, see p. 181. For more on shifts in pronouns, see 20d.

12   Sentence fragment

A sentence fragment is a part of a sentence that is written as if it were a whole sentence, with a capital letter at the beginning and a period, question mark, or exclamation point at the end. A fragment lacks a subject, a complete verb, or both. Or a fragment may begin with a subordinating word such as *because,* which indicates that it depends for its meaning on another sentence.

NO SUBJECT

> Marie Antoinette spent huge sums of money on herself and her favorites.
> *Her extravagance helped*
> ~~Helped~~ bring on the French Revolution.
> ^

NO COMPLETE VERB
> *was*
> The old aluminum boat sitting on its trailer.
> ^

Sitting cannot function alone as the verb of the sentence. The auxiliary verb *was* makes it a complete verb, *was sitting,* indicating continuing action.

BEGINNING WITH SUBORDINATING WORD
> *where*
> We returned to the drugstore/, ~~Where~~ we waited for our parents.
> ^

For guidelines on editing for sentence fragments, see p. 260. For more detailed information on sentence fragments, see Chapter 31.

13   Wrong tense or verb form

Errors of wrong tense or wrong verb form include using a verb that does not indicate clearly when an action or condition is, was, or will be completed—for example, using *walked* instead of *had walked,* or *will go* instead of *will have gone.* Some varieties of English use the verbs *be* and *have* in ways that differ significantly from their use in standard academic or professional English; these uses may also be labeled as wrong verb forms. Finally, many errors of this kind involve verbs with irregular forms (like *begin, began, begun* or *break, broke, broken*). Errors may occur when a writer confuses these forms or treats these verbs as if they followed the regular pattern—for example, using *beginned* instead of *began,* or *have broke* instead of *have broken.*

▶ By the time Ian arrived, Jill ~~died.~~ **had**

The verb *died* does not clearly indicate that the death occurred *before* Ian arrived.

▶ The poet ~~be~~ **is** looking at a tree when she has a sudden inspiration.

▶ Mia Hamm has ~~broke~~ **broken** many soccer records.

▶ The Greeks ~~builded~~ **built** a wooden horse that the Trojans ~~taked~~ **took** into the city.

The verbs *build* and *take* have irregular past-tense forms.

For guidelines on editing verb tenses, see p. 224. For more detailed information about verb tenses and forms, see 24b and Chapters 25 and 26.

14 Lack of subject-verb agreement

A verb must agree with its subject in number and person. In many cases, the verb must take a form depending on whether the subject is singular or plural: *The old man is angry and stamps into the house,* but *The old men are angry and stamp into the house.* Lack of subject-verb agreement is often just a matter of leaving the *-s* ending off the verb out of carelessness, or of using a form of English that does not have this ending. Sometimes, however, this error results from particular sentence constructions.

When other words come between a subject and a verb, be careful: the noun nearest to the verb is not always the verb's subject.

▶ A central part of my life goals ~~have~~ **has** been to go to law school.

The subject is the singular noun *part,* not *goals.*

>   *are*
> ► The two main goals of my life ~~is~~ to be generous and to have no regrets.
>
> Here, the subject is the plural noun *goals,* not *life.*

If a subject has two or more parts connected by *and,* the subject is almost always plural. Sometimes the parts of the subject refer to the same person or thing; in such cases, as in the second example below, the subject should be treated as singular.

> ► The senator and her husband commutes every day from the suburbs.
>
>   *commutes*
> ► Our senator and friend ~~commute~~ every day from New York.

If a subject has two or more parts joined by *or* or *nor,* the verb should agree with the part nearest to the verb.

>   *comes*
> ► My brothers or my sister ~~come~~ every day to see Dad.
>
> Here, the noun closest to the verb is a singular noun. The verb must agree with that singular noun. If this construction sounds awkward, consider the next edit.

>   *sister*   *brothers*
> ► My ~~brothers~~ or my ~~sister~~ commute every day from Phoenix.
>
> Now the noun closest to the verb is plural, and the verb agrees with it.

Collective nouns such as *committee* and *jury* can be singular or plural, depending on whether they refer to a single unit or multiple individuals.

>   *were*
> ► The committee ~~was~~ taking all the responsibility themselves.
>
>   *was*
> ► The committee ~~were~~ honored for its fund-raising.

Some writers stumble over words like *measles* and *mathematics,* which look plural but are singular in meaning.

>   *has*
> ► Measles ~~have~~ become much less common in the United States.

Pronoun subjects cause problems for many writers. Most indefinite pronouns, such as *each, either, neither,* or *one,* are always singular and take a singular verb. The indefinite pronouns *both, few, many, others,* and *several* are always plural and take plural verb forms. Several indefinite pronouns (*all, any, enough, more, most, none, some*) can be singular or plural depending on the context in which they are used.

▶ Each of these designs ~~coordinate~~ with the others.
                 coordinates ^

▶ Many of these designs coordinates with the others.

The relative pronouns *who, which,* or *that* take verbs that agree with the word the pronoun refers to.

▶ Johnson was one of the athletes who ~~was~~ disqualified.
                                were ^

For guidelines on editing for subject-verb agreement, see p. 228. For additional information about subject-verb agreement, see Chapter 26.

15   Missing comma in a series

When three or more items appear in a series, they should be separated from one another with commas. Many newspapers do not use a comma between the last two items, but the best advice is that you'll never be wrong to use a series comma because a sentence can be ambiguous without one.

▶ Sharks eat mostly squid, shrimp, crabs, and other fish.

For guidelines on editing for series commas, see p. 314. For more on parallel structures in a series, see 19a; on using commas in a series, see 38d.

16   Lack of agreement between pronoun and antecedent

Pronouns are words such as *I, it, you, her, this, themselves, someone,* and *who* that replace another word (the antecedent) so that it does not have to be repeated. Pronouns must agree with their antecedents in gender (for example, using *he* or *him* to replace *Frederick Douglass,* and *she* or *her* to replace *Queen Elizabeth*) and in number (for example, using *it* to replace *a book,* and *they* or *them* to replace *fifteen books*).

Some problems occur with words like *each, either, neither,* and *one,* which are singular and take singular pronouns.

     its
▶ Each of the puppies thrived in ~~their~~ new home.
                  ^

Problems can also occur with antecedents that are joined by *or* or *nor.*

     she
▶ Neither Jane nor Susan felt that ~~they~~ had been treated fairly.
                            ^

Some problems involve words like *audience* and *team,* which can be either singular or plural depending on whether they are considered a single unit or multiple individuals.

     their
▶ The team frequently ~~changed~~ ~~its~~ positions to get varied experience.
                      ^

     Because *team* refers to the multiple members of the team rather than to the team as a single unit, *its* needs to change to *their.*

The other kind of antecedent that causes problems is an antecedent such as *each* or *employee,* which can refer to either men or women. Use *he or she, him or her,* and so on, or rewrite the sentence to make the antecedent and pronoun plural or to eliminate the pronoun altogether.

     or her
▶ Every student must provide his own uniform.
                       ^

   All students   *their*   *uniforms*
▶ ~~Every student~~ must provide ~~his~~ own ~~uniform.~~
   ^   ^   ^

                         a
▶ Every student must provide ~~his own~~ uniform.
                           ^

For guidelines on editing for pronoun-antecedent agreement, see p. 244. For more information on pronoun-antecedent agreement, see 29f.

17   Unnecessary comma(s) with a restrictive element

A restrictive element is one that is essential to the basic meaning of the sentence. It is *not* set off from the rest of the sentence with commas.

▶ People/who wanted to preserve wilderness areas/opposed the plan to privatize national parks.

The reader needs the clause *who wanted to preserve wilderness areas* because it announces which people opposed the plan. As an essential element, the clause should *not* be set off by commas.

▶ **Shakespeare's tragedy/** *Othello/* **deals with the dangers of jealousy.**

The reader needs to know which of Shakespeare's many tragedies this sentence is talking about. The title *Othello* is therefore essential and should *not* be set off by commas.

For guidelines on editing out unnecessary commas with restrictive elements, see p. 314. For additional information about restrictive phrases and clauses, see 38c and 38j.

18 Fused sentence

A fused sentence (also called a run-on sentence) is created when clauses that could each stand alone as a sentence are joined with no punctuation or words to link them. Fused sentences must either be divided into separate sentences or joined by adding words or punctuation.

▶ **The current was swift.** *He* **he could not swim to shore.**

▶ **Klee's paintings seem simple,** *but* **they are very sophisticated.**

▶ **She doubted the value of meditation;** *nevertheless,* **she decided to try it once.**

▶ **I liked the movie very much,** *for* **it made me laugh throughout.**

For guidelines on revising fused sentences, see p. 254. For more information about ways to revise fused sentences, see Chapter 30.

19 Misplaced or dangling modifier

Check every modifier (whether a word, phrase, or clause) to make sure that it is as close as possible to the word it describes or relates to. Be on the lookout for misplaced modifiers that may confuse your readers by seeming to modify some other word, phrase, or clause.

▶ ~~T~~hey could see the eagles swooping and diving ~~with binoculars~~, *With*

Who was wearing the binoculars—the eagles?

▶ ~~H~~e had decided he wanted to be a doctor ~~when he was ten years old~~, *When*

What kind of doctor would he be at age ten?

▶ The architect (only) considered using pine paneling.

Did the architect only consider but then reject pine paneling?

A dangling modifier hangs precariously from the beginning or end of a sentence and is attached to no other word in the sentence. The word that it modifies may exist in your mind but not on paper. Proofread carefully to ensure that each modifier refers to some other word in the sentence.

                                       you are
▶ A doctor should check your eyes for glaucoma every year if over fifty.

                 we see that
▶ Looking down the sandy beach, people are tanning themselves.

For guidelines on editing misplaced and dangling modifiers, see p. 240.

20   *Its/It's* confusion

Use *its* to mean *belonging to it;* use *it's* only when you mean *it is* or *it has.*

              its   *It's*
▶ The car is lying on ~~it's~~ side in the ditch. ~~Its~~ a white 2000 Subaru.

For more on distinguishing *its* and *it's,* see 41b.

4

Considering Rhetorical Situations

What do a magazine article, a letter to MasterCard complaining about an error on your bill, and an engineering report have in common? The writers of all three must analyze their rhetorical situations and then respond to them in appropriate ways. As a careful and effective writer, you will want to understand as much as possible about your purposes for writing, the audience you are addressing, the genre you are using, and the other crucial elements of any writing situation.

4a Consider your task or assignment.

- If you have a specific writing assignment, what does it ask you to do? Look for words such as *analyze, classify, compare, contrast, define, describe, discuss, explain,* and *survey.* Keep in mind that these words may differ in meaning from discipline to discipline or from job to job: *analyze* might mean one thing in literature and something rather different in biology—and something else still in a corporate report.
- What information do you need to complete the assignment or task? Do you need to do any research?
- Should you limit—or broaden—the topic you're writing about to make it more compelling to you and your audience? What problem(s) does the topic suggest to you? If you wish to redefine the assignment in any way, check with the person who came up with the assignment.
- What are the assignment's specific requirements? Consider length, format, organization, and deadline.
- What graphics or other visual information does the assignment call for?

4b Consider your purpose.

- What is the primary purpose the assignment calls for—to explain? summarize? persuade? recommend? entertain? some other purpose? If you are unclear about the primary purpose, think about what you want to accomplish, or talk with the person who came up with the assignment. Are there secondary purposes to keep in mind?
- What is the purpose of the person who gave you this assignment—to make sure you have understood certain materials? to evaluate your thinking and

writing abilities? to determine whether you can evaluate certain materials critically? How can you fulfill these expectations?

- What are your own purposes in this piece of writing—to respond to a question adequately and accurately? to learn as much as possible about a topic? to communicate your ideas clearly and forcefully? to make recommendations? to express certain feelings? How can you achieve these goals?

4c Consider your audience.

- Whom do you most want to reach—people already sympathetic to your views? people who disagree with your views? members of a group you belong to? or a group you don't belong to?
- In what ways are the members of your audience different from you? from one another? Think in terms of education, region, age, gender, occupation, social class, ethnic and cultural heritage, politics, religion, marital status, sexual orientation, and such.
- What assumptions can you legitimately make about your audience? What might they value? Think of qualities such as brevity, originality, conformity, honesty, adventure, wit, seriousness, thrift, and so on.
- What languages and dialects does your audience use, and what special language, if any, will they expect you to use? What knowledge do they have about your topic? Do you need to provide any special background information or define any terms?
- What response(s) do you want to evoke?

4d Consider your rhetorical stance.

- What is your overall attitude toward the topic—approval? disapproval? curiosity? indifference? How strong are your opinions?
- What social, political, religious, personal, or other factors account for your attitude?
- What do you know about the topic? What questions do you have?
- What interests you *most* about the topic? Why?
- What interests you *least* about it? Why?
- What seems important—or unimportant—about the topic?
- What preconceptions, if any, do you have about it?
- What do you expect to conclude about the topic?
- Think about your audience. Will they have similar attitudes and interests, or not?

4e Consider genre and language.

- What genre, or kind, of writing does your task call for—a report? a review? a poem? a letter? a blurb?
- If you need to produce academic writing, should you use any specialized varieties of English along with standard academic English? any occupational, professional, regional, or ethnic varieties? any words from a language other than English?

For Multilingual Writers: *Bringing in Other Languages*

Even when you write in English, you may want or need to include words, phrases, or whole passages in another language. If so, consider whether your readers will understand that language and whether you need to provide a translation, as in this example from John (Fire) Lame Deer's "Talking to the Owls and Butterflies":

> Listen to the air. You can hear it, feel it, smell it, taste it. *Woniya waken*—the holy air—which renews all by its breath. *Woniya, woniya waken*—spirit, life, breath, renewal—it means all that.

In this instance, translation is necessary because the phrase Lame Deer is discussing has multiple meanings in English. (See 34e for more on bringing in other languages.)

4f Consider specific online issues.

- In what ways does your task call for online work—to find information on the Internet? to email someone asking for information or response? to create or contribute to a Web document? to participate in a MUD?
- If you are sending email, is your subject line explicitly clear? Does your signature line identify you fully? Remember that email isn't completely private. If you are forwarding an email message, do you have permission to do so (59b)?
- If you are writing for the Web, what formats should you use—a certain template? frames? navigation buttons? (See Chapter 16.)
- What visual elements should you use—color to signal response to email? colors and graphics that can be easily downloaded in a Web document (15c)?
- If you are writing in a MUD, MOO, or listserv, are you following the expected conventions? Refer to the welcome page or to any FAQs for a list of the expected conventions.

◎ **A Matter of Style:** *Considering Tone Online*

Remember that closeness to online readers doesn't happen automatically. Your tone in online exchanges, then, should be based on how well you really know your audience as well as on what is most appropriate in the context of a specific piece of online writing. The company president may also be your very good friend, but when you write to her about company business, you should adopt an appropriately businesslike tone.

- Have you paid attention to your netiquette—the good manners of the digital world? In addition to not flaming readers with angry messages and not SHOUTING with all-cap messages, learn the policies of the school or company whose online services you are using (14a).
- If you are using information obtained online, how reliable is it (12c)?

5

Exploring Ideas

The point is so simple that we often forget it: we write best about topics we know well. One of the most important parts of the entire writing process, therefore, is choosing a topic that will engage your strengths and your interest and then exploring that topic by surveying what you know and determining what you need to find out.

5a Try brainstorming.

One of the best ways to begin exploring a topic is also the most familiar: *talk it over* with others. One way to begin is in a brainstorming session. Used widely in business and industry, brainstorming means tossing out ideas—often with several other people, either in person or online. You can also brainstorm by yourself.

1. Within a time limit of five or ten minutes, in a group with several others, list *every* word or phrase that comes to mind about the topic. Just jot

down key words and phrases, not sentences. No one has to understand the list but you and your group. Don't worry about whether or not something will be useful. Just list as much as you can in this brief span of time.
2. If very little occurs to you and your group, try calling out thoughts about the opposite side of your topic. If you are trying, for instance, to think of reasons to reduce tuition and are coming up blank, try concentrating on reasons to *increase* tuition. Once you start generating ideas in one direction, you can usually move back to the other side of the topic fairly easily.
3. When the time is up, stop and read over the lists you have made. If anything else comes to mind, add it to your list. Then reread the list, looking for patterns of interesting ideas or one central idea.

Here is what one student came up with after brainstorming with her classmates for an essay on prejudice.

Some prejudice in everyone

Where does it come from?

Learned—we aren't born with it

Examples: against some races or other groups

against some ways of thinking

against some ways of dressing

5b Try freewriting.

Freewriting is a method of exploring a topic by writing about it for a period of time *without stopping*.

1. Write for ten minutes or so. Think about your topic, and let your mind wander; write down whatever occurs to you. Don't stop, and don't worry about grammar or spelling. If you get stuck, write anything—just don't stop.
2. When the time is up, look at what you have written. You may discover some important insights and ideas.

5c Try looping.

Looping is a kind of directed freewriting that narrows a topic through a process of five-minute stages, or loops.

1. Spend five minutes freewriting about your topic *without stopping*. This is your first loop.

2. Look at what you have written. Find the central or most intriguing thought, and summarize it in a single sentence.
3. Starting with the summary sentence from your first loop, spend another five minutes freewriting. This second loop circles around the first loop, just as the first loop circled around your topic. Look for the central idea within your second piece of freewriting. That idea will form the basis of a third loop.
4. Keep this process going until you discover a clear angle on your topic or something about the topic that you can pursue in a full-length piece of writing.

For Multilingual Writers:
Using Your Native Language to Explore Ideas

For generating and exploring ideas—the work of much brainstorming, freewriting, looping, and clustering—you may be most successful at coming up with good ideas quickly and spontaneously if you work in your native language. Later in the process of writing, you can choose the best of these ideas and begin working with them in English.

5d Try clustering.

Clustering is a way of generating ideas using a visual scheme or chart. It is especially helpful for understanding the relationships among the parts of a broad topic and for developing subtopics.

1. Write down your topic in the middle of a blank piece of paper and circle it.
2. In a ring around the topic circle, write down what you see as the main parts of the topic. Circle each one, and then draw a line from it to the topic.
3. Think of more ideas, examples, facts, or other details relating to each main part. Write each of these near the appropriate part, circle each one, and draw a line from it to the part.
4. Repeat this process with each new circle until you can't think of any more details. Some trails may lead to dead ends, but you will still have various trains of thought to follow and many useful connections among ideas.

Here is an example of the clustering one student did for an essay about prejudice:

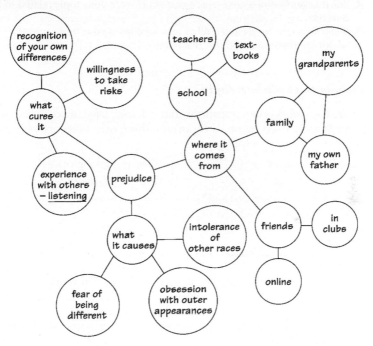

5e Ask questions.

Another basic strategy for exploring a topic and generating ideas is simply to ask and answer questions. Here are two widely used sets of questions to get you started.

Questions to describe a topic

Originally developed by Aristotle, the following questions can help you explore a topic by carefully and systematically describing it:

1. *What is it?* What are its characteristics, dimensions, features, and parts?
2. *What caused it?* What changes occurred to create your topic? How is it changing? How will it change?

3. *What is it like or unlike?* What features differentiate your topic from others? What analogies does your topic support?
4. *What larger system is your topic a part of?* How is your topic related to this system?
5. *What do people say about it?* What reactions does your topic arouse? What about the topic causes those reactions?

Questions to explain a topic

These are the well-known questions that ask *who, what, when, where, why,* and *how.* Widely used by news reporters, these questions are especially helpful for explaining a topic.

1. *Who* is doing it?
2. *What* is at issue?
3. *When* does it begin and end?
4. *Where* is it taking place?
5. *Why* does it occur?
6. *How* is it done?

5f   Work collaboratively.

Most work today is done collaboratively, whether that work is on a basketball court, at a corporate meeting, or in a classroom. Writers often work together to come up with ideas, to respond to one another's drafts, or even to coauthor something. Here are some strategies for working with others:

1. Fix a regular meeting time and a system for contacting one another.
2. If you are working over a computer network, exchange email addresses, and consider exchanging ideas and drafts electronically.
3. Establish ground rules for the group. Be sure every member has an equal opportunity — and responsibility — to contribute.
4. Assign duties at each meeting: one person to take notes, another to keep the discussion on track, and so on.
5. With final deadlines in mind, set an agenda for each group meeting.
6. Listen carefully to what each person says. If disagreements arise, try paraphrasing to see if everyone is hearing the same thing.
7. Use group meetings to work together on particularly difficult problems. If an assignment is complex, have each member explain one section to all the others. If the group has trouble understanding part of the task, check with whoever made the assignment.
8. Expect disagreement, and remember that the goal is not for everyone just to "go along." The challenge is to get a really spirited debate going and to argue through all possibilities.

9. If you are preparing a group-written document, divide up the drafting duties. Set reasonable deadlines for each stage of work. Schedule at least two meetings to iron out the final draft, reading it aloud and working for consistency of tone. Have everyone proofread the final draft, with one person making the corrections.
10. If the group will be making a presentation, be sure you know exactly how much time you will have. Decide how each member will contribute to the presentation, making sure everyone has a role. Leave time for at least two practice sessions.
11. Make a point of assessing the group's effectiveness. What has the group accomplished? What has it done best? What has it been least successful at? What has each member contributed? How could the group function more effectively?

6
Drafting

One of our students defines drafting as that time in a writing project "when the rubber meets the road." In this sense, drafting begins the moment you start shaping your ideas for presentation to your readers. As you decide on your thesis (or central idea), organize materials to support that idea, and sketch out a plan for your writing, you have already begun the drafting process.

6a   Establish a working thesis.

As noted, a thesis states the central idea of a piece of writing. Most academic or professional writing contains a thesis statement, often near the beginning. The thesis functions as a promise to readers, letting them know what the writer will discuss. Though you may not have a final thesis when you begin to write, you should establish a tentative working thesis early on in your writing process.

The word *working* is important here because the working thesis may well change as you write. Even so, a working thesis focuses your thinking and research, and helps keep you on track.

A working thesis should have two parts: a topic part, which states the topic, and a comment part, which makes an important point about the topic.

┌─────────── TOPIC ────────────┐┌─────────── COMMENT ────────────┐
▶ **Recent studies of depression suggest that it is much more closely**

related to physiology than scientists had previously thought.

┌─────────── TOPIC ───────────┐┌─────────── COMMENT ───────────┐
▶ **The current health care crisis arises from three major causes.**

A successful working thesis has three characteristics:

1. It is potentially *interesting* to the intended audience.
2. It is as *specific* as possible.
3. It limits the topic enough to make it *manageable.*

You can evaluate a working thesis by checking it against each of these characteristics, as in the following example:

PRELIMINARY WORKING THESIS

▶ **Theories about global warming are being debated around the world.**

INTERESTING? The topic itself holds interest, but it seems to have no real comment attached to it. The thesis merely states a bare fact, and the only place to go from here is to more bare facts.

SPECIFIC? The thesis is not specific. Who is debating these theories? What is at issue in this debate?

MANAGEABLE? The thesis is not manageable; it would require research on global warming in many countries.

ASSESSMENT: This thesis can be narrowed by the addition of a stronger comment and a sharper focus.

REVISED WORKING THESIS

▶ **Scientists from several countries have challenged global-warming theories, claiming that they are more propaganda than science.**

For Multilingual Writers: *Stating a Thesis*

In some cultures, it is considered rude to state an opinion outright. In the United States, however, academic and business practices require writers to make key positions explicitly clear.

6b Gather information to support your thesis.

Writing will often call for research. An assignment may specify that you conduct research on your topic and cite your sources. Or you may find that you do not know enough about your topic to write about it effectively without doing some research. Sometimes you need to do research at various stages of the writing process—early on, to help you understand or define your topic, or later on, to find additional examples to support your thesis. Once you have a working thesis, consider what additional information, including any visuals or graphics, you might need. (For more on conducting research and working with sources, see Chapters 11 and 12. For more on organizing your support into paragraphs, see Chapter 7. For more on supporting your thesis, see Chapter 9.)

6c Write out a plan.

At this point, you may find it helpful to write out a plan or informal outline. To do so, simply write down your thesis, review your exploratory notes and research materials, and then list all the examples and other good reasons you have to support the thesis. Here, for example, is another working thesis and its writer's plan:

WORKING THESIS

▶ **Increased motorcycle use demands reorganization of parking lots.**

INTRODUCTION

give background and overview (motorcycle use up dramatically)
state purpose—to fulfill promise of thesis by offering solutions

BODY

describe the current situation (tell of my research at area parking lots)
describe the problem in detail (report on statistics; cars vs. cycles)
present two possible solutions (enlarge lots or reallocate space)

CONCLUSION

recommend against first solution because of cost and space
recommend second solution, and summarize benefits of it

Outlines

Even if you have made an informal written plan before drafting, you may also wish to prepare a formal outline, which can help you see exactly how the parts of your writing will fit together—how your ideas relate, where you need examples, and what the overall structure of your work will be.

Most formal outlines follow a conventional format of numbered and lettered headings and subheadings, using roman numerals, capital letters, arabic numerals, and lowercase letters to show the levels of importance of the various ideas and their relationships. Each new level is indented to show its subordination to the preceding level.

Thesis statement
  I. First main idea
   A. First subordinate idea
     1. First supporting detail or point
     2. Second supporting detail
     3. Third supporting detail
   B. Second subordinate idea
     1. First supporting detail
     2. Second supporting detail
  II. Second main idea
   A. First subordinate idea
     1. First supporting detail
     2. Second supporting detail
   B. Second subordinate idea
     1. First supporting detail
     2. Second supporting detail
       a. First supporting detail
       b. Second supporting detail

Each level contains at least two parts, so there is no *A* without a *B*, no *1* without a *2*. Comparable items are placed on the same level—all capital letters, for instance, or all arabic numerals. Each level develops the idea before it. Points *1, 2,* and *3* under *IA*, for example, are the points that develop, explain, or demonstrate *IA*. Headings are stated in parallel form—either all sentences or all grammatically parallel structures.

Whatever form your plan takes, you may want or need to change it along the way. Writing has a way of stimulating thought, and the process of drafting may generate new ideas. Or you may find that you need to reexamine some data or information or gather more material.

Outlining on a computer

Outlining on a computer will allow you to rearrange or experiment with various options easily and efficiently. In addition, your software may have an outline template and the capability to produce a complete table of contents based on the headings and subheadings you use in your draft.

6d Write out a draft.

No matter how good your planning, investigating, and organizing have been, chances are you will need to do more work as you draft. This fact of life leads to the first principle of successful drafting: be flexible. If you see that your plan is not working, do not hesitate to alter it. If some information now seems irrelevant, leave it out—even if you went to great lengths to obtain it. Throughout the drafting process, you may need to refer to points you have already written about. You may learn that you need to do more research, that your whole thesis must be reshaped, or that your topic is too broad and should be narrowed. Very often you will continue planning, investigating, and organizing throughout the writing process.

Some Guidelines for Drafting

- Keep all your information close at hand and arranged according to your plan.

- Draft with a computer if possible; additions and revisions will be easier later on. Remember to save your text to your hard drive or a disk, labeling it *draft* or dating it for easy identification.

- Try to write in stretches of at least thirty minutes. Writing can provide momentum, and once you get going, the task becomes easier.

- Don't let small questions bog you down. As you write, questions that need to be answered will come up. But unless they are major ones, just make a note of them or a tentative decision, and move on.

- Keep a plan in mind for any graphics or visual information that you might add to your draft.

- Remember that a first draft need not be perfect. In order to keep moving and get a draft done, you must often sacrifice some fine points of writing at this stage. Concentrate on getting all your ideas down on paper.

- Stop writing at a logical place—where you know exactly what will come next. If you do, it will be easier for you to start writing when you return to the draft.

7

Constructing Paragraphs

Paragraphs serve as signposts—pointers that help guide readers through a piece of writing. A look through a popular magazine will show paragraphs working this way: the first paragraph almost always aims to get our attention and to persuade us to read on, and subsequent ones often indicate a new point or a shift in focus or tone.

Put simply, a paragraph is a group of sentences or a single sentence set off as a unit. Usually all the sentences in a paragraph revolve around one main idea.

Editing Paragraphs

- Is there a sentence that makes the main idea of each paragraph clear? If not, should there be? (7a)

- Does the first sentence of each paragraph let readers know what that paragraph is about? Does the last sentence in some way conclude that paragraph's discussion? If not, does it need to?

- Within each paragraph, how does each sentence relate to the main idea? Revise or eliminate any that do not. (7a)

- How completely does each paragraph develop its main idea? What details are used? Are they effective? Do any paragraphs need more detail? (7b) What other methods of development might be used— narration? description? comparison and contrast? analogy? (7c)

- Is each paragraph organized in a way that is easy to follow? Are sentences within each paragraph clearly linked? Do any of the transitions try to create links between ideas that do not really exist? (7e)

- Are the paragraphs clearly linked? Do any links need to be added? Are any of the transitions from one paragraph to another artificial? (7e)

- How does the introductory paragraph catch readers' interest? (7f)

- How does the last paragraph draw the piece to a conclusion? (7f)

7a Focus on a main idea.

An effective paragraph often focuses on one main idea. A good way to achieve such paragraph unity is to state the main idea clearly in one sentence and then relate all the other sentences in the paragraph to that idea. The sentence that presents the main idea is called the topic sentence.

Announcing the main idea in a topic sentence

The following paragraph opens with a clear topic sentence, and the rest of the paragraph builds on the idea stated in that sentence:

> *Our friendship was the source of much happiness and many memories.* We danced and snapped our fingers simultaneously to the soul tunes of the Jacksons and Stevie Wonder. We sweated together in the sweltering summer sun, trying to win the championship for our softball team. I recall the taste of pepperoni and sausage pizza as we discussed the highlights of our team's victory. Once we even became attracted to the same person, but luckily we were able to share his friendship.

A topic sentence does not always come at the beginning of a paragraph; it may come at the end. Occasionally a paragraph's main idea is so obvious that it need not be stated explicitly in a topic sentence.

Relating each sentence to the main idea

Whether the main idea of a paragraph is stated in a topic sentence or is only implied, make sure that all other sentences in the paragraph contribute to the main idea. The first sentence in the following paragraph announces the topic. All of the other sentences clearly relate to that topic, resulting in a unified paragraph.

> When I was a teenager, there were two distinct streams of popular music: one was black, and the other was white. The former could only be heard way at the end of the radio dial, while white music dominated everywhere else. This separation was a fact of life, the equivalent of blacks sitting

A Matter of Style: *Marking Online Paragraphs*

Long chunks of text are often hard for readers to process. Break online text into block paragraphs, leaving an extra line of space between each one and arranging them so that plenty of white space rests readers' eyes. You can also help readers by stating the most important information clearly at the beginning of each paragraph or chunk of text.

www.bedfordstmartins.com/lunsford

in the back of the bus and "whites only" signs below the Mason-Dixon line. Satchmo might grin for days on "The Ed Sullivan Show" and certain historians hold forth *ad nauseam* on the black contribution to American music, but the truth was that our worlds rarely twined.
—MARCIA GILLESPIE, "They're Playing My Music, but Burying My Dreams"

7b   Provide details.

An effective paragraph develops its main idea by providing enough details to hold the reader's interest. Without such development, a paragraph may seem lifeless and abstract.

A POORLY DEVELOPED PARAGRAPH

No such thing as human nature compels people to behave, think, or react in certain ways. Rather, from the time of our infancy to our death, we are constantly being taught, by the society that surrounds us, the customs, norms, and mores of our distinct culture. Everything in culture is learned, not genetically transmitted.

This paragraph is boring. Although its main idea is clear and its sentences hold together, it fails to gain our interest or hold our attention because it lacks any specific examples or details. Now look at the paragraph revised to include needed specifics.

THE SAME PARAGRAPH, REVISED

Imagine a child in Ecuador dancing to salsa music at a warm family gathering while a child in the United States is decorating a Christmas tree with bright, shiny red ornaments. Both of these children are taking part in their countries' cultures. It is not by instinct that one child knows how to dance to salsa music, nor is it by instinct that the other child knows how to decorate the tree. No such thing as human nature compels people to behave, think, or react in certain ways. Rather, from the time of our infancy to our death, we are constantly being taught, by the society that surrounds us, the customs, norms, and mores of our distinct culture. A majority of people feel that the evil in human beings is human nature. However, the Tasaday, a Stone Age tribe discovered not long ago in the Philippines, do not even have equivalents in their language for the words *hatred, competition, acquisitiveness, aggression,* and *greed.* Such examples suggest that everything in culture is learned, not genetically transmitted.

Though both paragraphs present the same point, only the second one comes to life. It does so by bringing in specific details *from* life. We want to read this paragraph because it appeals to our senses (a child dancing; bright, shiny red ornaments) and our curiosity (who are the Tasaday?).

7c Use effective patterns of development.

Here are several common patterns you can use to develop paragraphs.

Narration

A narrative paragraph uses a story to develop a main idea. Here is one student's narrative paragraph that tells a personal story to support a point about the dangers of racing bicycles with flimsy alloy frames.

> People who have been exposed to the risk of dangerously designed bicycle frames have paid too high a price. I saw this danger myself in the 1984 Putney Race. An expensive graphite frame failed, and the rider was catapulted onto Vermont pavement at fifty miles per hour. The pack of riders behind him was so dense that other racers crashed into a tangled, sliding heap. The aftermath: four hospitalizations. I got off with some stitches, a bad road rash, and severely pulled tendons. My Italian racing bike was pretzled, and my racing was over for that summer. Others were not so lucky. An Olympic hopeful, Brian Stone of the Northstar team, woke up in a hospital bed to find that his cycling was over—and not just for that summer. His kneecap had been surgically removed. He couldn't even walk.

Description

A descriptive paragraph uses specific details to create a clear impression. Thus, descriptive paragraphs often *show* rather than tell, using sensory details to help the reader see what something looks like and perhaps how it sounds, smells, tastes, or feels. Notice how the following paragraph includes details about an old schoolroom; they convey a strong impression of a room where "time had taken its toll."

> The professor's voice began to fade into the background as my eyes wandered around the classroom in the old administration building. The water-stained ceiling was cracked and peeling, and the splitting wooden beams played host to a variety of lead pipes and coils. My eyes followed these pipes down the walls and around corners until I eventually saw the electric outlets. I thought it was strange that they were exposed, and not

built in, until I realized that there probably had been no electricity when the building was built. Below the outlets the sunshine was falling in bright rays across the hardwood floor, and I noticed how smoothly the floor was worn. Time had taken its toll on this building.

Definition

You may often need to write an entire paragraph in order to define a word or concept, as in the following paragraph:

> Economics is the study of how people choose among the alternatives available to them. It's the study of little choices ("Should I take the chocolate or the strawberry?") and big choices ("Should we require a reduction in energy consumption in order to protect the environment?"). It's the study of individual choices, choices by firms, and choices by governments. Life presents each of us with a wide range of alternative uses of our time and other resources; economists examine how we choose among those alternatives.
>
> —TIMOTHY TREGARTHEN, *Economics*

Example

One of the most common ways of developing a paragraph is by illustrating a point with one or more examples.

> The Indians made names for us children in their teasing way. Because our very busy mother kept my hair cut short, like my brothers', they called me Short Furred One, pointing to their hair and making the sign for short, the right hand with fingers pressed close together, held upward, back out, at the height intended. With me this was about two feet tall, the Indians laughing gently at my abashed face. I am told that I was given a pair of small moccasins that first time, to clear up my unhappiness at being picked out from the dusk behind the fire and my two unhappy shortcomings made conspicuous.
>
> —MARI SANDOZ, "The Go-Along Ones"

Division and classification

Division breaks a single item into parts. Classification groups many separate items according to their similarities. A paragraph evaluating one history course might divide the course into several segments—textbooks, lectures, assignments—and examine each one in turn. A paragraph giving an overview of many history courses might classify the courses in a number of ways—by time periods, by geographic areas, by the kinds of assignments demanded, by the number of students enrolled, or by some other principle.

DIVISION

We all listen to music according to our separate capacities. But, for the sake of analysis, the whole listening process may become clearer if we break it up into its component parts, so to speak. In a certain sense, we all listen to music on three separate planes. For lack of a better terminology, one might name these: (1) the sensuous plane, (2) the expressive plane, (3) the sheerly musical plane. The only advantage to be gained from mechanically splitting up the listening process into these hypothetical planes is the clearer view to be had of the way in which we listen.
                              —AARON COPLAND, *What to Listen for in Music*

CLASSIFICATION

Many people are seduced by fad diets. Those who have always been overweight turn to them out of despair; they have tried everything, and yet nothing seems to work. A second group to succumb appear perfectly healthy but are baited by slogans such as "look good, feel good." These slogans prompt self-questioning and insecurity—do I really look good and feel good?—and as a direct result, many healthy people fall prey to fad diets. With both types of people, however, the problems surrounding such diets are numerous and dangerous. In fact, these diets provide neither intelligent nor effective answers to weight control.

Comparison and contrast

When you compare two things, you look at their similarities; when you contrast two things, you focus on their differences. You can structure paragraphs that compare or contrast in two basic ways. One way is to present all the information about one item and then all the information about the other item, as in the following paragraph:

You could tell the veterans from the rookies by the way they were dressed. The knowledgeable ones had their heads covered by kerchiefs, so that if they were hired, tobacco dust wouldn't get in their hair; they had on clean dresses that by now were faded and shapeless, so that if they were hired they wouldn't get tobacco dust and grime on their best clothes. Those who were trying for the first time had their hair freshly done and wore attractive dresses; they wanted to make a good impression. But the dresses couldn't be seen at the distance that many were standing from the employment office, and they were crumpled in the crush.
                              —MARY MEBANE, "Summer Job"

Or you can switch back and forth between the two items, focusing on particular characteristics of each in turn.

> Malcolm X emphasized the use of violence in his movement and employed the biblical principle of "an eye for an eye and a tooth for a tooth." King, on the other hand, felt that blacks should use nonviolent civil disobedience and employed the theme "turning the other cheek," which Malcolm X rejected as "beggarly" and "feeble." The philosophy of Malcolm X was one of revenge, and often it broke the unity of black Americans. More radical blacks supported him, while more conservative ones supported King. King thought that blacks should transcend their humanity. In contrast, Malcolm X thought they should embrace it and reserve their love for one another, regarding whites as "devils" and the "enemy." King's politics were those of a rainbow, but Malcolm X's rainbow was insistently one color—black. The distance between Martin Luther King Jr.'s thinking and Malcolm X's was the distance between growing up in the seminary and growing up on the streets, between the American dream and the American reality.

Analogy

Analogies (comparisons that explain an unfamiliar thing in terms of a familiar one) can also help develop paragraphs. In the opening sentences of the following paragraph, the writer draws an unlikely analogy—between dogs and laboratories—to introduce readers to an examination of what keeps laboratories young.

> Like dogs, laboratories age considerably faster than people. But while dogs age at a factor of seven, I would say labs age at a factor of 10, which makes the MIT Media Lab 100 years old last month. When we officially opened our doors for business in October 1985, we were the new kids on the block, considered crazy by most. Even *The New York Times* called us "charlatans." While I was slightly hurt at being referred to as "all icing and no cake," it secretly pleased me because I had no doubt that computing and content would merge together into everyday life. Now, 10 years later, "multimedia" is old hat. The term appears in the names and advertising jingles of some of the most staid corporations. But becoming part of the establishment is a lot less fun than experiencing the risk and abuse of pioneering.
> —NICHOLAS NEGROPONTE, "Being Digital"

Cause and effect

You can often develop paragraphs by explaining the causes of something or the effects that something brings about. The following paragraph discusses the effects of television on the American family:

Television's contribution to family life has been an equivocal one. For while it has, indeed, kept the members of the family from dispersing, it has not served to bring them together. By its domination of the time families spend together, it destroys the special quality that distinguishes one family from another, a quality that depends to a great extent on what a family does, what special rituals, games, recurrent jokes, familiar songs, and shared activities it accumulates.

–MARIE WINN, *The Plug-in Drug: Television, Children, and the Family*

Process

Paragraphs often serve to depict or explain a process, sometimes using chronology to order the stages in that process.

By the late 20s, most people notice the first signs of aging in their physical appearance. Slight losses of elasticity in facial skin produce the first wrinkles, usually in those areas most involved in their characteristic facial expressions. As the skin continues to lose elasticity and fat deposits build up, the face sags a bit with age. Indeed, some people have drooping eyelids, sagging cheeks, and the hint of a double chin by age 40 (Whitbourne, 1985). Other parts of the body sag a bit as well, so as the years pass, adults need to exercise regularly if they want to maintain their muscle tone and body shape. Another harbinger of aging, the first gray hairs, is usually noticed in the 20s and can be explained by a reduction in the number of pigment-producing cells. Hair may become a bit less plentiful, too, because of hormonal changes and reduced blood supply to the skin.

–KATHLEEN STASSEN BERGER, *The Developing Person through the Life Span*

7d Consider paragraph length.

Paragraph length is determined by content and purpose. Paragraphs should develop an idea, create any desired effects (such as suspense or humor), and advance the larger piece of writing. Fulfilling these aims will sometimes require short paragraphs, sometimes long ones. For example, if you are writing a persuasive piece, you may put all your evidence into one long paragraph to create the impression of a solid, overwhelmingly convincing argument. In a story about an exciting event, on the other hand, you may use a series of short paragraphs to create suspense, to keep the reader rushing to each new paragraph to find out what happens next.

Reasons to start a new paragraph

- to turn to a new idea
- to emphasize something (such as an idea or an example)
- to change speakers (in dialogue)
- to lead readers to pause
- to take up a subtopic
- to start the conclusion

7e   Make paragraphs flow.

A paragraph has coherence—or flows—if its details fit together clearly in a way that readers can easily follow. Here are several ways to achieve paragraph coherence.

Using spatial order

Paragraphs organized in spatial order look at something from top to bottom, left to right, or near to far. Spatial order is a common way of organizing descriptive paragraphs, as in the descriptive paragraph in 7c.

Using chronological order

Paragraphs organized chronologically arrange events as they occurred, from the earliest event to later ones. Chronological order is used frequently in narrative paragraphs, as in the process paragraph in 7c.

Using logical order

One common way to organize paragraphs logically is to follow a general-to-specific pattern, which usually opens with a general or abstract idea followed by a number of more specific points that substantiate or elaborate on the generalization. See the narrative paragraph in 7c for an example. This pattern is also useful for opening paragraphs (see 7f).

Using associational order

Paragraphs that organize information associationally do so by means of a series of associations from the writer's own experiences. This chain of association often relies on a central image or memory—a particular aroma, for instance. The following paragraph links a series of memories to one central image—that of children being left alone:

> Walking from Bartlett to John Lee's hand laundry, alone. Maybe aged four. From Bartlett to somewhere. Near the Myrtle Avenue el. Shortest person on street corners. The only one waiting for lights to turn green. No memory of anyone asking where his Mommy is. Just last week, 1992, Flagstaff, Arizona. A little three- or four-year-old child is wandering around a supermarket. A concerned woman bends over: "Did you lose your Mommy?" The same week, the same store, a little three- or four-year-old American Indian child is wandering, bawling loudly. People stop and stare. No one asks.
>
> —VICTOR VILLANUEVA, *Bootstraps*

Note that the writer uses a series of sentence fragments to suggest the fragmented nature of his memories.

Repeating key words and phrases

Weaving in repeated key words and phrases—or pronouns that point to them—not only links sentences but also alerts readers to the

---

A Matter of Style: *Reiterating*

One pattern you may recognize from political discourse and some forms of preaching is known as reiterating. In this pattern, the writer states the main point of a paragraph and then reiterates it in a number of different ways, hammering home the point and often building in intensity as well. This strategy finds particular power in the writing and preaching of Martin Luther King Jr., as in the following example:

> We are on the move now. The burning of our churches will not deter us. We are on the move now. The bombing of our homes will not dissuade us. We are on the move now. The beating and killing of our clergymen and young people will not divert us. We are on the move now. The arrest and release of known murderers will not discourage us. We are on the move now. Like an idea whose time has come, not even the marching of mighty armies can halt us. We are moving to the land of freedom.
>
> —MARTIN LUTHER KING JR., "Our God Is Marching On"

importance of those words or phrases in the larger piece of writing. Notice in the following example how the repetition of the italicized key words helps hold the paragraph together:

> Over the centuries, *shopping* has changed in function as well as in style. Before the Industrial Revolution, most consumer goods were sold in open-air *markets*, *customers* who went into an actual *shop* were expected to *buy* something, and *shoppers* were always expected to *bargain* for the best possible *price*. In the nineteenth century, however, the development of the department *store* changed the relationship between buyers and sellers. Instead of visiting several *market* stalls or small *shops*, *customers* could now *buy* a variety of merchandise under the same roof; instead of feeling expected to *buy*, *they* were welcome just to look; and instead of *bargaining* with several merchants, *they* paid a fixed *price* for each *item*. In addition, *they* could return an *item* to the *store* and exchange *it* for a different one or get *their* money back. All of these changes helped transform *shopping* from serious requirement to psychological recreation.

Using parallelism

Parallel structures can help connect the sentences within a paragraph. As readers, we feel pulled along by the force of the parallel structures in the following example:

> William Faulkner's "Barn Burning" tells the story of a young boy trapped in a no-win situation. If he betrays his father, he loses his family. If he betrays justice, he becomes a fugitive. In trying to free himself from his trap, he does both.

Using transitions

Transitions are words such as *so, however,* and *thus* that signal relationships between sentences and paragraphs. Transitions help guide the reader from one idea to another. To understand how important transitions are in directing readers, try reading the following paragraph, from which all transitions have been removed.

A PARAGRAPH WITH NO TRANSITIONS

> In "The Fly," Katherine Mansfield tries to show us the real personality of the boss beneath his exterior. The fly helps her to portray this real self. The boss goes through a range of emotions and feelings. He expresses these feelings to a small but determined fly, whom the reader realizes he unconsciously relates to his son. The author basically splits up the story into three parts, with the boss's emotions and actions changing quite measurably.

With old Woodifield, with himself, and with the fly, we see the boss's manipulativeness. Our understanding of him as a hard and cruel man grows.

We can, if we work at it, figure out the relationship of these sentences to one another, for this paragraph is essentially unified by one major idea. But the lack of transitions results in an abrupt, choppy rhythm; the paragraph lurches from one detail to the next, dragging the confused reader behind. See how much easier the passage is to read and understand with transitions added.

THE SAME PARAGRAPH WITH TRANSITIONS

In "The Fly," Katherine Mansfield tries to show us the real personality of the boss beneath his exterior. The fly in the story's title helps her to portray this real self. In the course of the story, the boss goes through a range of emotions. At the end, he finally expresses these feelings to a small but determined fly, whom the reader realizes he unconsciously relates to his son. To accomplish her goal, the author basically splits up the story into three parts, with the boss's emotions and actions changing measurably throughout. First with old Woodifield, then with himself, and last with the fly, we see the boss's manipulativeness. With each part, our understanding of him as a hard and cruel man grows.

Commonly used transitions

TO SIGNAL SEQUENCE

again, also, and, and then, besides, finally, first . . . second . . . third, furthermore, last, moreover, next, still, too

TO SIGNAL TIME

after a few days, after a while, afterward, as long as, as soon as, at last, at that time, before, earlier, immediately, in the meantime, in the past, lately, later, meanwhile, now, presently, simultaneously, since, so far, soon, then, thereafter, until, when

TO SIGNAL COMPARISON

again, also, in the same way, likewise, once more, similarly

TO SIGNAL CONTRAST

although, but, despite, even though, however, in contrast, in spite of, instead, nevertheless, nonetheless, on the contrary, on the one hand . . . on the other hand, regardless, still, though, yet

TO SIGNAL EXAMPLES

after all, for example, for instance, indeed, in fact, of course, specifically, such as, the following example, to illustrate

TO SIGNAL CAUSE AND EFFECT

accordingly, as a result, because, consequently, for this purpose, hence, so, then, therefore, thereupon, thus, to this end

TO SIGNAL PLACE

above, adjacent to, below, beyond, closer to, elsewhere, far, farther on, here, near, nearby, opposite to, there, to the left, to the right

TO SIGNAL CONCESSION

although it is true that, granted that, I admit that, it may appear that, naturally, of course

TO SIGNAL SUMMARY, REPETITION, OR CONCLUSION

as a result, as has been noted, as I have said, as mentioned earlier, as we have seen, in any event, in conclusion, in other words, in short, on the whole, therefore, to summarize

For Multilingual Writers: *Distinguishing among Transitions*

Distinguishing among some very similar common transition words can be difficult. The difference between *however* and *nevertheless,* for example, is a subtle one: while each introduces statements that contrast with what comes before it, *nevertheless* emphasizes the contrast whereas *however* tones it down. Check the usage of transitions in *The American Heritage Dictionary of the English Language,* which provides usage notes for easily confused words. Remember that you won't need to use an explicit transition in every sentence.

7f Work on opening and closing paragraphs.

Opening paragraphs

Even a good piece of writing may remain unread if it has a weak opening paragraph. In addition to announcing your topic, an introductory paragraph must engage readers' interest and focus their attention on what is to follow. At their best, introductory paragraphs serve as hors d'oeuvres, whetting the appetite for the following courses.

One common kind of opening paragraph follows a general-to-specific sequence, ending with a thesis. In such an introduction, the writer opens with a general statement and then gets more and more specific, concluding with the thesis. The following paragraph illustrates such an opening:

> Throughout Western civilization, places such as the ancient Greek agora, the New England town hall, the local church, the coffeehouse, the village square, and even the street corner have been arenas for debate on public affairs and society. Out of thousands of such encounters, "public opinion" slowly formed and became the context in which politics was framed. Although the public sphere never included everyone, and by itself did not determine the outcome of all parliamentary actions, it contributed to the spirit of dissent found in a healthy representative democracy. Many of these public spaces remain, but they are no longer centers for political discussion and action. They have largely been replaced by television and other forms of media—forms that arguably isolate citizens from one another rather than bringing them together.
>
> —MARK POSTER, "The Net as a Public Sphere"

In this paragraph, the opening sentence introduces a general subject—sites of public debate throughout history; subsequent sentences focus more specifically on the roles public spaces have played in democratic societies; and the last sentence presents the thesis, which the rest of the essay will develop.

OTHER EFFECTIVE WAYS OF OPENING

- with a quotation
- with an anecdote
- with a question
- with an opinion

Concluding paragraphs

A good conclusion wraps up a piece of writing in a meaningful and memorable way. If a strong opening paragraph arouses readers' curiosity, a strong concluding paragraph satisfies readers.

A common and effective strategy for concluding is to restate the central idea (but not word for word) and then move to several more general statements. The following paragraph uses this strategy, opening with a final point of comparison between Generals Grant and Lee, specifying it in several sentences, and then ending with a much more general statement:

> Lastly, and perhaps greatest of all, there was the ability, at the end, to turn quickly from war to peace once the fighting was over. Out of the way these two men behaved at Appomattox came the possibility of a peace of reconciliation. It was a possibility not wholly realized, in the years to come, but which did, in the end, help the two sections to become one nation again . . . after a war whose bitterness might have seemed to make such a reunion wholly impossible. No part of either man's life became him more than the part he played in this brief meeting in the McLean house at Appomattox. Their behavior there put all succeeding generations of Americans in their debt. Two great Americans, Grant and Lee—very different, yet under everything very much alike. Their encounter at Appomattox was one of the great moments of American history.
>
> —BRUCE CATTON, "Grant and Lee: A Study in Contrasts"

OTHER EFFECTIVE WAYS OF CONCLUDING

- with a quotation
- with a question
- with a vivid image
- with a call for action
- with a warning

8

Revising and Editing

Whether you are writing a wedding invitation, an email to a client, or a history essay, you will want to make time to revise, edit, and proofread what you write. Revising involves taking a fresh look at your draft, making sure that it includes all the necessary information and that the presentation is clear and effective. Editing involves fine-tuning your prose, attending to details of sentence structure, grammar, usage, punctuation, and spelling. Finally, careful proofreading aims at a perfect copy.

A Matter of Style: *Revising Online Writing*

The revising you do online will depend on your rhetorical situation. If a lot is at stake (a promotion or a contract, for example), then you will want to devote time and effort to revising: the writing must be correct, accurate, and persuasive. However, many less formal situations (casual email or newsgroup messages, for example) may call for conveying information quickly and easily; in such cases, the messages you write probably need to be revised only for clarity. In MUDs, your writing may be so short and so quick that revising is not even expected.

8a Revise.

If at all possible, put the draft away for a day or two to clear your mind and get some distance from your writing.

Rereading for meaning

At this point, don't worry about small details. Instead, concentrate on your message and how clearly you have expressed it. Note any places where the meaning seems unclear.

Remembering your purpose

Does your draft achieve its purpose? If you wrote for an assignment, go back to it to make sure that you did what was asked. If you set out to prove something, make sure you have done so. If you intended to propose a solution to a problem, make sure you have indeed set forth a well-supported solution rather than, for instance, an analysis of the problem.

Reconsidering your stance

Take time to look at your draft with one central question in mind: where are you coming from in this draft? Articulate the stance you take, and ask yourself what factors have led you to that position.

Considering your audience

How appropriately do you address your audience? Think carefully about your audience's experiences and expectations. Will you catch their interest, and will they be able to follow your discussion? Is the language formal or informal enough for these readers? Have you defined any terms they may not know? What objections might they raise?

Analyzing organization

One way to check the organization of a draft is to outline it, jotting down the main idea of each paragraph. Do the main ideas clearly relate to the thesis and to one another? Can you identify any confusing leaps from point to point? Have any important points been left out?

Considering your use of visuals

Have you used any visuals (graphs, maps, photographs, and so on)? If so, do they help make a point and get your meaning across? Are all visuals clearly labeled? Are their sources given? Are they referred to in the text? Consider whether there is any information in your draft that would be better presented as a visual.

Getting response

In addition to your own critical appraisal and that of an instructor or supervisor, you may want to get responses to your draft from friends, classmates, or colleagues. The questions on the next page can be used to respond to someone else's draft or to analyze your own. If you ask other people to evaluate your draft, be sure that they know your assignment, intended audience, and purpose.

For Multilingual Writers:
Asking a Native Speaker to Review Your Draft

One good way to make sure that your writing is well developed and easy to follow is to have someone else read it. You might find it especially helpful to ask a native speaker to read over your draft and to point out any words or patterns that are unclear or not idiomatic. (See Chapter 62 for more on words used idiomatically.)

Some Guidelines for Peer Response

- *Assignment and purpose.* Does the draft carry out the assignment? Does it accomplish its purpose?

- *Title and introduction.* Does the title tell readers what the draft is about? How does it catch readers' interest? Does the opening make readers want to continue? How else might the draft begin?

- *Thesis.* What is the central idea? Is it stated explicitly? Should it be?

- *Audience.* How does the draft interest and appeal to its audience? Is it written at the right level for the intended readers?

- *Rhetorical stance.* Where does the writer stand? What words indicate the stance? What influences have likely contributed to that stance?

- *Supporting points.* List the main points, and review them one by one. How does each one support the thesis? Do any need to be explained more or less? Do any seem confusing or boring? Do any make you want to know more? Should any points be eliminated or added? How well is each point supported by details?

- *Visuals.* Do any visuals add to the key points? Are they clearly referred to in the draft?

- *Organization and flow.* Is the writing easy to follow? Are the ideas presented in an order that will make sense to readers?

- *Transitions.* Are there effective transitions within sentences, between paragraphs, and from one idea to the next?

- *Conclusion.* Does the draft conclude in a memorable way, or does it seem to end abruptly or trail off into vagueness? How else might it end?

- *Final thoughts.* What are the main strengths and weaknesses of the draft? What might still be confusing to readers? What is the single most important thing you say in the draft? What will readers want to know more about?

8b Edit.

Once you have revised a draft for content and organization, it is time to look closely at your sentences and words. Turning a "blah" sentence into a memorable one—or finding exactly the right word to express a thought—can result in writing that is really worth reading.

As with life, variety is the spice of sentences. You can add variety to your sentences by looking closely at their length, structure, and opening patterns.

Varying sentence length

Too many short sentences, especially one following another, can sound like a series of blasts on a car horn, whereas a steady stream of long sentences may tire or confuse readers. Most writers aim for some variety in length, breaking up a series of fairly long sentences with a very brief one.

In examining the following paragraph, the writer discovered that all five of its sentences were almost exactly the same length. See how varying the lengths of two sentences makes the paragraph easier to read:

The incident, which occurred when I was six and

my sister was seven, has changed me in many ways.

~~Primarily as a~~ result of ~~the~~ harsh appraisal ~~my~~
↑*One*   ↑*that*
has been an extreme concern for
~~father's acquaintance gave me, I have always been~~
↑

~~very concerned about~~ my appearance. Conceivably,

a concern about my appearance can be beneficial;

however, at times it is a bit of an obsession. I

have become overly critical of my own appearance and

even more critical of the appearance of those around

me. I instantly judge a person by the way he or she

looks, a ~~prejudice that includes everyone, not just~~
practice that is the basis for prejudice and one that limits
↑
my appreciation of myself as well as of others.
~~minorities.~~

Varying sentence openings

Opening sentence after sentence in the same way results in a jerky, abrupt, or choppy rhythm. You can vary sentence openings by beginning with a dependent clause, a phrase, an adverb, a conjunctive adverb, or a coordinating conjunction (23b).

The following paragraph provides vivid description and imaginative dialogue, but see how revising some of the sentence openings improves the flow and makes the paragraph easier to read and more memorable.

> "Your daughter is absolutely beautiful!" the woman
> gushed as she talked to my father. ~~She was a~~ friend of
> his from work, ~~and~~ had heard much about my sister Tracy
> and me but had never met us before. I could tell that
> she was one of those blunt, elderly women, the type
> that pinches cheeks, because as soon as she finished
> appraising my sister, she turned to me with a
> deductive look in her eye. Her face said it all. ~~Her~~
> ~~beady~~ brown eyes ~~traveled~~ slowly from my head to my
> toe, ~~as~~ she sized me up and said rather condescend-
> ingly, "Oh, and she must be the smart one." I looked
> down at my toes as I rocked nervously back and forth.
> Then, looking at my sister, I realized for the first
> time that she was very pretty and that I was, well,
> the smart one.

Inserted above the text:
- *A* (above "She was a")
- *she* (above "and")
- *Beady* (above "Her")
- *traveling* (above "traveled")

Checking for sentences opening with it *and* there

As you go over the opening sentences of your draft, look especially at those beginning with *it* or *there*. Sometimes these words can create a special emphasis, as in *It was a dark and stormy night.* But they can also be easily overused or misused. Another, more subtle problem with these openings is that they may be used to avoid taking responsibility for a statement. The following sentence can be improved by editing:

> *The university must*
> ▶ ~~It is necessary to~~ raise student fees.
>   ^

Examining words

Even more than paragraphs and sentences, word choice—or diction—offers writers an opportunity to put their personal stamp on a piece of writing. Study your word choice carefully, making sure you get the most mileage out of each word. The following questions should help you become aware of the kinds of words you use:

- Are the nouns primarily abstract and general or concrete and specific? Too many abstract and general nouns can result in boring prose. To say that you bought a new car is much less memorable and interesting than to say you bought a new red convertible or a new Nissan.

- Are there too many nouns in relation to the number of verbs? The *effect* of the *overuse* of *nouns* in *writing* is the *placing* of too much *strain* on the inadequate *number* of *verbs* and the resultant *prevention* of *movement* of the *thought.* In the preceding sentence, one tiny verb (*is*) has to drag along the entire weight of eleven nouns. The result is a heavy, boring sentence. Why not say instead, *Overusing nouns places a big strain on the verbs and consequently slows down the prose*?

- How many verbs are forms of *be*—*be, am, is, are, was, were, being, been*? If *be* verbs account for more than about a third of your total verbs, you are probably overusing them (25a, b).

- Are verbs *active* wherever possible? Passive verbs are harder to read and remember than active ones. Although the passive voice has many uses, your writing will often be stronger, more lively, and more energetic if you use active verbs (25g).

- Are your words *appropriate*? Check to be sure they are not too fancy—or too casual.

Using spell checkers and style checkers

While these software tools won't catch every spelling error or identify all problems of style, they can be very useful. Most professional writers use their spell checkers religiously. Remember, however, that spell checkers are limited; they don't recognize most proper names, foreign words, or specialized language, and they do not recognize homonym errors (misspelling *there* as *their,* for example). Most commercial style checkers will highlight clichés, repetitions, or expressions like *it is* and *there are,* but they are not very sophisticated and sometimes give bad advice. (For additional advice on using style checkers, see p. 139.)

Examining tone

Tone refers to the attitude that a writer's language conveys toward the topic and the audience. In examining the tone of your draft, think about the nature of the topic, your own attitude toward it, and that of your intended audience. Check for connotations, or specific associations, of words as well as slang, jargon, emotional language, and the level of formality. Is your language creating the tone you want to achieve (humorous, serious, impassioned, and so on), and is that tone an appropriate one, given your audience and topic? You may discover from examining the tone of your draft that your own attitude toward the topic is different from what you originally thought.

Proofreading the final draft

Take time for one last, careful proofreading, which means reading to correct any typographical errors or other slips, such as inconsistencies in spelling and punctuation. To proofread most effectively, read through the copy aloud, making sure that punctuation marks are used correctly and consistently, that all sentences are complete—except for intentional fragments in narrative writing—and that no words are missing. Then go through it again, this time reading backward so that you can focus on each individual word and its spelling. This final proofreading aims to make your written product letter-perfect—something you can be proud of.

9
Thinking Critically: Constructing and Analyzing Arguments

In one important sense, all language use has an argumentative edge. When you greet friends warmly, you wish to convince them that you are genuinely glad to see them. By putting a particular story on the front page, a newspaper argues that it is more important than other stories; by using emotional language and focusing on certain details in reporting an event, a newscaster tries to persuade us to view the event in a particular way. What one reporter might call a *massive demonstration* another might call a *noisy protest* and yet another, an *angry march*.

Some Guidelines for Thinking Critically

All information carries some perspective or spin. Examine all ideas carefully—including your own.

- What is the agenda or underlying plan?
- Why does the writer hold these ideas or beliefs? What social, economic, political, or other conditions may have influenced these beliefs?
- What does the writer want readers to do—and why?
- What reasons does the writer offer in support of his or her ideas? Are they good reasons?
- What sources does the writer rely on? How current and reliable are they? What agendas do these sources have? Are any perspectives left out?
- What objections might be made to the argument?
- What are the writer's underlying values or unstated assumptions? Are they acceptable? Why, or why not?
- Be especially careful to examine all the information you find on the Web. What individual or group is responsible for this site and the argument?
- Study any photographs, drawings, graphs, or other visual images carefully. What do they contribute to the argument?
- Remember to consider your own beliefs. Once you make up your own mind, question the ideas and evidence that led to your conclusions.

9a Understand what counts as argument.

For many years, traditional Western notions of argument tended to highlight one purpose—winning. Although winning is still one important purpose of argument, it is by no means the only purpose.

TO WIN The most traditional purpose of academic argument, arguing to win is used in campus debating societies, in political debates, in trials, and often in business. The writer or speaker aims to present a position that prevails over some other position.

TO CONVINCE Often, out-and-out defeat of another's position is not only unrealistic but undesirable. Instead, the goal might be to convince another person to change his or her mind. Doing so calls on a writer to provide *compelling reasons* for an audience to accept the writer's conclusion.

TO EXPLORE AN ISSUE Argument to explore an issue or reach a decision seeks a sharing of information and perspectives in order to make informed choices—from deciding which computer to buy to exploring with your family the best health care system for an elderly relative.

TO MEDITATE Sometimes you may argue with yourself in the form of intense meditations or even prayer—to reach peace of mind on a troubling subject, for example.

Checking whether a statement can be argued

In much of your work at school or on the job, you will be asked to take a position and argue for that position—whether to prove a mathematical equation or analyze a trend in your company's sales. Such work will usually call for you to convince or decide and will therefore require you to consider an arguable statement, to make a claim based on the statement, and finally to present good reasons in support of the claim. An arguable statement, to begin with, should have three characteristics:

1. It should attempt to convince readers of something, change their minds about something, or urge them either to do something or to explore a topic in order to make a wise decision.
2. It should address a problem for which no easily acceptable solution exists or ask a question to which no absolute answer exists.
3. It should present a position that readers might realistically have varying perspectives on.

ARGUABLE   Video games lead to violent behavior.

This statement seeks to convince, suggests a causal relationship that is difficult to prove, and takes a position many disagree with.

UNARGUABLE   Video games earn millions of dollars every year for the
companies that produce them.

This statement can easily be verified and thus does not offer a basis for
argument.

9b Formulate an argumentative thesis.

Once you have an arguable statement, you need to make a claim about
it, one you will then ask readers to accept. For example, look at the
following statement:

The use of pesticides endangers the lives of farm workers.

This statement is arguable because it aims to convince, it addresses
an issue with no easily identifiable answer, and it can realistically be
disputed.

It makes a comment—that pesticides threaten lives; the comment is
just a factual statement about *what is*. To develop a claim that can
become the working thesis for an argument, you often need to direct
this kind of statement toward some action; that is, your claim needs to
move from *what is* to *what ought to be*, as in the following thesis:

┌──────────── TOPIC ─────────────┐
▶ **Because pesticides endanger the lives of farm workers,**
┌──── COMMENT ────┐
their use should be banned.

In academic writing, you will often make a claim that urges readers
not to take action but to interpret something in a certain way. In such
cases, the claim about what ought to be is usually implied rather than
stated.

▶ **Moral opposition to slavery was the major cause of the Civil War.**

Implied, but not stated, is the claim that economic or constitutional causes
were far less important than this one was.

9c Shape your appeal to your audience.

Arguments and the claims they make are effective only insofar as they
appeal to particular audiences. For example, if you want to argue for
increased lighting in parking garages on campus, you might appeal to

students on a listserv by citing examples drawn from student experiences of the safety problems in such dimly lit garages. If you are writing to university administrators, however, you might focus on the negative publicity associated with past attacks in campus garages and evoke the anger that such attacks cause in parents, alumni, and other important groups.

Keep your audience in mind as you develop any argument.

- Establish common ground with your readers wherever possible.
- Show that you respect your audience's interests and views.
- Choose examples and other pieces of verbal and visual evidence that your audience will understand and relate to.
- Choose language, style, and the level of formality most appropriate to your audience.

9d Formulate good reasons to support your claim.

Torture, wrote Aristotle, makes for a very convincing argument but not one that reasonable people will resort to. In effecting real changes in minds and hearts, we need instead to rely on *good reasons* — reasons that establish our credibility, reasons that appeal to logic, and reasons that appeal to emotion.

9e Establish your credibility.

To make your argument convincing, you must first gain the respect and trust of your readers, or establish your credibility with them. The ancient Greeks called this particular kind of character appeal *ethos* and valued it highly. In general, writers can establish credibility in three ways.

Demonstrating knowledge

A writer can establish credibility first by establishing his or her credentials. To decide whether you know enough to argue an issue credibly, consider the following questions:

- Can you provide information about your topic from sources other than your own knowledge?
- What are the sources of your information?
- How reliable are your sources?

- Do any sources contradict one another? If so, can you account for or resolve the contradictions?
- If you have personal experience relating to the issue, would telling about this experience help support your claim?

These questions may well show that you must do more research, check sources, resolve contradictions, refocus your working thesis, or even change your topic.

Establishing common ground

Many arguments between people or groups are doomed to end without resolution because the two sides occupy no common ground, no starting point of agreement. The following questions can help you find common ground in presenting an argument:

- What are the differing perspectives on this issue?
- What common ground can you find—aspects of the issue on which all sides agree?
- How can you express such common ground clearly to all sides?
- How can you discover—and consider—opinions on this issue that differ from your own?
- How can you use language—occupational, regional, or ethnic varieties of English, or languages other than English—to establish common ground with those you address?

You can read more about common ground in Chapter 33.

Demonstrating fairness

In arguing a position, writers must demonstrate fairness toward opposing arguments. Audiences are more inclined to give credibility to writers who seem to be considering and representing their opponents' views fairly than to those who seem to be ignoring or distorting such views. The following questions can help you avoid such unfair tactics and establish yourself as open-minded and evenhanded:

- How can you show that you are taking into account all significant points of view?
- How can you demonstrate that you understand and sympathize with points of view other than your own?
- What can you do to show that you have considered evidence carefully, including evidence that does not support your position?

> **For Multilingual Writers:** *Counting Your Own Experience*
>
> You may have been told that your own personal experience doesn't count in making academic arguments. If so, reconsider this advice, for showing an audience that you have personal experience with a topic can carry strong persuasive appeal with many English-speaking readers. As with all evidence used in an argument, however, evidence based on your own experience must be pertinent to the topic, understandable to the audience, and clearly related to your purpose.

9f Use logical appeals.

Our credibility alone cannot and should not carry the full burden of convincing readers. Indeed, many view the logic of the argument—the reasoning behind it—as equally, if not more, important.

Providing examples, precedents, and narratives

Just as a picture can sometimes be worth a thousand words, so can a well-conceived example be extremely valuable in arguing a point. Examples are used most often to support generalizations or to bring abstractions to life. In an argument about violence and video games in which you make the general statement that such games send a message that violence is fun, you might then illustrate that generalization with these examples:

> For instance, the makers of the game *Quake* present deadly and deranged acts of violence as fun entertainment, while the makers of *Postal* imply that preying on the defenseless is acceptable behavior by marketing a game in which players kill innocent, helpless victims.

Precedents are particular kinds of examples taken from the past. If, as part of a proposal for increased lighting in the library garage, you point out that the university has increased lighting in four similar garages in the past year, you are arguing on the basis of precedent.

In research writing (see Chapters 10–13), you must usually list your sources for any examples or precedents not based on your own knowledge.

Because storytelling is universal, narratives can be very persuasive in helping readers understand and accept an argument. In arguing for increased funding for the homeless, for instance, you might include a brief narrative about a day in the life of a homeless person to dramatize the issue and help readers *see* the need for more funding. Stories drawn from your own experience can have particular appeal to readers, for they not only help make your point in true-to-life, human terms but also establish your credibility by helping readers know you better and therefore identify with you more closely (9e).

The following questions can help you check any use of example, precedent, and narrative:

- How representative are the examples?
- Are they sufficient in strength or number to lead to a generalization?
- In what ways do they support your point?
- How closely does the precedent relate to the point you're trying to make? Are the situations really similar?
- How timely is the precedent? (What would have been applicable in 1920 is not necessarily applicable today.)
- Does the narrative support your thesis?
- Will the story's significance to the argument be clear to your readers?
- Is the story one of several good reasons, or does it have to carry the main burden of the argument?

Citing authority and testimony

Another way to support an argument logically is to cite an authority. In recent decades, the use of authority has figured prominently in the controversy over smoking. Since the U.S. surgeon general's 1964 announcement that smoking is hazardous to health, followed by a series of court decisions supporting that link, many Americans have quit smoking, largely convinced by the authority of the scientists offering the evidence.

Ask yourself the following questions to be sure you are using authorities effectively:

- Is the authority timely? (The argument that the United States should pursue a policy just because it was supported by Thomas Jefferson will probably fail because Jefferson's time was so radically different from ours.)
- Is the authority qualified to judge the topic at hand? (To cite a fan's Web site on Tom Cruise in an essay on film history is not likely to strengthen your argument.)
- Is the authority likely to be known and respected by readers? (To cite an unfamiliar authority without some identification will lessen the impact of the evidence.)

- Are the authority's credentials clearly stated and verifiable? (Especially with Web-based sources, it is crucial to know whose authority guarantees the reliability of the information.)

Testimony—the evidence that an authority presents in support of a claim—is a feature of much contemporary argument. If testimony is timely, accurate, representative, and provided by a respected authority, then it, like authority itself, can add powerful support to an argument.

In research writing (see Chapters 10–13), you should list your sources for authority and testimony not based on your own knowledge.

For Multilingual Writers: *Bringing in Other Voices*

Sometimes quoting authorities will prompt you to use language other than standard academic English, and in ways that support your own authority. For instance, if you're writing about political relations between Mexico and the United States, you might quote a leader of a Mexican American organization; using that person's *own words*—which may be partly or entirely in Spanish or a regional variety of English—can carry extra power, calling up a voice from a pertinent community. See Chapter 32 for advice about using varieties of English and other languages.

Establishing causes and effects

Showing that one event is the cause—or the effect—of another can sometimes help support an argument. Suppose you are trying to explain, in a petition to change your grade in a course, why you were unable to take the final examination. In such a case, you would probably try to trace the causes of your failure to appear—the death of your grandmother followed by the theft of your car, perhaps—so that the committee reading the petition would consider anew the effect—your not taking the examination.

Tracing causes often lays the groundwork for an argument, particularly if the effect of the causes is one we would like to change. In an environmental science class, for example, a student may argue that a national law regulating smokestack emissions from utility plants is needed because (1) acid rain on the East Coast originates from emissions at utility plants in the Midwest, (2) acid rain kills trees and other vegetation, (3) utility lobbyists have prevented midwestern states from passing strict laws controlling emissions from such plants, and (4) in the absence of such laws, acid rain will destroy most eastern forests by 2020. In this case, the fourth point ties all of the previous points together to provide an overall argument from effect: unless X, then Y.

Using inductive and deductive reasoning

Traditionally, logical arguments are classified as using either inductive or deductive reasoning, both of which almost always work together. Inductive reasoning, most simply, is the process of making a generalization based on a number of specific instances. If you find you are ill on ten occasions after eating seafood, for example, you will likely draw the inductive generalization that seafood makes you ill. It may not be an absolute certainty that seafood was the culprit, but the *probability* lies in that direction.

Deductive reasoning, on the other hand, reaches a conclusion by assuming a general principle (known as a major premise) and then applying that principle to a specific case (the minor premise). In practice, this general principle is usually derived from induction. The inductive generalization *Seafood makes me ill,* for instance, could serve as the major premise for the deductive argument *Since all seafood makes me ill, the plate of it just put before me is certain to make me ill.*

Deductive arguments like this one have traditionally been analyzed as syllogisms—three-part statements containing a major premise, a minor premise, and a conclusion.

MAJOR PREMISE   All people die.

MINOR PREMISE   I am a person.

CONCLUSION   I will die.

Syllogisms, however, are too rigid and absolute to serve in arguments about questions that have no absolute answers, and they often lack any appeal to an audience. From Aristotle came a simpler alternative, the enthymeme, which calls on the audience to supply the implied major premise. Consider the following example:

> Since violent video games can be addictive and cause psychological harm, players and their parents must carefully evaluate such games and monitor their use.

You can analyze this enthymeme by restating it in the form of two premises and a conclusion.

MAJOR PREMISE	Games that cause harm to players should be evaluated and monitored.
MINOR PREMISE	Violent video games cause addiction and psychological harm to players.
CONCLUSION	These games should be evaluated and monitored.

Note that the major premise is one the writer can count on an audience agreeing with or supplying: safety and common sense demand that potentially harmful games should be used with great care. By implicitly asking an audience to supply this premise to an argument, a writer engages the audience's participation.

Another way to use deductive arguments is from the system developed by philosopher Stephen Toulmin, which looks for claims, reasons, and warrants instead of major and minor premises. In Toulmin's terms, the argument about video games would look like this:

CLAIM	Violent video games should be carefully evaluated and their use monitored.
REASON(S)	Violent video games cause addiction and psychological harm to players.
WARRANT	Games that cause harm to players should be evaluated and monitored.

Whether it is expressed as a syllogism, an enthymeme, or a claim, a deductive conclusion is only as strong as the premise or reasons on which it is based.

9g Use effective emotional appeals.

Most successful arguments appeal to our hearts as well as to our minds. This principle was vividly demonstrated a number of years ago, when we began hearing about famine in Africa. Facts and figures (logical appeals) convinced many that the famine was real and serious. What brought an outpouring of aid, however, was the arresting emotional power of televised images and photographs of starving children.

Using concrete descriptive details

Like photographs, vivid description can bring a moving immediacy to any argument. A student may amass facts and figures, including diagrams and maps, to illustrate the problem of wheelchair access to the library. But only when the student asks a friend who uses a wheelchair to accompany her to the library does the writing gain the concrete descriptive details necessary to move readers. The student can write, "Marie inched her heavy wheelchair up the narrow, steep entrance ramp, her arms straining to pull up the last twenty feet, her face pinched with the sheer effort."

Using figurative language

Figurative language, or figures of speech, paint a detailed and vivid picture by making striking comparisons between something you are writing about and something else that helps a reader visualize, identify with, or understand it (35d).

Figures of speech include metaphors, similes, and analogies. Most simply, metaphors compare two things directly: *Richard the Lion-Hearted; old age is the evening of life.* Similes make comparisons using *like* or *as: Richard is as brave as a lion; old age is like the evening of life.* Analogies are extended metaphors or similes that compare an unfamiliar concept or process to a more familiar one. Metaphors, similes, and analogies are crucial to understanding.

> I see the Internet as a city struggling to be built, its laws only now being for-mulated, its notions of social order arising out of the needs of its citizens and the demands of their environment. Like any city, the Net has its char-latans and its thieves as well as its poets, engineers, and philosophers[. . .]. Our experience of the Internet will be determined by how we master its core competencies. They are the design principles that are shaping the electronic city.
>
> —PAUL GILSTER, *Digital Literacy*

9h Recognize the use and misuse of fallacies.

Fallacies have traditionally been thought of as errors in argument, but they often work very effectively to convince or affect audiences. As both a writer and a reader of arguments, you will want to think critically about how fallacies work.

Recognizing ethical fallacies

Some arguments focus not on establishing the credibility of the writer but on destroying the credibility of an opponent. At times, such attacks are justified: if a nominee for the Supreme Court has acted dishonestly in law school, for example, that information is a legitimate argument against the nominee's confirmation. Many times, however, someone attacks a person's character in order to avoid dealing with the issue at hand. Be extremely careful about attacking an opponent's credibility, for doing so without justification can harm your own credibility. Such unjustified attacks are called ethical fallacies. They take two main forms: ad hominem charges and guilt by association.

AD HOMINEM

Ad hominem (Latin for "to the man") charges directly attack someone's character rather than focusing on the issue at hand, suggesting that because something is wrong with this person, whatever he or she says must also be wrong.

▶ **Patricia Ireland is just a hysterical feminist. We shouldn't listen to her views on abortion.**

Labeling Ireland *hysterical* and linking that label with *feminist* focuses on Ireland's character rather than on her views on the issue at hand.

GUILT BY ASSOCIATION

Guilt by association attacks someone's credibility by linking that person with a person or activity the audience considers bad, suspicious, or untrustworthy.

▶ **Senator Fleming does not deserve reelection; one of her assistants turned out to be involved with organized crime.**

Is there any evidence that the senator knew about the organized-crime involvement?

Recognizing logical fallacies

Readers who detect fallacious appeals may reject an otherwise worthy argument that relies on them. Your time will be well spent, therefore, in learning to recognize logical fallacies.

BEGGING THE QUESTION

Begging the question is a kind of circular argument that treats a question as if it has already been answered.

▶ **That TV news provides accurate and reliable information was demonstrated conclusively on last week's *60 Minutes*.**

This statement says in effect that TV news is accurate and reliable because TV news says so.

POST HOC FALLACY

The *post hoc* fallacy, from the Latin *post hoc, ergo propter hoc* ("after this, therefore caused by this"), assumes that just because B happened *after* A, it must have been *caused* by A.

▶ **We should not rebuild the docks. Every time we do, a hurricane comes along and damages them.**

Does the reconstruction cause hurricanes?

NON SEQUITUR

A non sequitur (Latin for "it does not follow") attempts to tie together two or more logically unrelated ideas as if they *were* related.

▶ **If we can send a spacecraft to Mars, then we can discover a cure for cancer.**

These are both scientific goals, but do they have anything else in common?

EITHER-OR FALLACY

The either-or fallacy asserts that a complex situation can have only two possible outcomes, one of which is necessary or preferable.

▶ **If we do not build the aqueduct, businesses in the tri-cities will be forced to shut down because of lack of water.**

Do no other alternatives exist?

HASTY GENERALIZATION

A hasty generalization bases a conclusion on too little evidence or on bad or misunderstood evidence.

▶ **I couldn't understand the lecture today, so I'm sure this course will be impossible.**

How can the writer be so sure based on only *one* piece of evidence?

OVERSIMPLIFICATION

Oversimplification of the relation between causes and effects is another fallacy based on careless reasoning.

▶ **If we prohibit the sale of alcohol, we will get rid of drunkenness.**

This claim oversimplifies the relation between laws and human behavior.

Recognizing emotional fallacies

Unfair or overblown emotional appeals attempt to overcome readers' good judgment.

BANDWAGON APPEAL

A common emotional fallacy is bandwagon appeal, which suggests that a great movement is under way and the reader will be a fool or a traitor not to join it.

▶ **Voters are flocking to candidate X by the millions, so you'd better cast your vote the right way.**

Why should you jump on this bandwagon? Where is the evidence to support this claim?

FLATTERY

Flattery is an emotional fallacy that tries to persuade readers to do something by suggesting that they are thoughtful, intelligent, or perceptive enough to agree with the writer.

▶ **We know you have the taste to recognize that an investment in an Art-Form ring will pay off in the future.**

How will it pay off?

IN-CROWD APPEAL

In-crowd appeal, a special kind of flattery, invites readers to identify with an admired and select group.

▶ **Want to know a secret that more and more of Middletown's successful young professionals are finding out about? It's Mountainbrook Manor, the condominiums that combine the best of the old with the best of the new.**

Who are these "successful young professionals," and will you become one by moving to Mountainbrook Manor?

VEILED THREATS

Veiled threats try to frighten readers into agreement by hinting that they will suffer adverse consequences if they don't agree.

▶ **If Public Service Electric Company does not get an immediate 15 percent rate increase, its services to you, its customers, may be seriously affected.**

How serious is this possible effect? Is it likely—or even legal?

FALSE ANALOGIES

False analogies make comparisons between two situations that are *not* alike in most or important respects.

▶ **If the United States gets involved in a land war in the Middle East, it will turn out just like Vietnam.**

Is there any point of analogy except military engagement? This example was written in 1988. The Persian Gulf War of 1991 demonstrates well the weaknesses of such analogies.

9i Cite sources in an argument.

In constructing a written argument, it is usually necessary—and often essential—to use sources. The key to persuading people to accept your argument is good reasons; and even if your assignment doesn't specify that you must consult outside sources, they are often the most effective way of finding and establishing these reasons. Sources can help you in a number of ways:

- to provide background information on your topic
- to demonstrate your knowledge of the topic to readers
- to cite authority and testimony in support of your thesis
- to find opinions that differ from your own, which can help you sharpen your thinking, qualify your thesis if necessary, and demonstrate fairness to opposing arguments

For a thorough discussion of finding, gathering, and evaluating sources, both off- and online, see Chapter 12.

9j Organize an argument.

Once you have assembled good reasons in support of an argumentative thesis, you must organize your material in order to present the argument convincingly. Although there is no ideal or universally favored organizational framework, you may find it useful to try one of the following ones.

The classical system

The system of argument often followed by ancient Greek and Roman orators is now referred to as *classical*. You can adapt the ancient format to written arguments as follows:

1. Introduction
   - Gain readers' attention and interest.
   - Establish your qualifications to write about your topic.
   - Establish common ground with readers.

- Demonstrate fairness.
- State or imply your thesis.
2. Background
   - Present any necessary background information, including pertinent personal narrative.
3. Lines of argument
   - Present good reasons (including logical and emotional appeals) in support of your thesis.
   - Generally present reasons in order of importance.
   - Demonstrate ways your argument may be in readers' best interest.
4. Consideration of alternative arguments
   - Examine alternative points of view.
   - Note advantages and disadvantages of alternative views.
   - Explain why one view is better than other(s).
5. Conclusion
   - Summarize the argument if you choose.
   - Elaborate on the implication of your thesis.
   - Make clear what you want readers to think or do.
   - Reinforce your credibility.

The Toulmin system

Another useful system of argument was developed by philosopher Stephen Toulmin. This simplified form of the Toulmin system can help you organize an argumentative essay:

1. Make your claim (a statement that is debatable or controversial).

   ▶ **The federal government should ban smoking.**

2. Qualify your claim if necessary.

   ▶ **The ban would be limited to public places.**

3. Present good reasons to support your claim.

   ▶ **Smoking causes serious diseases in smokers.**
   ▶ **Nonsmokers are endangered by others' smoke.**

4. Explain the warrant (underlying assumptions) that connects your claim and your reasons. If the warrant is controversial, provide backing for it.

   WARRANT   The Constitution was established to "promote the general welfare."

WARRANT	Citizens are entitled to protection from harmful actions by others.
BACKING	The United States is based on a political system that is supposed to serve the basic needs of its people, including their health.

5. Provide additional grounds to support your claim (facts, statistics, testimony, and the use of other logical, ethical, or emotional appeals).

STATISTICS	Cite the incidence of deaths attributed to secondhand smoke.
FACTS	Cite lawsuits won recently against large tobacco companies, including one that awarded billions of dollars to states in reparation for smoking-related health care costs.
FACTS	Cite bans on smoking already imposed in many public institutions and places of employment—such as Ohio State University and restaurants in California.
AUTHORITY	Cite the surgeon general and the president.

6. Acknowledge and respond to possible counterarguments.

COUNTERARGUMENT	Smokers have rights, too.
RESPONSE	The suggested ban applies only to public places; smokers would be free to smoke in private.

7. Finally, draw your conclusion, stated in the strongest way possible.

9k A sample argument essay

Asked to write an essay addressed to her classmates—one that makes an argumentative claim and supports it with good reasons—Heather Ricker decided to follow up on her interest in current debates over whether and how video games may affect users' behavior. Her essay is organized according to the classical system and annotated to point out the various parts of her argument as well as her use of good reasons and appeals to logic, credibility, and emotion.

Ricker 1

Heather Ricker

Professor Lunsford

English 167

August 16, 1999

Video Games: Buyers Beware!

"Stay alive at all costs! Find the key! .... Opening gets
reader's
Kill the bad guys!" This is how one eighth- attention and
provides
grader describes the principles of playing background
information
video games. Such games might seem like

harmless fun, but what if the violence

attracts and addicts young players, affecting

their behavior and their view of reality?

Some say that violent video games have

minimal impact on young teenagers, pointing

out that most video game players live

completely normal lives. The weaknesses in

that argument are almost too obvious: first,

"most" is not "all." More important, just

because a player does not immediately

imitate specific violent acts found in video

games does not mean the games will have no

long-term negative impact on that player's

views and behavior. Because of this .... States
argumenta-
possibility, parents should assume tive thesis

responsibility for evaluating video games

and should prohibit young teenagers from

purchasing those that are especially

violent.

To begin with, a number of authorities .... Introduces
good reason:
claim that playing a violent video game does violent video
games can
be a threat to
health

Ricker 2

present a threat to the user's psychological
health. As early as 1983, Geoffrey and
Elizabeth Loftus, in their book Mind at
Play: The Psychology of Video Games, warned
about the dangers of violent video games:
"Although we can never be sure in any
individual case, a substantial body of
evidence indicates that viewing excessive
violence on the screen is associated with
aggression and violent behavior among
children and teenagers" (98). More recently,
studies have measured changes in behavior
and emotional responses to video games,
Cites sources ┈┈┈┈ ranging from "assertiveness" (Journal of
Child Study qtd. in Boal, "Shooters") and
withdrawal (Jeanne Funk qtd. in Boal, "One
Step") to "aggression, anger, and hostility"
(A. Mehrabian and W. J. Wixen qtd. in
"Social," sec. I). While in its survey of
the research on video game playing,
Mediascope, the publication of a nonprofit
research organization, concludes that there
are not sufficient studies, especially of
current games, to make any definitive
statements about the dangers of video game
use, parents should be concerned--maybe more
so because so few studies have been
conducted.

In addition, playing violent video
games adversely affects psychological health

Ricker 3

by actually addicting players. One of the
most troubling influences video games have
on players is the medium's remarkable
ability to fixate a player's attention or,
to borrow psychologist Sherry Turkle's term,
its "holding power" (30). Addictive
reactions in the body can be linked to some
of the visual and aural signals found in
video games--signals that cause the eyes,
for example, to stop blinking for extended
periods. This phenomenon triggers the
release of dopamine, a neurotransmitter
thought by some to be the "master molecule
of addiction" (Quittner 3). Is this chemical
association the reason forty out of the
forty-seven top-rated Nintendo games have
violence as their theme (Cesarone)?

Admittedly, according to a report in
the New York Times, the very best-selling
games are nonviolent (Miller). But even
without being top sellers, the violent games
sell well. The National Coalition on
Television Violence (NCTV) rates the violent
content of games and concludes that violence
is indeed a theme in more than half of the
games on the market. As reported by
Cesarone, the NCTV rates 55.7 percent of
games as unfit or highly violent.

Games that mimic military combat
training not only encourage brutality but

Good reason: video games can be addictive

Cites authority

Cites scientific data as evidence

Presents counterargument

Offers refutation to counterargument

Uses statistic as support

Ricker 4

Good reason: what games *don't* teach

also totally ignore teaching players about restraint--one more reason violent games should be off-limits. One of the main proponents of this claim has been Lieutenant Colonel David Grossman, an expert witness in federal and state cases dealing with violence. He worries that video games expose young people to combat-style training without teaching them when to put nonviolent alternatives into play (316). As Grossman points out, the military used Pavlovian methods of desensitization during World War II to train soldiers to kill other human beings against their natural tendencies. Repetitive conditioning such as

Analogy used in support of claim: repetitive conditioning in World War II led to desensitization; it can do so with video games as well

"killing" cadences and unit songs as well as referring to people as "targets" helped to dehumanize the enemy in the soldier's mind. Then there was the positive reinforcement of three-day passes for good marksmanship. It is not hard to see the similarities between military conditioning and desensitization and the conditioning that could come from shooting and harming video game targets. In fact, the military now uses such games in training its soldiers. Though video games may not transform players magically into virtual marines, Grossman's argument stresses that adolescents do learn from the

Ricker 5

games they play and thus violent games are
cause for concern.

In fact, rather than teaching when and
where to show restraint, the games and
promotion for the games teach that violence ············· Good reason:
can be fun. For instance, the game Resident   advertising
                                                             stresses
Evil promotes violence as entertainment.   violence
The publishers of the game invite players
to "face your fear" using "a vast selection ············· Introduces
of weapons." The makers of Carmageddon   examples as
                                                             evidence
imply that preying on the defenseless is
acceptable behavior: they market a game that
involves killing helpless civilians. Even
less violent games like Klingon Honor Guard
appeal to the notion that violence carried
out honorably is ennobling: "[. . .] you
must fulfill your blood oath--become the
ultimate warrior and exact glorious
revenge [. . .]" (Klingon).

Real killing may sometimes be an
inevitable evil, but it certainly should not
be considered fun or trivial. Parents should
not accept violence as entertainment in
games--and they should not think that such
violence can't affect the way their children
look at the world and at other human beings.

Recent protests--some coming from
senators--against the sale of violent video
games to minors have resulted in the

Ricker 6

Cites legisla-
tion that
responds to
the risk

formulation of the 21st Century Media
Responsibility Act. This bill, if passed,
would criminalize selling or lending violent
media to children under seventeen years of
age. In addition, it would require a common
rating system among various media (music,
video, TV) and a description of video game
contents. This required package labeling
might force retailers to curtail sales to
young teenagers.

The video game industry, however, claims
that it can censor itself with its own
labels. Its goal, of course, is to prevent
restrictive legislation that would cost it
"hordes of young gamers" (Boal, "One Step").
The makers of Kingpin, a particularly
violent game, have tried to protect the sale
of their game by declaring that it was
never intended for young audiences. But
before the Littleton shootings heightened
public awareness of video game violence,
this game could have been purchased easily
by young teens like the one described
by Salon's Mark Boal: "Once inside [the
store], Dave, who is 14 and has spiked
hair, makes a beeline for the box with the
large yellow [warning] sticker" ("One Step").
Clearly, by leaving enforcement of existing
ratings up to retailers, the video game

Ricker 7

industry hopes to avoid legislation and
protect its own interests.

Video games are not the only ························· Reiterates
contributing factor to society's tendencies   argumenta-
toward violence, but they are having an   tive thesis

influence. For this reason, we all must take ········· Makes direct
responsibility for the way we use video   appeal to
                                                    audience by
games.   using "we"

Ricker 8

Works Cited

Boal, Mark. "One Step Ahead of the Law."
    Salon 19 July 1999. 27 July 1999
    <http://www.salonmagazine.com/tech/
    feature/1999/07/19/kingpin/index.htm>.

---. "The Shooters and the Shrinks." Salon
    6 May 1999. 1 Aug. 1999 <http://
    www.salonmagazine.com/tech/feature/
    1999/05/06/game_violence/>.

Carmageddon. Interplay Productions. 1998.

Cesarone, Bernard. "Video Games and
    Children." Jan. 1994. 27 July 1999
    <http://www.parenthoodweb.com/articles/
    phw83.htm>.

Grossman, David. On Killing: The
    Psychological Cost of Learning to Kill
    in War and Society. New York: Little,
    Brown, 1995.

Kingpin. Interplay Productions. 1999.

Klingon Honor Guard. MacSoft, Microprose,
    1998.

Loftus, Geoffrey R., and Elizabeth F.
    Loftus. Mind at Play: The Psychology of
    Video Games. New York: Basic, 1983.

Miller, Stephen C. "Most-Violent Video Games
    Are Not Biggest Sellers." New York
    Times July 1999. 10 Aug. 1999.

Ricker 9

Quittner, Joshua. "Are Video Games Really So
    Bad?" <u>Time</u> 10 May 1999. 27 July 1999
    <http://www.pathfinder.com/time/
    magazine/articles/0,3266,23885,00.html>.

<u>Resident Evil</u>. Capcom Entertainment. 1998.

"The Social Effects of Electronic Interactive
    Games: An Annotated Bibliography."
    <u>Mediascope</u> 27 July 1999 <http://
    www.mediascope.org/pubs/bseeig.htm>.

Turkle, Sherry. <u>Life on the Screen: Identity
    in the Age of the Internet</u>. New York:
    Simon, 1995.

Some Guidelines for Analyzing an Argument

Here are some questions that can help you judge the effectiveness of an argument:

- What gains readers' interest? (9c)
- How has the writer established qualifications to write about the topic—by showing personal experience with it? by citing authoritative sources? What in the introduction establishes common ground with readers? What background information is given? Is it sufficient? (9e)
- What is the claim? Is the claim qualified? Is a thesis stated? If not, will readers be able to recognize it? Is it sufficiently focused? (9b)
- What good reasons support the claim? (9d)
- What warrants or assumptions support these reasons? What backs up any warrants? (9e,f)
- What support is offered for the thesis—examples? facts? statistics? authorities? testimony? (9f)
- How has the writer appealed to readers' emotions? (9g)
- How has the writer used images, graphics, or other visuals to support the argument?
- Are there any fallacies? (9h)
- Are opposing points of view acknowledged and responded to? Has the writer noted both their advantages and disadvantages? (9e)
- How does the essay conclude—by summarizing the argument? elaborating on its implications? making an emotional appeal? Has the writer made clear what readers should think or do? (9j)

10

Preparing for a Research Project

Your employer asks you to recommend the best new intercom system. You need to plan a week's stay in Tokyo. Your twins want a clown or a magician for their fifth birthday party. An instructor assigns a term paper about a musician. Each of these situations calls for research, for examining various kinds of sources. And each of these situations calls for you to assess the data you collect, to synthesize your findings, and to come up with your own, original recommendation or conclusion. Many tasks that call for research, such as a term paper or a business report, require that your work culminate in a written document.

10a   Analyze a research assignment.

If you have been assigned a research project, be sure you understand the requirements and limits of the assignment before you begin your research. For example, in an introductory writing course, you might receive the following assignment:

> Choose a subject of interest to you, and use it as the basis for a research essay that makes and substantiates a claim.

In response to questions, the instructor might explain that the essay should use information from both print and online sources to support the claim, should be roughly ten to fifteen pages in length, and should be written for members of the writing class.

Before beginning a research project, you should also map out a rough but realistic schedule for your research.

Scheduling a Research Project

Date assigned: _____   Try to complete by:

Analyze project; decide on primary purpose and
audience; choose topic if necessary.   _____
Set aside library time; develop search strategy.   _____
Send for materials needed by mail.   _____

(continues on next page)

Do background research; narrow topic if necessary.   _____

Decide on research question, tentative hypothesis.   _____

Start working bibliography; track down sources.   _____

Gather or develop graphics or visuals needed.   _____

Develop working thesis and rough outline.   _____

If necessary, conduct interviews, make observations,
or distribute and collect questionnaires.   _____

Read and evaluate sources; take notes.   _____

Draft explicit thesis and outline.   _____

Prepare first draft, including visuals.   _____

Obtain and evaluate critical responses.   _____

Do more research if necessary.   _____

Revise draft.   _____

Prepare list of works cited.   _____

Edit revised draft; use spell checker.   _____

Prepare final draft.   _____

Do final proofreading.   _____

Final draft due: _____

10b   Consider the context of the research project.

Purpose

If you have been assigned a specific research project, keep in mind the cue words in that assignment. Does the assignment ask that you *describe, survey, analyze, explain, classify, compare,* or *contrast*? What do such words mean in this field (4a)?

Audience

Who will be the audience for your research project?

- Who will be interested in the information you gather, and why?
- What do you know about their backgrounds?

- What will they want to know? What will they already know?
- What response do you want to elicit from them?
- What assumptions might they hold about the topic?
- What kinds of evidence will you need to convince them of your view?
- What will your supervisor or instructor expect?

Rhetorical stance

Think about your own attitude toward your topic. Are you just curious about it? Do you like it? dislike it? find it troubling? What influences have shaped your stance?

Scope

How many or what kind(s) of sources should you use? What kind of visuals—charts, maps, photographs, and so on—will you need to include? Will you be doing any field research—interviewing, surveying, or observing? Will the Web be a good (or bad) place to look?

Length

The amount of research and writing time you need for a five-page essay differs markedly from that for a fifteen-page essay. And you may need more time if materials are not available or if you discover that you must do more research.

Deadline

When is the project due? Are any preliminary materials—a working bibliography, a thesis, an outline, a first draft—due before this date? When you are preparing a research project for an employer, your supervisor may want to see part of your work at an early stage.

Research log

In a research log—either print or electronic—jot down thoughts about your topic, lists of things to do, and ideas about possible sources; also use it to keep track of library materials. Record online sources in your log, including the URL and a brief annotation, especially if you are unable to bookmark Web materials on your personal computer.

10c Formulate a research question and hypothesis.

Once you have analyzed your task and chosen a topic, formulate a research question that you can tentatively answer with a hypothesis, a statement of what you anticipate your research will show. As you do your research, you will move from a hypothesis to a working thesis (10e). Like a working thesis, a hypothesis must be not only manageable but interesting and specific. In addition, it must be arguable—it must be a debatable proposition that can be proved or disproved by a manageable amount of research evidence.

Here is an example of the move from general topic to hypothesis:

TOPIC	Heroes in U.S. films
ISSUE	Changes in heroes in U.S. films
RESEARCH QUESTION	How have heroes changed since they found a home in Hollywood?
HYPOTHESIS	As real-life heroes have been dethroned in popular U.S. culture over the last century, so have film heroes, and current films suggest that the hero may not have a future at all.

10d Investigate what you know about your topic.

Once you have formulated a hypothesis, marshal everything you know about it. Here are some strategies for getting all your initial thoughts about the topic down on paper.

- *Brainstorming.* For five minutes, alone or in a group, list everything you know, think of, or wonder about your hypothesis (5a).
- *Freewriting.* For five minutes, write about every reason for believing your hypothesis to be true; then, for five minutes, write down every argument that someone opposed to your hypothesis might make (5b).
- *Tapping your memory for sources.* List everything you can remember about *where* you learned about your topic: computer bulletin boards, email, books, magazines, courses, conversations, television. What you know comes from somewhere, and "somewhere" can serve as a starting point.

10e Move from hypothesis to working thesis.

As you gather information and begin reading and evaluating sources, you will probably refine your research question and change your hypothesis significantly. Only after you have explored your hypothesis, tested it, and sharpened it by reading, writing, and talking with others does the hypothesis become a working thesis.

For example, after an examination of contemporary films, you may decide that your hypothesis about the future of heroes in U.S. films will not hold up in an interesting, original research essay (10c). Consequently, you might shift your attention to what forms future heroes might take:

WORKING   Although a case of mistaken identity dealt a near-fatal blow
THESIS   to the hero in U.S. films, a study of recent movies suggests
            that the hero lives on—in two startlingly different forms.

11

Conducting Research

A few minutes' thought may bring to mind some piece of everyday research you have done. One couple with a passion for ice cream decided to carry out some research on their city's ice cream, and after some preliminary reading at the local library about the history of making ice cream, they literally ate their way through the research project, ending up with an article they sold to a local magazine. This chapter describes the kinds of research you will most often be called on to conduct—library or database research and field research.

11a Explore library and database resources.

The library is one of a researcher's best friends, especially in an age of electronic communication. Your college, public, or corporate library houses a great number of print materials: books, journals and periodicals, and reference works of all kinds. In addition, computer terminals there will give you access to electronic catalogs and indexes—and access to many other libraries via the Internet. Many libraries provide tours, workshops, and free instructional programs full of lessons, examples, and guides for those learning to use the library and the Internet for research. Reference librarians are valuable resources who can help you determine which of the library's materials you might consult and where to find them. Your library probably has many of these resources and services: check them out.

Directory of Library and Database Resources

Many of the following resources are available online through your library or on your own via the Web (though sometimes for a fee). Additional Internet resources are listed in the Writer's Almanac at the back of this book.

- guides to reference books and databases (11c)
- encyclopedias (11c)
- biographical resources (11c)
- almanacs, yearbooks, news digests, and atlases (11c)
- indexes to books and reviews (11c)
- periodical indexes (11c)
- library catalog (11d)
- vertical file
- special collections
- audio and video collections
- art collections
- interlibrary loans
- computer databases (11c, e, f)
- Internet and World Wide Web (11f)

11b **Develop a research strategy.**

Especially in an age of information, having a set of clear research strategies is invaluable to any researcher.

Kinds of sources

Before you plunge into a research project, ask these questions:

- Will you need primary sources (historical documents, literary works, diaries, letters, eyewitness accounts, raw data from experiments), secondary sources (accounts produced by other investigators, such as lab reports, biographies, reviews), or both? Often what constitutes a primary or secondary source will depend on your purpose or field. A critic's evaluation of a painting, for example, serves as a secondary work if you are writing an essay on that painting but as a primary work if you are conducting a study of the critic's writing.

- What kinds of sources does the assignment require? If you must use primary or nonprint sources, find out their location, availability, and any prerequisites for using them. If you need to use Internet sources, make sure you have good access and that you know how to use those sources (11f).

- How current do your sources need to be? If you must investigate the latest findings in your field, check periodicals and online. If you need broader, more detailed coverage and background information, you may need to look more to books.

- Do you need to consult sources contemporary with an event or a person's life? If your research deals with a specific time period, you may need to examine newspapers, magazines, and books written during that period.

- How many sources should you consult? Make sure you have enough sources to prove your thesis, and check to see whether your assignment specifies the number of sources.

Managing your search

Considering logistics can help you complete a project in the time allowed. If you have only two weeks to do research, for instance, you will need to be very selective. If you have several months, however, you can follow a broader course, perhaps conducting some field research. Also consider issues of access: can you get to the materials, people, works of art, or other items you need in the time allowed? How can you speed up access? For library searches, find out whether you can print the results of the searches you conduct and whether you can copy these results onto your own disc. Finally, consider any advance contacts you may need to make—to set up an interview, to secure materials through interlibrary loan, to use a friend's computer with a speedy connection, to see materials in a rare-book room.

11c Select reference works.

Libraries provide two necessary kinds of reference information: general background materials, which will give an overview of your topic, and specialized materials, which may help answer your research question and develop your working thesis. There is also a broad variety of reference material available on the Web; since the quality of such materials can vary widely, reference information found on the Web should be evaluated with special care (12c). Check with a librarian to determine which appropriate reference materials are available electronically.

GUIDES TO REFERENCE WORKS

Gale Directory of Databases; Guide to Reference Books; Walford's Guide to Reference Material

Among the types of sources most often consulted are encyclopedias, biographical dictionaries, summaries of current events, and indexes listing books. Many of these reference materials are available either online or on CD-ROM; your librarian can help you access them. Here are examples of each.

GENERAL ENCYCLOPEDIAS

Compton's Interactive Encyclopedia <www.comptons.com>; *Grolier Multimedia Encyclopedia* <www.grolier.com>; *Microsoft Encarta* <www.encarta .com>; *New Encyclopedia Britannica* <www.britannica.com>

SPECIALIZED ENCYCLOPEDIAS

Cambridge History of Africa; Encyclopedia of Asian History; Encyclopedia of Computer Science and Technology; Encyclopedia of Education; Harvard Guide to American History; Oxford Companion to English Literature

Consult a reference librarian about other specialized encyclopedias that may relate to the discipline you are researching.

BIOGRAPHICAL RESOURCES

African American Biographies; Chicano Scholars and Writers; Dictionary of American Biography; Dictionary of National Biography; Notable American Women; Who's Who in America

ALMANACS, YEARBOOKS, NEWS DIGESTS, ATLASES

Atlas of World Cultures: A Geographical Guide to Ethnographic Literature; Facts on File: News Digest; National Geographic Atlas of the World; Statistical Abstracts of the United States

INDEXES TO BOOKS AND REVIEWS

Book Review Digest; Book Review Index; Books in Print; Cumulative Book Index; Film Index International; Index to Book Reviews in the Humanities; Index to Book Reviews in the Social Sciences; Paperbound Books in Print

PERIODICAL INDEXES

GENERAL *Access: The Supplementary Index; Alternative Press Index; InfoTrac; NewsBank; Newspaper Abstracts Ondisc; New York Times Index; NEXIS/LEXIS;*

Periodical Abstracts; Poole's Index to Periodical Literature; Readers' Guide to Periodical Literature

SPECIALIZED INDEXES AND ABSTRACTS *America: History and Life; Arts and Humanities Citation Index; Biological Abstracts; ERIC (Educational Resources Information Center); PsycLIT; United States Government Publications*

11d Use the library catalog.

A library catalog lists all the library's materials. Some libraries still have their catalogs on cards or microfiche, but most have transferred (or are in the process of transferring) their holdings to a circulation computer, which allows you to use public terminals—on site or remote—to search for material. If your library is in the process of computerizing its catalog, ask a reference librarian which catalog to check for recently published materials.

Most circulation computers provide clear instructions on how and when to type in information. You can search for holdings by author, title, or subject. Note that many circulation computers, like the one the example below comes from, indicate whether a book has been checked out and, if so, when it is due to be returned.

```
AUTHOR        Rushing, Janice Hocker.
TITLE         Projecting the shadow : the cyborg hero in American
              film / Janice Hocker Rushing, Thomas S. Frentz.
PUBLISH INFO  Chicago : University of Chicago Press, 1995.
DESCRIPTION   x, 261 p. : ill. ; 24 cm.
SERIES        New practices of inquiry.
NOTES         Includes bibliographical references (p. 222-244)
              and index.
SUBJECTS      Cyborgs in motion picures.
              Myth in motion pictures.
ADD AUTHORS   Frentz, Thomas S.
OCLC #        32737837.
ISBN          0226731669 (cloth : alk. paper)

      LOCATION        CALL NO.          YEAR      STATUS
1 > JOU Stacks        PN1995.9.C9 R57   1995      DUE 01-05-00
```

Besides identifying a book's author, title, subject, and publication information, each catalog entry also lists a call number—the book's identification number. Most academic libraries now use the Library of Congress system, which begins call numbers with letters of the alphabet. Some libraries, however, still use the older Dewey decimal system;

others combine systems. Once you have printed out the circulation-computer entry for the book or written down the call number, look for a library map or shelving plan to tell you where your book is housed. When you find it, take the time to browse through the books around it. Very often you will find the immediate area a more important treasure trove than any bibliography or index.

11e   Search with keywords.

Many important resources are now available to you in databases, either online or on CD-ROMs. Especially if you have to pay a fee for these searches, it is important to limit each search as carefully as you can.

Doing efficient searches requires that you choose your keywords carefully. Sometimes you may search by author or title—then the keywords are obvious. More often, however, you will probably be searching subject headings. Many smaller databases, such as library catalogs, include a thesaurus of keywords to help you as you start your search.

Reading the instructions for using a particular search engine or database is also a good idea, since to search efficiently you need to understand its search logic. The Boolean system of search logic offers terms and punctuation that make it easy to compose search expressions that carefully specify the information you need. For instance, using *and* usually indicates that two items (for example, *Shakespeare* and *guns*) must be present for an article to be called up. *Or* instructs the computer to include every article in which either one word *or* the other shows up. And *not* indicates that when a particular word appears, the article should be excluded (*firearms* not *swords*). Other search engines use a plus sign (+) or a minus sign (–) instead of *and* or *not*.

Another element of search logic is the use of parentheses or quotation marks to indicate keywords made up of more than one word; if you are searching for information on Lois Lane, for example, you might type "*Lois Lane*" to search for that exact phrase. You can also use parentheses to search for multiple terms, typing *dogs* and (*training* or *obedience*). Other functions enable you to call up every instance in which a keyword (*Clinton,* for example) appears near another keyword (*veto,* for example). For advice on the search logic of a specific search engine, read the engine's tips on searching (sometimes labeled *advanced search*), which describe the search logic for that particular system.

Suppose you were checking the *MLA International Bibliography* database using the keyword *film hero.* The database might return to you eighty-one initial entries, including the following one:

```
You searched for the WORD: film hero                        MLA
                                            Record 2 of 81
AUTHOR          Abele, Elizabeth.
TITLE           Rescuing the Hero: Shifting Expectations for Men in
                the '90s.
APPEARS IN      The Mid-Atlantic Almanac: The Journal of the
                Mid-Atlantic Popular/American Culture Association.
                1996, 5, p. 107-22 MAA 1063-1763 Greencastle, PA.
PUB TYPE        journal article.
LANGUAGE        English.
SUBJECT         dramatic arts -- film -- treatment of masculinity --
                of hero.
ISSN            1063-1763.
SEQUENCE #      96-4-225.
UPD CODE        9601.
```

If you continued this search using the same keyword to search two other CD-ROM databases, a *PsycLIT* search would yield five entries, and an *ERIC* search would yield six. An example of this search using the search engine *Yahoo!* appears on p. 104.

Searching with subject directories

While you are choosing a topic or forming a research question, a useful alternative to searching the Internet with keywords is to browse or search subject directories. Subject directories let you limit your search by choosing from broad categories, which lead to directories of more focused subjects and lists of relevant sites. Useful subject directories are often part of search engines such as *Yahoo!*, but there are many others such as the *Argus Clearinghouse* <www.clearinghouse.net> (see p. 104).

11f   Use the Internet to gather research material.

The Internet is essentially a global patchwork quilt of linked computer networks. The World Wide Web is a part of the Internet that is hyper-textual, allowing users to leap from place to place by pointing a cursor at onscreen *links* (usually designated by highlighting or underlining) and clicking a mouse.

Access to the Internet

Internet access requires a modem and a Web browser software package. With a modem, you can either access a school's, company's, or organization's computer system or subscribe to an Internet provider, such as America Online or Prodigy.

Web Guides and Search Engines

Yahoo! <http://www.yahoo.com> is a Web guide that allows you either to search directories related to particular subjects (such as entertainment or education) or to enter keywords that *Yahoo!* uses to search its directories and the entire Web.

AltaVista <http://www.altavista.com> lets you search the Web using either their subject directories or keywords and phrases.

Ask Jeeves <http://www.ask.com> lets you search using questions or keywords, posing your question to several search engines simultaneously.

Dogpile <http://www.dogpile.com> allows you to search using multiple search engines at the same time.

Excite <http://www.excite.com> allows you to search over 250 million indexed Web pages and multimedia items.

Google <http://www.google.com> allows you to search with keywords using a powerful ranking search logic.

HotBot <http://www.hotbot.com> lets you search using their subject directories, or keywords or phrases, names, or URLs in 110 million Web sites and to narrow the search to specific dates, media, and other criteria.

Infoseek <http://infoseek.go.com> lets you search Web sites, their directory of reviewed sites, news stories, company biographies, or Usenet groups (see p. 106).

Lycos <http://www.lycos.com> allows you to search a huge catalog of Web sites, and Advanced Search lets you narrow a search to music, homepages, news downloads, and other multimedia documents.

Magellan <http://magellan.excite.com> allows you to search the Web and Web sites that have been evaluated for the quality of their content and organization by keywords and related concepts.

MetaCrawler <http://www.metacrawler.com> performs keyword searches using multiple search engines simultaneously and then eliminates any duplicate listings from the results.

WebCrawler <http://www.webcrawler.com> lets you search with an easy-to-use "natural language" procedure that is especially helpful for those new to keyword searching.

For additional advice on searching the Internet, see 14b.

Every site on the Internet has its own address, called a Uniform Resource Locator (URL), which must be typed *exactly* as it appears— using the exact capital or lowercase letters, spacing, and so on. Here, for example, is the URL for a helpful Web site that offers answers to a multitude of questions about computer terminology:

<http://www.whatis.com>

The first part of this address, (http:), is the protocol, or hypertext transfer protocol, which announces the kind of Internet link that is being made; the next part, (www.whatis.com), is the domain name, which announces the owner of the site and identifies it, in this case, as a commercial site (com). Some addresses have a third part, a directory path, which leads you to a particular part of the larger site.

Web browsers, guides, and search engines

Browsers, such as Netscape Navigator and Microsoft Explorer, give you access to powerful Web guides (which search subject directories of sites) and search engines (which allow you to carry out keyword searches).

Choosing the search engine best suited to your research task may take some experimenting, since different search engines give a variety of different results. Suppose you were conducting a search using *Yahoo!* for the keyword *film hero*. You might first narrow the search using "Search Options" to search only listings added during the past four years. By entering the keyword *film +hero* (using a plus sign rather than *and,* following *Yahoo!* style), your results from *Yahoo!* would include one category and twenty-six sites.

Several search engines, such as *MetaCrawler* and *Ask Jeeves,* perform metasearches, using several search engines simultaneously and collecting the results. These engines are useful when you are performing more general searches since they often return a limited set of results and do not offer the special options to construct advanced searches as standard search engines do.

Other Web research tools

Search engines are powerful tools, but because they search millions of sites on the Web, the quantity of information they retrieve can seem overwhelming. But there are many other credible, noncommercial sites that can serve as manageable starting points on the Web for your research. Check out the following resources, ranging from online libraries and catalogs to reference sites sponsored by universities and government organizations. This list includes just a sampling.

SAMPLE *YAHOO!* SEARCH QUERY

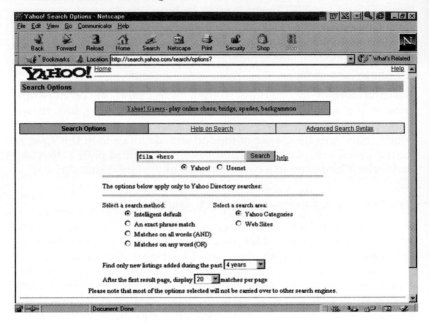

The Internet Public Library <http://www.ipl.org/> offers a carefully edited and organized selection of subject directories.

The Voice of the Shuttle: Web Page for Humanities Research <http://humanitas.ucsb.edu/> offers helpful links to humanities-related resources, including links to subject areas, universities, libraries, and reference resources.

Library of Congress <http://www.lcweb.loc.gov/> is best for research related to American history and culture.

The Universal Library <http://www.ul.cs.cmu.edu/> links to books, various collections, journals, and multimedia resources.

The Argus Clearinghouse <http://www.clearinghouse.net/> offers a large collection of carefully selected subject guides with helpful ratings.

Doing Research on the Web <http://www.cohums.ohio-state.edu/english /People/Locker.1/research.htm> lists general search engines and provides hints for locating people and businesses. It is especially helpful for those interested in business and economics.

Bedford/St. Martin's English Research Room <http://www.bedfordstmartins .com/english_research/> is a helpful source for information on research and writing.

SAMPLE *YAHOO!* SEARCH RESULTS

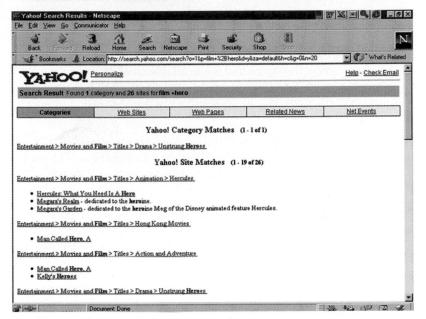

Beyond the Web: other Internet tools

The Internet provides access not only to the Web but to a number of other means of accessing and sharing information.

GOPHER, FTP, AND TELNET

Until recently, gopher, FTP, and telnet could be accessed only through special software for each one. Now, however, they are assimilated into most Web browsers.

Using gopher, a hierarchical system that organizes files in menus, often involves following a path from one menu to another before you get to a specific document. At times, you may lose track of how you actually located the material of interest to you. To simplify matters, you can use a bookmark to identify an important gopher location you want to revisit. Over time, you may create a bookmark list, a sort of custom menu, that makes it easy for you to get to particular gopher sites.

File transfer protocol (FTP) is a method for calling up and copying (at no cost) a huge number of public files from host computers all over the Internet. The files, which may not be available via gopher or the Web, can be short documents (such as government statistics), whole books, or online magazines that include graphics, sound, and video.

A telnet program allows you to make a telephone connection with another computer on the Internet. Through telnet, you can use your computer to access resources that are available on another computer. To log on using telnet, you usually need a special account, but some sites, such as libraries, allow you to log on as a guest.

EMAIL

Short for "electronic mail," email is a sped-up postal system that allows you to communicate with people or groups all over the world via the Internet (59b). It can also be very helpful in conducting research.

LISTSERVS

Listservs are groups that use email to carry on discussions among people who have similar interests—and you can find a listserv on the Internet for almost every subject under the sun. You can check out potentially interesting listservs by using the subject directory on a search engine such as *AltaVista*. To join a listserv, you must subscribe by sending a message to a subscription address. After subscribing, you should read postings for a few days before becoming an active participant; this procedure, known as lurking, will give you a sense of the discussion and of the rules, if any, that are governing it. Once you feel comfortable posting a message, you can use the listserv to get responses to questions or tips on other resources related to your topic of interest.

USENET

Usenet is a network with links to thousands of discussion newsgroups that, unlike listservs, are open to visitors without subscriptions. Although you can visit a newsgroup by using a Web browser or search engine, you must subscribe to receive postings from it automatically. Like listservs, newsgroups can be very helpful in conducting research. But you should be aware that the information on them is only as reliable as the people who are doing the posting. For this reason, you should look carefully at a group's frequently asked questions, or FAQs, which will tell you something about its topics of interest and procedures, and read postings for a while so that you can test their reliability and credibility.

MUDS, MOOS, AND IRCS

Whereas communication via email is asynchronous, meaning that there is a time gap between the posting and the receiving of a message, communication via the Internet software systems for MUDs, MOOs, and IRCs is synchronous, with messages received as they are being typed. MUDs (multi-user domains or dungeons) are now being used for distance education and other academic projects. MOOs (MUDs, object-oriented) let participants create complex virtual spaces for conferencing and all kinds of collaborations. IRCs (Internet relay chats), also called *chat rooms,* are another way for people at far-flung sites to talk or hold a conference.

11g Conduct field research.

For many research projects, particularly those in the social sciences and business, you will need to collect field data. The "field" may be many things—a classroom, a church, an ice-cream parlor, a laboratory, or the corner grocery store. As a field researcher, you will need to discover *where* you can find relevant information, *how* to gather it, and *who* might be your best providers of information.

Interviews

Some information is best obtained by asking direct questions of other people. If you can talk with an expert—in person, on the telephone, or via the Internet—you might get information you could not have obtained through any other kind of research. In addition to getting an "expert opinion," you might ask for firsthand accounts or suggestions of other places to look or other people to consult.

Planning an Interview

- Determine your exact purpose, and be sure it relates to your research question and your hypothesis.
- Set up the interview well in advance. Specify how long it will take, and if you wish to tape-record the session, ask permission to do so.
- Prepare a written list of factual and open-ended questions. Brainstorming or freewriting can help you come up with questions. (5a, b) Leave plenty of space for notes after each question. If the interview proceeds in a direction that seems fruitful, do not feel that you have to ask all of your prepared questions.
- Record the subject, date, time, and place of the interview.
- Thank those you interview, either in person or in a follow-up letter or email.

Observation

Trained observers report that making a faithful record of an observation requires intense concentration and mental agility. Here are some tips.

Conducting Observation

- Determine the purpose of the observation, and be sure it relates to your research question and hypothesis.
- Brainstorm about what you are looking for, but don't be rigidly bound to your expectations.
- Develop an appropriate system for recording data. Consider using a split notebook or page: on one side, record your observations directly; on the other, record your thoughts or interpretations.
- Be aware that the way you record data will affect the final report, if only in respect to what you include in the notes and what you omit.
- Record the date, time, and place of observation.

Opinion surveys

Surveys usually depend on questionnaires. On any questionnaire, the questions should be clear and easy to understand and designed so that you can analyze the answers easily. Questions that ask respondents to say *yes* or *no* or to rank items on a scale are particularly easy to tabulate.

Designing a Questionnaire

- Write out your purpose, and review your research question and hypothesis to determine the kinds of questions to ask.
- Figure out how to reach the respondents you need.
- Draft potential questions, and check to see that each question calls for a short, specific answer.
- Test the questions on several people, and revise questions that are ambiguous, too hard to answer, or take too much time.
- For a questionnaire that is to be mailed, draft a cover letter explaining your purpose. Provide a self-addressed, stamped envelope, and be sure to state a deadline.
- On the final version of the questionnaire, leave adequate space for answers.
- Proofread the questionnaire.

12

Evaluating and Using Sources

Every time you check out *Consumer Reports* for its evaluation of an appliance or use the Internet to talk to owners of a software program you are interested in, you are calling on sources for help. All research builds on the careful and sometimes inspired use of sources—that research done by others. You will want to make the most of your sources, using the insights you gain from them to help you create powerful prose of your own. This chapter will guide you in this effort.

12a Keep clear records of sources.

As you locate and consider research sources—books, articles, Web sites, and so on—you should create a working bibliography, which is a list of the sources that seem most likely to address your research question. The emphasis here is on *working,* for this list will include materials that may end up not being useful. As you use reference books, bibliographic sources, periodical indexes, computer databases, search engines, or the circulation computer, make a bibliography entry for every source you think you might use.

Guidelines for Creating a Working Bibliography

- Before you begin a working bibliography, check to see whether you are to follow a particular style for documenting sources. Chapters 48–55 provide guidelines on four major documentation styles: MLA, APA, CBE, and Chicago.

- Use index cards (one for each source), a notebook, or a computer file. Record information on one side only so that you can arrange the entries alphabetically when you prepare the bibliography or works cited.

- For each *book,* record the following: call number or other location information; author(s) and/or editor(s); title and subtitle, if any; publisher's name and location; year of publication; and other information you may find—translator, volume number, edition, and so on. If the book is made up of selections by a variety of authors, record the author(s) and title of the piece you are using and its inclusive page numbers.

(continues on next page)

- For each *periodical article,* list author(s); editor(s); article title and subtitle; periodical name, volume number, and date; and inclusive page numbers.
- For sources you find listed in *reference books,* note the name of the reference work and its location in case you need to check it again.
- For entries from *electronic sources,* get a printout, making sure that it includes all of the following items of information about the source that are applicable and available: author(s) of the text; title; name of the site or discussion group; editor of the site or database, if any; date published or last updated; publication information for the print version, if any; URL or other information to access the source; inclusive page, paragraph, screen, or other section numbers, or the total number of sections; name of any sponsoring organization; date accessed; and copyright information. Check electronic sources carefully to determine their publication information. Remember that when using sources accessed through your library or school network, what looks like a Web site may be a CD-ROM or other source. Ask a librarian if you are unsure.
- For *films, recordings,* or *works of art,* list the information required by the documentation system you are using (see Chapters 48–55), and note where you found the information.

For a research essay about film and heroes (using the Modern Language Association style of documentation), you might generate the following working-bibliography cards:

BOOK

PN1995.9
R57
1995

Rushing, Janice Hocker, and Thomas S. Frentz. Projecting the
    Shadow: The Cyborg Hero in American Film. Chicago:
    U Chicago P, 1995.

ARTICLE

> Prats, Armando J. "Back from the Sunset: The Western, the
> Eastwood Hero, and 'Unforgiven.'" Journal of Film and
> Video. Sp-Fall 1995: 106–23. ERIC Database.

12b Assess the usefulness of a source.

Since you want the information you glean from sources to be reliable
and persuasive, you must evaluate each potential source carefully. Use
these guidelines to assess the usefulness of a source.

- *Relevance.* Is the source closely related to your research question?
- *Author's and publisher's credentials and stance.* Is the author an expert on the
  topic? What is the author's stance on the issue(s) involved, and how does
  this influence the information in the source? Does the author support or
  challenge your own views? If you are evaluating a book published by a corporation, government agency, or interest group, what is the publisher's
  position on the topic? If you are evaluating an article, what kind of periodical published it—popular? academic? alternative?
- *Date of publication.* Recent sources are often more useful than older ones,
  particularly in the sciences. However, in some fields, the most authoritative
  works may be the older ones.
- *Level of specialization.* General sources can be helpful as you begin your
  research, but you may then need the authority or currentness of more specialized sources. On the other hand, extremely specialized works may be
  too hard to understand.
- *Audience.* Was the source written for the general public? specialists? advo-
  cates or opponents?
- *Cross-referencing.* Is the source cited in other works?
- *Length.* Is the source long enough to provide adequate detail?
- *Availability.* Do you have access to the source?

12c   Evaluate electronic sources with special scrutiny.

Unlike most library-based research tools, much material on the Internet in general and the World Wide Web in particular is still the work of enthusiastic amateurs or commercial entrepreneurs. Advertisements, one-sided statements, and careless or even false information are all jumbled together with solid, reliable data. In this frontier electronic environment, you must be the judge of just how accurate and trustworthy the materials are. In making such judgments, you can rely on the same kind of critical thinking you use to assess the usefulness of any source. In addition, you can improve your evaluation of electronic sources by keeping some key questions in mind.

- Who has posted this document or site—an individual? an interest group? a company? a government agency?

- What can you determine about the credibility of the individual or group posting the document? What evidence can you find to show that the authors are knowledgeable and credible?

- Who can be held accountable for the information in the document? How well and thoroughly does the document credit its own sources?

- How effectively is the document or site designed? How user-friendly is it? Is it easy to navigate? If it is a Web page, are the links helpful? What effects do design, visuals, and sound have on the message?

- What is missing or omitted from the document or site? Does the document or site include, for example, an email address or way to contact those responsible for it? How do such exclusions affect how you can or cannot use the information?

- What perspective(s) are represented? If only one perspective is represented, how can you balance or expand this viewpoint?

- Does the source list revision dates? Is it regularly updated? Does it archive earlier editions or documents?

For additional guidelines on evaluating Internet sources, see p. 135.

12d   Read critically, and synthesize data.

After you have identified a potential source and decided to read it, you still need to determine if it merits a place in your research essay. Keeping these questions in mind can save you time as you dig into sources.

- How does the source material—visual as well as verbal—address your research question?

- How does it provide support for your working thesis?

- Does the source offer counterarguments to your working thesis? If so, what responses can you make?
- What is the author's stance or perspective? Is he or she an advocate of something? a strong opponent? an amused onlooker? a specialist? Are there any clues to what forces may have shaped the author's perspective?
- How does this stance affect the author's presentation?
- In what ways do you share—or not share—the author's stance?
- What is the author's tone—cautious? angry? flippant? serious? What words express this tone?
- What is the author's main point?
- How much and what kind of evidence does the author use to support that point?
- How persuasive do you find the evidence?
- Do any of your other sources disagree with this source? If so, how are you going to handle this disagreement?
- What patterns or trends do the author's argument and evidence fall into? Can you synthesize, or group, this author's argument and evidence with arguments and evidence from other sources?
- What inferences, or conclusions, can you draw from those patterns or trends?

12e Take notes: quote, paraphrase, summarize.

When you decide that a source is useful, take careful notes on it. While note-taking methods vary from one researcher to another, you should (1) get down enough information to help you recall the major points of the source; (2) put the information in the form in which you are most likely to incorporate it into your research essay; and (3) note all the information you will need to cite the source accurately.

When you have become more familiar with the general guidelines for taking accurate notes (see p. 114), then you must decide in each case what kind of notes to take from each source.

Quotation

Quoting involves bringing a source's exact words into your text. Use an author's exact words when the wording is so memorable or expresses a point so well that you cannot improve or shorten it without weakening it, when the author is a respected authority whose opinion supports

Guidelines for Taking Accurate Notes

- Using index cards, a notebook, or a computer file, list the author's name and a shortened title of the source. Your working-bibliography entry for the source will contain full bibliographic information, so you need not repeat it in each note. (12a)

- Record the exact page number from which your note comes. If your note refers to more than one page, indicate which part of the note comes from which page. For an electronic source for which page or reference numbers are unavailable, record the URL and other relevant location information carefully.

- Label each note card or page with a subject heading.

- After you have written your note, identify it as a quotation, a paraphrase, a summary, a combination of these forms, or some other form—such as your own critical comment—to avoid confusion later. Mark quotations accurately with quotation marks, or paraphrase and summarize completely in your own words to be sure you do not inadvertently plagiarize the source. (12g)

- Read each completed note carefully, and recheck it against the source for the accuracy of quotations, statistics, and specific facts.

your own ideas, or when an author challenges or disagrees profoundly with others in the field.

Here is an example of an original passage and a note card recording a quotation from it. Note quotation marks; square brackets to show an added word, changed capitalization, and which part of the quotation came from which page; and ellipses enclosed in brackets to mark omitted words.

> It is not clear who makes and who is made in the relation between human and machine. It is not clear what is mind and what body in machines that resolve into coding practices. In so far as we know ourselves in both formal discourse (for example, biology) and in daily practice (for example, the homework economy in the integrated circuit), we find ourselves to be cyborgs, hybrids, mosaics, chimeras. Biological organisms have become biotic systems, communications devices like others. There is no fundamental, ontological separation in our formal knowledge of machine and organism, of technical and organic. The replicant Rachel in the Ridley Scott film *Blade Runner* stands as the image of a cyborg culture's fear, love, and confusion.
> —DONNA J. HARAWAY, *Simians, Cyborgs, & Women* (177–78)

Cyborg heroes

Haraway, <u>Simians</u>, pp. 177–178

[177]"In so far as we know ourselves [...], we find ourselves to
be cyborgs, hybrids [...]. [178][Thus, t]he replicant Rachel in
the Ridley Scott film <u>Blade Runner</u> stands as the image of a
cyborg culture's fear, love, and confusion."

Quotation

Guidelines for Quoting Accurately

- Copy quotations carefully, with punctuation, capitalization, and spelling exactly as in the original. (42a)
- It is especially important to enclose the quotation in quotation marks; don't rely on your memory to distinguish your own words from those of the source. (42a)
- Use brackets if you introduce words of your own into the quotation or make changes in it. (43b)
- Use ellipses enclosed in brackets if you omit material. (43f)
- If you later incorporate the quotation into your research essay, copy it from the note precisely, including brackets and ellipses.
- Record the author's name, shortened title, and page number(s) on which the quotation appears.
- Make sure you have a corresponding working-bibliography entry with complete source information. (12a)
- Label the note with a subject heading.

Paraphrase

When you paraphrase, you put an author's material (including major and minor points, usually in the order they are presented) into *your own words and sentence structures.* If you wish to cite some of the author's words within the paraphrase, enclose them in quotation marks. Here are examples of paraphrases that resemble an original paragraph too closely.

ORIGINAL

It is not clear who makes and who is made in the relation between human and machine. It is not clear what is mind and what body in machines that resolve into coding practices. In so far as we know ourselves in both formal discourse (for example, biology) and in daily practice (for example, the home-work economy in the integrated circuit), we find ourselves to be cyborgs, hybrids, mosaics, chimeras. Biological organisms have become biotic systems, communications devices like others. There is no fundamental, ontological separation in our formal knowledge of machine and organism, of technical and organic. The replicant Rachel in the Ridley Scott film *Blade Runner* stands as the image of a cyborg culture's fear, love, and confusion.

         —DONNA J. HARAWAY, *Simians, Cyborgs, & Women*

UNACCEPTABLE PARAPHRASE: USING THE AUTHOR'S WORDS

As Haraway explains, in a high-tech culture like ours, *who makes and who is made, what is mind or body, becomes unclear.* When we look at ourselves in relation to the real or the mechanical world, we must admit we are cyborgs, and even *biological organisms* are now *communications systems.* Thus our beings can't be separated from machines. A fine example of this cyborg image is Rachel in Ridley Scott's *Blade Runner.*

Because the italicized phrases are either borrowed from the original without quotation marks or changed only superficially, this paraphrase is unacceptable.

UNACCEPTABLE PARAPHRASE: USING THE AUTHOR'S SENTENCE STRUCTURES

As Haraway explains, it is unclear who is the maker and who is the made. It is unclear what in the processes of machines might be the mind and what the body. Thus in order to know ourselves at all, we must recognize ourselves to be cyborgs. Biology then becomes just another device for communicating. As beings, we can't separate the bodily from the mechanical anymore. Thus Rachel in Ridley Scott's *Blade Runner* becomes the perfect symbol of cyborg culture.

Although this paraphrase does not rely on the words of the original, it does follow the sentence structures too closely. The paraphrase must represent your own interpretation of the material and thus must show your own thought patterns.

    Now look at a paraphrase that expresses the author's ideas accurately and acceptably. It is in the writer's own words but includes a quotation from the original.

Cyborg heroes

Haraway, <u>Simians</u>, p. 181

As Haraway's entire chapter demonstrates, today the line between person and machine is forever blurred, especially in terms of the binary coding systems used by computers to "know." If knowing thyself is still important, then, we must know ourselves as "cyborgs, hybrids, mosaics, chimeras." Moviemaker Ridley Scott provides a good example of this mixture in the character of Rachel in <u>Blade Runner.</u>

Paraphrase

Guidelines for Paraphrasing Accurately

- Include all main points and any important details from the original source in the same order in which the author presents them.
- State the meaning in your own words and sentence structures. If you want to include especially memorable language from the original, enclose it in quotation marks.
- Save for another note your own comments, elaborations, or reactions.
- Record the author, shortened title, and the page number(s) on which the original material appeared.
- Make sure you have a corresponding working-bibliography entry. (12a)
- Label the note with a subject heading, and identify it as a paraphrase to avoid confusion with a summary.
- Recheck the paraphrase against the original to be sure that the words and sentence structures are your own and that they express the author's meaning accurately.

Summary

A summary is a significantly shortened version of a passage or even a whole chapter or work that captures main ideas *in your own words.* Unlike a paraphrase, a summary uses just enough information to record the points you wish to emphasize. The note card on p. 118 shows a summary of the preceding passage by Haraway. It states the author's main points selectively and without using her words.

Cyborg heroes

Haraway, <u>Simians</u>, pp. 177–178

Haraway says humans today are already part machine, and she cites the Ridley Scott movie <u>Blade Runner</u> as an example.

Summary

Guidelines for Summarizing Accurately

- Include just enough information to recount the main points you want to cite. A summary is usually far shorter than the original.
- Use your own words. If you include any language from the original, enclose it in quotation marks.
- Record the author, shortened title, and page number(s) on which the original material appeared.
- Make sure you have a corresponding working-bibliography entry for the material.
- Label the note with a subject heading, and identify it as a summary to avoid confusion with a paraphrase.
- Recheck against the original any material you plan to use to be sure you have captured the author's meaning and that your words are entirely your own.

12f Photocopy and download material: consider issues of copyright.

Nearly all libraries provide photocopying machines that you can use to copy pages or even whole articles or chapters. You can then annotate the photocopies with your thoughts and questions and highlight interesting quotations and key terms. However, try not to rely too heavily on photocopying—you still need to read the material carefully. And resist the temptation to treat photocopied material as notes, an action that could lead to inadvertent plagiarizing as well as to wasting time looking for information you only vaguely remember having read. If you read and take careful notes on your sources rather than relying primarily on photocopies, your drafting process will be more efficient. If you do photocopy material, note on the photocopy all the information you need to cite the material in your list of sources cited. (And check that the page numbers are clearly legible.)

Printing out the pages of source material you gather from the Internet can make it easier to take notes. But if you are downloading source material—saving it to your computer— check to see whether you are allowed to copy the source without asking for permission. Many sites include copyright guides. Most sites allow students to download one copy for personal use; do not email copies of material to discussion lists or other public forums without first getting permission. In addition, remember that Web sites change frequently, so what is there one day may not be there the next. It's especially important, then, to print out or take down all the information you will need to document those sources you download. For specific guidelines and help in requesting permission to use materials on the Internet, see p. 122.

12g Recognize plagiarism, and acknowledge sources.

Plagiarism, the use of someone else's words without crediting the other person, breaks trust within the research conversation you are a part of and with readers as well. As a mark of dishonesty, it can destroy the credibility of both research and researcher and can result in serious consequences.

You are probably already aware of cases of deliberate plagiarism—writers who have copied passages directly from source materials. In addition, however, you should be aware of unintended plagiarism—a quotation accidentally used without quotation marks, a paraphrase that too closely resembles the original, background details used without acknowledgment in the mistaken belief that none was necessary. You can avoid unintended plagiarism by understanding what material you must document; by taking systematic, accurate notes; and by giving full credit to sources in both in-text citations and in your list of sources cited.

For Multilingual Writers: *Plagiarism as a Cultural Concept*

Many cultures do not recognize Western notions of plagiarism, which rest on a belief that language can be owned by writers. Indeed, in many countries, and even within some communities in the United States, using the words of others without attribution is considered a sign of deep respect as well as an indication of knowledge. In academic writing in the United States, however, you should credit all materials except those that are common knowledge, that are available in a wide variety of sources, or that are your own findings from field research.

Materials not requiring acknowledgment

COMMON KNOWLEDGE

If most readers would be likely to know something, you need not mention the source. For example, you do not need to credit a source for the statement that Bill Clinton was reelected president in 1996. If, on the other hand, you give the exact number of popular votes he received, you should cite the source for the figure.

FACTS AVAILABLE IN A VARIETY OF SOURCES

If a number of reference books include a certain piece of information, you need not cite a specific source for it. For instance, you do not need to cite a source for the fact that the Japanese bombing of Pearl Harbor failed to destroy the oil tanks and submarines. You would, however, need to credit a source that argued that the failure to destroy the submarines meant that Japan was destined to lose the war.

YOUR OWN FINDINGS FROM FIELD RESEARCH

If you conduct interviews, observation, or surveys, simply announce your findings as your own.

Materials requiring acknowledgment

DIRECT QUOTATIONS

When you use another person's words directly, credit the source. If you quote some of the author's words within a paraphrase or summary, you need to cite the quotation separately, after the closing quotation mark.

FACTS NOT WIDELY KNOWN; ARGUABLE ASSERTIONS

If your readers would be unlikely to know a fact or if an author presents as fact an assertion that may or may not be true, cite the source. To claim, for instance, that Switzerland is amassing an offensive nuclear arsenal would call for the citation of a source, since Switzerland has long been an officially neutral state.

JUDGMENTS, OPINIONS, AND CLAIMS OF OTHERS

Whenever you summarize or paraphrase anyone else's opinion, give the source. Even though the wording should be completely your own, you must acknowledge the source.

STATISTICS, CHARTS, TABLES, AND GRAPHS FROM ANY SOURCE

Credit all statistical and graphic material not derived from your own fieldwork, even if you yourself create the graph from data in another source (15c).

HELP FROM FRIENDS, INSTRUCTORS OR SUPERVISORS, AND OTHERS

A conference with an instructor may give you the idea you need to clinch an argument. Give credit. Friends may help you conduct surveys. Credit them, too.

Recognizing Plagiarism and Acknowledging Sources

- Maintain an accurate and thorough working bibliography. (12a)
- Establish a consistent note-taking system, listing sources and page numbers and clearly identifying all quotations, paraphrases, summaries, statistics, and graphics. (12e)
- Identify all quotations with quotation marks—both in your notes and in your essay. (12e)
- Be sure your summaries and paraphrases use your own words and sentence structures. (12e)
- Give a citation or note for each quotation, paraphrase, summary, arguable assertion or opinion, statistic, and graph that is from a source. (See Chapter 48, 52a, 54a, and 55a.)
- Prepare an accurate and complete list of sources cited according to the required documentation style. (See Chapter 50, 52c, 54b, and 55b.)

Acknowledging the source of each piece of information you incorporate into your essay will be much easier if you double-check each working-bibliography entry as you examine a source and if your notes accurately identify direct quotations, paraphrases, and summaries.

Materials requiring permission

The concept of fair use in copyright laws allows you to use brief excerpts of copyrighted material (generally 300 words from a book, 150 words from an article, or 4 lines from a poem—or even more if your work is for a class and not intended to be published), as long as you provide a full citation. To cite personal communication such as email or listserv postings, however, you should ask permission of the writer before you include any of his or her material in your own text. To use someone else's graphics or images in your text, it is safest to request permission from the creator or owner. Here is a sample email permission request:

MAIL TO: litman@mindspring.com

CC TO: lunsford.2@osu.edu

SUBJECT: Request for permission

Dear Professor Litman:

I am writing to request permission to quote from your essay, "Copyright, Owners' Rights and Users' Privileges on the Internet: Implied Licenses, Caching, Linking, Fair Use, and Sign-on Licenses." I want to quote some of your work in a hypertext essay I am writing for students in my composition class in order to explain the complex debates over ownership on the Internet and to argue that students in my class should be participating in these debates. My essay, like all the others in my class, will be linked to our class Web page. I will give full credit to you and will cite the URL where I first found your work: <http://www.msen.com/~litman/dayton/htm>.

Please let me know if you are willing to grant me permission to quote from your essay. Thank you very much for considering my request.

Raul Sanchez <sanchez.32@osu.edu>

In all cases, remember the difference between an assignment that you will submit to a teacher and classmates and a document that you will publish on the Internet or in print. For your class, you might include the text of an entire song in an essay, but you cannot put such an essay—with the copyrighted song—on the Internet without infringing on the rights of the copyright owner.

13

Writing a Research Essay

Everyday decisions often call for research and writing. In trying to choose between two jobs in different towns, for example, one person made a long list of questions to answer: which job location had the lower cost of living? how did the two locations compare in terms of schools, cultural opportunities, major league sports, and so on? After conducting careful and thorough research, he was prepared to draw up a letter of acceptance to one place and a letter of regret to the other. This chapter aims to help you move effectively from research to writing.

13a Refine your writing plans.

For most research writing, drafting should begin well before the deadline. Growing understanding of the subject and response from others may call not only for more drafting but for gathering more information or even refining your research question. Start by reconsidering your purpose, audience, stance, and working thesis:

- What is your central purpose? other purposes, if any?
- What is your stance? Are you an advocate, a critic, a reporter, an observer?
- What audience are you addressing?
- How much background information do you need to present to your audience?
- What support will your readers find convincing—examples? quotations from authorities? statistics? graphs, charts, or other visuals? data from your own observation or from interviews?
- Should your tone be that of a colleague, an expert, or a friend?
- How can you establish common ground with your audience?
- What is your working thesis trying to establish? Will your audience accept it?

13b Organize, outline, and draft.

To group the many pieces of information that you have collected, examine your notes for connections, finding what might be combined with what, which notes will be more useful and which less useful, which ideas lend support to your working thesis and which should be put aside.

Outlines can take various forms and be done at various stages. You may group your notes, as just mentioned; write a draft; and only then outline the draft to study its tentative structure. Or you may develop a working outline from your notes, listing the major points in a tentative order with support for each point. Such a working outline may see you through the rest of the writing process, or you may decide to revise your outline as you go along. Yet another way to proceed is to plot out your organization early on in a formal outline (6c).

Begin drafting wherever you feel most confident. If you have an idea for an introduction, begin there. If you are not sure how you want to introduce the essay but do know how you want to approach one point, begin with that, and return to the introduction later.

If you will be doing most of your drafting with a word-processing program, remember that most software programs now come with an outlining function as well as capabilities for formatting endnotes, footnotes, and lists of sources cited. You may want to begin by copying your outline into a new document and using it to help guide your drafting: you can always jump back and forth from one part of the outline to the next. You can also open up more than one window, putting notes in one window, your draft in another, your bibliography in another, your outline in yet another. If you have been keeping your notes in a computer file, you can copy them directly into your document and then rework them so that they fit appropriately into your draft. And, if you have kept your source information in a computer file as well, you can have that file handy as you add entries to your list of sources cited.

Working title and introduction

The title and introduction play special roles, for they set the stage for what is to come. Ideally, the title announces the subject of the essay in an intriguing or memorable way. The introduction should draw readers into the essay and provide any background they will need to understand your discussion. Here are some tips for drafting an introduction to a research essay.

- It is often effective *to open with a question,* especially your research question. Next, you might explain what you will do to answer the question. Then *end with your thesis statement*—in essence, the answer—which grows out of your working thesis.
- Help readers get their bearings by *forecasting your main points.*
- *Establish your own credibility* by telling how you have become knowledgeable about the topic.

- In general, you may *not* want to open with a quotation. In the course of a research essay, you may want to quote several sources, and opening with a quotation from one source may give it too much emphasis.

Conclusion

A good conclusion to a research essay helps readers know what they have learned. Here are some strategies that may help.

- A specific-to-general pattern is frequently appropriate. Open with a reference to your thesis statement, and then expand to a more general conclusion that reminds readers of the significance of your discussion.
- If you have covered several main points, you may want to remind readers of them. Be careful, however, to provide more than a mere summary.
- Try to end with something that will have an impact—a provocative quotation or question, a vivid image, a call for action, or a warning. But guard against sounding preachy.

13c Incorporate source materials.

Many fields have specific rules for incorporating source materials. Here are some general guidelines.

Direct quotations

Because your essay is primarily your own work, limit your use of quotations. Use direct quotations for the following purposes:

- to incorporate a statement expressed so effectively by the author that it cannot be paraphrased without altering the meaning
- to allow the words of an authority on your topic to contribute to your researching credibility
- to allow an author to state a position in his or her own words
- to create a particular effect

BRIEF QUOTATIONS

Short quotations should run in with your text, enclosed by quotation marks (42a).

> In Miss Eckhart, Welty recognizes a character who shares with her "the love of her art and the love of giving it, the desire to give it until there is no more left" (10).

LONG QUOTATIONS

Quotations longer than four lines (MLA) or forty words (APA), or ten lines, or more than one paragraph (Chicago), should be set off from the regular text. Begin such a quotation on a new line, and indent every line ten spaces (MLA) or five to seven spaces (APA) from the left margin. This indentation sets off the quotation clearly, so quotation marks are unnecessary. Type the quotation to the right margin, and double-space it as you do the regular text. Introduce long quotations by a signal phrase or a sentence followed by a colon.

> A good seating arrangement can prevent problems; however, *withitness,* as defined by Woolfolk, works even better:
>
> > Withitness is the ability to communicate to students that you are aware of what is happening in the classroom, that you "don't miss anything." With-it teachers seem to have "eyes in the back of their heads." They avoid becoming too absorbed with a few students, since this allows the rest of the class to wander. (359)
>
> This technique works, however, only if students actually believe that their teacher will know everything that goes on.

INTEGRATING QUOTATIONS INTO YOUR TEXT

Carefully integrate quotations into your text so that they flow smoothly and clearly into the surrounding sentences. Use a signal phrase or verb, such as those underlined in the following examples and listed below.

> In *Death of a Salesman,* Willy Loman dreams the wrong dreams and idealizes the wrong ideals. His misguided perceptions are well captured by Brown: "He has lived on his smile and on his hopes, survived from sale to sale, been sustained by the illusion that he has countless friends in his territory, that everything will be all right [. . .]" (97).
>
> As Eudora Welty notes, "learning stamps you with its moments. Childhood's learning," she continues, "is made up of moments. It isn't steady. It's a pulse" (9).

Notice that the examples alert readers to the quotations by using signal phrases that include the author's name. When you cite a quotation in this way, you need put only the page number in parentheses.

SIGNAL VERBS

acknowledges	allows	believes	concludes
advises	answers	charges	concurs
agrees	asserts	claims	confirms

SIGNAL VERBS

criticizes	emphasizes	offers	reveals
declares	expresses	opposes	says
describes	interprets	remarks	states
disagrees	lists	replies	suggests
discusses	objects	reports	thinks
disputes	observes	responds	writes

When you write about literary and artistic works created in the past, generally follow Modern Language Association (MLA) style and use present-tense verbs, as above. (See Chapter 48.) However, if you are using the style recommendations of the American Psychological Association (APA), use signal phrases in the past tense or the present-perfect form. (See Chapter 52.)

> In *Abnormal Psychology,* Comer (1995) <u>emphasized</u> that Shakespeare's Othello blamed behavior on the moon: "She comes more near the earth than she was wont / And makes men mad."

BRACKETS AND ELLIPSES

In direct quotations, enclose in brackets any words you change or add, and indicate any deletions with ellipsis points enclosed in brackets (43f).

> A farmer, Jane Lee, spoke to the Nuclear Regulatory Commission about the occurrences. "There is something wrong in the [Three Mile Island] area. It is happening within nature itself," she said, referring to human miscarriages, stillbirths, and birth defects in farm animals ("Legacy" 33).

> Economist John Kenneth Galbraith has pointed out that "large corporations cannot afford to compete with one another [. . .]. In a truly competitive market someone loses[. . .]. American big business has finally learned that everybody has to protect everybody else's investment" (Key 17).

Paraphrases and summaries

Introduce paraphrases and summaries clearly, usually with a signal phrase that includes the author of the source, as the underlined words in this example indicate.

> Professor of linguistics Deborah Tannen <u>says</u> that she offers her book *That's Not What I Meant!* to "women and men everywhere who are trying their best to talk to each other" (19). <u>Tannen goes on to illustrate</u> how communication between women and men breaks down <u>and then to suggest</u> that a full awareness of "genderlects" can improve relationships (297).

Graphics and visuals

If you are using graphics (such as bar or line graphs, clip art, cartoons, illustrations, maps, photographs, pie charts, tables, or time lines), as with quotations, you need to incorporate them smoothly into your text.

- Make sure the graphic conveys information more efficiently than words alone could do.
- Position the graphic near the text it illustrates or refers to.
- Label each graphic clearly and consistently (*Figure 1: Photograph of the New York Skyline*).
- Make sure that your text introduces each graphic clearly and concisely.
- Make sure that your graphic will be easily readable and will reproduce clearly.
- Check the documentation system you are using to make sure you label graphics appropriately; MLA, for instance, asks that you number and title tables and figures (*Table 1: Average Amount of Rainfall by Region*).
- If you are posting your document or essay on a Web site, make sure you have permission to use any images or photographs that are covered by copyright (see p. 122 for an example of a letter requesting permission).

(For information on how to insert images from the World Wide Web into your text, see 16f.)

13d Revise and edit your draft.

Try to get feedback from at least two or three readers. Then reread your draft very carefully, making notes for necessary changes and additions. Pay particular attention to how you have used sources, and make sure you have full documentation for all of them. (For more detailed information on revising and editing, see Chapter 8. For an example of a student research essay, see Chapter 51.)

13e Prepare a list of sources.

Once you have a final draft with your source materials in place, you are ready to prepare your list of works cited (MLA), your references (APA or CBE), or your bibliography (Chicago style). Create an entry for each source used in your essay. Then double-check your essay against your list of sources cited to see that you have listed every source mentioned in the in-text citations or notes and that you have not listed any sources not cited in your essay. (For guidelines on MLA, APA, CBE, and Chicago styles, see Chapters 50, 52, 54, and 55.)

14

FAQs about Writing Online

How do you judge the reliability of a source you find on the Web? How do you quote part of an email message? For that matter, how do you even spell *email: email*? *E-mail*? *e-mail*? New modes of electronic communication raise these and many other questions for writers.

With such issues for writers a concern, a survey of students and instructors across the country about their online work was undertaken. Their responses inform this chapter, which offers up-to-date advice on conventions of language and style for the digital world. The sections of the chapter offer answers to some questions you may have about these evolving online conventions.

14a General questions about writing online

Online writing takes many forms, including email and listserv messages, newsgroup postings, homepages, hypertexts, MUDs, MOOs, and IRCs. Before you apply the following advice, be sure it is appropriate for the particular form you're using.

What online format conventions should you know?

- SUBJECT LINES. In email and postings, make sure your subject line states your purpose as clearly and succinctly as possible.

  Subject: Sorry to miss the meeting 10/3/00

  This subject line announces that you've made a mistake and is much more helpful than a subject line such as "oops."

- REPLIES. In email, when you use the "reply" function to send a message back about a subject that is entirely different from the one stated in the original subject line, you should change the subject line. Suppose a colleague has written you under the subject of *trading work shifts*. In your reply, if you are changing the subject to ask something about vacation days in 2001, change the subject line to read *Vacation days '01*.

- .SIG FILES. Conclude your online communications with a signature block (known as a *.sig file*) that gives your name, title, address, phone and fax numbers, and so on. These signature files establish your credentials and thus your authority. Keep your signature block concise.

- **BREVITY.** Because readers need to scroll to read online text, shorter is often better. Consider limiting your lines to sixty to seventy characters in order to avoid one- or two-word lines that sometimes occur when one system downloads to another.

- **SHOUTING.** Typing words in all capital letters can seem like SHOUTING and can work effectively only if used judiciously. (Using all lowercase letters can also be annoying.)

- **ATTACHMENTS AND GRAPHICS.** Before sending any attachments or graphics, check to see that the recipients will be able and willing to download them. Some recipients (and many listservs) may refuse to open attachments for fear of viruses unless the attachments come from someone well-known to them.

- **TYPE FONTS.** For most academic and professional work that you plan to print, choose readable fonts such as Courier or Times New Roman in eleven- or twelve-point size. Use clean, modern fonts such as Arial or Helvetica for headings or work that is to be read online. More exotic fonts such as Impact or Chicago are interesting but hard for many people to read.

- **MUDs AND MOOs.** Learn from other participants what format conventions are in place.

What should you pay special attention to when you represent yourself online?

- **INTRODUCTIONS.** Include a brief introduction to any messages, especially if you are new to a group or aren't known to readers (*Hello from an interested participant in a recent workplace seminar at which you spoke. I am writing to . . .*). Doing so can help clarify the purpose of your message and thus encourage prompt response.

- **FLAMING.** Sometimes writers say things online that they would never say in face-to-face communication. Be careful not to slip into the kind of inconsiderate language known as flaming.

- **PROOFREADING.** Unless you are part of a speedy MUD or MOO conversation, proofread and spell-check your messages before you send them. The higher the stakes of the message, especially if it's likely to be printed out, the more careful you should be about its accuracy and clarity.

How do online audiences differ from print audiences?

- **PRIVACY.** Remember that the Internet is public and that online readers can take quick action in regard to your messages and postings including printing or forwarding them. If privacy is a prerequisite for a message, think twice before emailing or posting it.

- **TONE.** Though informal online exchanges can seem a lot like talking, remember that closeness to others doesn't happen instantly, online or off. Write according to how well you really know your audience and according to the specific context. The company president may also be your good friend; when you write to her about company business, however, you should use an appropriately businesslike tone.

How do you mark paragraphs online?

Long chunks of text are often difficult for readers to process. If you can't indent your online paragraphs, break your text into blocks, leaving an extra space between them. You can also help readers by stating the most important information at the beginning of each paragraph.

14b Research online

How do you gain access to the Internet?

In addition to a computer, you'll need two basic tools: a modem (or a network connection to some other faster form of access) and a browser, such as Netscape Navigator, Microsoft Explorer, Mosaic, or Lynx. Then you'll need an Internet service provider (ISP)—a computing center, telephone or cable company, or other communal or government service—to connect your computer to the Internet and provide you with a username. Your campus computer lab or corporate computer center is a good place to find people who can help you get started.

Where can you get more information and detailed help for navigating the Internet?

Check out Andrew Harnack and Eugene Kleppinger's *Online! A Reference Guide to Using Internet Sources* or check online at

<http://www.bedfordstmartins.com/online>

Another helpful online source can be found at

<http://dir.yahoo.com/computers_and_internet/internet/world_wide_web/searching_the_web/>

How do you begin online research efficiently?

Narrow your topic, and then come up with a list of specific keywords as soon as possible. Rather than searching for instances of a broad term like *cancer,* for example—which would call up thousands of possibilities—begin with the most specific topic you can, such as *metastatic colon cancer in teenagers.* (For more on keywords, see 11e.)

How do you begin searching the Internet?

Start by choosing the most appropriate and efficient search engines for your topic; you can find a catalog of specialty search engines listed by category at <http://www.search.com>. (See also 11f.)

- SUBJECT DIRECTORY SEARCH TOOLS. The following sources are especially helpful if you need to narrow a general topic to a specific subtopic.

  Yahoo! <http://www.yahoo.com> allows you to search broad subject categories or to search with keywords.

  WWW Virtual Library <http://vlib.org/> provides searchable directories to resources for hundreds of subject areas.

  The Library of Congress <http://lcweb.loc.gov> provides useful information on Internet sources and extensive subject directories.

- TEXT INDEX SEARCH ENGINES. The following tools help you look for specific keywords and give links to documents containing those words. Some also offer their own subject directories. These engines are particularly helpful when you have already carefully limited your topic.

  AltaVista is huge, indexing millions of Web pages and newsgroup messages; it allows you to search for a single term or for terms in combinations:

  <http://www.altavista.com>

  Other popular and user-friendly engines include:

  Excite <http://www.excite.com>
  Google <http://www.google.com>
  HotBot <http://www.hotbot.com>
  Infoseek <http://www.infoseek.go.com>
  LookSmart <http://www.looksmart.com>
  Lycos <http://www.lycos.com>

NetscapeSearch <http://search.netscape.com>

WebCrawler <http://www.webcrawler.com>

Several search engines allow you to perform a metasearch, which involves using a single term to search with several search engines at once.

Ask Jeeves <http://www.ask.com>

Dogpile <http://www.dogpile.com>

MetaCrawler <http://www.metacrawler.com>

The BigHub <http://www.thebighub.com>

For Apple users, Sherlock software includes an Internet channel that also allows you to search using several search engines at once.

- SEARCH ENGINE KEYWORDS. When you search, begin simply, without complicating the search with *and*'s and *or*'s. Enter the most specific term first: *Hitchcock movies* instead of *movies Hitchcock*. Make sure you know if your search engine is case sensitive—whether it distinguishes lowercase from uppercase letters. Use proper names when possible, in quotation marks if necessary (11e).

How do you evaluate online sources?

Because almost anything—regardless of quality—may be published on the Internet, online research calls for careful evaluation of sources (12c).

- AUTHORITY. Who is the author of this site? What are the author's credentials? Who or what does the author represent? Check for information about the author, which is included often at the bottom of a Web page. Also try entering the author's name in a search engine to see what links it provides; if the author has a homepage that might offer further credential information, you'll find it this way. For newsgroup postings you find on Usenet, you can try using DejaNews to search for other messages written by the author.

- RELEVANCE. How directly related to your topic is the online source? If it isn't specifically relevant, don't use it.

- SPONSOR. Who sponsors the site? Read the Web address for clues. If a comparative review of new VCRs, for example, gives an address of <http://maritav@mitsubishi.com>, the review *may* favor Mitsubishi products. The final suffix in a domain name also tells something about the kind of group sponsoring the site.

  .com (commercial)

  .org (nonprofit organizations)

.edu (educational institutions, usually universities)

.gov (government agencies)

.mil (military groups)

.net (networks)

Geographical domains indicate country of origin: *.ca* (Canada), *.ie* (Republic of Ireland), and so on.

- LINKS TO OTHER SOURCES. Does the site provide references and links to other sources? If possible, check out those sources.
- VERIFIABILITY AND CURRENCY. Can the information in the site be verified? How accurate and complete is the information? How current is it? Is it updated regularly? Check links to the sources of a site's information whenever possible.

Do you need permission to use online texts, graphics, or images in your own work?

The concept of fair use in copyright law allows you to use brief excerpts of copyrighted material (generally 300 words from a book, 150 words from an article, or 4 lines from a poem—or even more if your work is for a class and not intended to be published), as long as you provide a full citation. To quote from personal communication such as email, however, you should ask permission of the writer. To use someone else's graphics or images in your text, it is safest to request permission from the creator or owner. (See 12g for an example of a request for permission.)

In all cases, remember the difference between an assignment that you will submit to a teacher and classmates and a document that you will post or publish on the Internet or in print. For your class, you might include the text of an entire song in an essay, but you cannot put such an essay—with the copyrighted song—on the Internet without infringing on the rights of the copyright owner.

What if page numbers aren't included in an online source you want to cite?

If the source has internal divisions such as parts, paragraphs, or screens, you can include the number or name of the division(s) you are citing, such as (Selfe, par. 8) or (Selfe, abstract). But be careful not to list divisions that come from your browsing software. Here are some additional examples, following MLA style (see Chapter 48):

As Richard deCordova notes in a memorable phrase, the studios wanted to convince millions of moviegoers that "the real hero behave[d] just like the reel hero" (qtd. in Gallagher, part 2).

Brian Gallagher cites a remark by Cary Grant that sums up the strain many stars must have felt: "Everybody wants to be Cary Grant. Even I want to be Cary Grant" (part 3).

Here is the works-cited entry for these citations:

Gallagher, Brian. "Some Historical Paradoxes of
      Stardom in the American Film Industry, 1910-
      1960." Images: A Journal of Film and Popular
      Culture 3 (1997): 7 parts. 7 Aug. 1997
      <http://www.qni.com/~ijournal/issue03/infocus/
      stars1.htm>.

How do you cite texts that may exist in different versions or that are subject to change?

If possible, include the *date of print publication,* if any; the *publication date on the Web*—sometimes a version number or revision date; and the *date you accessed the document.* This information lets readers know that any material you used was part of the document on the date you accessed it—and it allows them to look at other versions to see whether changes have occurred. (See Chapter 50 for more on citing electronic sources.)

Brewer, E. Cobham. The Dictionary of Phrase and Fable.
      London, 1894. 1996. Bibliomania. 9 Oct. 1997
      <http://www.bibliomania.com/Reference/
      PhraseAndFable/>.

14c Design and graphics online

How do you find and use images and graphics from the Web?

Graphic browsers (Microsoft Explorer, Netscape Navigator, HotJava) let you roam the Web in search of images or graphics to use, and many of them are in the public domain, meaning that you can use them without requesting permission or paying a fee. *Yahoo!* is one good source for links to clip art and other graphics:

<http://dir.yahoo.com/computers_and_internet/graphics/>

Choose images and graphics selectively: many take a long time to download. In addition, it's easy to indulge in overkill, especially with clip art, which many people find irritating or clichéd. Choose only those images or graphics that are thoroughly relevant to your topic, and integrate them into your text so that they support but do not dominate the point you are trying to make.

If an image or graphic you want to use is marked with a copyright symbol (©), and if you are going to disseminate your text in print or on the Web, you will need to ask permission and acknowledge its use in any list of references. (See p. 122 for a sample letter requesting permission.)

What art or drawing programs exist for developing effective graphics?

Almost all word-processing programs allow you to create simple visuals such as boxes, charts, or graphs. Other software such as Microsoft Excel, ClarisWorks, or FrontPage offers increasingly sophisticated image composers. In addition, drawings you make by hand can be quickly scanned into your computer and inserted into any document. (See Chapter 15 for advice on creating graphics.)

14d Sentence style online

Does all online writing need to be very concise?

- EMAIL AND POSTINGS. Much online communication is meant to be instantaneous, composed of short and quick exchanges. The speed of communication, small screens, even scarce bandwidth all encourage concise, directly stated messages. Unless your writing is meant to be printed out, use screen space efficiently.

- HOMEPAGES. Homepages must use space to maximum effect, giving necessary information via images and words and including links to other pages and documents. Though these linked documents may be quite lengthy, the homepage leading you to them needs to be concise.

- MUDS AND MOOS. Brevity is even more important in MUDs and MOOs, where many people interact simultaneously. MUDs and MOOs tend to invite very short exchanges, often just a sentence or two.

How much stylistic polishing does online writing call for?

As always, the answer depends on your rhetorical situation. If the outcome of a piece of online writing is very important to you (an award or promotion, say, or a Web page you are responsible for designing), then the more polished your prose the better. Make sure it's correct, accurate, and persuasive.

Many email or newsgroup postings, however, seek to convey information in the quickest and easiest way possible. Such messages need only be polished enough to be clear. And in MUDs and MOOs, writing contributions are so short and done so rapidly that polished prose is not expected.

When and how should you use a style or grammar checker?

Editing programs like Writer's Workbench offer information on issues such as sentence length, verb voice, and sentence openers. Grammar checkers in word processors such as Microsoft Word can also be helpful, checking your drafts for common sentence-level errors and flagging wordy sentences or fragments. But these programs and tools are giving advice out of context and may suggest corrections—such as flagging fragments used intentionally as part of a list—where none are needed. Beware, then, and remember that such advice may *not* be appropriate to your specific writing goals.

14e   Grammar online

What do the various parts of URLs and email addresses mean? Is there an underlying grammar that helps you read them?

Just as word order is important to the grammar of English sentences, so too is the order of the parts of a URL or email address. You can read a URL for its meaning just as you can read a sentence, so knowing the grammar of URLs can help you use this locator, especially if you are trying to identify an error in an address.

PROTOCOL   DOMAIN NAME   DIRECTORY PATH   FILE NAME

http://www.bedfordstmartins.com/lunsford/everyday_writer

SLASHES END PROTOCOL   SLASHES END DOMAIN NAME, DIRECTORY PATH

USERNAME   DOMAIN NAME

eaashdown@earthlink.com

AT SIGN SEPARATES USER NAME FROM DOMAIN NAME

Of particular importance is the final designation of the domain name: *com* for commercial sites or *edu* for educational institutions, for example (14b). Note, however, that domain names differ in other countries and the domain name may also identify a country of origin (*ca* for Canada, *ar* for Argentina).

Most important of all, remember that a URL or email address must be typed *exactly* as it appears, without any extra spaces or changes to punctuation.

How important are sentence conventions online?

The answer to this question depends on the kind of online writing you are doing (email? Web page? MOO? hypertext essay?) and on your rhetorical situation—the context of your writing, your purpose, your audience and their expectations, the genre you are using, and the level of formality appropriate to your message.

- EMAIL. If in doubt, stick to the conventions of standard academic English, including clear, complete sentences, even if you use more informal language. Much email is appropriately informal; it's often conversational and like talk in its use of fragments and run-on sentences: *Long time, no see— gimme some news, will you?* But if you're emailing your boss in response to a request, you will want to be more formal and to observe conventions: *I am responding to your request for an update on sales in the northern region.*

- POSTINGS. If you're posting to a listserv or newsgroup whose members are largely unknown to you, look for any available FAQs before you begin: the information there may provide ground rules for postings, including expectations about writing conventions. It's also a good idea to look at other postings for a few days to get a sense of style and audience before posting anything yourself. If you are too casual or don't pay attention to conventions, you may send a message that you don't intend to—that you are satisfied with sloppy work, for instance.

  Remember that postings, like email, can easily be printed out and circulated offline. In print, carelessness about conventions may send unintentional signals to an even wider audience.

- MUDS AND MOOS. In the fast-paced real-time communication of a MUD or MOO, paying careful attention to all conventions is very difficult. As a result, sentence fragments, comma splices, dangling modifiers, and so on are more likely to be ignored.

How do you deal with acronyms such as HTML or MOO that need to be made into verbs?

The digital revolution has spawned many acronyms that are used routinely by online writers. To make them into verb forms, just follow the grammar of English verbs, with a few variations.

- To make an acronym into a past-tense verb, add an apostrophe + *d: FTP'd, HTML'd* (but *MUDded*).
- To make an acronym into a present participle, just add *ing: FTPing, CCing.*

14f Words online

How and when should you use digital jargon?

Like all jargon, the terms emerging in the digital age can be irritating and incomprehensible—or extremely helpful. If the jargon is concrete and specific, it can help clarify concepts, providing a useful shorthand for an otherwise lengthy explanation.

Frequently used terms (such as *asynchronous communication* and *email*) are the ones online writers should know. Other terms, like the jargon in this sentence—"Savvy wavelet compression is the fiber signpost of the virtual chillout room"—may be appropriate for techies talking to one another, but they are not very useful to those trying to communicate with a nontechnical or general audience. Before you use technical jargon, remember your readers: if they will not understand the terms, or if you don't know them well enough to judge, then take the time to say what you need to say in everyday language.

How do you spell the plurals of acronyms such as MOO or URL?

The digital revolution has spawned many technical acronyms that are used routinely by online writers. To make them plural, just add a lowercase -s (without an apostrophe): *MOOs, URLs.* As with other jargon, though, if your readers may not understand, write the term out.

When is it appropriate to use digital acronyms like IMHO and F2F?

Along with the new jargon have come quite a few new acronyms that serve as a kind of shorthand for everyday expressions. Such acronyms may be appropriate for some informal online communication, but you should avoid them in most academic or other formal writing. Here are some of them:

BTW	by the way
FWIW	for what it's worth
F2F	face-to-face
IMHO	in my humble opinion
OTOH	on the other hand
RL	real life

14g Punctuation and mechanics online

What do the punctuation marks in electronic addresses indicate?

/   The forward slash separates parts of URLs.

•   The dot separates parts of email addresses and URLs.

@   The *at* sign is part of every email address, indicating that you are *at* an electronic address.

<>   Angle brackets can be used in printed texts to frame email addresses and URLs, making it possible to use them within sentences and with other punctuation.

_   The underscore is used in many URLs (and around titles in online text in place of italics).

~   The tilde appears in many URLs as an indicator of the user or owner of the directory path.

These marks are crucial for finding what you want, so treat them with care—they are not optional!

What are the strange combinations of punctuation marks that you often see in online writing?

Some online writers combine punctuation marks and other keyboard characters to create (when viewed sideways) facial expressions that signal tone or attitude. For example, a smile :-) signals a friendly hello or nod. These little online punctuation marks, called *emoticons* (or *smileys*), are used primarily for fun (43g). Use them as you would other online shorthand: only if they are appropriate to your topic and purpose and only if they will be understood and accepted by your audience. As a general rule, leave emoticons out of most academic writing.

How do you show italics online?

For programs that don't allow you to use italics, you can substitute other devices. To add emphasis to a word or phrase, use asterisks:

▶ **The company homepage simply *must* be updated!**

To indicate a title, use the underline mark before and after the title:

▶ **Thanks for the copy of _EasyWriter_, which arrived today.**

Because underlining on the World Wide Web signals an active hypertext link, you should not underline words to signal italics in Web documents.

Are there special rules for using capital letters online?

In general, follow the same conventions online that you would in print, capitalizing the first word of each sentence and proper nouns and adjectives. Some writers treat email almost like talk, writing hurriedly and not using any capital letters. This practice can be hard on your readers, however, and looks unprofessional if it is printed out. Since email *is* often printed out, you should follow the print conventions of capitalization. Here are some other tips for using capital letters online:

- ELECTRONIC ADDRESSES. Follow the capitalization *exactly* in address lines: systems that are case sensitive may not recognize <*Lunsford.8@Osu.edu*> if the actual address is <*lunsford.8@osu.edu*>.

- SHOUTING. Capitalizing whole words or phrases for emphasis comes across to readers as SHOUTING. So, instead of uppercase letters, use asterisks to add emphasis: *Sorry for the abrupt response, but I am *very* busy.*

- INTERCAPS. Some companies use capitals in the middle of their own or their products' names, often turning two words into one. Leave the capitals in, following the style you see in company advertising or on the product itself—*HotJava, WordPerfect, EasyWriter.*

How do you know when to use hyphens with new compound words that are not yet in any dictionaries?

Many new compounds, especially those pertaining to technology, appear as one word, without hyphenation. Helpful advice comes from the editors of *Wired* magazine in their style manual *Wired Style:* "When in doubt, close it up." Hence *videogame, desktop, download, toolbar.*

How do you break a URL if it won't all fit on one line of printed text?

First, remember to signal the beginning and end of the URL with angle brackets (<>). If you are using MLA style and you need to divide a long Internet address at the end of a line, break it only after a slash:

> <http://www.bedfordstmartins.com/lunsford/
> everyday_writer>

An alternate style from the editors of *Wired* magazine is to break the URL in one of the following places:

- *after* the beginning protocol: <http://
- *before* a punctuation mark: <http://www.bedfordstmartins
  .com/online>

Wherever you break a URL, be sure not to add a hyphen at the break and to delete a hyphen added by your word processor.

How do you deal with money, weights and measures, phone numbers, and dates on the Internet?

Because the Internet reaches readers around the globe, you may need to use non-U.S. units. When using monetary figures online, use the currency of the nation you are writing about or to. For weights and measures, remember that the system of inches and pounds is largely limited to the United States; use metric measurements (meters, grams) when they are appropriate. Begin phone numbers with a plus sign (+) followed by the international access code, if any; then add the area, province, or city code in parentheses; and then add the local number, with spaces between: *+1 (212) 846 3119.* Readers outside the United States follow different conventions for dates, inverting the order of the month and day. Avoid potential confusion from abbreviating dates (*6/7/99*) and spell out the name of the month instead: *June 7, 1999* or *7 June 1999.*

15

Document Design

Computers have given us new ease in using headings, lists, graphics, and other visuals. Because these visual elements can help us get and keep a reader's attention, they bring a whole new dimension to writing—what some refer to as *visual rhetoric*. This chapter will help you to use visual rhetoric effectively in creating various documents, including online documents that can be printed out.

Some Guidelines for Using Visuals

- Use visuals as part of your written presentation, not as decoration. Preparing visuals should be part of your process of generating ideas and planning for the complete document.

- Refer to the visual in your text before the visual itself appears, explaining its main point. For example: *As Table 1 demonstrates, the cost of a college education has risen dramatically in the last decade.*

- Number and title your visuals.

- If you did not create a particular visual yourself, or if you created a visual using someone else's research, credit your source fully—and ask permission if necessary. (12g)

- Use clip art sparingly if at all. Computer clip art is so easy to cut and paste that you may be tempted to fancy up your text, but do so only if the addition contributes to your argument.

15a Create a visual structure.

Effective writers use visual elements such as white space and color, and choose type styles and sizes that guide readers, presenting them with documents that are easy on the eye and easy to understand.

White space and margins

For most documents, frame your page with margins of white space of between one inch and one and one-half inches. Since the eye takes in only so much data in one movement, very long lines can be hard to read. Wider margins help, particularly if the information is difficult or dense. You can also use white space around graphics or lists to make them stand out.

Each page should be a unit. You would not want to put a heading at the very bottom of a page, forcing the readers to turn the page to get to the text that the heading is announcing. And try not to end a page with a hyphenated word, leaving readers to guess at the second part as they turn the page.

Double-space most academic documents you prepare, with the first line of each paragraph indented one-half inch or five spaces. Certain kinds of writing for certain disciplines may call for different spacing. Letters and memorandums, for example, are usually single-spaced, with no paragraph indentation but with an extra line space between paragraphs. Lab reports in some disciplines are also single-spaced. Other kinds of documents, such as flyers and newsletters, may call for multiple columns of print.

Computers allow you to decide whether or not you want both side margins justified, or squared off, as they are on this page. Except in posters and other writing where you want to achieve a distinctive visual effect, you should always justify the left margin, though you may decide to indent lists and blocks of text that are set off. However, most writers, and many instructors, prefer the right margin to be *ragged,* or unjustified.

Color

Many software programs, printers, and copiers offer the possibility of using color to add emphasis in your documents. Keep in mind the following tips:

- Use color to draw attention to elements you want to emphasize: headings and subheadings, bullets, text boxes, or parts of charts or graphs.
- For most documents, keep the number of colors to a minimum (one or two in addition to white and black).
- Be consistent in your use of color; use the same color for all subheads, for example.

Paper

The quality of the paper and the readability of the print affect the overall look and feel of your document. Although you may well want to use inexpensive paper for your earlier drafts, when your college writing is ready for final presentation, use eight-and-a-half by eleven-inch good-quality white bond paper. On some occasions, you may wish to use a parchment or cream-colored bond—for a résumé perhaps. For brochures and posters, colored paper may be most appropriate. Try to use the best-quality printer available to you for your final product.

Pagination

Except for a separate title page, which is usually left unnumbered, number every page of your document. Your instructor may ask that you follow a particular format (APA or MLA, for example); if not, beginning with the first page of text, place your last name and an arabic numeral in the upper-right-hand corner of the page, about one-half inch from the top and aligned with the right margin. Do not put the number in parentheses or follow it with a period. Most personal computers will paginate a document for you.

Selecting type

Most personal computers allow writers to choose among a great variety of type sizes and typefaces, or fonts. For most college writing, the easy-to-read ten to twelve point type sizes are best, as is a serif font (this is serif type; this is sans serif type). Although a smaller or more unusual style—such as *italics* or *cursive*—might seem attractive at first glance, readers may find such styles distracting and hard to read. Most important, be consistent in the size and style of typeface you choose. Unless you are striving for some special effect, shifting sizes and fonts can give an appearance of disorderliness.

15b   Use headings effectively.

In longer documents, headings (set-off words and phrases) call attention to the organization of the text and thus aid comprehension. Some genres of reports have set headings, which readers expect (and writers therefore must provide). If you use headings, you need to decide on typeface and size, wording, and placement.

Type size and style

This book uses various levels of headings. For your college writing, you might distinguish levels of headings using type—all capitals for the first-level headings, capital and lowercase underlined for the second level, plain capitals and lowercase for the third level, and so on. With a computer, you have even more options, including color. For example:

ON A TYPEWRITER	ON A COMPUTER
FIRST-LEVEL HEADING	FIRST-LEVEL HEADING
<u>Second-Level Heading</u>	**Second-Level Heading**
Third-Level Heading	<u>Third-Level Heading</u>
	Fourth-Level Heading

Consistent headings

Look for the most succinct way to word your headings. Most often, state the topic in a single word, usually a noun (*Toxicity*); in a phrase, usually a noun phrase (*Levels of Toxicity*) or a gerund phrase (*Measuring Toxicity*); in a question that will be answered in the text (*How Can Toxicity Be Measured?*); or in an imperative that tells readers what steps to take (*Measure the Toxicity*). Whichever structure you choose, make sure you use it consistently for all headings of the same level: all questions, for example, or all gerund phrases and *not* a mixture of the two.

Typically, place a first-level heading at the left margin; indent a second-level heading five spaces from the left; and center a third-level head. Other positions are possible; just remember to place each level of heading consistently throughout your paper.

15c Use visuals effectively.

In some cases, visuals may be the primary text you present; in other cases, they will be of equal or supplemental importance to your text. In every case, they can help make a point vividly and emphatically by presenting information more succinctly and more clearly than words alone could.

In deciding when and where to use visuals, the rule of thumb is simply to use ones that will make your points most emphatically and will most help your audience understand your document. Researchers who have studied the use of visuals offer some tips about when a particular kind of visual is most appropriate.

- *Use graphs* or *charts* to draw attention to relationships among data. *Pie charts* compare a part to the whole. *Bar charts* and *line graphs* compare one element with another, compare elements over time, demonstrate correlations, and illustrate frequency.

- *Use tables* to draw attention to particular numerical information.

- *Use drawings* or *diagrams* to draw attention to dimensions and to details.

- *Use maps* to draw attention to location and to spatial relationships.

- *Use cartoons* to illustrate or emphasize a point dramatically or to amuse.

- *Use photographs* to draw attention to a graphic scene (such as devastation following an earthquake) or to depict people or objects.

Number your visuals (*Figure 1* or *Fig. 1*). Give them titles (*Racial and Ethnic Origin in the United States, 1990*) and perhaps subtitles that provide a link to the text. Here are examples of several kinds of visuals labeled following MLA style.

PIE CHART

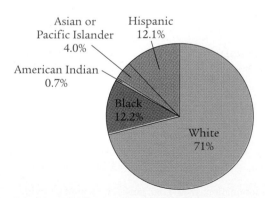

Figure 1. Racial and Ethnic Origin in the United States (Projected), 2001, U.S. Census Bureau, 2000.

TABLE

Table 1
Word Choice by Race: *Seesaw* and *Teeter-totter*, Chicago 1986

	Black	*White*	*Total*
Seesaw	47 (78%)	4 (15%)	51
Teeter-totter	13 (22%)	23 (85%)	36
Total	60	27	87

Source: Michael I. Miller, "How to Study Black Speech in Chicago." *Language Variation in North American English.* Ed. A. Wayne Glowka and Donald M. Lance. New York: MLA, 1993. 166.

BAR GRAPH

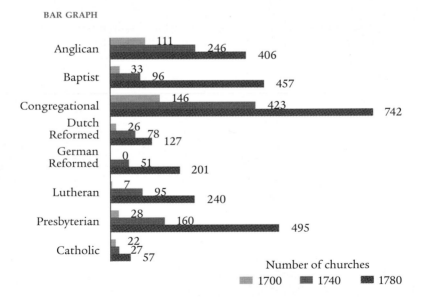

Figure 2. Church Growth by Denomination, 1700–1780, James A. Henretta, David Brody, Susan Ware, and Marilynn S. Johnson, *America's History* (New York: Worth, 1997) 119.

LINE GRAPH

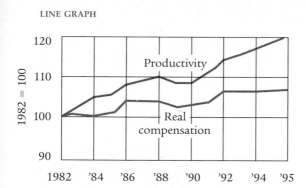

Figure 3. Productivity and Wages, 1982–1995, *New York Times,*
2 Jan. 1996: C20. Copyright © 1996 by The New York Times Co.
Reprinted by permission.

DIAGRAM

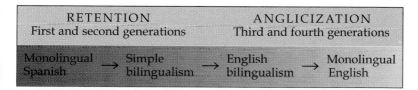

Figure 4. Spanish-English Bilingualism and the Language Shift Process,
D. Letticia Galindo. "Bilingualism and Language Variation," *Language Variation
in North American English,* ed. A. Wayne Glowka and Donald M. Lance (New
York: MLA, 1993) 202.

15d Sample documents

Interested in creating a flyer advertising your company's services? Want
to put together a newsletter for a campus group you belong to? What
follows is a catalog of documents collected from college students and
others, along with annotations intended to guide you in creating similar documents for yourself.

NEWSLETTER

Specific issue identified

Sponsoring organization identified

Title in vivid color box and largest type

Mission statement featured prominently

Title of lead article highlighted

Eye-catching photo included

Triple columns make text easy to read

Second color sets off sidebar

URL for group Web site listed

Housatonic Habitat

Front Porch

Fall 1999

Housatonic Habitat for Humanity

Working Together to Help Build Dreams

Jeffrey Home Dedicated in Newtown

Fairfield County—and the Danbury area in particular—was still recovering from the storm once known as Hurricane Floyd when Housatonic Habitat dedicated its first Newtown home on Sunday, September 19th. That's why Kim Philbin, a volunteer for HHfH's Family Partnership Committee, chose to read Matthew 7: 25 before presenting Jim and Sarah Jeffrey with a Bible: "Jesus said that though the rains come down and the floodwaters rise, and the wind beat against the walls, the house will not collapse because it is built

on solid rock."

The passage was appropriate, not only because of the recent deluge, but because Floyd—which arrived just as Sarah, Jim, Brian, and Paul Jeffrey were attempting to move in—was only the most recent meteorological obstacle hurdled by the builders of Newtown One. Torrential rains, ice storms, 110-degree heat; the house has already survived a decade's worth of bad weather, because it's built on rock—literally as well as figuratively. As Project Manager Larry Coleman noted while giving the Jeffreys their Habitat toolkit—filled with tools used on their new home—67 Philo Curtis Road sits on solid Connecticut ledge.

Many dignitaries spoke—among them Newtown First Selectman Herb Rosenthal, the Reverend Kathleen Adams-Shephard of Newtown's Trinity Episcopal Church, and the Rever-

end Dr. Louise Parsons Pietsch, whose St. Stephen's Episcopal Church in Ridgefield sponsored the home. But the most moving words came from the Jeffreys themselves. "Truly this is a miracle," said Jim, after he and Sarah had attempted to name the many people ("lots of Jims and Chrises") who had helped with the home: "People of all ages and faiths coming together to help a family they didn't know." Added Sarah, "This house is more than we could have hoped for. It's amazing that people who started out as strangers grew to become our friends."

Welcome Aboard!

Housatonic Habitat is proud to welcome two new partners to the affiliate's fold. **John Jay High School** of Cross River, New York, is now a Campus Chapter; and the **Congregational Church of Brookfield** has become HHfH's tenth Covenant Church.

We thank these new partners... and be sure to watch this space for further developments!

www.danbury-ct/habitat

BROCHURE

COVER   **INTERIOR PAGE**

···· Informative title in large, eye-catching type

Eating Vegetarian

𝒜 Vegetarian

IS A PERSON WHO EATS ···· Definition used to organize information
mainly plant foods such as grains, beans, nuts, fruits and vegetables.

There are several ways of eating vegetarian.

• **Semi-vegetarians** exclude some but not all ···· Further explanation presented in bulleted list
  foods of animal origin.* They may not eat
  beef, for example, but will sometimes eat
  poultry or seafood.
• **Lacto-ovovegetarians** include milk or milk
  products and eggs in their diets, but omit
  meat, fish and poultry.
• **Lactovegetarians** include milk products, but
  don't eat eggs, meat, poultry or seafood.
• **Vegans** don't eat any animal products.

*Foods of animal origin = meat, fish, poultry, eggs, milk, milk products, honey, bouillon

Vegetarian Food Guide Pyramid
Always eat at least the minimum number of servings from each level.

fats, oils, sweets
Use sparingly. But
have at least 3 tsp.
of fat a day.

milk, yogurt,
cheese
0–3 servings
daily

dry beans, nuts,
seeds, eggs, meat
substitutes
2–3 servings daily

vegetables
3–5 servings
daily

fruits
2–4 servings
daily

bread,
cereal,
rice, pasta
6–11
servings
daily

···· Useful information presented in a clear illustration

1 ···· Page number

···· Ample space around title and illustration

···· Appropriate illustration in central spot

LISTSERV POSTING (FOR A CLASS)

To: alenglh167@lists.acs.ohio-state.edu
From: Kristen Convery <convery.8@osu.edu>
Subject: Re: class discussion of "self"
Cc:
Bcc:

At 03:48 PM 11/17/00 -0500, Kate wrote:

>Has anyone had any interesting or pertinent discussions
>of the "self" in other classes this term?

I'm taking psychology this quarter and have found some
information that pertains to our discussion on the self.

Carl Rogers studied the self and self-concept, theorizing
that people do things in line with their concept of themselves in order to avoid having to rework that self-
concept. For instance, if I think of myself as an artist
and not as a musician and I want to go to a concert, I
will go to the art museum just so that I do not have to
rethink and maybe change the way I view myself.

Comments from other class members? It strikes me as
interesting that we seem to feel as if we must fit one
mold, and that that mold nullifies all other concepts of
the self. Why can't we be both artists and musicians?
But it's true--especially when I look at families. How
many families do you guys know where the parents proudly
introduce members as "the scientist (writer/artist/
musician/thinker) of the family"? And how does this
inhibit other siblings who might also want to be scientists, writers, artists, musicians, thinkers, but fear
taking over someone else's place?

Just a few thoughts . . .

Kristen C.

Annotations (left margin):

Subject line provides specific information

Writer includes the part of an earlier posting she is responding to

Double space indicates new paragraph

Posting responds to query and calls for further comments; tone is engaged, friendly, and polite

Writer gives only first name and initial because this is a closed listserv for class members

PORTFOLIO COVER

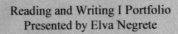

Reading and Writing I Portfolio
Presented by Elva Negrete

.... Colorful
graphic
encloses title
and author

Table of Contents

- Cover Letter
- Argumentative Essay
- Stylistic Analysis
- Imitation/Parody
- Exploratory Essay
- Final Exam

.... Bulleted
list gives
portfolio's
contents

.... Clip art is
appropriate to
the course
subject

English 1310
Reading and Writing I
Professor Jaime Mejía
March 10, 2000

.... Course
information
and date

"Until I take pride in my language, I cannot take pride in myself."
–Gloria Anzaldúa, "How to Tame a Wild Tongue"

.... Relevant
quotation
gets readers'
attention

16

Web Texts

As more and more people go to school, work, play, and shop online, the uses of the World Wide Web are expanding exponentially. In school, you might read and analyze Web documents for classes; you may also create Web texts for clubs or groups you belong to—a homepage for a women's soccer team, for example, or a résumé template for the undergraduate engineering club. On the job, you might help maintain a Web site, create advertising material for the Web, or respond to queries posted to the company's Web site. You even may author Web texts for yourself, your family, or your friends—a homepage with a journal page for friends to read or a family tree that all members can contribute to.

The feature that distinguishes the World Wide Web from other media is its hypertextuality, what you might think of as its "linkability." Because of links that authors build into their Web sites, users can click on highlighted words or images to go immediately to other parts of the site—or to other sites on the Web. Web sites can also include color, sound, and still or moving images, making them multimedia experiences. To help your audience move around within your Web text, to embed links in the text, and to incorporate multimedia, you must be familiar with the basics of hypertext markup language (HTML) and its codes. To present your Web text to an audience, you must make it available on a Web server. This chapter provides an overview of how to write a text suited to the Web, as well as an introduction to these technical issues.

16a Planning Web texts

You should plan a Web text much as you would any text (see Chapter 4).

- Think about the purpose of your text, and let those purposes help determine your overall format, the length of your text, and the links you create. If your purpose is to explain, for example, how current cartoonists make fun of politicians, you might provide links to caricatures of ten contemporary politicians to enhance the explanation.

- Remember that Web texts are dynamic rather than static texts. You will most likely need to plan for ongoing reassessment and maintenance of your Web text.

- Identify as clearly as possible the audience for your Web document. If your intended audience is your instructor, classmates, colleagues, or other people you know, you can make certain assumptions about their background knowledge and likely responses to your text. If your audience is broader than that, however, you may need to provide more explicit information. Always structure your text to fit the needs of your audience.

- Consider how clearly and concisely you can state the topic of your Web document. A topic that is vague or overly broad—such as *American movies*—will require far too much text and too many links to make it useful to others. Narrow your topic and clarify your stance on it until you have something with practical scope: *The rise of cyborg movies, 1975–2000.*

- What is your rhetorical stance? Are you presenting yourself as an expert or as a novice seeking information from audience members? What information will you need to seem credible and persuasive to your audience?

- What impression do you intend to create with the design of your Web document? Articulating this impression clearly can guide your decisions about how much text and what kinds of navigation aids to use, as well as your choices of images, colors, sound clips, and so on. How detailed should your menus be? What colors, images, and sounds will speak best to your audience?

- What are the technical limitations facing readers of your Web text? If you include graphics and images, how much memory will your document occupy? How long will it take readers to download? Will they be able to access images and sound?

For more information about these basic rhetorical principles, see Chapter 4.

16b Mapping Web texts

Just as you might outline an essay, you should develop an outline of your Web text. Such an outline can take the form of a map, allowing you to lay out your Web text in a general way and to make sure the parts of it are related to one another in appropriate and reader-friendly ways.

- Take an inventory of the content material you have, and make a list of material you need to find or create. Then set a realistic schedule for developing the content material of your text.

- Think of your Web text as a series of pages. The homepage is the introduction or overview that the user will encounter by pointing a browser to your main Web address. From the homepage, users can reach all the other pages. Each page can be as long or as short as you need it to be. It may fit on one screen, or it may require the user to scroll through multiple screens.

- Sketch the basic text and graphics for each page of your document, beginning with the homepage. You can use the drawing functions in your word processor, or you can use one five- by seven-inch card or eight-and-a-half by eleven-inch piece of paper for each page.
- Arrange the pages on a bulletin board, a large desk, or the floor. Then indicate the links among the pages using string or paper arrows.
- Check to see if the pages cover your purpose thoroughly and that their relationship to one another will be appealing and understandable to your audience.

16c   Designing Web texts

In matters of design, you will be wise to stick to a few basic principles with every page and link you create. In particular, always include the title, your name, contact information, and date, and provide one link back to the homepage on each page.

Homepages

The homepage of any Web document is extremely important, for it introduces your topic and sets out the various paths readers can use to explore the rest of the document.

- At the top of the homepage, include a title (and subtitle, if necessary) along with a simple, eye-catching graphic or statement that makes the subject of the document clear to readers. Below this, include an overview of what is in the document. (See p. 161 for an example of a homepage.)
- On the right or left of the page, list the links that readers can use to access other parts of the document or other sites. You may also want to include a link to a site map from your homepage. Use a site map to diagram or display the hierarchy of pages on your site.
- In the body of the page, include any introductory text related to your site, such as a welcome statement or overview of the site's purpose.
- At the bottom of the page, include a logo, if appropriate, along with your name, contact information (such as your email address), and the date you created the document. (You will later need to add dates on which you have updated it.) If the page is long, you may also want to add a button to return to the top of the page.
- Consider using your homepage as the basis for a template, or model, to save time and to help make the design of all your pages consistent. You can

download such templates from shareware Web sites or create a template that imitates the design of a page you find particularly effective. (See 16f for more on templates.) In any case, decide now how you will highlight links throughout your site—with <u>underlining</u>, **bold text,** color, icons (✎), or labeling (*for additional readings, click here*). Choose background and text colors that are appropriate to your topic and that are contrasting so that your text is easy to read.

Basic page design

- Use simple graphics that can be downloaded quickly and easily by your readers. (See 16f for more on graphics.)

- Use bullets, numbered lists, and headings as signposts for readers.

- Use fonts that are easy to read: decorative fonts may be fine for headings, but they are tiring for readers in long passages. If you use different fonts and type sizes for emphasis and variety, make sure that they add to the effectiveness of the page. When you do vary fonts and sizes, do so consistently.

- Use color carefully and consistently. In general, use light colors for background so that the text will stand out, and use colors to guide readers—one color to signal headings, for example, and another to signal subheadings. Remember that white text on a dark background will not print well.

- Group related information and images in the same area of a page.

- Remember that readers of English are used to reading left to right and top to bottom. Place your most important text or images at the top left of a page—or at the lower right.

- Include a link to the homepage and your name and contact information on every page.

- Maintain consistency among your pages to make them easier to navigate and read. Use the same title or navigation graphics on each page.

- Ask some readers to respond to a rough draft of your pages, especially the homepage. How understandable are the pages? How easy are they to navigate? How effective is the use of color, font, and graphics? (16f)

16d Adding links and navigation tools

The success of any Web document is tied to the effectiveness of its links, including those to other pages in the same site (internal links) and those to other sites (external links). It may help to think of such links as the elements that add depth and texture to your document: the opening page provides an overview and announces the general aim of the document, but the links bring this aim to life, providing a level of detail not possible in the homepage. Links may lead to explanations, lists of supporting statistics, bibliographies, and additional readings or other relevant sites.

Especially as you begin working with Web documents, be conservative in the number of links you plan. Although it can be tempting to add numerous links to a page of Web text—just as it might be tempting to add many footnotes to a page of print text—too many links can overwhelm both you and your readers.

As noted above, you can signal links with underlining, **bold text,** color, icons (☺), or labeling (*for additional readings, click here*). In any event, make sure readers will know what the purpose of the link is and, if it leads to an external site, who its author is.

Finally, remember to add clear internal links so that readers can return to the homepage, for example, or to a previous page. These internal links may take the form of navigation buttons, pictures, or icons such as arrows (→), stars (★), or other symbols designed to help readers move quickly through your Web document. Such buttons should be placed at the top, bottom, or side of a page. Remember to add text to the button if its meaning will not be instantly clear: an arrow alone, for instance, may not tell readers that clicking on it will take them to the next page. In such cases, label the arrow button *Next.* (See 16f for more detailed information on links.)

16e   Checking out Web sites

One good way to prepare for creating your own Web text is, of course, to browse the Web, noting the elements of sites you find particularly effective. In addition, take a look at a homepage and one other page from a student Web project shown on pp. 161–162.

16f   Writing Web texts

After you plan, map, and design your Web text, you have other important decisions to make. You'll need to have access to the necessary software—a basic text-editing program such as NotePad or SimpleText as well as word-processing software. Many writers new to the Web like to

HOMEPAGE FOR A CLASS PROJECT

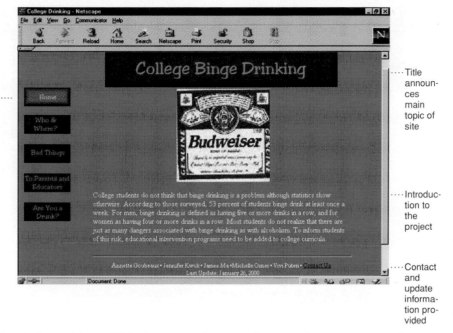

···· Title announces main topic of site

···· Introduction to the project

···· Contact and update information provided

begin by writing a Web document in a word-processing program such as WordPerfect or Microsoft Word and then saving the material in hypertext markup language (HTML).

More experienced Web writers prefer to use HTML to create a Web document themselves. To do so most effectively, you will need a software program for creating HTML called an HTML editor, such as Netscape's Composer, which your Internet browser may already include. Many others are available; descriptions and downloading information can be found at sites such as the CWSApps List of Basic HTML Editors <http://cws.internet.com/32html.html> or SoftSeek <http://www.softseek.com/internet/web_publishing_tools/>.

HTML CODES

HTML codes act like traffic signals, turning on a feature of a text and then turning it off again. One set of codes (usually called document tags) governs the larger aspects of the text (such as the title, body elements, background color, and so on) while another set (usually called

SECOND PAGE FOR A CLASS PROJECT

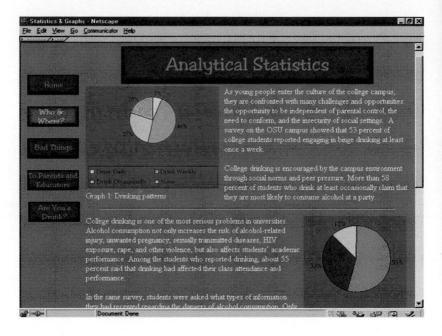

appearance tags) governs smaller aspects (italics, boldface, underlining, and so on). Here's what the basic tags for an HTML document look like:

```
<HTML>
<HEAD>
<TITLE> title of your site goes here</TITLE>
</HEAD>
<BODY>
Your text and images go here
</BODY>
</HTML>
```

The *<title>* field contains information about your document that Web search tools can use to locate it. Other tags help you create and organize the body of the document.

SECTION HEADING TAGS

Use these tags to create headings and to indicate levels of importance.

<H1> Level one heading text </H1>

<H2> Level two heading text </H2>

<H3> Level three heading text </H3>

<H4>Level four heading text </H4>

DIVISIONAL TAGS

Use these tags to format and to help organize your pages.

<CENTER></CENTER>	centers elements and text
<P></P>	indicates a paragraph
<BLOCKQUOTE></BLOCKQUOTE>	indicates a long quotation
 	indicates a line break (no closing tag)
<HR>	indicates a horizontal rule (no closing tag)

TYPOGRAPHY TAGS

<B></B>	**bold text**
<I></I>	*italics text*
<U></U>	<u>underlined text</u>

LIST TAGS

<UL></UL>	bulleted list
<OL></OL>	numbered list

The following sources will help you use HTML and design your site:

A BEGINNER'S GUIDE TO HTML

<http://www.ncsa.uiuc.edu/General/Internet/WWW/HTMLPrimer.html>

UNIVERSITY OF VIRGINIA LIBRARY, HTML AND WEB DOCUMENT CREATION

<http://www.lib.virginia.edu/usered/docs.html>

FOR COLOR IN YOUR DOCUMENT

<http://www.bagism.com/colormaker/>

<http://home.netscape.com/assist/net_sites/bg/index.html>

FOR BACKGROUND IMAGES AND COLORS

<http://home.netscape.com/assist/net_sites/bg/backgrounds.html>
<http://www.infi.net/wwwimages/colorindex.html>

FOR TABLES

<http://www.bagism.com/tablemaker/>

TEMPLATES

A template can serve as a model for all the pages of your Web document. Using your carefully edited homepage as a guide, you can develop a template that will help give consistency to your pages and thus make them easier to read. You can also download Web page templates from shareware Web sites, or you may imitate the design of an existing Web page you find particularly effective. Basically, a template sets the background color, heading information, navigation buttons, and contact information—all the elements you want to appear on every page. Once this template is saved in your directory or folder, you can resave it using the "save as" command to create new pages.

GRAPHICS AND IMAGES

Graphics are particularly important on Web pages. Make sure, however, that the graphics you use are closely related to your purposes.

- Tables, pie charts, and other graphs can often be created in your word-processing program and then saved as HTML, or your HTML editor can help you create such visuals.

- Photographs or other printed graphics can be scanned and saved as files to be inserted into your Web text. A scanner should be available to you in a campus computer lab. If a picture file will not fit into your document, you can use a program such as Adobe Photoshop to change its size and quality.

- Most browsers can view JPEG or GIF images, saved as .jpeg or .gif files—the most common image file formats. However, remember that the file space an image takes up may make it slow or difficult to download; limit individual images to 20 kilobytes to be safe, or use a smaller thumbnail image and link users to the original, larger file.

- If you have not taken a photograph or created a graphic yourself, you will need to see if it is copyrighted and, if so, to ask permission to scan or download and use it.

- Free icons, clip art, and other images are widely available from sites such as the Clip Art Connection, or you can check most search engines for other free image archives. You should not, however, export images from other Web texts without asking permission (12g). Also, be aware that clip art can be tiresome; use it only if it contributes something to your text.

- To download and save an image from the Web when using Windows, position your cursor over the image and right click with your mouse, and select "save image as." To download an image when using a Macintosh, hold down the mouse until a menu appears, and select "save this image as."

LINKS

Providing links that transfer readers effortlessly from place to place calls for a lot of thought on the part of the Web writer. You will probably need to practice creating links or even take a tutorial to learn how to do so. The following steps, however, will get you started:

- Choose a format for your links. Will you use an icon or button to signal them? a change of color? underlining or bold text?

- For basic links, include an anchor tag:

  <A HREF="file name or URL">text or item to be a button</A>

ANCHOR TAG	REFERENCE TAG	LINK TEXT	ANCHOR TAG

- For internal links to other places on the same Web page, use "jump-to" anchor tags:

  <A HREF="#JUMP-to-Bibliography">bibliography</A>

ANCHOR TAG	REFERENCE TAG	JUMP-TO TAG	LINK TEXT	ANCHOR TAG

- For internal links to other pages in your Web site, use relative links:

  <A HREF="julio2.html">next page </A>

ANCHOR TAG	REFERENCE TAG	FILE NAME	LINK TEXT	ANCHOR TAG

- For external links to other sites, use the complete URL:

  <A HREF="http://etext.lib.virginia.edu/">Electronic Text Center</A>

ANCHOR TAG	REFERENCE TAG	URL	LINK TEXT	ANCHOR TAG

Previewing your Web text

As with any text, asking for response from readers is crucial to your overall success. Before you make your Web document available on an Internet server, therefore, you should ask others to preview your text.

- Proofread every page, looking for any typos, errors, or confusing passages.
- Check the navigation of the site, verifying that all links work and that readers can find their way around with ease.
- Check your site using several different browsers, if possible, to see that each page is displayed properly for users of both graphic and text-only browsers.
- Examine all graphics and images. Do all images load quickly and accurately? Do all graphics and images convey the meaning you have intended? For images or graphics that you did not create, is appropriate credit given to your source?

Some Guidelines for Evaluating Your Web Text

- Does your Web text accomplish its purpose? Is every page relevant to your topic? (16a)
- Who is the intended audience? Does the homepage invite those readers in? (16a)
- Does your homepage clearly introduce the topic and give an overview of what is on the site? Is it clear when the site was last updated? Is your name and contact information on every page? (16c)
- How easy is it to navigate your Web site? How accessible and quick to download will it be for your readers? (16d)
- Are all links clear and working? (16d)
- How have you used images, graphics, and color? Do they all help convey the meaning you intended? Do the graphics and background contribute to the site's readability? Check to be sure you have struck an appropriate balance between the graphics and text of your document. If you have used graphics created by someone else, have you given proper credit to your source? (16f)

Your final step is to publish your document on the Web, transferring your files to your Internet server. Methods for posting files can vary; check with your Internet service provider or campus computer service for instructions.

17

Consistency and Completeness

If you listen carefully to the conversations around you, you will hear inconsistent and incomplete structures all the time, particularly during a lively or heated discussion. For instance:

> "Those hits could make Chad Curtis's whole year," Paul O'Neill said. "When you hit a walk-off homer in the World Series, that's something he's going to remember for a long time."

In the flow of conversation after a World Series game, the incomplete structures in O'Neill's comments pose few problems for listeners. But in writing, these sentences can seem mixed up, incoherent, even nonsensical. This chapter provides guidelines for recognizing and editing mixed and incomplete structures.

Editing for Consistency and Completeness

- If you find an especially confusing sentence, check to see whether it has a subject and a predicate. If not, revise as necessary. (17a) If you find both a subject and a predicate, and you are still confused, see whether the subject and verb make sense together. If not, revise so that they do. (17b)
- Revise any *is when, is where,* and *reason . . . is because* constructions. (17b)

             a practice in which
  - ▶ Spamming is ~~where~~ companies send electronic junk mail.
         ^

- Check all comparisons for completeness. (17e)

             we like
  - ▶ We like Lisa better than Margaret.
                  ^

17a Make grammatical patterns consistent.

One inconsistency that poses problems for writers and readers is a mixed structure, which results from beginning a sentence with one grammatical pattern and then switching to another one. For example:

MIXED   The fact that I get up at 5:00 a.m., a wake-up time that explains why I'm always tired in the evening.

The sentence starts out with a subject (*The fact*) followed by a dependent clause (*that I get up at 5:00 a.m.*). The sentence needs a predicate to complete the independent clause, but instead it moves to another phrase followed by a dependent clause (*a wake-up time that explains why I'm always tired in the evening*), and what results is a fragment.

REVISED   The fact that I get up at 5:00 a.m. explains why I'm always tired in the evening.

Deleting *a wake-up time that* changes the rest of the sentence into a predicate.

REVISED   I get up at 5:00 a.m., a wake-up time that explains why I'm always tired in the evening.

Deleting *The fact that* turns the beginning of the sentence into an independent clause.

17b Make subjects and predicates consistent.

Another kind of mixed structure, called faulty predication, occurs when a subject and predicate do not fit together grammatically or simply do not make sense together. Many cases of faulty predication result from using forms of *be* when another verb would be stronger.

▶ A characteristic that I admire is ~~a person who is generous.~~ *generosity.*

A person is not a characteristic.

▶ The rules of the corporation ~~expect~~ employees ~~to~~ be on time. *require that*

Rules cannot expect anything.

Is when, is where, reason . . . is because

Although you will often hear expressions such as *home is where the heart is* in everyday use, these constructions are illogical and thus are inappropriate in academic or professional writing.

▶ A stereotype is ~~when someone characterizes~~ a group. ~~unfairly.~~ *an unfair characterization of*

▶ A confluence is where two rivers join to form one. *a place*

▶ ~~The reason~~ I like to play soccer ~~is~~ because it provides aerobic exercise.

17c Use elliptical structures carefully.

Sometimes writers omit certain words in compound structures. When the word omitted is common to all parts of the compound, this type of structure, known as an elliptical structure, is appropriate. In the following sentence, the omitted word is in brackets:

▶ **That bell belonged to the figure of Miss Duling as though it grew directly out of her right arm, as wings grew out of an angel or a tail [grew] out of the devil.**   –EUDORA WELTY, *One Writer's Beginnings*

If the omitted word does not match all parts of the compound, readers might be confused, and so the omission is inappropriate.

                                        is
▶ **His skills are weak, and his performance only average.**
                                        ^

The omitted verb *is* does not match both parts of the compound (*skills are . . . performance is*), and so the writer must include it.

17d Check for missing words.

The best way to catch inadvertent omissions is to proofread carefully.

                                        at
▶ **The catalog's Web site makes it easier to look and choose from their**
                                        ^
inventory.

For Multilingual Writers: *When Are Articles Necessary?*

Do you say "I'm at university now" or "I'm at *the* university now"? Deciding when to use the articles *a, an,* and *the* can be challenging for multilingual writers since many languages have nothing directly comparable to them. See 60d for help using articles.

17e Make comparisons complete, consistent, and clear.

When you compare two or more things, the comparison must be complete, logically consistent, and clear.

▶ I was embarrassed because my parents were so different⟋ *from my friends' parents.*
  ⌄

Different from what? Adding *from my friends' parents* tells readers what the comparison is being made to.

▶ Woodberry's biography is better than *the one by* Fields.
  ⌄

This sentence illogically compares a book with a person. The editing makes the comparison logical.

UNCLEAR   Aneil always felt more affection for his brother than his sister.

Did Aneil feel more affection for his brother than his sister did—or more affection for his brother than he felt for his sister?

CLEAR   Aneil always felt more affection for his brother than *he did for his sister.*

CLEAR   Aneil always felt more affection for his brother than his sister *did.*

18

Coordination and Subordination

If you think about how you build sentences, you may notice a difference between your spoken and your written language. In speech, people tend to use *and* and *so* as all-purpose connectors.

I'm going home now, and I'll see you later.

The meaning of this sentence may be perfectly clear in speech, which provides clues with voice, facial expressions, and gestures. But in writing, the actual meaning might not be clear. The sentence could, for instance, have two rather different meanings.

Because I'm going home now, I'll see you later.

I'm going home now because I'll see you later.

The first sentence links two ideas with *and,* a coordinating conjunction; the other two sentences link ideas with *because,* a subordinating conjunction. These examples show two different ways of combining ideas in a sentence: a coordinating conjunction gives the ideas equal emphasis, and a subordinating conjunction emphasizes one idea more than another.

Editing for Coordination and Subordination

How do your ideas flow from one sentence to another? Do they connect smoothly and clearly? Are the more important ideas given more emphasis than less important ones? These guidelines will help you edit with such questions in mind.

- How often do you link ideas with *and?* If you use *and* excessively, decide whether all the ideas are equally important. If they are not equal, edit to subordinate the less important ones. (18b)

- Look for strings of short sentences that might be combined to join related ideas. (18a)

  ▶ The report was short*but it*. It was persuasive*i*. It changed my mind.

- Are the most important ideas in independent clauses? If not, edit so that they are. (18b)

  ▶ *Even though the* The report was short, even though it changed my mind.

18a Use coordination to relate equal ideas.

When you want to give equal emphasis to different ideas in a sentence, link them with a coordinating conjunction (*and, but, for, nor, or, so, yet*) or a semicolon.

▶ They acquired horses, *and* their ancient nomadic spirit was suddenly free of the ground.

▶ There is perfect freedom in the mountains, *but* it belongs to the eagle and the elk, the badger and the bear.

▶ No longer were they slaves to the simple necessity of survival; they were a lordly and dangerous society of fighters and thieves, hunters and priests of the sun.   −N. SCOTT MOMADAY, *The Way to Rainy Mountain*

Coordination can help make explicit the relationship between two separate ideas.

▶ My son watches *The Simpsons* religiously; Forced to choose, he would probably choose Homer Simpson over his sister.

Connecting these two sentences with a semicolon strengthens the connection between two closely related ideas.

When you connect ideas in a sentence, make sure that the relationship between the ideas is clear.

▶ Watching television is a common way to spend leisure time, ~~and~~ it makes viewers apathetic.

The relationship between the two ideas in the original sentence is unclear: what does being a common form of leisure have to do with making viewers apathetic? Changing *and* to *but* better relates the two ideas.

18b   Use subordination to emphasize main ideas.

Subordination allows you to distinguish major points from minor points or to bring in supporting details. If, for instance, you put your main idea in an independent clause, you might then put any less significant ideas in dependent clauses, phrases, or even single words. The following sentence shows the subordinated point in italics:

▶ Mrs. Viola Cullinan was a plump woman *who lived in a three-bedroom house somewhere behind the post office.*
  −MAYA ANGELOU, "My Name Is Margaret"

The dependent clause adds important information about Mrs. Cullinan, but it is subordinate to the independent clause.

Notice that the choice of what to subordinate rests with the writer and depends on the intended meaning. Angelou might have given the same basic information differently.

▶ Mrs. Viola Cullinan, *a plump woman,* lived in a three-bedroom house somewhere behind the post office.

Subordinating the information about Mrs. Cullinan's size to that about her house would suggest a slightly different meaning, of course. As a writer, you must think carefully about what you want to emphasize and must subordinate information accordingly.

Subordination also establishes logical relationships among ideas. These relationships are often specified by subordinating conjunctions.

SOME COMMON SUBORDINATING CONJUNCTIONS

after	if	though
although	in order that	unless
as	once	until
as if	since	when
because	so that	where
before	than	while
even though	that	

The following sentence is shown with the subordinate clause italicized and the subordinating word underlined:

▶ She usually rested her smile until late afternoon *when her women friends dropped in and Miss Glory, the cook, served them cold drinks on the closed-in porch.* —MAYA ANGELOU, "My Name Is Margaret"

Using too many coordinate structures can be monotonous and can make it hard for readers to recognize the most important ideas. Subordinating lesser ideas can help highlight the main ideas.

▶ Many people come home tired in the evening, and so they turn on the
Though they
TV to relax. ~~They~~ may intend to watch just the news, ~~but then~~ a game
              ^   *which*
show comes on next, ~~and~~ they decide to watch ~~it~~ for just a short
        Eventually, ^
while ~~and~~ they get too comfortable to get up, and they end up
    ^
spending the whole evening in front of the TV.

The editing subordinates some of the less important ideas, making clear to the reader that some of the ideas are more important than others.

Subordinating less important ideas

> *Although our*
> ▶ ~~Our~~ new boss can be difficult, ~~although~~ she has revived and maybe
>   ^
>   even saved the division.

The editing puts the more important information—that she has saved part of the company—in an independent clause and subordinates the other information.

Excessive subordination

When too many subordinate clauses are strung together, readers may have trouble keeping track of the main idea expressed in the independent clause.

TOO MUCH SUBORDINATION

▶ **Philip II sent the Spanish Armada to conquer England, which was ruled by Elizabeth, who had executed Mary because she was plotting to overthrow Elizabeth, who was a Protestant, whereas Mary and Philip were Roman Catholics.**

A Matter of Style: *Subordination*

Carefully used subordination can create powerful effects. Some particularly fine examples come from Martin Luther King Jr.

> Perhaps it is easy for those who have never felt the stinging darts of segregation to say, "Wait." But *when* you have seen vicious mobs lynch your mothers and fathers at will and drown your sisters and brothers at whim; *when* you have seen hate-filled policemen curse, kick, and even kill your black brothers and sisters; . . . *when* you have to concoct an answer for a five-year-old son who is asking: "Daddy, why do white people treat colored people so mean?"; *when* you take a cross-country drive and find it necessary to sleep night after night in the uncomfortable corners of your automobile because no motel will accept you; . . . *when* your first name becomes "nigger," your middle name becomes "boy" (however old you are) and your last name becomes "John," and your wife and mother are never given the respected title "Mrs."; . . . *when* you are forever fighting a degenerating sense of "nobodiness"—then you will understand why we find it difficult to wait.
> —MARTIN LUTHER KING JR., "Letter from Birmingham Jail"

REVISED

▶ Philip II sent the Spanish Armada to conquer England, which was ruled by Elizabeth, a Protestant. She had executed Mary, a Roman Catholic like Philip, because Mary was plotting to overthrow her.

Putting the facts about Elizabeth executing Mary into an independent clause makes key information easier to recognize.

19

Parallelism

Parallel grammatical structures are used in many of our most familiar phrases: *sink or swim, rise and shine, shape up or ship out*. If you look and listen for these structures, you will see parallelism in everyday use. Bumper stickers often use parallel grammatical structures to make their messages memorable (*Minds are like parachutes; both work best when open*), as do song lyrics and jump-rope rhymes. This chapter will help you use parallel structures to create pleasing rhythmic effects in your own writing.

Editing for Parallelism

- Look for any series of three or more items, and make all of the items parallel in structure. If you want to emphasize one particular item, try putting it at the end of the series. (19a)
- Be sure items in lists are parallel in form. (19a)
- Be sure all headings are parallel in form. (19a)
- Check for places where two ideas are compared, contrasted, or otherwise paired in the same sentence. Often these ideas will appear on either side of *and, but, or, nor, for, so,* or *yet,* or after each part of *both . . . and, either . . . or, neither . . . nor, not only . . . but also, whether . . . or,* or *just as . . . so.* Edit to make the two ideas parallel in structure. (19b)
- Check all parallel structures to be sure you have included all necessary words—articles, prepositions, the *to* of the infinitive, and so on. (19c)

19a Make items in a series parallel.

Parallelism makes a series both graceful and easy to follow.

▶ In the eighteenth century, armed forces could fight *in open fields* and *on the high seas.* Today, they can clash *on the ground anywhere, on the sea, under the sea,* and *in the air.*
—DONALD SNOW AND EUGENE BROWN, *The Contours of Power*

The parallel phrases, as well as the parallel structure of the sentences themselves, highlight the contrast between warfare in the eighteenth century and warfare today.

In the sentences below, note how the revisions make all items in the series parallel.

▶ The quarter horse skipped, pranced, and ~~was sashaying~~ *sashayed* onto the track.

▶ The children ran down the hill, skipped over the lawn, and *jumped* into the swimming pool.

▶ The duties of the job include baby-sitting, house-cleaning, and *preparing* ~~preparation of~~ meals.

Items in a list, on a formal outline, and in headings should be parallel (6c).

▶ Kitchen rules: (1) Coffee to be made only by library staff. (2) Coffee service to be closed at 4:00 P.M. (3) Doughnuts to be kept in cabinet. *Coffee materials not to be handled by faculty.* (4) ~~No faculty members should handle coffee materials.~~

19b Use parallel structures to pair ideas.

Parallel structures can help you pair two ideas effectively. The more nearly parallel the two structures are, the stronger the connection between the ideas will be.

▶ History became popular, and historians became alarmed.
—WILL DURANT

▶ I type in one place, but I write all over the house.
                                                        —TONI MORRISON

                                                   the flesh
▶ Writers are often more interesting on the page than in ~~person.~~
                                                                    ^

In these examples, the parallel structures help readers see an important contrast between two ideas or acts.

With coordinating conjunctions

When you link ideas with *and, but, or, nor, for, so,* or *yet,* try to make the ideas parallel in structure.

            who is
▶ Consult a friend in your class or who is good at math.
              ^

                                                    accepts
▶ The wise politician promises the possible and ~~should accept~~ the
                                                          ^
inevitable.

In both sentences, the editing links the two ideas by making them parallel.

A Matter of Style: *Parallelism*

Parallel structures can help a writer emphasize important ideas, as Joan Didion does in the following sentence:

> I would like to promise her that she will grow up with a sense of her cousins and of rivers and of her great-grandmother's teacups, would like to pledge her a picnic on a river with fried chicken and her hair uncombed, would like to give her *home* for her birthday, but we live differently now and I can promise her nothing like that.
> —JOAN DIDION, "On Going Home"

The first two parallel phrases—*would like to promise her, would like to pledge her*—introduce a series of specific concrete details and images that lead up to the general statement in the last phrase, that she *would like to give her* daughter a sense of "home." Although Didion could have stated this general point first and then gone on to illustrate it with concrete details, she achieves greater emphasis by making it the last in a series of parallel structures.

With correlative conjunctions

Use the same structure after both parts of the following correlative conjunctions: *either . . . or, both . . . and, neither . . . nor, not . . . but, not only . . . but also, just as . . . so,* and *whether . . . or.*

live in
▶ I wanted not only to go away to school but also to New England.
                                                        ^

Balancing *to go* with *to live* links the two ideas and makes the sentence easier to read.

19c Include all necessary words.

In addition to making parallel elements grammatically similar, be sure to include any words—prepositions, articles, verb forms, and so on— that are necessary for clarity, grammar, or idiom.

                                          in
▶ We'll move to a town in the Southwest or Mexico.
                                              ^

To a town in Mexico or to Mexico in general? The editing clarifies the meaning.

20

Shifts

A shift in writing is an abrupt change of some sort that results in inconsistency. Sometimes a writer will shift deliberately, as Dave Barry does in noting he "would have to say that the greatest single achievement of the American medical establishment is nasal spray." Barry's shift in tone from the serious (the American medical establishment) to the banal (nasal spray) makes us laugh, as Barry wishes us to. Although writers sometimes deliberately make such shifts for good reasons, unintentional shifts can be jolting and confusing to readers. This chapter helps you edit out unintentional shifts in verbs, pronouns, and tone.

Editing Out Confusing Shifts

- If you shift from one verb tense to another, check to be sure there is a reason for doing so. (20a)
- Do you see any shifts in mood—perhaps from an indicative statement to an imperative—and, if so, are they necessary? (20b)
- Check for shifts from active (*She asks questions*) to passive voice (*Questions are asked*). Are they intentional—and, if so, for what reason? (20c)
- Do you see any shifts in point of view—from *we* to *you*, for example—and, if so, what are the reasons for the shifts? (20d)
- Check your writing for consistency in tone. If your tone is serious, is it consistently so? (20f)

20a Check for unnecessary shifts in tense.

If the verbs in a passage refer to actions occurring at different times, they may require different tenses. Be careful, however, not to change tenses for no reason.

> A few countries produce almost all of the world's illegal drugs, but
>   *affects*
> addiction ~~affected~~ many countries.
>   ^

For Multilingual Writers: *Shifting Tenses in Reported Speech*

If Al said to Maria, "I will marry you," why did she then correctly tell her mom, "He said that he *would* marry me"? For guidelines on reporting speech, see 61b.

20b Check for shifts in mood.

Be careful not to shift from one mood to another without good reason. The mood of a verb can be indicative (he *closes* the door), imperative (*close* the door), or subjunctive (if the door *were closed*) (25h).

▶ Keep your eye on the ball, and ~~you should~~ bend your knees.

The sentence shifts from the imperative to the indicative; the editing makes both verbs imperative since the writer's purpose is to give orders.

20c Check for shifts in voice.

Do not shift without reason between the active voice (she *sold* it) and the passive voice (it *was sold*). Sometimes a shift in voice is justified, but often it may only confuse readers (25g).

▶ Two youths approached me/ and ~~I was~~ asked for my wallet.
　　　　　　　　　　　　　me

The original sentence shifts from the active (*youths approached*) to the passive (*I was asked*), so it is unclear who asked for the wallet. Making both verbs active clears up the confusion.

20d Check for shifts in point of view.

Unnecessary shifts between first-person point of view (*I, we*), second-person (*you*), and third-person (*he, she, it, one*, or *they*), or between singular and plural subjects can be very confusing to readers.

　　　　You
▶ ~~One~~ can do well on this job if you budget your time.

It was not clear whether the writer was making a general statement or giving advice to someone. Eliminating the shift eliminates this confusion.

　　　　　　　　　　　　　　　　　nurses have
▶ Nurses receive much less pay than doctors, even though ~~a nurse has~~

the primary responsibility for daily patient care.

The writer had no reason to shift from third-person plural (*nurses*) to third-person singular (*a nurse*).

20e Check for shifts between direct and indirect discourse.

When you quote someone's exact words, you are using direct discourse: *She said, "I'm an editor."* When you report what someone says without repeating the exact words, you are using indirect discourse: *She said she is an editor.* Shifting between direct and indirect discourse in the same sentence can cause problems, especially with questions.

>   *he*
> ▶ Bob asked what could ~~he~~ do to help~~?~~**.**
>   ^   ^

The editing eliminates an awkward shift by reporting Bob's question indirectly. It could also be edited to quote him directly: *Bob asked, "What can I do to help?"*

20f Check for shifts in tone and diction.

Tone (a writer's attitude toward a topic or audience) is related to diction, or word choice, and to overall formality or informality. Watch out for tone or diction shifts that could confuse readers and leave them wondering what your real attitude is (8b).

INCONSISTENT TONE

The question of child care forces a society to make profound decisions about its economic values. Can most families with children actually live adequately on only one salary? If some conservatives had their way, June Cleaver would still be stuck in the kitchen baking cookies for Wally and the Beaver and waiting for Ward to bring home the bacon, except that, with only one income, the Cleavers would be lucky to afford hot dogs.

In this version, the first two sentences set a serious, formal tone, discussing child care in fairly general, abstract terms. But in the third sentence, the writer shifts suddenly to sarcasm, to references to television characters of an earlier era, and to informal language like *stuck* and *bring home the bacon.* Readers cannot tell whether the writer is presenting a serious analysis or preparing for a humorous satire. See how the passage was revised to make the tone consistent.

REVISED

The question of child care forces a society to make profound decisions about its economic values. Can most families with young children actually live adequately on only one salary? Some conservatives believe that women with young children should not work outside the home, but many mothers are forced to do so for financial reasons.

21

Emphasis

In speaking, we can easily indicate emphasis by raising our voices, putting extra stress on an important word, or drawing out a phrase. And much of the writing we see around us—in advertisements, on Web sites, and in magazines—gains emphasis in similar fashion by using color, graphics, or bold type, for instance.

Much academic or professional writing, however, can't rely on such graphic devices for emphasis. Luckily, writers have other tools at their disposal. This chapter will help you write emphatic sentences that put the spotlight on main ideas, letting readers know which elements are most important.

Editing for Sentence Emphasis

As you revise a draft, follow these steps to make sure that each sentence emphasizes the ideas you *want* emphasized.

- Identify the word or words you want to receive special emphasis. If those words are buried in the middle of a sentence, edit the sentence to change their position. The end and the beginning are generally the most emphatic. (21a)
- Note any sentences that include a series of three or more words, phrases, or clauses. Could the items in the series be arranged in climactic order, with the most important item last? (21b)

21a   Use closing and opening positions for emphasis.

When you read a sentence, what are you likely to remember? Other things being equal, you remember the ending. This is the part of the sentence that should move the writing forward by providing new information, as it does in the following example:

▶ To protect her skin, she took along *plenty of sunblock lotion.*

A less emphatic but still important position in a sentence is the opening.

▶ When Rosita went to the beach, she was anxious not to get a sunburn. *So plenty of sunblock lotion* went with her.

If you place relatively unimportant information in the memorable closing position of a sentence, you may undercut what you want to emphasize or give more emphasis to the closing words than you intend.

> *Last month, she*
> ▶ ~~She~~ gave [$500,000] ~~to the school capital campaign~~ ~~last month.~~
> ^
>
> Moving *$500,000* to the end of the sentence emphasizes the *amount*.

21b Use climactic order to emphasize important ideas.

When you arrange ideas in order of increasing importance, power, or drama, your writing builds to a climax. The following statement saves its most dramatic item for last, making its point forcefully:

> ▶ After they've finished with the pantry, the medicine cabinet, and the attic, [neat people] will throw out the red geranium (too many leaves), sell the dog (too many fleas), and send the children off to boarding school (too many scuffmarks on the hardwood floors).
>   —SUSANNE BRITT, "Neat People vs. Sloppy People"

The original version of the next sentence fails to achieve strong emphasis because its verbs are not sequenced in order of increasing power; the editing provides climactic order.

> *and*
> ▶ Soap operas assault our eyes, damage our brains~~,~~~~.~~ ~~and~~ offend our ears~~.~~~~,~~
> ^   ^   ^

A Matter of Style: *Anticlimax and Humor*

Sometimes it's fun to turn the principle of climactic order upside down, opening with grand or exaggerated language only to end anticlimactically, with everyday words.

> He is a writer for the ages—the ages of four to eight.
>   —DOROTHY PARKER

Parker builds up high expectations at the beginning of the sentence—only to undercut them unexpectedly by shifting the meaning of *ages*. Having led readers to expect something dramatic, she makes us laugh, or at least smile, with words that are decidedly undramatic.

22

Conciseness

You can see the importance of conciseness in directions, particularly those on medicines. Consider the following directions found on one common prescription drug:

> Take one tablet daily. Some nonprescription drugs may aggravate your condition, so read all labels carefully. If any include a warning, check with your doctor.

Squeezing words onto a three-inch label is probably not your ordinary writing situation, but more often than not, you will want to write as concisely as you can.

Editing for Conciseness

- Look for redundant words. If you are unsure about a word, read the sentence without it; if meaning is not affected, leave the word out. (22b)
- Take out empty words—words like *aspect* or *factor, definitely* or *very*. (22c)
- Replace wordy phrases with a single word. Instead of *because of the fact that,* try *because.* (22d)
- Reconsider any sentences that begin with *it is* or *there is/are*. Unless they create special emphasis, try recasting the sentences without these words. (22e)

22a   Eliminate unnecessary words.

Usually you'll want to make your point in the fewest possible words.

> ▶ **Her constant and continual use of vulgar expressions with obscene meanings indicated to her pre-elementary supervisory group that she was rather deficient in terms of her ability to interact in an efficient manner with peers in her potential interaction group.**

Why write that sentence when you could instead write the following?

> ▶ **Her constant use of four-letter words told the day-care workers she might have trouble getting along with other four-year-olds.**

◎ **A Matter of Style:** *Brevity in Email*

In general, keep your messages brief. Because readers need to scroll to read on-screen text, shorter is often better. Set your email format at sixty to seventy characters per line in order to avoid the one- or two-word lines that sometimes occur when one email system downloads to another.

22b Eliminate redundant words.

Sometimes writers add words for emphasis, saying that something is large *in size* or red *in color* or that two ingredients should be *combined together*. The deleted words below, however, are redundant—unnecessary for meaning.

>   A
> ~~Compulsory~~ A͏ttendance at assemblies is required.

> The auction featured ~~contemporary~~ "antiques" made recently.

> Many different forms of hazing occur, such as physical ~~abuse~~ and mental abuse.

22c Eliminate empty words.

Empty words are those that contribute no real meaning. In general, delete them.

EMPTY WORDS

angle, area, aspect, case, character, element, factor, field, kind, nature, scope, situation, thing, type

Many modifiers are so common that they have become empty words, adding no meaning to a statement.

MEANINGLESS MODIFIERS

absolutely, awesome, awfully, central, definitely, fine, great, literally, major, quite, really, very

When you cannot simply delete empty words, try to think of a more specific way to say what you mean.

▶ ~~The~~ Ĥousing ~~situation~~ can ~~have a really significant impact on the~~ *strongly influence*

~~social aspect of~~ ^social a student's life.

22d Replace wordy phrases.

Wordy phrases are those that can be reduced to a word or two with no loss in meaning.

WORDY	CONCISE
at all times	always
at the present time	now/today
at that point in time	then
due to the fact that	because
in order to	to
in spite of the fact that	although
in the event that	if
for the purpose of	for

22e Simplify sentence structure.

Using the simplest grammatical structures possible will tighten and strengthen your sentences considerably.

▶ **Kennedy, ~~who was~~ only the second Roman Catholic ~~to be~~ nominated**

for the presidency by a major party, had to handle the religion issue
delicately.
~~in a delicate manner.~~
^

Reducing a clause to an appositive, deleting unnecessary words, and replacing four words with one tighten the sentence and make it easier to read.

Using strong verbs

Be verbs (*is, are, was, were, been*) often result in wordiness.

▶ A high-fat, high-cholesterol diet ~~is bad for~~ your heart.

                   harms

Avoiding expletives

Sometimes expletive constructions—*there is, there are,* and *it is*—are an effective way to introduce a topic; often, however, your writing will be better without them.

▶ ~~There are~~ many people ~~who~~ fear success because they believe they do not deserve it.

       M

▶ ~~It is necessary for~~ presidential candidates to perform well on television.

     P   *need*

Using active voice

Some writing situations call for the passive voice, but it is always wordier than the active—and often makes for dull or even difficult reading (25g).

▶ ~~In Gower's research, it was~~ found that pythons often dwell in trees.

   Gower

23
Sentence Variety

Row upon row of trees identical in size and shape may appeal, at some level, to our sense of orderliness, but, in spite of that appeal, the rows soon become boring. Constant uniformity in anything, in fact, soon gets tiresome, while its opposite, variation, is usually pleasing to readers. Variety is important in sentence structures because too much uniformity results in dull, listless prose. This chapter examines ways to revise boring sentences—variety in length and variety in openings.

Editing for Sentence Variety

- Count the words in each sentence. If the difference between the longest and shortest sentences is fairly small—say, five words or fewer—try revising your sentences to create greater variety. (23a)
- If many sentences have fewer than ten words, consider whether any of them need more detail or should be combined with other sentences.
- How do your sentences open? If all or most of them open with a subject, try recasting some sentences to begin with a transition, a phrase, or a dependent clause. (23b)

23a Vary sentence length.

Deciding how and when to vary sentence length is not always easy. Is there a "just right" length for a particular sentence or idea? The answers depend on, among other things, your purpose, intended audience, and topic. Frequent alternation in sentence length characterizes much memorable writing. After one or more long sentences with complex ideas or images, the punch of a short sentence can be refreshing.

> ▶ **The fire of, I think, five machine-guns was pouring upon us, and there was a series of heavy crashes caused by the Fascists flinging bombs over their own parapet in the most idiotic manner. It was intensely dark.** —GEORGE ORWELL, *Homage to Catalonia*

A Matter of Style: *Technical Style*

For some types of writing, varying sentence structure and length is not always appropriate. Many technical writers, particularly those who write manuals that will be translated into other languages, must follow stringent rules for sentence structure and length. Technical writers working for Hewlett-Packard, for example, must adhere to a strict subject-verb-object order and limit all sentences to a maximum length of fifteen words. You will want to understand the style conventions of your field as fully as possible and bring them to bear on your own sentence revisions.

23b Vary sentence openings.

If sentence after sentence begins with a subject, a passage may become monotonous or even hard to read.

▶ The way football and basketball are played is as interesting as the
    Because football   *e*
players. ~~Football~~ is a game of precision/, Ȩach play is diagrammed to
  ^   *however,*
accomplish a certain goal. Basketball, is a game of endurance.
In fact, a   ^
A basketball game looks like a track meet; the team that drops of
^

exhaustion first loses. Basketball players are often compared to artists/,
their   ^
~~The players~~' moves and slam dunks ~~are~~ their masterpieces.
^

The editing adds variety by using subordinating words (*Because* in the second line) and a prepositional phrase (*In fact* in the fourth line) and by linking sentences. Varying sentence openings prevents the passage from seeming to jerk or lurch along.

You can add variety to your sentence openings by using transitions, various kinds of phrases, and introductory dependent clauses.

TRANSITIONAL EXPRESSIONS

▶ *In contrast,* our approach will save time and money.

▶ *Nevertheless,* the show must go on.

PHRASES

▶ *At each desk,* a computer printout provides necessary data.

▶ *Frustrated by the delays,* the drivers started honking their horns.

▶ *To qualify for flight training,* one must be in good physical condition.

▶ *Our hopes for snow shattered,* we started home.

DEPENDENT CLAUSES

▶ *What they want* is a place to call home.

▶ *Because the hills were dry,* the fire spread rapidly.

24

Basic Grammar

The grammar of our first language comes to us almost automatically, without our thinking much about it or even being aware of it. Listen in, for instance, on a conversation between two six-year-olds.

> CHARLOTTE: My new bike that Grandma got me has a red basket and a loud horn, and I love it.
>
> ANNA: Can I ride it?
>
> CHARLOTTE: Sure, as soon as I take a turn.

This simple conversation features sophisticated grammar—the subordination of one clause to another, a compound object, and a number of adjectives—used effortlessly. Though native speakers know the basic grammatical rules, these rules can produce a broad range of sentences, some more effective and artful than others. Understanding the grammatical structures presented in this chapter can help you produce sentences that are grammatical—and appropriate and effective as well.

24a The basic grammar of sentences

A sentence is a grammatically complete group of words that expresses a thought. To be grammatically complete, a group of words must contain a subject, which identifies what the sentence is about, and a predicate, which says or asks something about the subject or tells the subject to do something.

SUBJECT	PREDICATE
I	have a dream.
The rain in Spain	stays mainly in the plain.
Puff, the magic dragon,	lived by the sea.

Some brief sentences have a one-word predicate with an implied, or understood, subject (for example, *Stop!*). Most sentences, however, contain additional words that expand the basic subject and predicate. In the preceding example about the dragon, for instance, the subject might have been simply *Puff;* the words *the magic dragon* tell us more about the subject. Similarly, the predicate of that sentence could grammatically be *lived;* the words *by the sea* expand the predicate by telling us where Puff lived.

PARTS OF SPEECH

All English words belong to one or more of eight grammatical categories called parts of speech: verbs, nouns, pronouns, adjectives, adverbs, prepositions, conjunctions, and interjections. Many English words regularly function as more than one part of speech. Take the word *book,* for example: when you *book a plane flight,* it is a verb; when you *take a good book to the beach,* it is a noun; and when you *have book knowledge,* it is an adjective.

24b Verbs

Verbs are among the most important words because they move the meanings of sentences along. Verbs show actions of body or mind (*glance, speculate*), occurrences (*become, happen*), or states of being (*be, seem*). They can also change form to show *time, person, number, voice,* and *mood.*

TIME	we *work,* we *worked*
PERSON	I *work,* she *works*
NUMBER	one person *works,* two people *work*
VOICE	she *asks,* she *is asked*
MOOD	we *see,* if we *saw*

Auxiliary verbs (also called helping verbs) combine with other verbs (often called main verbs) to create verb phrases. Auxiliaries include the various forms of *be, do,* and *have* (which can also be used as main verbs) and the words *can, could, may, might, must, shall, should, will,* and *would.*

▶ You *do need* some sleep tonight!

▶ I *could have danced* all night.

▶ She *would prefer* to learn Italian rather than Spanish.

See Chapter 25 for a complete discussion of verbs.

24c Nouns

Nouns name persons (*aviator, child*), places (*lake, library*), things (*truck, suitcase*), and concepts (*happiness, balance*). Proper nouns name specific persons, places, things, and concepts: *Bill, Iowa, Supreme Court, Buddhism.* Collective nouns name groups: *team, flock, jury* (26d).

You can change most nouns from singular (one) to plural (more than one) by adding *-s* or *-es: horse, horses; kiss, kisses.* Some nouns, however, have irregular plural forms: *woman, women; alumnus, alumni; mouse, mice; deer, deer.* Noncount nouns, such as *dust, peace,* and *prosperity,* do not have a plural form because they name something that cannot easily be counted (36c, 60a).

To show ownership, nouns take the possessive form by adding an apostrophe plus *-s* to a singular noun or just an apostrophe to a plural noun: *the horse's owner, the boys' dilemma* (41a).

Nouns are often preceded by the articles *a, an,* or *the* (also known as determiners): *a rocket, an astronaut, the launch* (60c, d).

> **For Multilingual Writers:** *Count and Noncount Nouns*
>
> Is the hill covered with grass or grasses? See 60a for a discussion of count and noncount nouns.

24d Pronouns

Pronouns often take the place of nouns, serving as short forms so that you do not have to repeat a noun that you have already mentioned. A noun that a pronoun replaces or refers to is the antecedent of the pronoun. (See Chapter 29.)

ANTECEDENT   PRONOUN

▶ *Caitlin* **refused the invitation even though** *she* **wanted to go.**

Here are the categories of pronouns.

PERSONAL PRONOUNS

Personal pronouns refer to specific persons or things.

I, me, you, he, she, him, it, we, they

▶ **After the scouts made camp,** *they* **ran along the beach.**

POSSESSIVE PRONOUNS

Possessive pronouns indicate ownership.

my, mine, your, yours, her, hers, his, its, our, ours, their, theirs

▶ *My* **roommate lost** *her* **keys.**

REFLEXIVE PRONOUNS

Reflexive pronouns refer to the subject of the sentence or clause in which they appear. They end in -*self* or -*selves*.

myself, yourself, himself, herself, itself, oneself, ourselves, yourselves, themselves

▶ **The seals sunned *themselves* on the warm rocks.**

INTENSIVE PRONOUNS

Intensive pronouns have the same form as reflexive pronouns. They emphasize a noun or another pronoun.

▶ **He decided to paint the apartment *himself*.**

INDEFINITE PRONOUNS

Indefinite pronouns do not refer to specific nouns although they may refer to identifiable persons or things. The following is a partial list:

all, another, anybody, both, each, either, everything, few, many, most, neither, none, no one, nothing, one, some, something

▶ ***Somebody* screamed when the lights went out.**

DEMONSTRATIVE PRONOUNS

Demonstrative pronouns identify or point to specific nouns.

this, that, these, those

▶ ***These* are Peter's books.**

INTERROGATIVE PRONOUNS

Interrogative pronouns are used to ask questions.

who, which, what

▶ ***Who* can help set up the chairs for the meeting?**

RELATIVE PRONOUNS

Relative pronouns introduce dependent clauses and relate the dependent clause to the rest of the sentence (24m).

who, which, that, what, whoever, whichever, whatever

▶ **Margaret owns the car *that* is parked by the corner.**

The interrogative pronoun *who* and the relative pronouns *who* and *who-ever* have different forms depending on how they are used in a sentence. (See Chapter 29.)

Reciprocal pronouns refer to individual parts of a plural antecedent.

each other, one another

▶ **The business failed because the partners distrusted** *each other.*

24e Adjectives

Adjectives modify (limit the meaning of) nouns and pronouns, usually by describing, identifying, or quantifying those words.

▶ **The** *red* **Corvette ran off the road.** [describes]
▶ *That* **Corvette needs to be repaired.** [identifies]
▶ **We saw** *several* **Corvettes race by.** [quantifies]

In addition to their basic forms, most descriptive adjectives have other forms that allow you to make comparisons: *small, smaller, smallest; foolish, more foolish, most foolish, less foolish, least foolish* (27c). Many of the words functioning as pronouns (24d) can function as adjectives when they are followed by a noun.

▶ *That* **is a dangerous intersection.** [pronoun]
▶ *That* **intersection is dangerous.** [adjective]

Adjectives usually precede the words they modify, though they may follow linking verbs: *The car was defective.*

Other kinds of adjectives that identify or quantify are articles (*a, an, the*) and numbers (*three, sixty-fifth*).

Proper adjectives are adjectives formed from or related to proper nouns (*Egyptian, Emersonian*). Proper adjectives are capitalized (44b).

24f Adverbs

Adverbs modify verbs, adjectives, other adverbs, or entire clauses. Many adverbs have an *-ly* ending, though some do not (*always, never, very, well*), and some words that end in *-ly* are not adverbs but adjectives (*friendly, lovely*). One of the most common adverbs is *not.*

▶ Jabari *recently* visited his roommate's family in Maine. [modifies the verb *visited*]

▶ It was an *unexpectedly* exciting trip. [modifies the adjective *exciting*]

▶ He *very* soon discovered lobster. [modifies the adverb *soon*]

▶ *Frankly,* he would have liked to stay another month. [modifies the independent clause that makes up the rest of the sentence]

Many adverbs, like many adjectives, have other forms that can be used to make comparisons: *forcefully, more forcefully, most forcefully, less forcefully, least forcefully* (27c).

Conjunctive adverbs modify an entire clause and help connect the meaning between that clause and the preceding clause (or sentence). Examples of conjunctive adverbs include *however, furthermore, therefore,* and *likewise* (24h).

24g Prepositions

Prepositions are important structural words that express relationships—in time, space, or other senses—between nouns or pronouns and other words in a sentence.

▶ We did not want to leave *during* the game.

▶ The contestants waited nervously *for* the announcement.

▶ Drive *across* the bridge, go *down* the avenue *past* three stoplights, and then turn left *before* the Gulf station.

SOME COMMON PREPOSITIONS

about	at	down	near	since
above	before	during	of	through
across	behind	except	off	toward
after	below	for	on	under
against	beneath	from	onto	until
along	beside	in	out	up
among	between	inside	over	upon
around	beyond	into	past	with
as	by	like	regarding	without

SOME COMPOUND PREPOSITIONS

according to	except for	instead of
as well as	in addition to	next to
because of	in front of	out of
by way of	in place of	with regard to
due to	in spite of	

24h   Conjunctions

Conjunctions connect words or groups of words to each other and tell something about the relationship between these words.

Coordinating conjunctions

Coordinating conjunctions join equivalent structures—two or more nouns, pronouns, verbs, adjectives, adverbs, prepositions, conjunctions, phrases, or clauses (18a).

▶ A strong *but* warm breeze blew across the desert.
▶ Please print *or* type the information on the application form.
▶ Kristin worked two shifts today, *so* she is tired tonight.

COORDINATING CONJUNCTIONS

and	for	or	yet
but	nor	so	

Correlative conjunctions

Correlative conjunctions join equal elements, and they come in pairs.

▶ *Both* Bechtel *and* Kaiser submitted bids on the project.
▶ Jeff *not only* sent a card *but also* visited me in the hospital.

CORRELATIVE CONJUNCTIONS

both . . . and	neither . . . nor
either . . . or	not only . . . but also
just as . . . so	whether . . . or

Subordinating conjunctions

Subordinating conjunctions introduce adverb clauses and signal the relationship between an adverb clause and another clause, usually an independent clause (18a, 24m). For instance, in the following sentence, the subordinating conjunction *while* signals a time relationship between the two events in the sentence, letting us know that they happened simultaneously:

▶ Sweat ran down my face *while* I frantically searched for my child.

SOME SUBORDINATING CONJUNCTIONS

after	if	though
although	in order that	unless
as	once	until
as if	since	when
because	so that	where
before	than	whether
even though	that	while

Conjunctive adverbs

Conjunctive adverbs signal a logical relationship between parts of a sentence and, when used with a semicolon, can link independent clauses (24m).

▶ The cider tasted bitter; *however,* each of us drank a tall glass of it.
▶ The cider tasted bitter; each of us, *however,* drank a tall glass of it.

SOME CONJUNCTIVE ADVERBS

also	indeed	now
anyway	instead	otherwise
besides	likewise	similarly
certainly	meanwhile	still
finally	moreover	then
furthermore	namely	therefore
however	nevertheless	thus
incidentally	next	undoubtedly

24i   Interjections

Interjections express surprise or emotion: *oh, ouch, ah, hey.* Interjections often stand alone, as fragments. Even when interjections are part of a sentence, they do not relate grammatically to the rest of the sentence.

▶   The problem suggested, *alas,* no easy solution.

PARTS OF SENTENCES

Knowing a word's part of speech helps us understand how to use that word. But we also need to look at the way the word functions in a particular sentence. Consider, for instance, the word *description.*

SUBJECT
▶   This *description* evokes the ecology of the Everglades.

DIRECT OBJECT
▶   I need a *description* of the ecology of the Everglades.

Description is a noun in both sentences, yet in the first it serves as the subject of the verb *evokes,* while in the second it serves as the direct object of the verb *need.*

Basic sentence patterns

1. SUBJECT/VERB

S   V
▶   Babies cry.

2. SUBJECT/VERB/SUBJECT COMPLEMENT

S   V   SC
▶   Babies seem fragile.

3. SUBJECT/VERB/DIRECT OBJECT

S   V   DO
▶   Babies drink milk.

4. SUBJECT/VERB/INDIRECT OBJECT/DIRECT OBJECT

S   V   IO   DO
▶   Babies give grandparents pleasure.

5. SUBJECT/VERB/DIRECT OBJECT/OBJECT COMPLEMENT

      S   V   DO   OC
▶ **Babies make parents proud.**

24j   Subjects

The subject of a sentence identifies what the sentence is about. The simple subject consists of one or more nouns or pronouns; the complete subject consists of the simple subject (ss) with all its modifiers.

    ┌──── COMPLETE SUBJECT ────┐
                  SS
▶ *Sailing over the fence, the ball* **crashed through Mr. Wilson's window.**

    ┌─── COMPLETE SUBJECT ───┐
    SS
▶ *Stadiums with real grass* **are hard to find these days.**

    ┌──── COMPLETE SUBJECT ────┐
    SS
▶ *Those who sit in the bleachers* **have the most fun.**

A compound subject contains two or more simple subjects joined with a coordinating conjunction (*and, but, or*) or a correlative conjunction (*both . . . and, either . . . or, neither . . . nor*).

▶ *Baseball and softball* **developed from cricket.**
▶ *Both baseball and softball* **developed from cricket.**

The subject usually comes before the predicate, or verb, but not always. Sometimes writers reverse this order to achieve a particular effect.

▶ **Up to the plate stepped** *Casey.*

In imperative sentences, which express requests or commands, the subject *you* is almost always implied, not stated.

▶ **(***You***) Keep your eye on the ball.**

In questions and certain other constructions, the subject usually appears between the auxiliary verb (24b) and the main verb.

▶ **Did** *Casey* **save the game?**

In sentences beginning with *there* or *here* followed by a form of *be,* the subject always follows the verb. *There* and *here* in such sentences are never the subject.

▶ There was no *joy* in Mudville.

24k Predicates

In addition to a subject, every sentence has a predicate, which asserts or asks something about the subject or tells the subject to do something. The hinge, or key word, of a predicate is the verb. The simple predicate (SP) of a sentence consists of the main verb and any auxiliaries (24b); the complete predicate includes the simple predicate plus any modifiers of the verb and any objects or complements and their modifiers.

┌── COMPLETE PREDICATE ──┐
┌── SP ──┐
▶ Both of us *are planning to work at home.*

A compound predicate contains two or more verbs that have the same subject, usually joined by a coordinating or a correlative conjunction.

┌─ S ─┐ ┌────── COMPOUND PREDICATE ──────┐
▶ Charles *shut the book, put it back on the shelf, and sighed.*

┌── S ──┐ ┌── COMPOUND PREDICATE ──┐
▶ The Amish *neither drive cars nor use electricity.*

On the basis of how they function in predicates, verbs can be divided into three categories: linking, transitive, and intransitive.

Linking verbs

A linking verb links, or joins, a subject with a subject complement. A subject complement is a word or group of words that identifies or describes the subject.

┌── S ──┐ ┌V┐ ┌── SC ──┐
▶ Christine is a single mother.

┌S┐ ┌V┐ ┌─SC─┐
▶ She is patient.

If it identifies the subject, the complement is a noun or pronoun (*a single mother*). If it describes the subject, the complement is an adjective (*patient*).

The forms of *be*, when used as main verbs rather than as auxiliary verbs, are linking verbs (like *are* in this sentence). Other verbs—such as *appear, become, feel, grow, look, make, seem, smell,* and *sound*—can also function as linking verbs, depending on the sense of the sentence.

Transitive verbs

A transitive verb expresses action that is directed toward a noun or pronoun. The noun or pronoun that receives the action is called the direct object of the verb.

S———V———, ,———DO———
▶ **I will analyze three poems.**

In the preceding example, the subject and verb do not express a complete thought. The direct object completes the thought, saying *what* I will analyze.

A direct object may be followed by an object complement, a word or word group that describes or identifies the direct object. Object complements may be adjectives, as in the next example, or nouns, as in the second example.

S,—V—, ,————DO———, ,— OC—
▶ **I consider Marianne Moore's poetry exquisite.**

,————— S—————, ,—V—, ,—DO—, ,— OC—
▶ **Her poems and personality made Moore a celebrity.**

A transitive verb may also be followed by an indirect object, which tells to whom or what, or for whom or what, the verb's action is done. You might say the indirect object is the recipient of the direct object.

,————————— S—————————, ,—V—, ,IO, ,————— DO—————
▶ **Moore's poems about the Dodgers give me considerable pleasure.**

Intransitive verbs

An intransitive verb expresses action that is not directed toward an object. Therefore an intransitive verb does not have a direct object, though it is often followed by an adverb.

```
    ┌──── S ────┐ ┌─── V───┐
```
▶ **The Red Sox persevered.**

```
    ┌──── S ────┐ ┌── V──┐
```
▶ **Their fans watched helplessly.**

The action of the verb *persevered* has no object (it makes no sense to ask, *persevered what?* or *persevered whom?*), and the action of the verb *watched* is directed toward an object that is implied but not expressed.

24l Phrases

A phrase is a group of words that lacks either a subject or a predicate or both. Phrases function as adjectives, adverbs, or nouns to add information to a sentence.

Noun phrases

A noun phrase consists of a noun and all its modifiers. In a sentence, a noun phrase can function as a subject, object, or complement.

```
    ┌──────────── SUBJECT ───────────┐
```
▶ *Delicious, gooey peanut butter* **is surprisingly healthful.**

```
              ┌── OBJECT──┐
```
▶ **Dieters prefer** *green salad.*

```
                    ┌─ COMPLEMENT ─┐
```
▶ **A tuna sandwich is** *a popular lunch.*

Verb phrases

A main verb and its auxiliary verbs make up a verb phrase, which can function only one way in a sentence: as a predicate.

▶ **I** *can swim* **for a long time.**

▶ **His problem** *might have been caused* **by tension between his parents.**

Prepositional phrases

A prepositional phrase includes a preposition, a noun or pronoun (called the object of the preposition), and any modifiers of the object. Prepositional phrases usually function as adjectives or adverbs.

ADJECTIVE	Our house *in Maine* is a cabin.
ADVERB	*From Cadillac Mountain,* you can see the northern lights.

Verbal phrases

Verbals are verb forms that do not function as verbs. Instead, they function as nouns, adjectives, or adverbs. There are three kinds of verbals: participles, gerunds, and infinitives. A verbal phrase is made up of a verbal and any modifiers, objects, or complements.

PARTICIPIAL PHRASES

Participial phrases always function as adjectives. They can include a present participle (the *crying* child) or a past participle (the *spoken* word).

▶ A dog *howling at the moon* kept me awake.

▶ *Irritated by the delay,* Louise complained.

GERUND PHRASES

A gerund has the same form as a present participle, ending in *-ing*. But gerunds and gerund phrases always function as nouns.

———— SUBJECT ————
▶ *Opening their eyes to the problem* was not easy.

———— DIRECT OBJECT ————
▶ They suddenly heard *a loud wailing from the sandbox.*

INFINITIVE PHRASES

Infinitive phrases can function as nouns, adjectives, or adverbs. The infinitive is the *to*-form of a verb: *to be, to write.*

——— ADJECTIVE ———
▶ A vote would be a good way *to end the meeting.*

——— ADVERB ———
▶ *To perfect a draft,* always proofread carefully.

——— NOUN ———
▶ *To know him* is a pleasure.

Absolute phrases

Absolute phrases usually include a noun or pronoun and a participle. They modify an entire sentence rather than a particular word. Absolutes may appear almost anywhere in a sentence and are usually set off from the rest of the sentence with commas (38a).

▶ I stood on the deck, *the wind whipping my hair.*

▶ *My fears laid to rest,* I climbed into the plane for my first solo flight.

Appositive phrases

A noun phrase that renames the noun or pronoun immediately preceding it is called an appositive phrase.

▶ The report, *a hefty three-volume work,* included forty-five recommendations.

▶ A single desire, *to change the corporation's policies,* guided our actions.

24m Clauses

A clause is a group of words containing a subject and a predicate. There are two kinds of clauses: independent and dependent.

Independent clauses (also known as main clauses) can stand alone as complete sentences: *The window is open.* Pairs of independent clauses may be joined with a coordinating conjunction (*and, but, for, or, nor, so,* or *yet*) and a comma.

▶ The window is open, *so* we'd better be quiet.

Like independent clauses, dependent clauses (also known as subordinate clauses) contain a subject and a predicate. They cannot stand alone as complete sentences, however, for they begin with a subordinating word. Dependent clauses function as nouns, adjectives, or adverbs (18b).

▶ *Because the window is open,* the room feels cool.

In this combination, the subordinating conjunction *because* transforms the independent clause *the window is open* into a dependent adverb clause. In doing so, it indicates a causal relationship between the two clauses.

Noun clauses

Noun clauses can function as subjects, direct objects, subject complements, or objects of prepositions. Thus a noun clause does not stand
apart but is always contained within another clause. Noun clauses usually begin with a relative pronoun (*that, which, what, who, whom, whose,
whatever, whoever, whomever, whichever*) or with *when, where, whether, why,*
or *how.*

▶ *That she had a good job* was important to him.

▶ He asked *where she went to college.*

▶ The real question was *why he wanted to know.*

▶ He was looking for *whatever he could dig up.*

Notice that in each of these sentences the noun clause is an integral part
of the independent clause that makes up the sentence. For example, in
the second sentence, the independent clause is not just *he asked* but *he
asked where she went to college.*

Adjective clauses

Adjective clauses modify nouns and pronouns in other clauses. Usually
adjective clauses immediately follow the words they modify. Most of
these clauses begin with the relative pronouns *who, whom, whose, that,* or
which. Some begin with *when, where,* or *why.*

▶ The surgery, *which took three hours,* was a complete success.

▶ It was performed by the surgeon *who had developed the procedure.*

▶ The hospital was the one *where I was born.*

Sometimes the relative pronoun introducing an adjective clause may be
omitted.

▶ That is one book *[that] I intend to read.*

Adverb clauses

Adverb clauses modify verbs, adjectives, or other adverbs. They begin with a subordinating conjunction (*after, although, as, as if, because, before, even though, if, in order that, once, since, so that, than, that, though, unless, until, when, where, whether, while*).

▶ We hiked *where there were few other hikers.*

▶ My backpack felt heavier *than it ever had.*

▶ I climbed as swiftly *as I could under the weight of my backpack.*

TYPES OF SENTENCES

Like words, sentences can be classified in different ways: grammatically or functionally.

24n Classifying sentences grammatically

Grammatically, sentences may be classified as simple, compound, complex, and compound-complex.

Simple sentences

A simple sentence consists of one independent clause and no dependent clause.

┌─────────── INDEPENDENT CLAUSE ───────────┐
▶ **The trailer is surrounded by a wooden deck.**

Compound sentences

A compound sentence consists of two or more independent clauses and no dependent clause. The clauses may be joined by a comma and a coordinating conjunction (*and, but, or, nor, for, so, yet*) or by a semicolon.

┌─────────── IND CLAUSE───────────┐ ┌────── IND CLAUSE──────┐
▶ Occasionally a car goes up the dirt trail, and dust flies everywhere.

┌────── IND CLAUSE ──────┐ ┌────────── IND CLAUSE──────────┐
▶ Angelo is obsessed with soccer; he eats, breathes, and lives the game.

Complex sentences

A complex sentence consists of one independent clause and at least one dependent clause.

┌───── IND CLAUSE─────┐ ┌────── DEP CLAUSE──────┐
▶ Many people believe that anyone can earn a living.

Compound-complex sentences

A compound-complex sentence consists of two or more independent clauses and at least one dependent clause.

┌──── IND CLAUSE────┐ ┌────── DEP CLAUSE──────┐ ┌────── IND CLAUSE──────┐
▶ I complimented Joe when he finished the job, and he seemed pleased.

┌────────── IND CLAUSE──────────┐ ┌────── IND CLAUSE──────┐
▶ Sister Lucy tried her best to help Martin, but he was an undisciplined
┌──────────── DEP CLAUSE────────────┐
boy who drove many teachers to despair.

24o Classifying sentences functionally

In terms of function, sentences can be classified as declarative (making a statement), interrogative (asking a question), imperative (giving a command), or exclamatory (expressing strong feeling).

DECLARATIVE	He sings with the Grace Church Boys Choir.
INTERROGATIVE	How long has he sung with them?
IMPERATIVE	Comb his hair before the performance starts.
EXCLAMATORY	What voices those boys have!

25

Verbs

Restaurant menus are often a good source of verbs in action. One famous place in Boston, for instance, offers to bake, broil, pan-fry, deep-fry, poach, sauté, fricassee, blacken, or scallop any of the fish entrees on its menu. To someone ordering—or cooking—at this restaurant, the important distinctions lie entirely in the verbs.

When used skillfully, verbs can be the heartbeat of prose, moving it along, enlivening it, carrying its action. This chapter aims to help you use verbs in all these ways. (See Chapter 26 for advice on subject-verb agreement and Chapter 61 for further details about verbs for multilingual writers.)

25a The five forms of verbs

Except for *be,* all English verbs have five forms.

BASE FORM	PAST TENSE	PAST PARTICIPLE	PRESENT PARTICIPLE	-S FORM
talk	talked	talked	talking	talks
adore	adored	adored	adoring	adores

BASE FORM	We often *go* to Legal Seafood.
PAST TENSE	Grandpa always *ordered* bluefish.
PAST PARTICIPLE	Have you *tried* their oyster stew?
PRESENT PARTICIPLE	Juanita is *getting* the shrimp platter.
-S FORM	The chowder *needs* salt and pepper.

-s *and* -es *endings*

Except with *be* and *have,* the -s form consists of the base form plus -s or -es. This form indicates action in the present for third-person singular subjects. All singular nouns; the words *he, she,* and *it;* and many indefinite pronouns (such as *this, anyone,* or *someone*) are third-person singular.

> ### *Editing the Verbs in Your Own Writing*
> - Circle all forms of *be*, *do*, and *have* that you used as main verbs. Try in each case to substitute a stronger, more specific verb. (25a, b)
> - If you have trouble with verb endings, review the rules for using them in 25a and c.
> - Double-check forms of *lie* and *lay*, *sit* and *set*, *rise* and *raise*. See that the words you use are appropriate for your meaning. (25d)
> - If you have problems with verb tenses, use the guidelines on p. 224 to check your verbs.
> - If you are writing about a literary work, you should refer to the action in the work in the present tense. (25e)
> - Check all uses of the passive voice for appropriateness. (25g)
> - Check all verbs used to introduce quotations, paraphrases, and summaries. If you rely on *say*, *write*, and other very general verbs, try substituting more vivid, specific verbs (*claim*, *insist*, and *wonder*, for instance). (13c)

	SINGULAR	PLURAL
FIRST PERSON	I wish	we wish
SECOND PERSON	you wish	you wish
THIRD PERSON	he/she/it wishes	they wish
	Joe wishes	children wish
	someone wishes	

The third-person singular form of *have* is *has*.

Forms of be

Be has eight forms, including three forms in the present tense and two in the past tense.

BASE FORM	be
PAST PARTICIPLE	been
PRESENT PARTICIPLE	being
PRESENT TENSE	I am, he/she/it is, we/you/they are
PAST TENSE	I/he/she/it was, we/you/they were

A Matter of Style: *Be*

My sister at work. She be there every day 'til five.

These sentences illustrate two common usages of *be*. The first shows the absence of *be;* the same sentence in standard academic English would read "My sister's at work." The second shows the use of "habitual *be,*" indicating that something is always the case. The same sentence in standard academic English would read "She's there every day until five."

These usages of *be* follow the discourse rules of many African American speakers and some southern white speakers. You may well have occasion to quote dialogue featuring these patterns in your own writing; doing so can be a good way to evoke particular regions or communities. See Chapter 34 on using varieties of English appropriately.

25b Use the appropriate auxiliary verbs.

Auxiliary verbs are used with a base form, present participle, or past participle to form verb tenses, questions, and negatives. The most common auxiliaries are forms of *be, do,* and *have.*

▶ We *have considered* all viewpoints.
▶ The problem *is ranking* them fairly.
▶ *Do* you *have* a solution? No, I *do* not *have* one yet.

Modal auxiliaries—*can, could, might, may, must, ought to, shall, will, should, would*—indicate future actions, possibility, necessity, obligation, and so on.

▶ You *can see* three states from the top of the mountain.
▶ She *should visit* this spot more often.

For Multilingual Writers: *Using Modal Auxiliaries*

Why do we not say "Alice can to read Latin"? For discussion of *can* and other modal auxiliaries, see 61a.

25c Regular and irregular verb forms

A verb is regular when its past tense and past participle are formed by adding *-ed* or *-d* to the base form.

BASE FORM	PAST TENSE	PAST PARTICIPLE
love	loved	loved
honor	honored	honored
obey	obeyed	obeyed

A verb is irregular when it does not follow the *-ed* or *-d* pattern. If you are unsure about whether a verb form is regular or irregular, or what the correct form is, consult the following list or a dictionary. Dictionaries list any irregular forms under the entry for the base form.

Some common irregular verbs

BASE FORM	PAST TENSE	PAST PARTICIPLE
arise	arose	arisen
be	was/were	been
bear	bore	borne, born
beat	beat	beaten
become	became	become
begin	began	begun
bite	bit	bitten, bit
blow	blew	blown
break	broke	broken
bring	brought	brought
broadcast	broadcast	broadcast
build	built	built
burn	burned, burnt	burned, burnt
burst	burst	burst
buy	bought	bought
catch	caught	caught
choose	chose	chosen
come	came	come
cost	cost	cost

BASE FORM	PAST TENSE	PAST PARTICIPLE
cut	cut	cut
dig	dug	dug
dive	dived, dove	dived
do	did	done
draw	drew	drawn
dream	dreamed, dreamt	dreamed, dreamt
drink	drank	drunk
drive	drove	driven
eat	ate	eaten
fall	fell	fallen
feel	felt	felt
fight	fought	fought
find	found	found
fly	flew	flown
forget	forgot	forgotten, forgot
freeze	froze	frozen
get	got	gotten, got
give	gave	given
go	went	gone
grow	grew	grown
hang (suspend)[1]	hung	hung
have	had	had
hear	heard	heard
hide	hid	hidden
hit	hit	hit
keep	kept	kept
know	knew	known
lay	laid	laid
lead	led	led
leave	left	left
lend	lent	lent
let	let	let

---

[1]*Hang* meaning "execute by hanging" is regular: *hang, hanged, hanged.*

BASE FORM	PAST TENSE	PAST PARTICIPLE
lie (recline)[2]	lay	lain
lose	lost	lost
make	made	made
mean	meant	meant
meet	met	met
pay	paid	paid
prove	proved	proved, proven
put	put	put
read	read	read
ride	rode	ridden
ring	rang	rung
rise	rose	risen
run	ran	run
say	said	said
see	saw	seen
send	sent	sent
set	set	set
shake	shook	shaken
shoot	shot	shot
show	showed	showed, shown
shrink	shrank	shrunk
sing	sang	sung
sink	sank	sunk
sit	sat	sat
sleep	slept	slept
speak	spoke	spoken
spend	spent	spent
spread	spread	spread
spring	sprang, sprung	sprung
stand	stood	stood
steal	stole	stolen
strike	struck	struck, stricken

---

[2] *Lie* meaning "tell a falsehood" is regular: *lie, lied, lied.*

BASE FORM	PAST TENSE	PAST PARTICIPLE
swim	swam	swum
swing	swung	swung
take	took	taken
teach	taught	taught
tear	tore	torn
tell	told	told
think	thought	thought
throw	threw	thrown
wake	woke, waked	waked, woken
wear	wore	worn
win	won	won
wind	wound	wound
write	wrote	written

25d **Distinguish between *lie* and *lay*, *sit* and *set*, *rise* and *raise*.**

These pairs of verbs cause confusion because both verbs in each pair have similar-sounding forms and somewhat related meanings. In each pair, one of the verbs is transitive, meaning that it takes a direct object (*I lay the package on the counter*). The other is intransitive, meaning that it does not take an object (*He lies on the floor unable to move*). The best way to avoid confusing these verbs is to memorize their forms and meanings.

BASE FORM	PAST TENSE	PAST PARTICIPLE	PRESENT PARTICIPLE	-S FORM
lie (recline)	lay	lain	lying	lies
lay (put)	laid	laid	laying	lays
sit (be seated)	sat	sat	sitting	sits
set (put)	set	set	setting	sets
rise (get up)	rose	risen	rising	rises
raise (lift)	raised	raised	raising	raises

> *lie*
> ► The doctor asked the patient to ~~lay~~ on his side.
>   ^

>   *set*
> ► She ~~sat~~ the vase on the table.
>   ^

>   *raised*
> ► He ~~rose~~ himself to a sitting position.
>   ^

25e Verb tenses

Tenses show when the action expressed by a verb takes place. The three simple tenses are the present tense, the past tense, and the future tense.

PRESENT TENSE	I use
PAST TENSE	I used
FUTURE TENSE	I will use

More complex aspects of time are expressed through progressive, perfect, and perfect progressive forms of the simple tenses.

PRESENT PROGRESSIVE	she *is asking, writing*
PAST PROGRESSIVE	she *was asking, writing*
FUTURE PROGRESSIVE	she *will be asking, writing*
PRESENT PERFECT	she *has asked, written*
PAST PERFECT	she *had asked, written*
FUTURE PERFECT	she *will have asked, written*
PRESENT PERFECT PROGRESSIVE	she *has been asking, writing*
PAST PERFECT PROGRESSIVE	she *had been asking, writing*
FUTURE PERFECT PROGRESSIVE	she *will have been asking, writing*

The simple tenses locate an action only within the three basic time frames of present, past, and future. Progressive forms express continuing actions; perfect forms express actions completed before another action or time in the present, past, or future; perfect progressive forms express actions that continue up to some point in the present, past, or future.

Present tense

SIMPLE PRESENT

Use the simple present to indicate actions occurring now and those occurring habitually.

▶ They *are* very angry about the decision.
▶ I *eat* breakfast every day at 8:00 A.M.
▶ Love *conquers* all.

When writing about action in literary works, use the simple present.

      comes   is
▶ Ishmael slowly ~~came~~ to realize all that ~~was~~ at stake in the search for the white whale.

General truths or scientific facts should be in the simple present, even when the predicate of the sentence is in the past tense.

                       makes
▶ Pasteur demonstrated that his boiling process ~~made~~ milk safe.

When you are quoting, summarizing, or paraphrasing a work, use the present tense.

      writes
▶ Keith Walters ~~wrote~~ that the "reputed consequences and promised blessings of literacy are legion."

Note that documenting an essay using APA (American Psychological Association) style and reporting the results of your experiments or another researcher's work call for using the past tense (*wrote, noted*) or the present perfect (*has reported*). (See Chapter 52.)

        noted
▶ Comer (1995) ~~notes~~ that protesters who deprive themselves of food (for example, Gandhi and Dick Gregory) are seen not as dysfunctional but rather as "caring, sacrificing, even heroic" (p. 5).

PRESENT PROGRESSIVE

Use the present progressive to indicate actions that are ongoing in the present: *You are driving too fast.*

PRESENT PERFECT

Use the present perfect to indicate actions begun in the past and either completed at some unspecified time in the past or continuing into the present: *Uncontrolled logging has destroyed many forests.*

PRESENT PERFECT PROGRESSIVE

Use the present perfect progressive to indicate an ongoing action begun in the past and continuing into the present: *The two sides have been trying to settle the case out of court.*

Past tense

SIMPLE PAST

Use the simple past to indicate actions that occurred at a specific time and do not extend into the present: *Germany invaded Poland on September 1, 1939.*

PAST PROGRESSIVE

Use the past progressive to indicate continuing actions in the past: *Lenin was living in exile in Zurich when the tsar was overthrown.*

PAST PERFECT

Use the past perfect to indicate actions that were completed by a specific time in the past or before some other past action occurred: *By the fourth century, Christianity had become the state religion.*

PAST PERFECT PROGRESSIVE

Use the past perfect progressive to indicate continuing actions in the past that began before a specific time or before some other past action began: *Carter had been planning a naval career until his father died.*

Future tense

SIMPLE FUTURE

Use the simple future to indicate actions that have yet to begin: *The Vermeer show will come to Washington in September.*

FUTURE PROGRESSIVE

Use the future progressive to indicate continuing actions in the future: *The loans will be coming due in the next two years.*

FUTURE PERFECT

Use the future perfect to indicate actions that will be completed by a specified time in the future: *In ten years, your investment will have doubled.*

FUTURE PERFECT PROGRESSIVE

Use the future perfect progressive to indicate continuing actions that will be completed by some specified time in the future: *In May, I will have been working at IBM for five years.*

Editing Verb Tenses

If you have trouble with verb tenses, make a point of checking for these common errors as you proofread.

- Errors of verb form: writing *seen* for *saw,* for example, which is an instance of confusing the past-participle and past-tense forms. (25e)
- Errors in tense: using the simple past (*Uncle Charlie arrived*) when meaning requires the present perfect (*Uncle Charlie has arrived*). (25e)
- Other errors result from using a regional or ethnic variety of English (*she nervous*) in situations calling for standard academic English (*she is nervous*). (See p. 216 and Chapter 34.)

25f Sequence verb tenses accurately.

Careful and accurate use of tenses is important to clear writing. Even the simplest narrative describes actions that take place at different times. When you use the appropriate tense for each action, readers can follow such time changes easily.

> *had*
> ▶ **By the time he lent her the money, she declared bankruptcy.**
>   ^

The original sentence suggests that the two events occurred at the same time; the revised sentence makes clear that the bankruptcy occurred first.

Use an infinitive (*to* plus a base form: *to go*) to indicate actions occurring at the same time as or later than the action of the predicate verb.

> *to plant*
> ▶ We had hoped ~~to have planted~~ our garden by now.
>   ^
>
> The action of the infinitive *to plant* follows that of the sentence's main verb (*had hoped*).

Use a present participle (base form plus *-ing*) to indicate actions occurring at the same time as that of the predicate verb.

> ▶ **Seeking to relieve unemployment, Roosevelt established several public works programs.**
>
> The seeking and establishment of the programs occurred simultaneously.

A past participle or a present-perfect participle (*having* plus a past participle) indicates actions occurring before that of the predicate verb.

> *Flown*
> ▶ ~~Flying~~ **to the front, the troops joined their hard-pressed comrades.**
>   ^
>
> The past participle *flown* shows that the flying occurred before the joining.

> *Having crushed*
> ▶ ~~Crushing~~ **all opposition at home, he launched a war of conquest.**
>   ^
>
> He launched the war after he crushed the opposition.

25g Use active voice and passive voice appropriately.

Voice tells whether a subject is acting (*He questions us*) or being acted upon (*He is questioned*). When the subject is acting, the verb is in the active voice; when the subject is being acted upon, the verb is in the passive voice. Most contemporary writers use the active voice as much as possible because it livens up their prose.

> PASSIVE   Huge pine trees *were uprooted* by the storm.
>
> ACTIVE   The storm *uprooted* huge pine trees.

The passive voice can work to good advantage in some situations. Newspaper reporters often use the passive voice to protect the confidentiality of their sources, as in the familiar phrase *it is reported that*. You can also use the passive voice when you want to emphasize the recipient of an action rather than the performer of the action.

> DALLAS, Nov. 22—President John Fitzgerald Kennedy was shot and killed by an assassin today.   —TOM WICKER, *New York Times*

Wicker uses the passive voice with good reason: to focus on Kennedy, not on who killed him.

To shift a sentence from passive to active voice, make the performer of the action the subject of the sentence.

>   *Researchers told the*
> ► ~~The~~ test administrator ~~was told~~ to give students an electric shock
>   ^
>   *they gave*
> each time a wrong answer. ~~was given.~~
>   ^   ^

A Matter of Style: *Technical and Scientific Writing*

Much technical and scientific writing uses the passive voice effectively to highlight what is being studied rather than who is doing the studying. Look at the following example, from a description of geological movement:

> The Earth's plates are created where they separate and are recycled where they collide, in a continuous process of creation and destruction.
> —FRANK PRESS AND RAYMOND SIEVER, *Understanding Earth*

25h Select the appropriate mood.

The mood of a verb indicates the attitude of the writer toward what he or she is saying. The indicative mood is used for stating facts or opinions and for asking questions: *I did the right thing.* The imperative mood is used for giving commands and instructions: *Do the right thing.* The subjunctive mood (used primarily in dependent clauses beginning with *that* or *if*) expresses wishes and conditions that are contrary to fact: *If I were doing the right thing, I'd know it.*

Forming and using the subjunctive

The present subjunctive uses the base form of the verb with all subjects.

> ► It is important that children *be* psychologically ready for a new sibling.

The past subjunctive is the same as the simple past except for the verb *be*, which uses *were* for all subjects.

▶ He spent money as if he *had* infinite credit.
▶ If the store *were* better located, it would attract more customers.

Because the subjunctive creates a rather formal tone, many people today tend to substitute the indicative mood in informal conversation.

▶ If the store *was* better located, it would attract more customers.

For academic or professional writing, use the subjunctive in the following contexts:

CLAUSES EXPRESSING A WISH

▶ He wished that his mother ~~was~~ *were* still living nearby.

THAT-CLAUSES EXPRESSING A REQUEST OR DEMAND

▶ The job demands that employees ~~are~~ *be* in good physical condition.

IF-CLAUSES EXPRESSING A CONDITION THAT DOES NOT EXIST

▶ If the federal government ~~was~~ *were* to ban the sale of tobacco, tobacco companies and distributors would suffer a great loss.

One common error is to use *would* in both clauses. Use the subjunctive in the *if*-clause and *would* in the independent clause.

▶ If I ~~would have~~ *had* played harder, I would have won.

For Multilingual Writers: *Using the Subjunctive*

"If you were to practice writing every day, it would eventually seem much easier to you." For a discussion of this and other uses of the subjunctive, see 63g.

26

Subject-Verb Agreement

In everyday terms, the word *agreement* refers to an accord of some sort: you reach an agreement with your boss about salary; friends agree to go to a movie; the members of a family agree to share household chores. This meaning covers grammatical agreement as well. In the present tense, verbs agree with their subjects in number (singular or plural) and in person (first, second, or third). This chapter will take a closer look at subject-verb agreement.

26a Make verbs agree with third-person singular subjects.

To make a verb in the present tense agree with a third-person singular subject, add *-s* or *-es* to the base form.

> ### Editing for Subject-Verb Agreement
>
> - Check your drafts verb by verb, and identify the subject that goes with each verb.
>
>   *are*
>   ▶ **The players on our side is̶ sure to win.**
>   ^
>
>   Because the simple subject here is *players*, the verb needs to be *are*. When you take away the words between the subject and the verb, it is easier to identify agreement problems. (26b)
>
> - Check compound subjects. Those joined by *and* usually take a plural verb. With those subjects joined by *or* or *nor*, however, the verb agrees with the part of the subject closer or closest to the verb. *Neither Claire's parents nor Claire* <u>plans</u> *to vote.* (26c)
>
> - Check collective-noun subjects. These nouns take a singular verb when they refer to a group as a single unit, but they take a plural verb when they refer to the multiple members of a group. *The crowd* <u>screams</u> *its support.* (26d)
>
> - Check indefinite-pronoun subjects. Most take a singular verb. (*Both, few, many, others,* and *several* take a plural verb.) *Each of the singers* <u>rehearses</u> *for three hours daily.* (26e)

▶ A vegetarian diet *lowers* the risk of heart disease.

To make a verb in the present tense agree with any other subject, use the base form of the verb.

▶ I *miss* my family.
▶ They *live* in another state.

Have and *be* do not follow the -s or -es pattern with third-person singular subjects. *Have* changes to *has; be* has irregular forms in both the present and past tenses (25a).

▶ War *is* hell.
▶ The soldier *was* brave beyond the call of duty.

26b **Make subjects and verbs agree, even when separated by other words.**

Make sure the verb agrees with the subject and not with another noun that falls in between.

▶ A vase of flowers *makes* a room attractive.

A Matter of Style: -s *and* -es *Endings*

She go to work seven days a week.
He don't take it to heart.

These two sentences are typical of some varieties of African American English and of some regional white English, in which third-person singular verbs do not end with -s or -es. (In standard academic English, these verb forms are *she goes* and *he doesn't*.) You will often see verb forms such as those in the sentences above in African American literature, especially in dialogue, and you may well quote passages using these varieties of English in your own writing. In most academic and professional writing, however, add -s or -es to third-person singular verb forms.

have
▶ Many books on the best-seller list ~~has~~ little literary value.
     ^

The simple subject is *books*, not *list*.

The phrases as well as, along with, in addition to, together with

Be careful when you use these and other similar phrases. They do not make a singular subject plural.

was
▶ A passenger, as well as the driver, ~~were~~ injured in the accident.
                                    ^

Though this sentence has a grammatically singular subject, it suggests the idea of a plural subject. The sentence makes better sense with a compound subject: *The driver and a passenger were injured in the accident.*

26c Compound subjects generally take plural verbs.

were
▶ A backpack, a canteen, and a rifle ~~was~~ issued to each recruit.
                                   ^

When subjects joined by *and* are considered a single unit or refer to the same person or thing, they take a singular verb form.

▶ John Kennedy's closest friend and political ally *was* his brother.

remains
▶ Drinking and driving ~~remain~~ a major cause of highway fatalities.
                     ^

In this sentence, *drinking and driving* is considered a single activity, and a singular verb is used.

If the word *each* or *every* precedes subjects joined by *and,* the verb form is singular.

▶ Each boy and girl *chooses* one gift to take home.

With subjects joined by *or* or *nor,* the verb agrees with the part closer or closest to the verb.

▶ Neither my roommate nor my neighbors *like* my loud music.

▶ Either the witnesses or the defendant *is* lying.

If you find this sentence awkward, put the plural noun closer to the verb: *Either the defendant or the witnesses are lying.*

      am
▶ Either you or I ~~are~~ wrong.
       ^

26d **Collective nouns can be singular or plural, depending on meaning.**

Collective nouns—such as *family, team, audience, group, jury, crowd, band, class,* and *committee*—refer to a group. Collective nouns can take either singular or plural verbs, depending on whether they refer to the group as a single unit or to the multiple members of the group. The meaning of a sentence as a whole is your guide to whether a collective noun refers to a unit or to the multiple parts of a unit.

▶ After deliberating, the jury *reports* its verdict.

The jury acts as a single unit.

▶ The jury still *disagree* on a number of counts.

The members of the jury act as multiple individuals.

      scatter
▶ The family of ducklings ~~scatters~~ when the cat approaches.
       ^

Family here refers to the many ducks; they cannot scatter as one.

      has
▶ Two-thirds of the park ~~have~~ burned.
      ^

Two-thirds refers to the single unit of the park that burned.

      were
▶ Two-thirds of the students ~~was~~ commuters.
      ^

Two-thirds here refers to the students who commuted as many individuals.

The phrases the number of, a number of

Treat phrases starting with *the number of* as singular and with *a number of* as plural.

> SINGULAR   The number of applicants for the internship *was* unbelievable.
>
> PLURAL   A number of applicants *were* put on the waiting list.

26e Most indefinite pronouns take singular verbs.

Indefinite pronouns are those that do not refer to specific persons or things. Most take singular verb forms.

SOME COMMON INDEFINITE PRONOUNS

another	each	much	one
any	either	neither	other
anybody	everybody	nobody	somebody
anyone	everyone	no one	someone
anything	everything	nothing	something

▶ Of the two jobs, neither *holds* much appeal.

▶ Each of the plays ~~depict~~ *depicts* a hero undone by a tragic flaw.

Both, few, many, others, and *several* are plural.

▶ Though many *apply*, few *are* chosen.

All, any, enough, more, most, none, and *some* can be singular or plural, depending on the noun they refer to.

▶ All of the cake *was* eaten.

▶ All of the candidates *promise* to improve the schools.

26f Make verbs agree with the antecedents of *who*, *which*, and *that*.

When the relative pronouns *who, which,* and *that* are used as a subject, the verb agrees with the antecedent of the pronoun.

▶ Fear is an ingredient that *goes* into creating stereotypes.

▶ Guilt and fear are ingredients that *go* into creating stereotypes.

Problems often occur with the words *one of the.* In general, *one of the* takes a plural verb, while *the only one of the* takes a singular verb.

▶ Carla is one of the employees who always ~~works~~ *work* overtime.

> Some employees always work overtime. Carla is among them. Thus *who* refers to *employees,* and the verb is plural.

▶ Ming is the only one of the employees who always ~~work~~ *works* overtime.

> Only one employee always works overtime, and that employee is Ming. Thus *one,* and not *employees,* is the antecedent of *who,* and the verb form must be singular.

26g Make linking verbs agree with their subjects, not with their complements.

A linking verb should agree with its subject, which usually precedes the verb, not with the subject complement, which follows it.

▶ The signings of three key treaties ~~is~~ *are* the topic of my talk.

> The subject is *signings,* not *topic.*

▶ Nero Wolfe's passion ~~were~~ *was* orchids.

> The subject is *passion,* not *orchids.*

26h Words such as *physics* and *news* take singular verbs.

Some words that end in *-s* seem to be plural but are singular in meaning and thus take singular verbs.

      strikes
▶ Measles still ~~strike~~ many Americans.

Some nouns of this kind (such as *statistics* and *politics*) may be either singular or plural, depending on context.

SINGULAR   Statistics *is* a course I really dread.
PLURAL   The statistics in that study *are* highly questionable.

26i Make verbs agree with subjects that follow them.

In English, verbs usually follow subjects. When this order is reversed, make the verb agree with the subject, not with a noun that happens to precede it.

      stand
▶ Beside the barn ~~stands~~ silos filled with grain.

The subject is *silos*; it is plural, so the verb must be *stand*.

In sentences beginning with *there is* or *there are* (or *there was* or *were*), *there* serves only as an introductory word; the subject follows the verb.

▶ There *are* five basic positions in classical ballet.

The subject, *positions,* is plural, so the verb must also be plural.

26j Titles and words used as words take singular verbs.

      describes
▶ *One Writer's Beginnings* ~~describe~~ Eudora Welty's childhood.

      is
▶ *Steroids* ~~are~~ a little word that packs a big punch in the world of sports.

27

Adjectives and Adverbs

Adjectives and adverbs often bring indispensable differences in meaning to the words they modify. In basketball, for example, there is an important difference between a *flagrant* foul and a *technical* foul, a layup and a *reverse* layup, and an *angry* coach and a *really angry* coach. In each instance, the modifiers are crucial to accurate communication.

Adjectives modify nouns and pronouns, answering the questions *which? how many?* and *what kind?* Adverbs modify verbs, adjectives, and other adverbs; they answer the questions *how? when? where?* and *to what extent?* Many adverbs are formed by adding *-ly* to adjectives (*slight, slightly*) but many adverbs are formed in other ways (*outdoors*) or have forms of their own (*very*).

> ### *Editing Adjectives and Adverbs*
>
> - Carefully scrutinize each adjective and adverb in your writing to see whether it's the best word possible. Considering one or two synonyms for each adjective or adverb should help you decide.
> - Is each adjective necessary? Would a more specific noun eliminate the need for an adjective (*mansion* rather than *enormous house*, for instance)? Follow this same line of inquiry with the verbs and adverbs in your writing.
> - Look for places where you might make your writing more specific or vivid by adding an adjective or adverb.
> - Are all comparisons complete? (27c)
> - If English is not your first language, check that adjectives are in the right order. (60e)

27a Use adjectives after linking verbs.

When adjectives come after linking verbs, they usually serve as a subject complement, to describe the subject: *I am patient.* Note that in specific sentences, some verbs may or may not be linking verbs—*appear, become, feel, grow, look, make, prove, seem, smell, sound* and *taste,* for instance. When a word following one of these verbs modifies the subject, use an adjective; when it modifies the verb, use an adverb.

> **For Multilingual Writers: *Adjectives and Plural Nouns***
>
> In Spanish, Russian, and many other languages, adjectives agree in number with the nouns they modify. In English, however, adjectives do not change number this way: *her dogs are small* (not *smalls*).

ADJECTIVE   **Otis Thorpe looked *angry*.**

ADVERB   **He looked *angrily* at the referee.**

Linking verbs suggest a state of being, not an action. In the preceding examples, *looked angry* suggests the state of being angry; *looked angrily* suggests an angry action.

27b Use adverbs to modify verbs, adjectives, and adverbs.

In everyday conversation, you will often hear (and perhaps use) adjectives in place of adverbs. For example, people often say *go quick* instead of *go quickly*. When you write in standard academic English, however, use adverbs to modify verbs, adjectives, and other adverbs.

> ▶ You can feel the song's meter if you listen ~~careful~~ *carefully*.

> ▶ The audience was ~~real~~ *really* disappointed by the show.

The modifiers *good, well, bad,* and *badly* cause problems for many writers because the distinctions between *good* and *well* and between *bad* and *badly* are often not observed in conversation. Problems also arise because *well* can function as either an adjective or an adverb.

Good *and* well

> ▶ I look ~~well~~ *good* in blue.

> This sentence contains a linking verb and so requires an adjective. But the adjective *well* refers to health, which is not the context of this sentence.

> **For Multilingual Writers:** *Determining Adjective Sequence*
> Should you write *these beautiful blue kitchen tiles* or *these blue beautiful kitchen tiles*? See 60e for guidelines on adjective sequence.

well
▶ **Now that the fever has broken, I feel ~~good~~ again.**
                              ^

As an adjective, *well* means "in good health"; this sentence is about health and calls for *well*, not *good*.

well.
▶ **He plays the trumpet ~~good.~~**
                          ^

Bad *and* badly

bad   *badly.*
▶ **I feel ~~badly~~ for the Toronto fans. Their team played ~~bad.~~**
      ^   ^

27c Comparatives and superlatives

Most adjectives and adverbs have three forms: positive, comparative, and superlative.

POSITIVE	COMPARATIVE	SUPERLATIVE
large	larger	largest
early	earlier	earliest
careful	more careful	most careful
happily	more happily	most happily

▶ **Canada is *larger* than the United States.**
▶ **My son needs to be *more careful* with his money.**
▶ **They are the *most happily* married couple I know.**

As these examples show, you usually form the comparative and superlative of one- or two-syllable adjectives by adding *-er* and *-est*: *short, shorter, shortest*. With some two-syllable adjectives, with longer adjectives, and with most adverbs, use *more* and *most*: *scientific, more scientific, most scientific; elegantly, more elegantly, most elegantly*.

Irregular adjectives and adverbs

Some short adjectives and adverbs have irregular comparative and superlative forms.

POSITIVE	COMPARATIVE	SUPERLATIVE
good	better	best
well	better	best
bad, badly	worse	worst
little (quantity)	less	least
many, much	more	most

Comparatives vs. superlatives

Use the comparative to compare two things; use the superlative to compare three or more things.

▶ Rome is a much *older* city than New York.

▶ Damascus is one of the ~~older~~ cities in the world.
                                 oldest

Double comparatives and superlatives

Double comparatives and superlatives are those that unnecessarily use both the *-er* or *-est* ending and *more* or *most*. Occasionally, these forms can act to build a special emphasis, as in the title of Spike Lee's movie *Mo' Better Blues*. In academic and professional writing, however, do not use *more* or *most* before adjectives or adverbs ending in *-er* or *-est*.

▶ Paris is the ~~most~~ loveliest city in the world.

▶ Rome lasted ~~more~~ longer than Carthage.
                much

Incomplete comparisons

In speaking, we sometimes state only part of a comparison because the context makes the meaning clear. For example, after comparing your car with a friend's, you might say "Yours is better," but the context makes it clear that you mean "Yours is better *than mine*." In writing, such a context may not exist. So, when editing, take the time to check for incomplete comparisons—and to complete them if they are unclear.

than those receiving a placebo.
▶ The patients taking the drug appeared healthier/
                                                ∧

Absolute concepts

Some adjectives and adverbs—such as *perfect, final,* and *unique*—are absolute concepts, so it is illogical to form comparatives or superlatives of these words.

▶ The patient felt compelled to have ~~more~~ perfect control over his

thoughts.

       a
▶ Anne has ~~the most~~ unique sense of humor.
  ∧

A Matter of Style: *Multiple Negation*

Speakers of English sometimes use more than one negative at a time—saying, for instance, "I can't hardly see you." Multiple negatives, in fact, have a long history in English (and can be found in the works of Chaucer and Shakespeare, for example). It was only in the eighteenth century, in an effort to make English more logical, that double negatives came to be seen as incorrect.

In fact, the use of double negatives for emphasis is very popular in many areas of the South. Someone might say, for example, "Can't nothing be done." Emphatic double negatives—and triple, quadruple, and more—are used by many speakers of African American vernacular English, who may say, for instance, "Don't none of my people come from up North."

Even though they occur in many varieties of English (and in many other languages, including French and Russian), multiple negatives are not characteristic of standard academic English. In academic or professional writing, you may well have reason to quote passages that include multiple negatives—whether you're quoting Shakespeare, Toni Morrison, or your grandmother—but you will play it safe if you avoid other uses of multiple negatives.

28

Modifier Placement

Modifiers enrich writing by making it more concrete or vivid, often adding important or even essential details. To be effective, modifiers should refer clearly to the words they modify and be positioned close to those words. Consider, for example, a sign seen recently in a hotel:

DO NOT USE THE ELEVATORS IN CASE OF FIRE.

Should we really avoid the elevators altogether, in case there is ever a fire? Repositioning the modifier *in case of fire* eliminates such confusion—and makes clear that we are to avoid the elevators only if there is a fire: IN CASE OF FIRE, DO NOT USE THE ELEVATORS. This chapter reviews the conventions of accurate modifier placement.

Editing Misplaced or Dangling Modifiers

1. Identify all the modifiers in each sentence, and draw an arrow from each modifier to the word it modifies.
2. If a modifier is far from the word it modifies, try to move the two closer together. (28a)
3. Does any modifier seem to refer to a word other than the one it is intended to modify? If so, move the modifier so that it refers clearly to only the intended word. (28a, c)
4. If you cannot find the word to which a modifier refers, revise the sentence: supply such a word, or revise the modifier itself so that it clearly refers to a word already in the sentence. (28d)

28a Position modifiers close to the words they modify.

Modifiers can cause confusion or ambiguity if they are not close enough to the words they modify or if they seem to modify more than one word in the sentence.

► She teaches a seminar this term on voodoo at Skyline College.

Surely the voodoo was not at the college.

H   *billowing from every window.*
▶ ~~Billowing from every window,~~ he saw clouds of smoke/
                                ^   ^

People cannot billow from windows.

After he lost the 1962 gubernatorial race,
▶ Nixon told reporters that he planned to get out of politics. ~~after he lost~~
  ^   ^
  ~~the 1962 gubernatorial race.~~

The unedited sentence implies that Nixon planned to lose the race.

Limiting modifiers

Be especially careful with the placement of limiting modifiers such as *almost, even, just, merely,* and *only.* In general, these modifiers should be placed right before or after the words they modify. Putting them in other positions may produce not just ambiguity but a completely different meaning.

AMBIGUOUS	The court *only* hears civil cases on Tuesdays.
CLEAR	The court hears *only* civil cases on Tuesdays.
CLEAR	The court hears civil cases on Tuesdays *only.*

Placing *only* before *hears* makes the meaning ambiguous. Does the writer mean that civil cases are the only cases heard on Tuesdays or that those are the only days when civil cases are heard?

                        almost
▶ The city ~~almost~~ spent twenty million dollars on the new stadium.
           ^

The original sentence suggests the money was almost spent; moving *almost* makes clear that the amount spent was almost twenty million dollars.

Squinting modifiers

If a modifier could refer to the word before it and the word after it, it is called a squinting modifier. Put the modifier where it clearly relates to only a single word.

SQUINTING	Students who practice writing *often* will benefit.
REVISED	Students who *often* practice writing will benefit.
REVISED	Students who practice writing will *often* benefit.

28b Move disruptive modifiers.

Disruptive modifiers interrupt the connections between parts of a grammatical structure or a sentence, making it hard for readers to follow the progress of the thought.

▶ *If they are cooked too long, vegetables will*
~~Vegetables will, if they are cooked too long,~~ lose most of their
nutritional value.

28c Move modifiers that unnecessarily split an infinitive.

In general, do not place a modifier between the *to* and the verb of an infinitive (*to often complain*). Doing so makes it hard for readers to recognize that the two go together.

▶ Hitler expected the British to fairly quickly. *surrender.* *surrender*

In some sentences, however, a modifier sounds awkward if it does not split the infinitive. In such cases, it may be best to reword the sentence to eliminate the infinitive altogether.

SPLIT   I hope *to* almost *equal* my last year's income.

REVISED   I hope that I will earn almost as much as I did last year.

28d Revise dangling modifiers.

Dangling modifiers are words that modify nothing in particular in the rest of a sentence. They often *seem* to modify something that is implied but not actually present in the sentence. Dangling modifiers frequently appear at the beginnings or ends of sentences.

DANGLING   Driving nonstop, Salishan Lodge is located two hours from Portland.

REVISED   Driving nonstop from Portland, you can reach Salishan Lodge in two hours.

To revise a dangling modifier, often you need to add a subject that the modifier clearly refers to; sometimes you have to revise the modifier itself, turning it into a phrase or a clause.

> *our family gave away*
> ▶ Reluctantly, the hound ~~was given away~~ to a neighbor.
>   ^

In the original sentence, was the dog reluctant, or was someone else reluctant who is not mentioned?

> *When he was*
> ▶ ~~As~~ a young boy, his grandmother told stories of her years as a country
>   ^
> schoolteacher.

His grandmother was never a young boy.

>   M
> ▶ ~~Thumbing through the magazine,~~ my eyes automatically noticed the
>   *as I was thumbing through the magazine.*
> perfume ads ╱
>   ^

Eyes cannot thumb through a magazine.

29

Pronouns

As words that stand in for nouns, pronouns carry a lot of weight in everyday discourse. For example:

> Take the Interstate until you come to Exit 3 and Route 313. Go past it, and take the next exit, which will be Broadway.

These directions, intended to lead an out-of-towner to her friend's house, provide a good example of why it's important for a pronoun to refer clearly to a specific noun or pronoun antecedent. The little word *it* in this example could mean either Exit 3 or Route 313. Or does *it* mean that Exit 3 *is* Route 313? This chapter aims to help you use pronouns accurately.

29a Pronoun case

Most speakers of English know intuitively when to use *I*, when to use *me*, and when to use *my*. Our choices reflect differences in case, the form a pronoun takes to indicate its function in a sentence. Pronouns

► Reluctantly, the hound ~~was given away~~ to a neighbor.
  ^ *our family gave away*

In the original sentence, was the dog reluctant, or was someone else reluctant who is not mentioned?

► ~~As~~ a young boy, his grandmother told stories of her years as a country
  ^ *When he was*
schoolteacher.

His grandmother was never a young boy.

                                          M
► ~~Thumbing through the magazine,~~ my eyes automatically noticed the
                as I was thumbing through the magazine.
perfume ads/
           ^

Eyes cannot thumb through a magazine.

29

Pronouns

As words that stand in for nouns, pronouns carry a lot of weight in everyday discourse. For example:

> Take the Interstate until you come to Exit 3 and Route 313. Go past it, and take the next exit, which will be Broadway.

These directions, intended to lead an out-of-towner to her friend's house, provide a good example of why it's important for a pronoun to refer clearly to a specific noun or pronoun antecedent. The little word *it* in this example could mean either Exit 3 or Route 313. Or does *it* mean that Exit 3 *is* Route 313? This chapter aims to help you use pronouns accurately.

29a Pronoun case

Most speakers of English know intuitively when to use *I*, when to use *me*, and when to use *my*. Our choices reflect differences in case, the form a pronoun takes to indicate its function in a sentence. Pronouns

Editing Pronouns

- Are all pronouns after forms of the verb *be* in the subjective case? *It's me* is common in spoken English, but in writing it should be *It is I.* (29a)
- To check for correct use of *who* and *whom* (and *whoever* and *whomever*), try substituting *he* or *him*. If *he* is correct, use *who* (or *whoever*); if *him*, use *whom* or *whomever*. (29b)
- In compound structures, make sure any pronouns are in the same case they would be in if used alone. (*She and Jake were living in Spain.*) (29c)
- When a pronoun follows *than* or *as*, complete the sentence mentally. If the pronoun is the subject of an unstated verb, it should be subjective. (*I like her better than he [likes her].*) If it is the object of an unstated verb, make it objective. (*I like her better than [I like] him.*) (29d)
- Check any use of *anyone, each, everybody, many,* and other indefinite pronouns (see list in 26e) to be sure they are treated as singular or plural as appropriate. (29f)
- If you find *he, his,* or *him* used to refer to persons of either sex, revise the pronouns, or recast the sentences altogether. (29f)
- For each pronoun, identify a specific word that it refers to. If you cannot find one specific word, supply one. If the pronoun refers to more than one word, revise the sentence. (29g)
- Check any use of *it, this, that,* and *which* to be sure each pronoun refers to some specific word elsewhere in the sentence or prior sentence. (29g)
- Be sure that any use of *you* refers to your specific reader or readers.

functioning as subjects are in the subjective case (*I*); those functioning as objects are in the objective case (*me*); those functioning as possessives are in the possessive case (*my*).

SUBJECTIVE PRONOUNS	OBJECTIVE PRONOUNS	POSSESSIVE PRONOUNS
I	me	my/mine
we	us	our/ours
you	you	your/yours
he/she/it	him/her/it	his/her/hers/its
they	them	their/theirs
who/whoever	whom/whomever	whose

Subjective case

A pronoun should be in the subjective case (*I, you, he/she/it, we, they, who, whoever*) when it is a subject, a subject complement, or an appositive renaming a subject or subject complement.

SUBJECT

She was passionate about recycling.

SUBJECT COMPLEMENT

The main supporter of the recycling program was *she.*

APPOSITIVE RENAMING A SUBJECT OR SUBJECT COMPLEMENT

Three colleagues—Peter, John, and *she*—worked on the program.

Many Americans routinely use the objective case for subject complements, especially in conversation: *Who's there? It's me.* If the subjective case for a subject complement sounds stilted or awkward (*It's I*), try rewriting the sentence using the pronoun as the subject (*I'm here*).

    She was the
► ~~The~~ first person to see Monty after the awards. ~~was she.~~
    ^   ^

Objective case

A pronoun should be in the objective case (*me, you, him/her/it, us, them*) when it functions as a direct or indirect object, an object of a preposition, an appositive renaming an object, or a subject of an infinitive.

DIRECT OBJECT

The boss surprised *her* with a big raise.

INDIRECT OBJECT

The owner gave *him* a reward.

OBJECT OF A PREPOSITION

Several friends went with *me.*

APPOSITIVE RENAMING AN OBJECT

We elected two representatives, Joan and *me.*

SUBJECT OF AN INFINITIVE

The students convinced *him* to vote for the school bond.

Possessive case

A pronoun should be in the possessive case when it shows possession or ownership. Notice that there are two forms of possessive pronouns: adjective forms, which are used before nouns or gerunds (*my, your, his/her/its, our, their, whose*), and noun forms, which take the place of a possessive noun (*mine, yours, his/hers/its, ours, theirs, whose*).

BEFORE A NOUN

The sound of *her* voice came right through the walls.

IN PLACE OF A POSSESSIVE NOUN

The responsibility is *hers*.

Pronouns before a gerund should be in the possessive case.

▶ I remember ~~him~~ singing.
  his

His modifies the gerund *singing*.

29b Use *who, whoever, whom,* and *whomever* appropriately.

A common problem with pronoun case is deciding whether to use *who* or *whom*. Use *who* and *whoever*, which are subjective-case pronouns, for subjects or subject complements. Use *whom* and *whomever*, which are objective-case pronouns, for objects. Two particular situations lead to confusion with *who* and *whom*: when they begin a question and when they introduce a dependent clause.

In questions

You can determine whether to use *who* or *whom* at the beginning of a question by answering the question using a personal pronoun. If the answer is in the subjective case, use *who*; if it is in the objective case, use *whom*.

Whom

▶ ~~Who~~ did you visit?
  ∧

I visited *them*. *Them* is objective; thus *whom* is correct.

Who

▶ ~~Whom~~ do you think wrote the story?
  ∧

I think *she* wrote the story. *She* is subjective; thus *who* is correct.

In dependent clauses

The case of a pronoun in a dependent clause is determined by its function in the clause, no matter how that clause functions in the sentence. If the pronoun acts as a subject or subject complement in the clause, use *who* or *whoever*. If the pronoun acts as an object in the clause, use *whom* or *whomever*.

                                        who
▶ Anyone can hypnotize someone ~~whom~~ wants to be hypnotized.
                                  ∧

The verb of the clause is *wants,* and its subject is *who.*

Whomever

▶ ~~Whoever~~ the party suspected of disloyalty was executed.
  ∧

Whomever is the object of *suspected* in the clause *whomever the party suspected of disloyalty.*

If you are not sure which case to use, try separating the dependent clause from the rest of the sentence and looking at it in isolation. Then rewrite the clause as a new sentence, and substitute a personal pronoun for *who(ever)* or *whom(ever)*. If the personal pronoun you substitute is in the subjective case, use *who* or *whoever;* if it is in the objective case, use *whom* or *whomever.*

▶ The minister grimaced at (*whoever/whomever*) made any noise.

Isolate the clause *whoever/whomever made any noise.* Substituting a personal pronoun gives you *they made any noise. They* is in the subjective case; therefore, *The minister grimaced at whoever made any noise.*

▶ The minister smiled at (*whoever/whomever*) she greeted.

Isolate and transpose the clause to get *she greeted whoever/whomever.* Substituting a personal pronoun gives you *she greeted them. Them* is in the objective case; therefore, *The minister smiled at whomever she greeted.*

29c Use the appropriate case in compound structures.

When a pronoun is part of a compound subject, complement, object, or appositive, put it in the same case you would use if the pronoun were alone.

▶ When ~~him~~ *he* and Zelda were first married, they lived in New York.

▶ The boss invited ~~she~~ *her* and her family to dinner.

▶ This morning saw yet another conflict between my sister and ~~I.~~ *me.*

▶ Both panelists, Javonne and ~~me,~~ *I*, were stumped.

To decide whether to use the subjective or objective case in a compound structure, use each part of the compound alone in the sentence.

▶ Come to the park with Belinda and ~~I.~~ *me.*

> Separating the compound structure gives you *Come to the park with Belinda* and *Come to the park with me;* thus *Come to the park with Belinda and me.*

29d Use the correct case in elliptical constructions.

Elliptical constructions are those in which some words are understood but left out. When an elliptical construction ends in a pronoun, put the pronoun in the case it would be in if the construction were complete.

▶ His sister has always been more athletic than *he* [is].

In some elliptical constructions, the case of the pronoun depends on the meaning intended.

▶ Willie likes Lily more than *she* [likes Lily].

> *She* is the subject of the omitted verb *likes.*

▶ Willie likes Lily more than [he likes] *her.*

> *Her* is the object of the omitted verb *likes.*

29e Use *we* and *us* appropriately before a noun.

If you are unsure about whether to use *we* or *us* before a noun, recasting the sentence without the noun will give you the answer. Use whichever pronoun would be correct if the noun were omitted.

>   *We*
> ▶ ~~Us~~ fans never give up hope.
>   ^
> Without *fans, we* would be the subject.

>   *us*
> ▶ The Rangers depend on ~~we~~ fans.
>   ^
> Without *fans, us* would be the object of a preposition.

29f Make pronouns agree with their antecedents.

The antecedent of a pronoun is the noun or other pronoun the pronoun refers to. Pronouns and antecedents are said to agree when they match up in person, number, and gender.

SINGULAR   The *choirmaster* raised *his* baton.

PLURAL   The *boys* picked up *their* music.

Compound antecedents

Compound antecedents joined by *and* require plural pronouns.

▶ My parents and I tried to resolve *our* disagreement.

When a compound antecedent is preceded by *each* or *every,* however, it takes a singular pronoun.

▶ Every *plant* and *animal* has *its* own ecological niche.

With a compound antecedent joined by *or* or *nor,* the pronoun agrees with the nearer or nearest antecedent. If the parts of the antecedent are of different genders or persons, however, this kind of sentence can be awkward or ambiguous and may need to be revised.

▶ Neither *Annie* nor *Astrid* got *her* work done.

> AWKWARD   Neither Annie nor Barry got his work done.
> REVISED   Annie didn't get her work done, and neither did Barry.

When a compound antecedent contains both singular and plural parts, the sentence may sound awkward unless the plural part comes last.

▶ Neither the newspaper nor the radio stations would reveal *their* sources.

Collective-noun antecedents

A collective noun that refers to a single unit (*herd, team, audience*) requires a singular pronoun.

▶ The *audience* fixed *its* attention on center stage.

When such an antecedent refers to the multiple parts of a unit, however, it requires a plural pronoun.

▶ The director chose this cast because *they* had experience in the roles.

Indefinite-pronoun antecedents

Indefinite pronouns are those that do not refer to specific persons or things. Most indefinite pronouns are always singular; a few are always plural. Some can be singular or plural depending on the context.

▶ One of the ballerinas lost *her* balance.

▶ Many in the audience jumped to *their* feet.

> SINGULAR   Some of the furniture was showing *its* age.
> PLURAL   Some of the farmers abandoned *their* land.

Sexist pronouns

Indefinite pronouns often refer to antecedents that may be either male or female. Writers used to use a masculine pronoun, known as the generic *he,* to refer to such indefinite pronouns. In recent decades, however, many people have pointed out that such wording ignores or even excludes females — and thus should not be used.

Editing Out the Generic Use of He, His, or Him

Every citizen should know <u>his</u> legal rights.

Here are three ways to express the same idea without *his.*

1. Revise to make the antecedent plural.
   All citizens should know <u>their</u> legal rights.
2. Revise the sentence altogether.
   Every citizen should have some knowledge of basic legal rights.
3. Use both masculine and feminine pronouns.
   Every citizen should know <u>his</u> or <u>her</u> legal rights.

This third option, using both masculine and feminine pronouns, can be awkward, especially when repeated several times in a passage.

29g Maintain clear pronoun reference.

The antecedent of a pronoun is the word the pronoun substitutes for. If a pronoun is too far from its antecedent, readers will have trouble making the connection between the two.

Ambiguous antecedents

Readers have trouble when a pronoun can refer to more than one antecedent.

>   *Bowman*
> ▶ **The meeting between Bowman and Sonny makes ~~him~~ compare his**
>   ^
> **own unsatisfying domestic life with one that is emotionally secure.**

Who is the antecedent of *him* and *his:* Bowman or Sonny? The revision makes the reference clear by replacing a pronoun (*him*) with a noun (*Bowman*).

▶ Kerry told Ellen, ~~she~~ should be ready soon." *"I*

Reporting Kerry's words directly, in quotation marks, eliminates the ambiguity.

Vague use of it, this, that, *and* which

The words *it, this, that,* and *which* are often used as a shortcut for referring to something mentioned earlier. But such shortcuts can often cause confusion. Like other pronouns, each of these words must refer to a specific antecedent.

▶ When the senators realized the bill would be defeated, they tried to postpone the vote but failed. ~~It~~ was a fiasco. *The entire effort*

▶ Nancy just found out that she won the lottery, ~~which~~ explains her *an event that* sudden resignation from her job.

Indefinite use of you, it, *and* they

In conversation, we frequently use *you, it,* and *they* in an indefinite sense in such expressions as *you never know, in the paper, it said,* and *on television, they said.* In academic and professional writing, however, use *you* only to mean "you, the reader," and *they* or *it* only to refer to a clear antecedent.

▶ Commercials try to make ~~you~~ buy without thinking. *people*

▶ In Texas, ~~you~~ often ~~hear~~ about the influence of big oil corporations.
      one   *hears*

▶ ~~On~~ the Weather Channel, ~~it~~ reported that Hurricane Fran will hit
    T
  Virginia Beach tomorrow morning.

▶ ~~In France, they~~ allow dogs. ~~in many restaurants.~~
  Many restaurants in France

Implied antecedents

A pronoun must refer to a specific antecedent. Sometimes a possessive may *imply* a noun antecedent, but it does not serve as a clear antecedent.

▶ In ~~Welty's~~ story, ~~she~~ characterizes Bowman as a man unaware of his
    her   *Welty*
  own isolation.

30

Comma Splices and Fused Sentences

The error known as a comma splice occurs when two independent clauses are joined with only a comma. We often see comma splices in advertising, where they can give slogans a catchy rhythm.

> It's not just a job, it's an adventure.
>   –U.S. ARMY RECRUITING SLOGAN

> You add the love, they'll add the smiles!
>   –KOOL-AID ADVERTISEMENT

Another common error is a fused, or run-on, sentence, which occurs when two independent clauses are joined with no punctuation or no connecting word between them. The Army slogan as a fused sentence would be "It's not just a job it's an adventure."

You will seldom if ever profit from using comma splices or fused sentences in academic or professional writing. In fact, doing so will almost always be identified as an error. This chapter will guide you in recognizing and revising comma splices and fused sentences.

Editing for Comma Splices and Fused Sentences

Look for independent clauses—groups of words that can stand alone as a sentence—coming one after another. If you find no punctuation between two independent clauses, you have identified a fused sentence. If you find two such clauses joined only by a comma, you have identified a comma splice. Here are six methods of editing comma splices and fused sentences.

1. Separate the clauses into two sentences. (30a)

   ▶ *Education* is an elusive word*/.* ~~it~~ *It* often means different things to different people.

2. Link the clauses with a comma and a coordinating conjunction (*and, but, or, nor, for, so,* or *yet*). (30b)

   ▶ *Education* is an elusive word, *for* it often means different things to different people.

3. Link the clauses with a semicolon. (30c)

   ▶ *Education* is an elusive word*/;* it often means different things to different people.

   If the clauses are linked only with a comma and a conjunctive adverb—a word like *however, then, therefore*—add a semicolon.

   ▶ *Education* is an elusive word*/;* indeed, it often means different things to different people.

4. Recast the two clauses as one independent clause. (30d)

   ▶ *An elusive word, education*
   ~~*Education* is an elusive word, it~~ often means different things to different people.

5. Recast one independent clause as a dependent clause. (30e)

> *because*
> ▶ *Education* is an elusive word‚ it often means different
>   ∧
> things to different people.

6. In informal writing, link the clauses with a dash. (30f)

> ——
> ▶ *Education* is a slippery word‚ it often means different
>   ∧
> things to different people.

To choose among these methods, look at the sentences before and after the ones you are revising. Doing so will help you determine how a particular method will affect the rhythm of the passage. It may help to read the passage aloud to see how the revision sounds.

30a Separate the clauses into two sentences.

The simplest way to revise comma splices or fused sentences is to separate them into two sentences.

COMMA SPLICE	My mother spends long hours every spring tilling the soil and moving manure‚ this part of gardening is nauseating.
FUSED SENTENCE	My mother spends long hours every spring tilling the soil and moving manure. this part of gardening is nauseating.

If the two clauses are very short, making them two sentences may sound abrupt and terse, and some other method of revision would probably be preferable.

30b   Link the clauses with a comma and a coordinating conjunction.

If the two clauses are closely related and equally important, join them with a comma and a coordinating conjunction (*and, but, or, nor, for, so,* or *yet*).

COMMA SPLICE
and
I got up feeling bad, I feel even worse now.
                    ^

FUSED SENTENCE
but
I should pay my tuition, I need a new car.
                      ^

30c   Link the clauses with a semicolon.

If the ideas in the two clauses are closely related, and you want to give them equal emphasis, link them with a semicolon.

COMMA SPLICE
This photograph is not at all realistic/; it even uses
                                      ^
dreamlike images to convey its message.

FUSED SENTENCE
The practice of journalism is changing dramatically;
                                                  ^
advances in technology have sped up news cycles.

Be careful when you link clauses with a conjunctive adverb or a transitional phrase. You must use such words and phrases with a semicolon, with a period, or with a comma combined with a coordinating conjunction (24h).

COMMA SPLICE
Many Third World countries have very high birthrates/;
                                                    ^
therefore, most of their citizens are young.
         ^

FUSED SENTENCE
Many Third World countries have very high birthrates.
T   ^
ƒherefore, most of their citizens are young.
         ^

FUSED SENTENCE
and,
Many Third World countries have very high birthrates,
                                                    ^
therefore, most of their citizens are young.
         ^

SOME CONJUNCTIVE ADVERBS AND TRANSITIONAL PHRASES

also	in contrast	next
anyway	indeed	now
besides	in fact	otherwise
certainly	instead	similarly
finally	likewise	still
furthermore	meanwhile	then
however	moreover	therefore
in addition	namely	thus
incidentally	nevertheless	undoubtedly

For Multilingual Writers: *Judging Sentence Length*

If you speak a language that tends to use very long sentences, you may string together sentences in English in a way that results in comma-splice errors. (Arabic, Farsi, and Chinese are three such languages.) Note that in standard academic and professional English, a sentence should contain only one independent clause, *unless* the clauses are joined by a comma and a coordinating conjunction or by a semicolon. (See Chapter 63.)

30d Recast the two clauses as one independent clause.

Sometimes you can reduce two independent clauses that are spliced or fused to a single independent clause.

COMMA SPLICE
Most
A large part of my mail is advertisements, *and* most of the rest is bills.

FUSED SENTENCE
Most
A large part of my mail is advertisements *and* most of the rest is bills.

A Matter of Style: *Comma Splices*

As with almost all the choices you make in writing, considering what is appropriate for your purpose and audience will guide your use of comma splices and fused sentences. Spliced and fused sentences appear frequently in literary and journalistic writing, for, like many other structures we commonly identify as errors, each can be used to powerful effect. In the following passage, see how comma splices create momentum with a rush of details:

> Golden eagles sit in every tree and watch us watch them watch us, although there are bird experts who will tell you in all seriousness that there are NO golden eagles here. Bald eagles are common, ospreys abound, we have herons and mergansers and kingfishers, we have logging with percherons and belgians, we have park land and nature trails, we have enough oddballs, weirdos, and loons to satisfy anybody. —ANNE CAMERON

Suppose, however, that Cameron were writing this description for a college class. Then she might well decide to omit the comma splices altogether, yielding a passage like the following:

> Golden eagles sit in every tree and watch us watch them watch us, although there are bird experts who will tell you in all seriousness that there are NO golden eagles here. Bald eagles are common; ospreys abound. We have herons and mergansers and kingfishers; we have logging with percherons and belgians; we have park land and nature trails. We have enough oddballs, weirdos, and loons to satisfy anybody.

Neither of these passages is right or wrong out of context: depending on the audience, purpose, and situation, either can be appropriate and effective.

30e Recast one independent clause as a dependent clause.

When one independent clause is more important than the other, try converting the other one to a dependent clause (18b).

COMMA
SPLICE

Although
^
Zora Neale Hurston is regarded as one of America's
major novelists, she died in obscurity.

FUSED
SENTENCE

Although
^
Zora Neale Hurston is regarded as one of America's
major novelists**,** she died in obscurity.
^

In the revision, the writer chose to emphasize the second clause and to make the first one into a dependent clause by adding the subordinating conjunction *although.*

COMMA
SPLICE

, *which reacted against mass production,*
The arts and crafts movement called for handmade
^
objects**/.** ~~it reacted against mass production.~~
^

In the revision, the writer chose to emphasize the first clause, the one describing what the movement advocated, and to make the second clause, the one describing what it reacted against, into a dependent clause.

30f Link the two clauses with a dash.

In informal writing, you can use a dash to join the two clauses, especially when the second clause elaborates on the first clause.

COMMA
SPLICE

Exercise has become too much like work/ it's a bad trend.
^

31

Sentence Fragments

If you pay close attention to advertisements, you will find sentence fragments in frequent use. For example:

Our Lifetime Guarantee may come as a shock.
Or a strut. Or a muffler. Because once you pay to replace them, Toyota's Lifetime Guarantee covers parts and labor on any dealer-installed muffler, shock, or strut for as long as you own your Toyota! So if anything should ever go wrong, your Toyota dealer will fix it. *Absolutely free.*
—TOYOTA ADVERTISEMENT

The three fragments (italicized here) grab our attention, the first two by creating a play on words and the third one by emphasizing that something is absolutely free. As complete sentences, the information would be less clever and far less memorable.

As this ad illustrates, sentence fragments are groups of words that are punctuated as sentences but lack some element grammatically necessary to a sentence, usually either a subject or a verb. Though you will see fragments in literature, hear them in conversation, and see them everywhere in advertising, you will seldom, if ever, want to use them in academic or professional writing (where some readers might regard them as errors).

Editing for Sentence Fragments

A group of words must meet three criteria to form a complete sentence. If it does not meet all three, it is a fragment. Revise a fragment by combining it with a nearby sentence or by rewriting it as a complete sentence.

1. A sentence must have a subject. (24j)
2. A sentence must have a verb, not just a verbal. A verbal cannot function as a sentence's verb without an auxiliary verb. (24l)

   VERB   **The terrier** *is barking.*

   VERBAL   **The terrier** *barking.*

3. Unless it is a question, a sentence must have at least one clause that does not begin with a subordinating word. Following are some common subordinating words:

although	if	when
as	since	where
because	that	whether
before	though	who
how	unless	why

31a   Combine phrase fragments with an independent clause, or make them into sentences.

Phrases are groups of words that lack a subject, a verb, or both. When verbal phrases, prepositional phrases, noun phrases, and appositive phrases are punctuated like sentences, they become fragments. To revise these fragments, attach them to an independent clause, or make them a separate sentence.

▶ NBC is broadcasting the debates/ ~~With~~ discussions afterward.
  with

> The second word group is a prepositional phrase, not a sentence. The editing combines the phrase with an independent clause.

▶ The town's growth is controlled by zoning laws/, ~~A~~ strict set of regulations for builders and corporations.
  a

> *A strict set of regulations for builders and corporations* is an appositive phrase renaming the noun *zoning laws*. The editing attaches the fragment to the sentence containing the noun to which the appositive refers.

▶ Vivian stayed out of school for three months after Linda was born.
  She did so to
  ~~To~~ recuperate and to take care of her.

> *To recuperate and to take care of her* includes verbals, not verbs. The revision— adding a subject (*she*) and a verb (*did*)—turns the fragment into a separate sentence.

Fragments beginning with transitions

Transitional expressions sometimes lead to fragments. If you introduce an example or explanation with one of the following transitions, be certain you write a sentence, not a fragment.

again	but	like
also	finally	or
and	for example	specifically
as a result	for instance	such as
besides	instead	that is

▶ Joan Didion has written on many subjects/, ~~Such~~ as the Hoover Dam and migraine headaches.
  such

> The second word group is a phrase, not a sentence. The editing combines it with an independent clause.

31b Combine compound-predicate fragments with independent clauses.

A compound predicate consists of two or more verbs, along with their modifiers and objects, that have the same subject. Fragments occur when one part of a compound predicate is punctuated as a separate sentence although it lacks a subject. These fragments usually begin with *and, but,* or *or.* You can revise them by attaching them to the independent clause that contains the rest of the predicate.

> They sold their house/ ~~A~~nd moved into an apartment.

(edit mark: lowercase "a" above the capital A)

31c Combine dependent-clause fragments with independent clauses, or delete opening words.

Dependent clauses contain both a subject and a verb, but they cannot stand alone as sentences; they depend on an independent clause to complete their meaning. Dependent clauses usually begin with words

---

A Matter of Style: *Fragments*

We often find sentence fragments in narrative writing, where they call up the rhythms of speech. For example:

> On Sundays, for religion, we went up on the hill. Skipping along the hexagon-shaped tile in Colonial Park. Darting up the steps to Edgecomb Avenue. Stopping in the candy store on St. Nicholas to load up. Leaning forward for leverage to finish the climb up to the church. I was always impressed by this particular house of the Lord.
> —KEITH GILYARD, *Voices of the Self*

Here Gilyard uses fragments to move the narrative—and the reader—up the hill. He could have strung the fragments together into one long sentence, but the series of fragments (as well as the parallelism of *skipping, darting, stopping,* and *leaning*) is more effective: he creates a rhythm and a sense of movement that take us as readers to the "house of the Lord."

such as *after, because, before, if, since, though, unless, until, when, where, while, who, which,* and *that.* You can usually combine dependent-clause fragments with a nearby independent clause.

▶ When I decided to work part-time/, I gave up some earning potential.
　　　　　　　　　　　　　　　　　^

If you cannot smoothly attach a clause to a nearby independent clause, try deleting the opening subordinating word and turning the dependent clause into a sentence.

　　　　　　　　　　　　　　　　　　　　A
▶ Injuries in automobile accidents occur in two ways. ~~When~~ ⁄an occupant

either is hurt by something inside the car or is thrown from the car.

32

Writing to the World

When Marshall McLuhan referred to the world as a global village in 1967, the phrase seemed unfamiliar and highly exaggerated. A little more than thirty years later, his words are practically a cliché, part of our everyday language. People today can communicate, often instantaneously via the Internet, across vast distances and cultures. With speed and ease once unimaginable, businesspeople complete multinational transactions, students take classes at distant universities via the Web, and grandmothers check in with family members across four or five—or six—time zones.

In a time of such instantaneous communication, you might find yourself writing to (or with) students throughout the country, or even across the globe—and you may well be in classes with people from other cultures, language groups, and countries. In business, government, and education, writers increasingly operate on an international stage. As the CEO of Tupperware International recently told a group of new business graduates, "If you want to move into management in this company, you will need knowledge of at least several languages and cultures." Such situations call upon us to think hard about how to write to the world, how to become what might be called *world writers*, able to communicate across cultures.

Editing to Communicate across Cultures

- Recognize what you consider "normal." Examine your own customary behaviors and assumptions, and think about how they may affect what you think and say (and write). (32a)

- When speaking with someone from another culture, listen carefully for meaning. Ask for clarification if need be. (32b)

- Consider your own authority as a writer. Should you sound like an expert? a subordinate? something else? (32c)

- Think about your audience's expectations. How explicit does your writing need to be? (32d)

- What kind of evidence will count most with your audience? (32e)

- Organize your writing with your audience's expectations in mind. (32f)

- If in doubt, use formal style. (32g)

32a Think about what you consider "normal."

How do you decide what is "normal" in a given situation? More than likely, your judgment is based on assumptions you are not even aware of. But remember: behavior that is considered out of place in one community may appear perfectly normal in another. If you want to communicate with people across cultures, you need to try to learn something about the norms in those cultures and, even more important, to be aware of the norms that guide your own behavior.

- Be aware of the values and assumptions that guide your own customary ways of communicating. Remember that most of us tend to see our own way as the "normal" or right way to do things. Examine your own assumptions and become aware of the ways they guide your thinking and behavior. Keep in mind that if your ways seem inherently right, then—even without thinking about it—you may assume that other ways are somehow less than right.

- Know that most ways of communicating are influenced by cultural contexts and that they differ widely from one culture to the next.

- Pay close attention to the ways that people from cultures other than your own communicate, and be flexible and open to their ways.

- Pay attention to and respect the differences among individual people *within* a given culture. Do not assume that all members of a community behave in just the same way or value exactly the same things.

Don't overgeneralize. Even though it's true, for example, that Americans drink millions of gallons of Coca-Cola a year, it is a mistake to think that all Americans drink Coca-Cola. In the same way, knowing that empathy is a more important method of persuasion than explicit criticism for some Asians does not mean this cultural pattern holds true for all Asians. If you have read Amy Tan's books about her life in a Chinese household, you will remember the spirited arguments that took place (though it seems that such arguments occurred only in the home rather than in public). In the final analysis, people argue in every culture, but they do so in very different ways. As a world writer, you need to be aware of and sensitive to differences within—as well as across—cultures.

32b Listen for meaning.

Listening may be the most underrated communicative art of our time. Certainly, it is seldom taught in U.S. schools. A conversation heard recently suggests how important careful listening is to effective communication. Two students at a writing center were talking about comments their professor had written on their essays. "He keeps telling me to try for more originality!" said one student from the Philippines in exasperation. "I wonder what he really means by 'originality'?" said the other, who was from Massachusetts. In fact, the students came up with two very different definitions of this seemingly simple word. For the Filipina student, "originality" meant going back to the original, whatever it was, and understanding it as thoroughly as possible—and then relating that understanding in her essay. In contrast, the student from Massachusetts understood "originality" to be something she came up with herself, an idea she had on her own. As it turned out, the professor, who was from France, had a third definition: for him, "originality" meant the students were to read multiple sources and then come up with a critical point of their own about those sources. The students listened and then talked about what this all meant. The professor listened, too, and designed a handout for the class providing his own definition of "originality" and giving examples of student work he considered to be "original" along with an explanation of why he judged them to be so.

This brief example points to the challenges all writers face in trying to communicate across space, across languages, across cultures. While there are no foolproof rules, here are some tips for communicating with people from cultures other than your own:

- Don't hesitate to ask people to explain or even repeat a point if you're not absolutely sure you understand.
- Take care to be explicit about what you mean.
- Invite response—ask whether you're making yourself clear. This kind of back-and-forth is particularly easy (and necessary) in email.

32c Consider your own authority as a writer.

How should you sound to your readers—like an expert? a beginner? a subordinate? an angry employee or customer? a boss? The answer often depends on how much authority you as a writer have and how that authority relates to others. In the United States, students are often asked to establish authority in their writing—by drawing on certain kinds of personal experience, by reporting on research they or others have conducted, or by taking a position for which they can offer strong evidence and support. But this expectation about writerly authority is by no means universal. Indeed, some cultures position student writers as novices whose job is to reflect what they learn from their teachers—those who hold the most important knowledge, wisdom, and, hence, authority. One Japanese student, for example, said he was taught that it's rude to challenge a teacher: "Are you ever so smart that you should challenge the wisdom of the ages?"

As this student's comment reveals, a writer's tone also depends on his or her relationship with listeners and readers. In this student's case, the valued relationship is one of respect and deference, of what one Indonesian student called "good modesty." Similarly, a Navajo writer explained that he is extremely hesitant to disagree with or criticize a woman who is his elder: in his matriarchal community, he is expected to honor such elders. As a world writer, you need to remember that those you're addressing may hold very different attitudes about authority.

- Whom are you addressing, and what is your relationship to him or her?
- What knowledge are you expected to have? Is it appropriate for or expected of you to demonstrate that knowledge—and if so, how?
- What is your goal—to answer a question? to make a point? to agree? something else?
- What tone is appropriate? If in doubt, show respect: politeness is rarely if ever inappropriate.

32d Consider your responsibility to your audience.

In the United States, many audiences (and especially those in the academic and business worlds) expect a writer to "get to the point" as directly as possible and to take on the major responsibility of articulating that point efficiently and unambiguously. But not all audiences have such expectations. A Chinese student, for instance, who was considered a very good writer in China, found herself struggling in her American classes. Her problem was not with grammar or word choice or sentence structure; she was very proficient in all these. But comments by teachers left her confused: her writing, U.S. teachers said, was "vague" and "indirect," with too much "beating around the bush." As it turned out, this kind of indirectness and subtlety was prized by her teachers in China, where readers and writers are expected to have more shared knowledge—and readers are thus expected to be able to "read between the lines" to understand what is being said.

The point of this story (and note how swiftly that point is made!) is that world writers must think carefully about whether audience members expect the writer to make the meaning of a text explicitly clear or, rather, expect to do some of the work themselves, supplying some of the information necessary to the meaning. A typical BBC news report, for example, provides an example of a writer-responsible text, one that puts the overwhelming responsibility on the writer to present an unambiguous message. Such a report begins with a clear overview of all the points to be covered, follows with a discussion of each of the major points in order, and ends with a brief summary. Many cultures organize information in a different, more reader-responsible, way, expecting that the audience will take more responsibility for understanding what is being said. Here are tips for thinking about reader and writer responsibility.

- What general knowledge do members of your audience have about your topic? What information do they expect—or need—you to provide?

- Does your audience tend to be very direct, saying explicitly what they mean? Or are they more subtle, less likely to call a spade a spade? Look for cues to determine how much responsibility you have as the writer.

32e Consider what counts as evidence.

How do you decide what evidence will best support your ideas? The answer depends, in large part, on how you define *evidence*. Americans generally give great weight to factual evidence. In doing research at a U.S. university, a Chinese student reports she was told time and time again by her instructors that "facts, and facts alone, provide the sure route to truth." While she learned to document her work in ways her U.S. professors found persuasive, she also continued to value the kinds of evidence favored back home, especially those based on authority and on allusion.

Differing concepts of what counts as evidence can lead to arguments that go nowhere. One well-known example of such a failed argument occurred in 1979, when Oriana Fallaci, an Italian journalist, was interviewing the Ayatollah Khomeini. Fallaci argued in a way common in North American and Western European cultures: she presented what she considered strong assertions backed up with facts ("Iran denies freedom to people. . . . Many people we can name have been put in prison and even executed, just for speaking out in opposition"). In his response, Khomeini relied on very different kinds of evidence: analogies ("Just as a finger with gangrene should be cut off so that it will not destroy the whole body, so should people who corrupt others be pulled out like weeds so they will not infect the whole field") and, above all, the authority of the Qur'an. Partly because of these differing beliefs about what counts as evidence, the interview ended in a shouting match, leading not to understanding but to ongoing and serious misunderstanding.

Two lessons every writer can learn from such examples of failed communication are to think carefully about how he or she uses evidence in writing and to pay attention to what counts as evidence to members of other cultures.

- Do you rely on facts? concrete examples? firsthand experience?
- Do you include the testimony of experts? Which experts are valued most, and why?
- Do you cite religious or philosophical texts? proverbs or everyday wisdom? other sources?
- Do you use analogies as support? How much do they count?
- Once you determine what counts as evidence in your own thinking and writing, think about where you learned to use and value this kind of evidence. You can ask these same questions about the use of evidence by members of other cultures.

32f Consider organization.

As you make choices about how to organize your writing, remember that cultural influences are at work here as well: the patterns that you find pleasing are likely to be ones that are deeply embedded in your own culture. The organizational patterns favored by U.S. engineers, for example, hold many similarities to the organizational system recommended by Cicero some two thousand years ago. Indeed, the predominant pattern, highly explicit and leaving little or nothing unsaid or unexplained, is probably familiar to most U.S. students: introduction and thesis, necessary background, overview of the parts to follow, systematic presentation of evidence, consideration of other viewpoints, and conclusion. If a piece of writing follows this pattern, Anglo-American readers ordinarily find it "well organized" or "coherent," and they have been doing so for a very long time.

But writers who value different organizational patterns may not. To some, the writing done by U.S. engineers may seem overly simple. One writer from Chile, for instance, reports that this pattern of writing can even seem childish to those in her country, saying it's like " 'This is a watch; the watch is brown; da-da; da-da.' For us, that's funny. I think that, for Americans, it must be funny the way I describe things." Indeed, this writer is accustomed to writing that is more elaborate, that sometimes digresses from the main point, and that is elliptical, not spelling out every connection from point A to point B.

Cultures that value indirection and subtlety tend to use patterns of organization that display these values. One common pattern in Korean writing, for example, includes an introduction; a topic with development; a tangential topic, again with development; and then a conclusion—with the thesis appearing only at the end.

Some cultures value repetition. It is common for some Arabic speakers, for example, to reiterate a major point from several different perspectives as a way of making that point.

When writing for world audiences, think about how you can organize material to get your message across effectively. One expert in international business communication recommends, for example, that businesspeople writing to others in Japan should state their requests indirectly—and only after a formal and respectful opening. There are no hard and fast rules to help you organize your writing for effectiveness across cultures, but here are a couple of things for you to consider.

- Determine when to state your thesis—at the beginning? at the end? somewhere else? not at all?

- Consider whether digressions are a good idea, a requirement, or best avoided with your intended audience.

32g Consider style.

As with beauty, good style is most definitely in the eye of the beholder—and thus is always affected by language, culture, and rhetorical tradition. In fact, what constitutes effective style varies broadly across cultures, and depends on the rhetorical situation—purpose, audience, and so on. (See Chapter 4.) Even so, there is one important style question to consider when writing across cultures: what level of formality is most appropriate? In the United States, a fairly informal style is often acceptable, even appreciated. Many cultures, however, tend to value more formality. When in doubt, therefore, it may be wise to err on the side of formality, especially in writing to elders or to those in authority.

- Be careful to use proper titles:

  Dr. Beverly Moss   Professor Jaime Mejia

- Avoid slang and informal structures such as fragments.

- Do not use first names in correspondence (even in email) unless invited to do so. Note, however, that an invitation to use a first name could come indirectly; if someone signs an email message or letter to you with his or her first name, you are implicitly invited to do the same.

- For international business email, use complete sentences and words; avoid contractions. Open with the salutation "Dear Mr./Ms. _____." Write dates by listing the day before the month and spelling out the name of the month rather than using a numeral (*7 June 2000*).

Beyond formality, stylistic preferences vary widely. Many writers of Spanish, for example, show a preference for longer sentences than those written by English-speaking writers. Writers of Spanish also use more complex sentences and ornate language (which members of some cultures might find overdone or flowery—and others might find understated!). Japanese writing tends to be very polite and diplomatic, perhaps because the Japanese language has three forms—the honorific, the polite, and the everyday.

Other languages bring other stylistic differences. World writers take nothing about language for granted. To be an effective world writer, you will want to work to recognize and respect those differences as you move from culture to culture.

33
Using Language to Build Common Ground

As a child, you may have learned to "do to others what you would have them do to you." To that golden rule, we could add, "Say to others what you would have them say to you." For the language we use has power: it can praise, delight, inspire—and also hurt, offend, or even destroy. Language that offends breaks the golden rule of language use, preventing others from identifying with you and thus damaging your credibility as a writer.

Few absolute guidelines exist for using language that respects differences and builds common ground. Two rules, however, can help:

consider carefully the sensitivities and preferences of others, and watch for words that carry stereotypes and betray assumptions not directly stated.

Editing for Language That Builds Common Ground

- What unstated assumptions might come between you and your readers? Look, for instance, for language implying approval or disapproval and for the ways you use *we, you,* and *they.* (33a)
- Does your language carry offensive stereotypes or connotations? (33a)
- Have you eliminated potentially sexist language? (33b)
- Are your references to race, religion, gender, sexual orientation, and so on relevant or necessary to your discussion? If not, consider leaving them out. (33c, d)
- Are the terms you use to refer to groups accurate and acceptable? (33c, d)

33a Watch for stereotypes and other assumptions.

Children like to play; U.S. citizens value freedom; people who do not finish high school fare less well in the job market than those who graduate. These broad statements contain stereotypes—standardized or fixed ideas about a group.

Stereotyping becomes especially evident in the words we choose to refer to others. Stereotyped language can break the links between writers and readers—or between speakers and listeners.

Because stereotypes are often based on half-truths, misunderstandings, and hand-me-down prejudices, they can lead to bias, bigotry, and intolerance. Even positive or neutral stereotypes can hurt, for they inevitably ignore the uniqueness of an individual. Careful writers will want to make sure that language doesn't stereotype any group *or* individual.

Other kinds of unstated assumptions that enter into thinking and writing can destroy common ground by ignoring differences between others and ourselves. For example, a student in a religion seminar who uses *we* to refer to Christians and *they* to refer to members of other religions had better be sure that everyone in the class is Christian, or some of them may feel left out of the discussion.

A Matter of Style: *Online Etiquette*

In online exchanges, help build common ground by putting yourself in your readers' shoes: how will they interpret your message? Might they interpret it as a flame, an attack of some kind? Remember that online readers don't have your facial expression or gestures to help them know if you are teasing. On the other hand, if you feel you have been flamed, try never to respond in kind: what you think is a flame may not have been intended as one at all.

Sometimes stereotypes even lead writers to call special attention to a group affiliation when it is not relevant to the point, as in *a woman bus driver* or *a Jewish doctor.* Nevertheless, deciding whether to describe an individual as a member of a group is often difficult. The following sections invite you to think about how your language can build—rather than destroy—common ground.

33b   Consider assumptions about gender.

Powerful and often invisible gender-related elements of language affect our thinking and our behavior. At one time, for instance, speakers always labeled a woman who worked as a doctor a *woman doctor* or any man who worked as a nurse a *male nurse,* as if to say, "they're exceptions." Equally problematic was the traditional use of *man* and *mankind* to refer to people of both sexes and the use of *he, him, his,* and *himself* to refer to people of unknown sex. Because such usage ignores half the human race, it hardly helps a writer build common ground.

Sexist language, those words and phrases that stereotype or ignore members of either sex or that unnecessarily call attention to gender, can usually be revised fairly easily. There are several alternatives to using masculine pronouns to refer to persons of unknown sex. One option is to recast the sentence using plural forms.

> *Lawyers*   *they*
> ▶ ~~A lawyer~~ must pass the bar exam before ~~he~~ can begin to practice.
>   ^   ^

Another option is to substitute pairs of pronouns such as *he or she, him or her,* and so on.

>   *or she*
> ▶ A lawyer must pass the bar exam before he can begin to practice.
>   ^

> ### Editing for Sexist Language
>
> * Have you used *man* or *men* or words containing one of them to refer to people who may be female? If so, consider substituting another word—instead of *fireman,* for instance, try *firefighter.*
> * If you have mentioned someone's gender, is it necessary to do so? If you identify someone as a female architect, for example, do you (or would you) refer to someone else as a *male architect*? Unless gender and related matters—looks, clothes, parenthood—are relevant to your point, leave them unmentioned.
> * Do you use any occupational stereotypes? Watch for the use of female pronouns for nurses and male ones for engineers, for example.
> * Do you use language that patronizes either sex? Do you refer to a wife as *the little woman,* for instance, or to a husband as *her old man*?
> * Have you used *he, him, his,* or *himself* to refer to people who may be female?
> * Have you overused *he and she, him and her,* and so on? Frequent use of these pronoun pairs can irritate readers.

Yet another way to revise the sentence is to eliminate the pronouns.

> ► A lawyer must pass the bar exam before ~~he can begin~~ *beginning* to practice.

INSTEAD OF	TRY USING
anchorman, anchorwoman	anchor
businessman	businessperson, business executive
chairman, chairwoman	chair, chairperson
congressman	member of Congress, representative
mailman	mail carrier
male nurse	nurse
man, mankind	humans, human beings, humanity, the human race, humankind
manpower	workers, personnel
mothering	parenting
policeman, policewoman	police officer
salesman	salesperson, sales associate
woman engineer	engineer

33c Consider assumptions about race and ethnicity.

As we all know, generalizations about racial and ethnic groups can result in especially harmful stereotyping. Such assumptions underlie statements that suggest, for instance, that all Asian Americans excel in math and science or that all Germans are efficient. In building common ground, writers must watch for any language that ignores differences not only among individual members of a race or ethnic group but also among subgroups. Writers must be aware, for instance, of the many nations to which American Indians belong and of the diverse places from which Americans of Spanish-speaking ancestry have emigrated.

Preferred terms

Identifying preferred terms is sometimes not an easy task, for they can change often and even vary widely.

The word *colored,* for example, was once widely used in the United States to refer to Americans of African ancestry. By the 1950s, the preferred term had become *Negro;* in the 1960s, however, *black* came to be preferred by most, though certainly not all, members of that community. Then, in the late 1980s, some leaders of the American black community urged that *black* be replaced by *African American.*

The word *Oriental,* once used to refer to people of East Asian descent, is now often considered offensive. At the University of California at Berkeley, the Oriental Languages Department is now known as the East Asian Languages Department. One advocate of the change explained that *Oriental* is appropriate for objects like rugs but not for people.

Once widely preferred, the term *Native American* is being challenged by those who argue that the most appropriate way to refer to indigenous people is by the specific name of the tribe or pueblo, such as *Chippewa, Crow,* or *Dine.* In Alaska and parts of Canada, many indigenous peoples once referred to as *Eskimos* now prefer *Inuit,* or a specific term such as *Tlinget, Haida,* or *Tsimshian.* If you do not know a specific term, it's probably wise to use the term *American Indian* or *Indigenous Peoples.*

Among Americans of Spanish-speaking descent, the preferred terms are many: *Chicano/Chicana, Hispanic, Latin American, Latino/Latina, Mexican American, Dominican,* and *Puerto Rican,* to name but a few.

Clearly, then, ethnic terminology changes often enough to challenge even the most careful writers. The best advice may be to consider your words carefully, to *listen* for the way members of groups refer to themselves (or *ask* them their preferences), and to check any term you're unsure of in a current dictionary.

33d Consider other kinds of difference.

Age

Mention age if it is relevant, but be aware that age-related terms can carry derogatory connotations (*matronly, well-preserved,* and so on). Describing Mr. Fry as *elderly but still active* may sound polite to you, but chances are Mr. Fry would prefer being called *an active seventy-eight-year-old*—or just *a seventy-eight-year-old,* which eliminates the unstated assumption of surprise that he is active at his age.

Class

Take special care to examine your words for stereotypes or assumptions about class. As a writer, you should not assume that all your readers share your background or values—that the members of your audience are all homeowners, for instance. And avoid using any words—*redneck, blue blood,* and the like—that might alienate members of an audience.

Geographical areas

Stereotypes about geographical areas are very often clichéd and exaggerated. New Englanders are not all thrifty and tight-lipped; Florida offers more than retirement and tourism; midwesterners are not all hardworking; not all Californians care about the latest trends. Be careful not to make these kinds of simplistic assumptions.

Check also that you use geographical terms accurately.

AMERICA, AMERICAN Although many people use these words to refer to the United States *alone,* such usage will not necessarily be acceptable to people from Canada, Mexico, and Central or South America.

BRITISH, ENGLISH Use *British* to refer to the island of Great Britain, which includes England, Scotland, and Wales, or to the United Kingdom of Great Britain and Northern Ireland. In general, do not use *English* for these broader senses.

ARAB This term refers only to people of Arabic-speaking descent. Note that Iran is not an Arab nation; its people speak Farsi, not Arabic. Note also that *Arab* is not synonymous with *Muslim* or *Moslem* (a believer in Islam). Most (but not all) Arabs are Muslim, but many Muslims (those in Pakistan, for example) are not Arab.

Physical ability or health

When writing about a person with a serious illness or physical disability, ask yourself whether mentioning the disability is relevant to your discussion and whether the words you use carry negative connotations. You might choose, for example, to say someone *uses* a wheelchair rather than to say he or she *is confined to* one. Similarly, you might note a subtle but meaningful difference in calling someone a *person with AIDS* rather than an *AIDS victim*. Mentioning the person first and the disability second, such as referring to a *child with diabetes* rather than a *diabetic child* or a *diabetic,* is always a good idea.

Religion

Religious stereotypes are very often inaccurate and unfair. For example, Roman Catholics hold a wide spectrum of views on abortion, Muslim women do not all wear veils, and many Baptists are not fundamentalists. In fact, many people do not believe in or practice a religion at all, so be careful of such assumptions. As in other cases, do not use religious labels without considering their relevance to your point.

Sexual orientation

Writers who wish to build common ground should not assume that readers all share one sexual orientation. As with any label, reference to sexual orientation should be governed by context. Someone writing about Representative Barney Frank's economic views would probably have little if any reason to refer to his sexual orientation. On the other hand, someone writing about diversity in U.S. government might find it important to note that Frank is a representative who has made his homosexuality public.

34
Language Variety

English comes in many varieties that differ from one another in pronunciation, vocabulary, rhetoric, and grammar. Whether you order a hero, a poor boy, a hoagie, a submarine, a grinder, or a *cubano* reflects such differences. In addition to numerous varieties of English, many other languages are spoken in the United States. This chapter focuses on how you can appropriately use different dialects of English and different languages.

> ### Editing for Language Variety
>
> You can use different varieties of language to good effect for the following purposes:
> - to repeat someone's exact words
> - to evoke a person, place, or activity
> - to establish your credibility and build common ground
> - to make a strong point
> - to get your audience's attention

34a Standard varieties of English

One variety of English, often referred to as the "standard," is that taught prescriptively in schools, represented in this and all other textbooks, used in the national media, and written and spoken widely by those wielding the most social and economic power. As the language used in business and most public institutions, standard English is a variety you will want to be completely familiar with. Standard English, however, is only one of many effective varieties of English and itself varies according to purpose and audience, from the very formal style used in academic writing to the informal style characteristic of casual conversation.

34b Ethnic varieties of English

Whether you are a Native American or trace your ancestry to Europe, Asia, Africa, Latin America, or elsewhere, you have an ethnic heritage that probably lives on in the English language. See how one Hawaiian writer uses an ethnic variety of English to paint a picture of young teens hearing a scary "chicken skin" story about sharks told by their grandmother.

"—So, rather dan being rid of da shark, da people were stuck with many little ones, for dere mistake."

Then Grandma Wong wen' pause, for dramatic effect, I guess, and she wen' add, "Dis is one of dose times. . . . Da time of da sharks."

Those words ended another of Grandma's chicken skin stories. The stories she told us had been passed on to her by her grandmother, who had heard them from her grandmother. Always skipping a generation.

–RODNEY MORALES, "When the Shark Bites"

Notice how the narrator uses both standard and ethnic varieties of English—presenting information necessary to the story line mostly in standard English and using a local, ethnic variety to represent spoken language, which helps us hear the characters talk.

Zora Neale Hurston often mixes African American vernacular (sometimes referred to as Ebonics) with standard English:

My grandmother worried about my forward ways a great deal. She had known slavery and to her my brazenness was unthinkable.

"Git down offa dat gate-post! You li'l sow, you! Git down! Setting up dere looking dem white folks right in de face! They's gowine to lynch you, yet. And don't stand in dat doorway gazing out at 'em neither. Youse too brazen to live long."

Nevertheless, I kept right on gazing at them, and "going a piece of the way" whenever I could make it.

–ZORA NEALE HURSTON, *Dust Tracks on a Road*

In each of these examples, one important reason for the shift from standard English is to demonstrate that the writer is a member of the community whose language he or she is representing and thus to build credibility with others in the community.

Take care, however, in using the language of communities other than your own. When used inappropriately, such language can have an opposite effect, perhaps destroying credibility and alienating your audience.

34c Occupational varieties of English

From the fast-food business to taxi driving, from architecture to zoology, every job has its own special variety of English. Examples abound, from specialized words (*hermeneutics* in literary studies) to invented words (*quark* in physics). Here is an example from the computer world about a problem plaguing the World Wide Web.

Right now, even if you're using a fully stocked Pentium and have a T1 line running into your bedroom, the Web can seem overloaded and painfully slow. Conventional wisdom says the solution lies in new network technologies like ATM and fiber optics. But researchers are investigating how to change the way computers communicate to minimize pauses, stutters, and false starts. After all, using the Internet isn't just a matter of shouting, "Hey, hotwired.com, shoot me that GIF!"   —STEVE G. STEINBERG, *Wired*

The columnist writing here uses technical abbreviations (*T1*) and acronyms (*ATM, GIF*) as well as ordinary words that have special meanings (*pauses, stutters*). He also uses a quotation to capture the sound and rhythm of speech and to help make his point: the Internet is governed by specific rules that can speed up—or slow down—communication.

34d Regional varieties of English

Using regional language is an effective way to evoke a character or place. Look at the following piece of dialogue from an essay about Vermont:

"There'll be some fine music on the green tonight, don't ya know?"
"Well, I sure do want to go."
"So don't I!"

Here the regional English creates a homespun effect and captures some of the language used in a particular place.

See how an anthropologist weaves together regional and standard academic English in writing about one Carolina community.

For Roadville, schooling is something most folks have not gotten enough of, but everybody believes will do something toward helping an individual "get on." In the words of one oldtime resident, "Folks that ain't got no schooling don't get to be nobody nowadays."
    —SHIRLEY BRICE HEATH, *Ways with Words*

Notice that the researcher takes care to let a resident of Roadville speak her mind—and in her own words.

34e Bringing in other languages

You might use a language other than English for the same reasons you might use different varieties of English: to represent the actual words of a speaker, to make a point, to connect with your audience, or to get

> **For Multilingual Writers:** *Global English*
>
> English is used in many countries around the world, resulting in many global varieties. You may, for example, have learned a British variety. British English differs somewhat from U.S. English in certain vocabulary (*bonnet* for *hood* of a car), syntax (*to hospital* rather than *to the hospital*), spelling (*centre* rather than *center*), and, of course, pronunciation. If you have learned a British variety of English, you will want to recognize the ways in which it differs from the U.S. standard.

their attention. See how Gerald Haslam uses Spanish to capture his great-grandmother's words and to make a point about his relationship to her.

> *"Expectoran su sangre!"* exclaimed Great-grandma when I showed her the small horned toad I had removed from my breast pocket. I turned toward my mother, who translated: "They spit blood."
>
> *"De los ojos,"* Grandma added. "From their eyes," mother explained, herself uncomfortable in the presence of the small beast.
>
> I grinned, "Awwwwwww."
>
> But my Great-grandmother did not smile. *"Son muy toxicos,"* she nodded with finality. Mother moved back an involuntary step, her hands suddenly busy at her breast. "Put that thing down," she ordered.
>
> "His name's John," I said.
>
> —GERALD HASLAM, *California Childhood*

35

Using Appropriate and Precise Language

One restaurant's *down-home beef stew with spuds* may be similar to another restaurant's *boeuf bourguignon with butter-creamed potatoes*. Both describe beef dishes, but in each case the language aims to say something about how the beef is prepared as well as something about the restaurant serving it. This chapter will help you choose words that are clear and appropriate for your purpose, topic, and audience.

> **Editing to Make Your Language Appropriate and Precise**
>
> • Check to see that your language reflects the appropriate level of formality and courtesy for your audience, purpose, and topic. If you use slang or colloquial language (such as *yeah*), is it appropriate? (35a)
>
> • Check to be sure your audience will understand any necessary jargon or technical language. If not, either define the jargon, or replace it with words that will be understood. (35a)
>
> • Consider the connotations of words carefully. If you say someone is *pushy*, be sure you mean to be critical; otherwise, use a word like *assertive*. (35b)
>
> • Be sure to use both general and specific words. If you are writing about the general category of beds, for example, do you give enough concrete detail (*an antique four-poster bed*)? (35c)
>
> • Look for clichés. Are they effective or stale? If the latter, try to replace them with fresher language. (35d)

35a Use the appropriate level of formality.

You need to choose a level of formality that matches your audience and purpose. In an email or letter to a friend or close associate, informal language is often appropriate. For most academic and professional writing, however, more formal language is appropriate, since you are addressing people you do not know well. Compare the following responses to a request for information about a job candidate:

EMAIL TO SOMEONE YOU KNOW WELL

Myisha is great—hire her if you can!

LETTER OF RECOMMENDATION TO SOMEONE YOU DO NOT KNOW

I am pleased to recommend Myisha Fisher. She will bring good ideas and extraordinary energy to your organization.

Slang and colloquial language

Slang, or extremely informal language, is often confined to a relatively small group and usually becomes obsolete rather quickly, though some slang gains wide use (*yuppie, bummer*). Colloquial language, such as

A Matter of Style: *Online Jargon*

Frequently used terms such as *asynchronous communication* and *email* are examples of the jargon online writers should know. Other terms, like the jargon in this sentence — "Savvy wavelet compression is the fiber signpost of the virtual chillout room" — may be appropriate for techies talking to one another, but they are not useful to those trying to communicate with a nontechnical or general audience. Before you use technical online jargon, remember your readers: if they will not understand the terms, or if you don't know your audience well enough to judge, then say what you need to say in everyday language.

a lot, in a bind, or *snooze,* is less informal, more widely used, and longer lasting than most slang.

Writers who use slang and colloquial language run the risk of not being understood or of not being taken seriously. If you are writing for a general audience about arms-control negotiations, for example, and you use the term *nukes* to refer to nuclear missiles, some readers may not know what you mean, and others may be irritated by what they see as a frivolous reference to a deadly serious subject.

Jargon

Jargon is the special vocabulary of — or special meanings given to common words by members of — a trade, profession, or field. Reserve technical language as much as possible for an audience that will understand your terms, and replace or define terms that they will not.

Jargon can be useful for technical audiences. But sometimes writers use words in an attempt to sound expert, and these puffed-up words can easily backfire.

INSTEAD OF	TRY USING
ascertain	find out
commence	begin
factor	cause
finalize	finish or complete

INSTEAD OF	TRY USING
functionality	function
impact (as verb)	affect
methodology	method
operationalize	start, put into operation
optimal	best
parameters	boundaries
peruse	look at
prioritize	rank
ramp up	increase
utilize	use

Pompous language, euphemisms, and doublespeak

Stuffy or pompous language is unnecessarily formal for the purpose, audience, or topic. Hence, it often gives writing an insincere or unintentionally humorous tone, making a writer's ideas seem insignificant or even unbelievable.

POMPOUS

Pursuant to the August 9 memorandum regarding petroleum supply exigencies, it is incumbent upon us to endeavor to make maximal utilization of telephonic communication in lieu of personal visitation.

REVISED

As of August 9, petroleum shortages require us to use the telephone whenever possible rather than make personal visits.

Euphemisms are words and phrases that make unpleasant ideas seem less harsh. *Your position is being eliminated* seeks to soften the blow

For Multilingual Writers: *Avoiding Fancy Diction*

In writing standard academic English, which is fairly formal, you may be inclined to use the biggest and newest words that you know in English. Though your intention is good—to put new words to good use—resist the temptation to use flowery or high-flown diction in your college writing. Academic writing calls first of all for clear, concise prose.

of being fired or laid off. Other euphemisms include *pass on* for *die* and *sanitation engineer* for *garbage collector*. Although euphemisms can sometimes appeal to an audience by showing that you are considerate of people's feelings, they can also sound insincere or evasive.

Doublespeak, a word coined from the *Newspeak* and *doublethink* of George Orwell's novel *1984*, is language used to hide or distort the truth. During massive layoffs and cutbacks in the business world, companies speak of firings as *work reengineering, employee repositioning, proactive downsizing, deverticalization, smartsizing,* and *special reprogramming*. The public—and particularly those who lose their jobs—recognize these terms as doublespeak.

35b Be alert to a word's denotation and connotation.

Denotation signals the general, or dictionary, meaning of a word, connotation the associations that accompany the word. The words *maxim, epigram, proverb, saw, saying,* and *motto* all carry roughly the same denotation. Because of their different connotations, however, *proverb* would be the appropriate word to use in reference to a saying from the Bible, *saw* in reference to the kind of wisdom handed down anonymously, *epigram* in reference to a witty statement by someone like Dave Barry.

Note the differences in connotation among the following three statements:

▶ Students Against Racism erected a barrier on the campus oval, saying it symbolizes "the many barriers to those discriminated against by university policies."

▶ Left-wing agitators threw up an eyesore right on the oval to try to stampede the university into giving in to their demands.

▶ Supporters of human rights challenged the university's investment in racism by erecting a protest barrier on campus.

The first statement is the most neutral, merely stating facts (and quoting the assertion about university policy to represent it as someone's words rather than as facts); the second, by using words with negative connotations (*agitators, eyesore, stampede*), is strongly critical; the third, by using words with positive connotations (*supporters of human rights*) and presenting assertions as facts (*the university's investment in racism*), gives a favorable slant to the story.

35c Balance general and specific diction.

Effective writers balance general words (those that name groups or classes) with specific words (those that identify individual and particular things). Abstractions, which are types of general words, refer to things we cannot perceive through our five senses. Specific words are often concrete, naming things we can see, hear, touch, taste, or smell.

GENERAL	LESS GENERAL	SPECIFIC	MORE SPECIFIC
book	dictionary	abridged dictionary	my 1996 edition of *Webster's Collegiate Dictionary*

ABSTRACT	LESS ABSTRACT	CONCRETE	MORE CONCRETE
culture	visual art	painting	Van Gogh's *Starry Night*

In the following passage, the author might have simply made a general statement—*their breakfast was always liberal and good*—or simply given the details of the breakfast. Instead, he is both general and specific.

> There would be a brisk fire crackling in the hearth, the old smoke-gold of morning and the smell of fog, the crisp cheerful voices of the people and their ruddy competent morning look, and the cheerful smells of breakfast, which was always liberal and good, the best meal that they had: kidneys and ham and eggs and sausages and toast and marmalade and tea.
> —THOMAS WOLFE, *Of Time and the River*

35d Use figurative language to create vivid pictures.

Figurative language, or figures of speech, paints pictures in readers' minds, allowing readers to "see" a point readily and clearly. Far from being a frill, such language is crucial to understanding.

Similes, metaphors, and analogies

Similes use *like, as, as if,* or *as though* to make explicit the comparison between two seemingly different things.

▶ **The Digital Revolution is whipping through our lives like a Bengali typhoon.**　　　　　　　　　　　　　　　　　—LOUIS ROSSETTO

▶ **The comb felt as if it was raking my skin off.**
　　　　　　　　　　　　　　　—MALCOLM X, "My First Conk"

Metaphors are implicit comparisons, omitting the *like, as, as if,* or *as though* of similes.

▶ **Today, America Online might be called the Carnival Cruise Lines of interactivity, but in the spring of 1985 it was a tiny start-up called Quantum Computer Services, Inc.**　　　　　　　—*Wired Style*

Mixed metaphors make comparisons that are inconsistent.

▶ **The lectures were like brilliant comets streaking through the night sky,**
　　dazzling　　　　　　　　　　**flashes**
　　~~showering~~ **listeners with** ~~a torrential rain~~ **of insight~~s~~.**
　　^　　　　　　　　　　　　^

　　The images of streaking light and heavy precipitation are inconsistent; in
　　the revised sentence, all of the images relate to light.

Analogies compare similar features of two dissimilar things; they explain something unfamiliar by relating it to something familiar.

▶ **Unix is the Swiss Army Knife of the Net.**　　　—THOMAS MANDEL

▶ **One Hundred and Twenty-fifth Street was to Harlem what the Mississippi was to the South, a long traveling river always going somewhere carrying something.**　　　—MAYA ANGELOU, *The Heart of a Woman*

Clichés

A cliché is a frequently used expression such as *busy as a bee.* By definition, we use clichés all the time, especially in speech, and many serve usefully as shorthand for familiar ideas or as a way of connecting to your audience. In addition, one person's cliché can be another's fresh and vivid image. But if you depend on clichés to excess in your writing, readers may conclude that what you are saying is not very new or even that you are not sincere. To check your writing for clichés, use this rule of thumb: if you can predict exactly what the upcoming word or words in a phrase will be, the phrase stands a very good chance of being a cliché.

A Matter of Style: *Signifying*

One distinctive use of figurative language found extensively in African American English is signifying, in which a speaker cleverly and often humorously needles or insults the listener. In the following passage, two African American men (Grave Digger and Coffin Ed) signify on their white supervisor (Anderson), who ordered them to find the originators of a riot:

> "I take it you've discovered who started the riot," Anderson said.
> "We knew who he was all along," Grave Digger said.
> "It's just nothing we can do to him," Coffin Ed echoed.
> "Why not, for God's sake?"
> "He's dead," Coffin Ed said.
> "Who?"
> "Lincoln," Grave Digger said.
> "He hadn't ought to have freed us if he didn't want to make provisions to feed us," Coffin Ed said. "Anyone could have told him that."
> —CHESTER HIMES, *Hot Day, Hot Night*

Coffin Ed and Grave Digger demonstrate the major characteristics of effective signifying: indirection, ironic humor, fluid rhythm—and a surprising twist at the end. Rather than insulting Anderson directly by pointing out that he's asked a dumb question, they criticize the question indirectly by ultimately blaming a white man (and one they're all supposed to revere). This twist leaves the supervisor speechless, teaching him something *and* giving Grave Digger and Coffin Ed the last word.

You will find examples of signifying in the work of many African American writers. You may also hear signifying in NBA basketball, for it is an important element of trash talking; what Grave Digger and Coffin Ed do to Anderson, Reggie Miller regularly does to his opponents on the court. As with all figurative language, it is important to recognize this verbal strategy—and to understand the meaning it adds.

36

Spelling

Drive down any commercial street, and you are sure to see many intentionally misspelled words—from a *Kountry Kitchen* restaurant to a *drive-thru* bank. Such fanciful or playful spelling will get you no points, however, in academic or professional writing. This chapter provides some fairly straightforward rules and guidelines that answer the most common questions about English spelling.

36a Learn the most commonly misspelled words.

The three thousand college essays used in the research for this book revealed a fairly small number of persistently misspelled words. Look over the fifty words most commonly misspelled. If you have trouble with any of them, take a moment to create a special memory device, such as the following, to help you remember them correctly: *They're certain their coats were over there.*

The fifty most commonly misspelled words

1. their/there/they're	18. through	35. business/-es
2. too/to	19. until	36. dependent
3. a lot	20. where	37. every day
4. noticeable	21. successful/-ly	38. may be
5. receive/-d/-s	22. truly	39. occasion/-s
6. lose	23. argument/-s	40. occurrences
7. you're/your	24. experience/-s	41. woman
8. an/and	25. environment	42. all right
9. develop/-s	26. exercise/-s/-ing	43. apparent/-ly
10. definitely	27. necessary	44. categories
11. than/then	28. sense	45. final/-ly
12. believe/-d/-s	29. therefore	46. immediate/-ly
13. occurred	30. accept/-ed	47. roommate/-s
14. affect/-s	31. heroes	48. against
15. cannot	32. professor	49. before
16. separate	33. whether	50. beginning
17. success	34. without	

Guidelines for Using a Spell Checker

- Keep a dictionary near your computer, and look up any word the spell checker highlights that you are not absolutely sure of.
- If your program has a "learn" option, enter into your spell-checker dictionary any proper names, non-English words, or specialized language you use regularly and have trouble spelling.
- Because spell checkers do not recognize homonym errors, use the search function to identify homonyms for you to double-check. (36b)
- Spell checkers will not catch missing capital letters, so be sure to proofread carefully for capitalization.

36b Learn to distinguish among homonyms.

English has many homonyms—words that sound alike but have different spellings and meanings. But a relatively small number of them—just eight groups—cause writers frequent trouble.

The most troublesome homonyms

their (possessive form of *they*)
there (in that place)
they're (contraction of *they are*)

to (in the direction of)
too (in addition; excessive)
two (number between *one* and *three*)

weather (climatic conditions)
whether (introducing a choice)

accept (take or receive)
except (leave out)

who's (contraction of *who is* or *who has*)
whose (possessive form of *who*)

its (possessive form of *it*)
it's (contraction of *it is* or *it has*)

your (possessive form of *you*)
you're (contraction of *you are*)

affect (an emotion; to have an influence)
effect (a result; to cause to happen)

Other homonyms and frequently confused words

advice (suggestion)
advise (suggest [to])

all ready (fully prepared)
already (previously)

allude (refer indirectly [to])
elude (avoid or escape)

allusion (indirect reference)
illusion (false idea or appearance)

all ways (by every means)
always (at all times)

altar (sacred platform or table)
alter (change)

bare (uncovered; to uncover)
bear (animal; to carry or endure)

brake (device for stopping; to stop)
break (fracture; to fragment)

buy (purchase)
by (near; beside; through)

capital (principal city)
capitol (legislators' building)

cite (refer to)
sight (seeing; something seen)
site (location)

coarse (rough or crude)
course (plan of study; path)

complement (something that completes; to complete)
compliment (praise; to praise)

conscience (moral sense)
conscious (mentally aware)

council (leadership group)
counsel (advice; to advise)

desert (dry area; to abandon)
dessert (sweet course at end of a meal)

elicit (draw forth)
illicit (illegal)

eminent (distinguished)
imminent (expected in the immediate future)

every day (each day)
everyday (daily, ordinary)

forth (forward)
fourth (between *third* and *fifth*)

gorilla (ape)
guerrilla (irregular soldier)

hear (perceive with the ears)
here (in this place)

hoarse (sounding rough)
horse (animal)

know (understand)
no (opposite of *yes*)

lead (a metal; to go before)
led (past tense of *lead*)

loose (not tight; not confined)
lose (misplace; fail to win)

may be (might be)
maybe (perhaps)

passed (went by; received a passing grade)
past (beyond; events that have already occurred)

patience (quality of being patient)
patients (persons under medical care)

personal (private or individual)
personnel (employees)

plain (simple, not fancy; flat land)
plane (airplane; tool; flat surface)

presence (condition of being)
presents (gifts; gives)

principal (most important; head of a school)
principle (fundamental truth)

rain (precipitation)
reign (period of rule; to rule)
rein (strap; to control)

right (correct; opposite of *left*)
rite (ceremony)
write (produce words on a surface)

scene (setting; view)
seen (past participle of *see*)

stationary (unmoving)
stationery (writing paper)

than (as compared with)
then (at that time; therefore)

thorough (complete)
threw (past tense of *throw*)
through (in one side of and out the other; by means of)

waist (part of the body)
waste (trash; to squander)

weak (feeble)
week (seven days)

which (what; that)
witch (woman with supernatural power)

For Multilingual Writers: *Recognizing British Spellings*

The following are some words that are spelled differently in American and British English:

AMERICAN	BRITISH
center	centre
check	cheque
civilization	civilisation
color	colour
criticize	criticise
judgment	judgement
realize	realise
theater	theatre

36c   Take advantage of spelling rules.

i *before* e *except after* c

Use *i* before *e* except after *c* or when pronounced "ay" (as in *weigh*) or in *weird* exceptions.

I BEFORE *E*	achieve, brief, field, friend
EXCEPT AFTER *C*	ceiling, receipt, perceive
OR WHEN PRONOUNCED "AY"	eighth, neighbor, reign, weigh
OR IN WEIRD EXCEPTIONS	either, foreign, height, leisure, neither, seize

Prefixes

A prefix does not change the spelling of the word it is added to. (See 47e on using hyphens with some prefixes and suffixes.)

dis- + service = disservice   over- + rate = overrate

Suffixes

A suffix may change the spelling of the word it is added to.

FINAL SILENT *E*

Drop the final silent *e* on a word when you add a suffix that starts with a vowel.

imagine + -able = imaginable   exercise + -ing = exercising

Keep the final *e* if the suffix starts with a consonant.

force + -ful = forceful   state + -ly = stately

EXCEPTIONS argument, changeable, judgment, noticeable, truly

FINAL *Y*

If adding a suffix to a word that ends in *y,* change the *y* to an *i* if it is pre-ceded by a consonant.

try, tried   busy, busily

Keep the *y* if it follows a vowel, if it is part of a proper name, or if the suffix begins with *i.*

employ, employed   Kennedy, Kennedyesque   dry, drying

FINAL CONSONANTS

When adding a suffix to a word that ends in a vowel and a consonant, double the final consonant if the word contains only one syllable or ends in an accented syllable.

stop, stopping   begin, beginner   occur, occurrence

Do not double the final consonant if it is preceded by more than one vowel or by a vowel and another consonant or if the new word is not accented on the last syllable.

bait, baiting	start, started	refer, reference
benefit, benefiting	infer, inference	fight, fighter

Plurals

ADDING -S OR -ES

For most words, add -s. For words ending in *s, ch, sh, x,* or *z,* add *-es.*

pencil, pencils	church, churches	bus, buses

Add -s to words ending in *o* if the *o* is preceded by a vowel. Add *-es* if the *o* is preceded by a consonant.

rodeo, rodeos	patio, patios	veto, vetoes
potato, potatoes	hero, heroes	

EXCEPTIONS   memo, memos; piano, pianos; solo, solos

OTHER PLURALS

For words ending in *y,* change *y* to *i* and add *-es* if the *y* is preceded by a consonant. Keep the *y* and add *-s* if the *y* is preceded by a vowel or if it ends a proper name.

theory, theories	eighty, eighties	Kennedy, Kennedys
attorney, attorneys	guy, guys	

Memorize irregular plurals.

bacterium, bacteria	datum, data	criterion, criteria

For compound nouns written as separate or hyphenated words, make the most important part plural.

brothers-in-law	lieutenant governors

37

Glossary of Usage

Matters of usage, like other language choices you must make, depend on what your purpose is and on what is appropriate for a particular audience at a particular time. This glossary provides usage guidelines for some commonly confused words and phrases.

a, an   Use *a* with a word that begins with a consonant (*a book*), with a consonant sound such as "*y*" or "*w*" (*a euphoric moment, a one-sided match*), and with a sounded *h* (*a hemisphere*). Use *an* with a word that begins with a vowel (*an umbrella*), with a vowel sound (*an X-ray*), and with a silent *h* (*an honor*).

accept, except   The verb *accept* means "receive" or "agree to." Used as a preposition, *except* means "aside from" or "excluding." *All the plaintiffs except Mr. Kim decided to accept the settlement.*

advice, advise   The noun *advice* means an "opinion" or "suggestion"; the verb *advise* means "offer or provide advice." *Charlotte's mother advised her to become a secretary, but Charlotte, who intended to become a dancer, ignored the advice.*

affect, effect   As a verb, *affect* means "influence" or "move the emotions of"; as a noun, it means "emotion" or "feeling." *Effect* is a noun meaning "result"; less commonly, it is a verb meaning "bring about." *Many people are affected by the realization that a nuclear war would have far-reaching effects.*

aggravate   The formal meaning is "make worse." *Having another mouth to feed aggravated their poverty.* In academic and professional writing, avoid using *aggravate* to mean "irritate" or "annoy."

all ready, already   *All ready* means "fully prepared." *Already* means "previously." *We were all ready for Lucy's party when we learned that she had already left.*

all right   *All right* means "acceptable" or signals agreement. *Alright,* a less common variant of the term, is not the preferred spelling.

all together, altogether   *All together* means "all in a group" or "gathered in one place." *Altogether* means "completely" or "everything considered." *When the union members were all together in the room, their consensus was altogether obvious.*

allude, elude   *Allude* means "refer indirectly." *Elude* means "avoid" or "escape from." *The candidate alludes to his parents, who had eluded political oppression.*

allusion, illusion   An *allusion* is an indirect reference, as when a writer hints at a well-known event, person, or quotation, assuming the reader will recognize it (*a literary allusion*). An *illusion* is a false or misleading appearance (*an optical illusion*).

already   See *all ready, already.*

alright   See *all right.*

altogether   See *all together, altogether.*

among, between In referring to two things or people, use *between*. In referring to three or more, use *among*. *The relationship between the twins is different from that among the other three children.*

amount, number Use *amount* with quantities you cannot count; use *number* for quantities you can count. *A small number of volunteers cleared a large amount of brush within a few hours.*

an See *a, an*.

and/or Avoid this term except in business or legal writing, where it is a short way of saying that one or both of two terms apply.

any body, anybody, any one, anyone *Anybody* and *anyone* are indefinite pronouns. *Anyone* [or *anybody*] *could enjoy carving wood. Any body* is two words, an adjective modifying a noun. *Any body of water has its own ecology. Any one* is two adjectives or a pronoun modified by an adjective. *Customers could buy only two sale items at any one time.*

anyplace, anywhere In academic and professional discourse, use *anywhere*, not *anyplace*.

anyway, anyways In writing, use *anyway*, not *anyways*.

anywhere See *anyplace, anywhere*.

apt, liable, likely *Likely to* means "probably will," and *apt to* means "inclines or tends to." Either will do in many instances. *Liable to* often carries a more negative sense and is also a legal term meaning "obligated" or "responsible for."

as Avoid sentences in which it is not clear if *as* means "because" or means "when." For example, does *Carl left town as his father was arriving* mean "at the same time as his father was arriving" or "because his father was arriving"?

as, as if, like Use *as* to identify equivalent terms in a description. *Gary served as moderator at the meeting.* Use *like* as a preposition to indicate similarity but not equivalency. *Hugo, like Jane, was a detailed observer.* Like cannot act as a conjunction introducing a clause. *The dog howled like a wolf, just as if* [not *like*] *she were a wild animal.*

assure, ensure, insure *Assure* means "convince" or "promise"; its direct object is usually a person or persons. *She assured voters she would not raise taxes. Ensure* and *insure* both mean "make certain," but *insure* carries the sense of protection against financial loss. *When the city rationed water to ensure that the supply would last, the Browns could no longer afford to insure their car-wash business.*

as to Do not use *as to* as a substitute for *about*. *Karen was unsure about* [not *as to*] *Bruce's intentions.*

at, where See *where*.

awful, awfully *Awful* and *awfully* mean "awe-inspiring" and "in an awe-inspiring way." Casual usage dilutes *awful* to mean "bad" (*I had an awful day*) and *awfully* to mean "very" (*It was awfully cold*). Avoid these casual usages in academic and professional writing.

awhile, a while Always use *a while* after a preposition such as *for, in,* or *after. We drove <u>awhile</u> and then stopped for <u>a while</u>.*

bad, badly Use *bad* after a linking verb such as *be, feel,* or *seem.* Use *badly* to modify an action verb, an adjective, or another verb. *The hostess felt <u>bad</u> because the dinner was <u>badly</u> prepared.*

because of, due to Use *due to* when the effect, stated as a noun, appears before the verb *be. His illness was <u>due to</u> malnutrition.* (*Illness,* a noun, is the effect.) Use *because of* when the effect is stated as a clause. *He was sick <u>because of</u> malnutrition.* (*He was sick,* a clause, is the effect.)

being as, being that Do not use these expressions in academic or professional writing; use *because* or *since* instead. *<u>Because</u>* [not *<u>being as</u>*] *Romeo killed Tybalt, he was banished to Padua.*

beside, besides *Beside* is only a preposition, meaning "next to." *Besides* can be a preposition meaning "other than" or an adverb meaning "moreover." *No one <u>besides</u> Francesca knows whether the tree is still growing <u>beside</u> the house.*

between See *among, between.*

breath, breathe *Breath* is a noun; *breathe,* a verb. *"<u>Breathe</u>," said the nurse, so June took a deep <u>breath</u> of laughing gas.*

bring, take Use *bring* when an object is moved from a farther to a nearer place; use *take* when the opposite is true. *<u>Take</u> the box to the post office; <u>bring</u> back my mail.*

but, yet Don't use these words together. *He is strong <u>but</u>* [not *but yet*] *gentle.*

but that, but what Avoid using these as substitutes for *that* in expressions of doubt. *Hercule Poirot never doubted <u>that</u>* [not *but that*] *he would solve the case.*

can, may *Can* refers to ability and *may* to possibility or permission. *Since I <u>can</u> ski the slalom well, I <u>may</u> win the race.*

can't hardly, can't scarcely *Hardly* and *scarcely* are negatives; therefore *can't hardly* and *can't scarcely* are double negatives. These expressions are commonly used in some regional and ethnic varieties of English but are not used in standard academic English. *Tim <u>can</u>* [not *can't*] *<u>hardly</u> wait.*

can't help but This expression is redundant. Use the more formal *I cannot but go* or the less formal *I can't help going* rather than *I can't help but go.*

can't scarcely See *can't hardly, can't scarcely.*

censor, censure *Censor* means "remove that which is considered offensive." *Censure* means "formally reprimand." *The public <u>censured</u> the newspaper for <u>censoring</u> letters to the editor.*

compare to, compare with *Compare to* means "regard as similar." *Anna <u>compared</u> the loss to a kick in the head. Compare with* means "to examine to find differences or similarities." *The article <u>compares</u> Tim Burton's films <u>with</u> David Lynch's.*

complement, compliment *Complement* means "go well with." *Compliment* means "praise." *Guests <u>complimented</u> her on how her earrings <u>complemented</u> her gown.*

comprise, compose *Comprise* means "contain." *Compose* means "make up." *The class comprises twenty students. Twenty students compose the class.*

conscience, conscious *Conscience* means "a sense of right and wrong." *Conscious* means "awake" or "aware." *After lying, Lisa was conscious of a guilty conscience.*

consensus of opinion Use *consensus* instead of this redundant phrase. *The family consensus was to sell the old house.*

consequently, subsequently *Consequently* means "as a result"; *subsequently* means "then." *He quit, and subsequently his wife lost her job; consequently, they panicked.*

continual, continuous *Continual* refers to an activity repeated at regular or frequent intervals. *Continuous* describes an ongoing activity or an object connected without break. *The damage done by continuous erosion was increased by the continual storms.*

could of See *have, of.*

criteria, criterion *Criterion* means "standard of judgment" or "necessary qualification." *Criteria* is the plural form. *Image is the wrong criterion for choosing a president.*

data *Data* is the plural form of the Latin word *datum,* meaning "fact." Although *data* is used informally as either singular or plural, in academic or professional writing, treat *data* as plural. *These data indicate that fewer people smoke today than ten years ago.*

different from, different than *Different from* is generally preferred in academic and professional writing, although both phrases are used widely. *Her lab results were no different from* [not *than*] *his.*

discreet, discrete *Discreet* means "tactful" or "prudent." *Discrete* means "separate" or "distinct." *The manager's discreet words calmed all the discrete factions.*

disinterested, uninterested *Disinterested* means "unbiased." *Uninterested* means "indifferent." *I'm uninterested in the problem of finding disinterested jurors.*

distinct, distinctive *Distinct* means "separate" or "well defined." *Distinctive* means "characteristic." *Each of the distinct elements has its own distinctive properties.*

doesn't, don't *Doesn't* is the contraction for *does not.* Use it with *he, she, it,* and singular nouns. *Don't* stands for *do not;* use it with *I, you, we, they,* and plural nouns.

due to See *because of, due to.*

each other, one another Use *each other* in sentences involving two subjects and *one another* in sentences involving more than two.

effect See *affect, effect.*

elicit, illicit The verb *elicit* means "draw out." The adjective *illicit* means "illegal." *The police elicited from the criminal the names of others involved in illicit activities.*

elude See *allude, elude.*

emigrate from, immigrate to *Emigrate from* means "move away from one's country." *Immigrate to* means "move to another country and settle there." *We emigrated from Norway in 1957. We immigrated to the United States.*

ensure See *assure, ensure, insure.*

enthused, enthusiastic Avoid the term *enthused* in academic and professional writing.

equally as good Replace this redundant phrase with *equally good* or *as good as.*

every day, everyday *Everyday* is an adjective meaning "ordinary." *Every day* is an adjective and a noun, specifying a particular day. *I wore everyday clothes. I wore a dress every day.*

every one, everyone *Everyone* is an indefinite pronoun. *Every one* is an adjective and a noun referring to each member of a group. *Because he began the assignment after everyone else, David knew he could not finish every one of the problems.*

except See *accept, except.*

explicit, implicit *Explicit* means "directly or openly expressed." *Implicit* means "indirectly expressed or implied." *The explicit message of the ad urged consumers to buy the product, while the implicit message promised popularity.*

farther, further *Farther* refers to physical distance. *How much farther is it to Munich? Further* refers to time or degree. *I want to avoid further delays.*

fewer, less Use *fewer* with nouns that can be counted. Use *less* with general amounts that you cannot count. *The world will be safer with fewer bombs and less hostility.*

finalize *Finalize* is a pretentious way of saying "end" or "make final." *We closed* [not *finalized*] *the deal.*

firstly, secondly, thirdly These are common in British English; *first, second,* and *third* are more common in U.S. English.

flaunt, flout *Flaunt* means "show off." *Flout* means "mock" or "scorn." *The teens flouted convention by flaunting their multicolored wigs.*

former, latter *Former* refers to the first and *latter* to the second of two things previously introduced. *Kathy and Anna are athletes; the former plays tennis, and the latter runs.*

further See *farther, further.*

good, well *Good* is an adjective and should not be used as a substitute for the adverb *well. Gabriel is a good host who cooks well.*

good and   *Good and* is colloquial for "very"; avoid it in academic and professional writing.

hanged, hung   *Hanged* refers to executions; *hung* is used for all other meanings. *The old woman hung her head as she passed the tree where the murderer was hanged.*

hardly   See *can't hardly, can't scarcely.*

have, of   *Have,* not *of,* should follow *could, would, should,* or *might. We should have* [not *of*] *invited them.*

herself, himself, myself, yourself   Do not use these reflexive pronouns as subjects or as objects unless they are necessary. Compare *John cut him* and *John cut himself. Jane and I* [not *myself*] *agree. They invited John and me* [not *myself*].

he/she, his/her   Better solutions for avoiding sexist language are to write out *he or she,* to eliminate pronouns entirely, or to make the subject plural (*they*). Instead of writing *Everyone should carry his/her driver's license,* try *Drivers should carry driver's licenses* or *People should carry their driver's licenses.*

himself   See *herself, himself, myself, yourself.*

his/her   See *he/she, his/her.*

hisself   Replace with *himself* in academic or professional writing.

hopefully   *Hopefully* is often misused to mean "it is hoped," but its correct meaning is "with hope." *Sam watched the roulette wheel hopefully* [not *Hopefully, Sam will win*].

hung   See *hanged, hung.*

if, whether   Use *whether* or *whether or not* for alternatives. *She was considering whether or not to go.* Reserve *if* for the conditional. *If it rains tomorrow, we will meet inside.*

illicit   See *elicit, illicit.*

illusion   See *allusion, illusion.*

immigrate to   See *emigrate from, immigrate to.*

impact   Avoid the colloquial use of *impact* or *impact on* as a verb meaning "affect." *Population control may reduce* [not *impact*] *world hunger.*

implicit   See *explicit, implicit.*

imply, infer   To *imply* is to suggest. To *infer* is to make an educated guess. *The note implied they were planning a small wedding; we inferred we would not be invited.*

infer   See *imply, infer.*

inside, inside of, outside, outside of   Drop *of* after the prepositions *inside* and *outside. The class regularly met outside* [not *outside of*] *the building.*

insure   See *assure, ensure, insure.*

interact with, interface with   *Interact with* is a vague phrase meaning "do something that somehow involves another person." *Interface with* is computer jargon for "discuss" or "communicate." Avoid both expressions in academic and professional writing.

irregardless, regardless   *Irregardless* is a double negative. Use *regardless.*

is when, is where   These vague expressions are often incorrectly used in definitions. *Schizophrenia is a psychotic condition in which* [not *when* or *where*] *a person withdraws from reality.*

its, it's   *Its* is a possessive form, even though it, like *his* and *her*, does not have an apostrophe. *It's* is a contraction for *it is* or *it has. It's important to observe the rat before it has its meal.*

kind, sort, type   Modify these singular nouns with *this*, and follow them with other singular nouns. *Wear this kind of dress. Wear these kinds of hats.*

kind of, sort of   Avoid these colloquialisms. *Amy was somewhat* [not *kind of*] *tired.*

later, latter   *Later* means "after some time." *Latter* refers to the last of two items named. *Juan and Chad won early on, but the latter was injured later in the season.*

latter   See *former, latter* and *later, latter.*

lay, lie   *Lay* means "place" or "put." Its main forms are *lay, laid, laid.* It generally has a direct object, specifying what has been placed. *She laid her books on the desk. Lie* means "recline" or "be positioned" and does not take a direct object. Its main forms are *lie, lay, lain. She lay awake until two.*

leave, let   *Leave* means "go away." *Let* means "allow." *Leave alone* and *let alone* are interchangeable. *Let me leave now, and leave* [or *let*] *me alone from now on!*

lend, loan   *Loan* is a noun, and *lend* is a verb. *Please lend me your pen so that I may fill out this application for a loan.*

less   See *fewer, less.*

let   See *leave, let.*

liable   See *apt, liable, likely.*

lie   See *lay, lie.*

like   See *as, as if, like.*

like, such as   *Like* means "similar to"; use *like* when comparing a subject to examples. *A hurricane, like a flood or any other major disaster, may strain emergency resources.* Use *such as* when examples represent a general category; *such as* is often an alternative to *for example. A destructive hurricane, such as Floyd in 1999, may drastically alter an area's economy.*

likely   See *apt, liable, likely.*

literally   *Literally* means "actually" or "exactly as written." Use it to stress the truth of a statement that might otherwise be understood as figurative. Do not use *literally* as an intensifier in a figurative statement. *Mirna was literally at the* *edge of her seat* may be accurate, but *Mirna is so hungry that she could <u>literally</u> eat a horse* is not.

loan   See *lend, loan.*

loose, lose   *Lose* is a verb meaning "misplace." *Loose* is an adjective that means "not securely attached." *Sew on that <u>loose</u> button before you <u>lose</u> it.*

lots, lots of   These are informal expressions that mean "much" or "many"; avoid using them in academic or professional discourse.

man, mankind   Many people consider these terms sexist because they do not mention women. Replace such words with *people, humans, humankind, men and women,* or similar phrases.

may   See *can, may.*

may be, maybe   *May be* is a verb phrase, whereas *maybe* is an adverb that means "perhaps." *He <u>may be</u> the president today, but <u>maybe</u> he will lose the next election.*

media   *Media* is the plural form of the noun *medium* and takes a plural verb. *The <u>media are</u>* [not *<u>is</u>*] *being consolidated.*

might have   See *have, of.*

moral, morale   A *moral* is a succinct lesson. *The <u>moral</u> of the story is that generosity is rewarded. Morale* means "spirit" or "mood." *Office <u>morale</u> was low.*

Ms.   Use *Ms.* as a title before a woman's name unless the woman specifies another title (*Miss* or *Mrs.*). Use *Ms.* with a woman's first name, not with her husband's name: *<u>Ms.</u> Susan Hewitt* or *<u>Ms.</u> Hewitt* [not *<u>Ms.</u> Peter Hewitt*].

myself   See *herself, himself, myself, yourself.*

nor, or   Use *either* with *or* and *neither* with *nor.*

number   See *amount, number.*

of   See *have, of.*

off, off of   Use *off* rather than *off of. The spaghetti slipped <u>off</u>* [not *<u>off of</u>*] *the plate.*

OK, O.K., okay   All are acceptable spellings, but avoid this expression in academic and professional discourse.

on account of   Use this substitute for *because of* sparingly or not at all.

one another   See *each other, one another.*

or   See *nor, or.*

outside, outside of   See *inside, inside of, outside, outside of.*

owing to the fact that   Avoid this and other wordy expressions for *because.*

per   Use the Latin *per* only in standard technical phrases such as *miles per hour.* Otherwise, find English equivalents. *As mentioned in* [not *<u>as per</u>*] *the latest report, our town's average food expenses every week* [not *<u>per week</u>*] *are $40 <u>per capita</u>.*

percent, percentage   Both words indicate a fraction of one hundred. Use *percent* with a specific number; use *percentage* with an adjective such as *large* or *small. Last year, 80 <u>percent</u> of the club's members were female. A large <u>percentage</u> of the club's members are women.*

plenty   *Plenty* means "enough" or "a great abundance." *They told us America was a land of plenty.* Colloquially, it is used to mean "very," a usage you should avoid in academic and professional writing. *He was very [not plenty] tired.*

plus   *Plus* means "in addition to." *Your salary plus mine will cover our expenses.* Do not use *plus* to mean "besides" or "moreover." *That dress does not fit me. Besides [not Plus], it is the wrong color.*

precede, proceed   *Precede* means "come before"; *proceed* means "go forward." *Despite the storm that preceded the flooding of the parking lot, we proceeded to our cars.*

pretty   Avoid using *pretty* as a substitute for "rather," "somewhat," or "quite." *Bill was quite [not pretty] disagreeable.*

principal, principle   When used as a noun, *principal* refers to a head official or an amount of money; when used as an adjective, it means "most significant." *Principle* means "fundamental law or belief." *Albert went to the principal and defended himself with the principle of free speech.*

proceed   See *precede, proceed.*

quotation, quote   *Quote* is a verb, and *quotation* is a noun. *He quoted the president, and the quotation [not quote] was preserved in history books.*

raise, rise   *Raise* means "lift" or "move upward." (Referring to children, it means "bring up.") It takes a direct object; someone raises something. *The guests raised their glasses to toast their host. Rise* means "go upward." It does not take a direct object; something rises by itself. *She saw the steam rise from the pan.*

rarely ever   Use *rarely* by itself, or use *hardly ever. When we were poor, we rarely went to the movies.*

real, really   *Real* is an adjective, and *really* is an adverb. Do not substitute *real* for *really. The older man walked really [not real] slowly.*

reason . . . is because   Use either *the reason . . . is that* or the word *because*—not both. *The reason the copier stopped is that [not is because] the paper jammed.*

reason why   This expression is redundant. *The reason [not the reason why] this book is short is market demand.*

regardless   See *irregardless, regardless.*

respectfully, respectively   *Respectfully* means "with respect." *Respectively* means "in the order given." *Karen and David, respectively a juggler and an acrobat, respectfully greeted the audience.*

rise   See *raise, rise.*

scarcely   See *can't hardly, can't scarcely.*

secondly   See *firstly, secondly, thirdly.*

set, sit   *Set* means "put" or "place" and takes a direct object. *Sit* refers to taking a seat but does not take an object. *"Set your cup on the table, and sit down."*

should of   See *have, of.*

since   *Since* has two uses: (1) to show passage of time, as in *I have been home since Tuesday*; (2) to mean "because," as in *Since you are in a bad mood, I will leave.*

Be careful not to use *since* ambiguously. In *Since I broke my leg, I've stayed home,* *since* might be understood to mean "because" or "ever since."

sit   See *set, sit.*

so, so that   In academic and professional writing, follow *so* with *that* to show how the intensified condition leads to a result. *Aaron was so tired that he fell asleep at the wheel.*

some body, somebody, some one, someone   *Somebody* and *someone* are indefinite pronouns. *When somebody comes walking down the hall, I always hope that it is someone I know. Some body* is an adjective modifying a noun. *Some one* is two adjectives or a pronoun modified by an adjective. *In dealing with some body like the senate, arrange to meet consistently some one person who can represent the group.*

someplace, somewhere   Use *somewhere* in academic and professional writing.

some time, sometime, sometimes   *Some time* refers to a length of time. *Please leave me some time to dress. Sometime* means "at some indefinite later time." *Sometime I will take you to London. Sometimes* means "occasionally." *Sometimes I eat sushi.*

somewhere   See *someplace, somewhere.*

sort   See *kind, sort, type.*

sort of   See *kind of, sort of.*

so that   See *so, so that.*

stationary, stationery   *Stationary* means "standing still"; *stationery* is writing paper. *When the bus was stationary, Pat took out stationery and wrote a note.*

subsequently   See *consequently, subsequently.*

such as   See *like, such as.*

supposed to, used to   Both expressions require the final *-d. He is supposed to sing.*

sure, surely   Avoid using *sure* as an intensifier. Instead, use *surely* (or *certainly* or *without a doubt*). *Surely the doctor will prescribe an antibiotic.*

take   See *bring, take.*

than, then   Use *than* in comparative statements. *The cat was bigger than the dog.* Use *then* when referring to a sequence of events. *I won, and then I cried.*

that, which   A clause beginning with *that* singles out the object being described. *The book that is on the table is a good one* specifies the book on the table as opposed to some other book. A clause beginning with *which* may or may not single out the object, although some writers use *which* clauses only to add more information about an object being described. *The book, which is on the table, is a good one* contains a *which* clause between the commas. The clause simply adds extra, nonessential information about the book; it does not specify which book.

that, which, who Use *that* when referring to things or to a group of people. *A band that tours frequently will please its fans.* Use *which* only when referring to things. *The new album, which is the band's first in years, appeals to new listeners.* Use *who* to refer to people. *Alex is the band member who plays drums.* In conversation, *that* can be used to refer to an individual (*the man that plays drums*), but in academic and professional writing, use *who* (*the man who plays drums*).

theirselves, themselves Use *themselves* rather than *theirselves*.

then See *than, then*.

thirdly See *firstly, secondly, thirdly*.

to, too, two *To* generally shows direction. *Too* means "also." *Two* is the number. *We, too, are going to the meeting in two hours.* Avoid using *to* after *where*. *Where are you flying* [not *flying to*]?

to, where See *where*.

two See *to, too, two*.

type See *kind, sort, type*.

uninterested See *disinterested, uninterested*.

unique *Unique* means "the one and only." Do not use it with adjectives that suggest degree, such as *very* or *most*. *Mel's hands are unique* [not *very unique*].

used to See *supposed to, used to*.

very Avoid using *very* to intensify a weak adjective or adverb; instead, replace the adjective or adverb with a stronger, more precise, or more colorful word. Instead of *very nice*, for example, use *kind, warm, sensitive, endearing,* or *friendly*.

way, ways When referring to distance, use *way*. *May was a long way* [not *ways*] *off*.

well See *good, well*.

when, where See *is when, is where*.

where Use *where* alone, not with words such as *at* and *to*. *Where are you going?* [not *Where are you going to?*]

whether See *if, whether*.

which See *that, which* and *that, which, who*.

who See *that, which, who*.

who, whom In adjective clauses, use *who* if the next word is a verb. *Liv, who smokes incessantly, is my godmother. Liv, who is my godmother, smokes incessantly.* Use *whom* if the following word is a noun or pronoun. *I heard that Liv, whom I have not seen for years, wears only purple.* Exception: ignore an expression such as *I think* within the clause. *Liv, who I think wears nothing but purple, is my godmother.* [Ignore *I think*; use *who* because the next word is a verb, *wears*.]

who's, whose   *Who's* is the contraction of *who* and *is* or *has*. *Who's on the patio?* *Whose* is a possessive form. *Whose sculpture is in the garden? Whose is on the patio?*

would of   See *have, of.*

yet   See *but, yet.*

your, you're   *Your* shows possession. *Bring your sleeping bag along.* *You're* is the contraction of *you* and *are*. *You're in the wrong sleeping bag.*

yourself   See *herself, himself, myself, yourself.*

38

Commas

It's hard to go through a day without encountering directions of some kind, and commas often play a crucial role in how you interpret instructions. See how important the comma is in the following directions for making hot cereal:

Add Cream of Wheat slowly, stirring constantly.

The comma here tells the cook to *add the cereal slowly*. If the comma came before the word *slowly*, however, the cook might add all of the cereal at once and *stir slowly*—perhaps resulting in lumpy cereal. This chapter aims to help you use commas correctly and effectively.

Editing for Commas

Research has shown that five of the most common errors in college writing involve commas. Check your writing for these five errors.

1. Check every sentence that doesn't begin with the subject to see whether it opens with an introductory element (a word, phrase, or clause that tells when, where, how, or why the main action of the sentence occurs). An introductory element needs to be followed by a comma, separating the introduction from the main part of the sentence. (38a)

2. Look at every sentence that contains one of the conjunctions *and, but, or, nor, for, so,* and *yet.* If the groups of words before and after the conjunction both function as complete sentences, you have a compound sentence. Make sure to use a comma before the conjunction. (38b)

3. Look at all adjective clauses beginning with *which, who, whom, whose, when,* or *where,* and at phrases and appositives (24l). Consider each element, and decide whether it is essential to the meaning of the sentence. If the rest of the sentence would be unclear without it, you should *not* set off the element with commas. (38c)

4. Identify all adjective clauses beginning with *that,* and make sure they are *not* set off with commas. (38c, j)

5. Check every *and* and *or* to see whether it comes before the last item in a series of three or more words, phrases, or clauses. Be sure that each item in a series (except the last) is followed by a comma. (38d)

38a Use commas to set off introductory words, phrases, and clauses.

▶ Slowly, she became conscious of her predicament.

▶ In fact, only you can decide.

▶ Eventually, John wondered whether he should change careers.

▶ In Fitzgerald's novel, the color green takes on great symbolic qualities.

▶ Sporting a pair of specially made running shoes, Brendan prepared for the race.

▶ To win the game, Connor needed skill and luck.

▶ Pen poised in anticipation, Shuli waited for the test to be distributed.

▶ Since Liz's mind was not getting enough stimulation, she decided to read some good literature.

Note that some writers omit the comma after an introductory element if it is short and does not seem to require a pause after it. However, you will never be wrong if you use a comma.

▶ At the racetrack, Jason lost nearly his entire paycheck.

In general, do *not* set off an adverb clause that follows a main clause unless it begins with *although, even though, while,* or another conjunction expressing the idea of contrast.

▶ Remember to check your calculations/before you submit the form.

▶ He uses semicolons frequently, while she prefers periods and short sentences.

38b Use commas to separate clauses in compound sentences.

A comma usually precedes a coordinating conjunction (*and, but, or, nor, for, so,* or *yet*) that joins two independent clauses in a compound sentence (24m).

▶ The title may sound important, but *administrative clerk* is only a euphemism for *photocopier.*

▶ The climbers have to reach the summit today, or they must turn back.

▶ The show started at last, and the crowd grew quiet.

With very short clauses, you can sometimes omit the comma.

▶ She saw her chance and she took it.

Always use the comma if there is any chance the sentence will be misread without it.

▶ I opened the junk drawer, and the cabinet door jammed.

Use a semicolon rather than a comma when the clauses are long and complex or contain their own commas.

▶ When these early migrations took place, the ice was still confined to the lands in the far north; but eight hundred thousand years ago, when man was already established in the temperate latitudes, the ice moved southward until it covered large parts of Europe and Asia.
—ROBERT JASTROW, *Until the Sun Dies*

38c Use commas to set off nonrestrictive elements.

Nonrestrictive elements are clauses, phrases, and words that do not limit, or restrict, the meaning of the words they modify. Since such elements are not essential to the meaning of a sentence, they should be set off from the rest of the sentence with commas. Restrictive elements, on the other hand, *do* limit meaning; they should *not* be set off with commas.

RESTRICTIVE   Drivers *who have been convicted of drunken driving*
                       should lose their licenses.

In the preceding sentence, the clause *who have been convicted of drunken driving* is essential to the meaning because it limits the word it modifies, *Drivers,* to only those drivers who have been convicted of drunken driving. Therefore, it is *not* set off with commas.

NONRESTRICTIVE   The two drivers involved in the accident, *who have
                       been convicted of drunken driving,* should lose their
                       licenses.

In this sentence, however, the clause *who have been convicted of drunken driving* is not essential to the meaning because it does not limit what it modifies, *The two drivers involved in the accident,* but merely provides additional information about these drivers. Therefore the clause *is* set off with commas.

To decide whether an element is restrictive or nonrestrictive, mentally delete the element, and then see if the deletion changes the meaning of the rest of the sentence or makes it unclear. If the deletion does change the meaning, the element is probably restrictive, and you should not set it off with commas. If it does not change the meaning, the element is probably nonrestrictive and requires commas.

Adjective and adverb clauses

An adjective clause that begins with *that* is always restrictive; do not set it off with commas. An adjective clause beginning with *which* may be either restrictive or nonrestrictive; however, some writers prefer to use *which* only for nonrestrictive clauses, which they set off with commas.

NONRESTRICTIVE CLAUSES

▶ **I borrowed books from the rental library of Shakespeare and Company,**
   which was the library and bookstore of Sylvia Beach at 12 rue de
   l'Odeon.   —ERNEST HEMINGWAY, *A Moveable Feast*

The adjective clause describing Shakespeare and Company is not necessary to the meaning of the independent clause and therefore is set off with a comma.

As noted earlier, an adverb clause that follows a main clause usually does *not* require a comma to set it off *unless* the adverb clause expresses contrast.

▶ The park soon became a popular gathering place‚ although some
nearby residents complained about the noise.

The adverb clause *although some nearby residents complained about the noise*
expresses the idea of contrast; therefore it is set off with a comma.

RESTRICTIVE CLAUSES

▶ The claim *that men like seriously to battle one another to some sort of
finish* is a myth.
            —JOHN MCMURTRY, "Kill 'Em! Crush 'Em! Eat 'Em Raw!"

The adjective clause is necessary to the meaning of the sentence because it
explains which claim is a myth; therefore the clause is not set off with a
comma.

▶ The man⁄ who rescued Jana's puppy⁄ won her eternal gratitude.

The adjective clause *who rescued Jana's puppy* is necessary to the meaning
because only the man who rescued the puppy won the gratitude; the clause
is restrictive and so takes no commas.

Phrases

Participial phrases may be restrictive or nonrestrictive. Prepositional
phrases are usually restrictive, but sometimes they are not essential to
the meaning of a sentence and are therefore set off with commas (24l).

NONRESTRICTIVE PHRASES

▶ The bus drivers‚ rejecting the management offer‚ remained on strike.

Using commas around the phrase makes it nonrestrictive, telling us that all
of the drivers remained on strike.

▶ Frédéric Chopin‚ in spite of poor health‚ composed prolifically.

The phrase *in spite of poor health* does not limit the meaning of *Frédéric
Chopin* and so is set off with commas.

RESTRICTIVE PHRASES

▶ The bus drivers⁄rejecting the management offer⁄remained on strike.

If the phrase *rejecting the management offer* limits the meaning of *The bus drivers,* the commas should be deleted. The revised sentence says that only

some of the bus drivers, the ones who rejected the offer, remained on strike, implying that the other drivers went back to work.

Appositives

An appositive is a noun or noun phrase that renames a nearby noun. When an appositive is not essential to identify what it renames, it is set off with commas.

NONRESTRICTIVE APPOSITIVES

▶ Ms. Bentley**,** my high school English teacher**,** inspired my love of literature.

Ms. Bentley's name identifies her; the appositive *my high school English teacher* simply provides extra information.

RESTRICTIVE APPOSITIVES

▶ Mozart's opera*/* The Marriage of Figaro*/* was considered revolutionary.

The phrase *The Marriage of Figaro* is essential to the meaning of the sentence because Mozart wrote more than one opera. Therefore it is *not* set off with commas.

38d Use commas to separate items in a series.

▶ He has plundered our seas, ravaged our coasts, burnt our towns, and destroyed the lives of our people.   –Declaration of Independence

You may see a series with no comma after the next-to-last item, particularly in newspaper writing. Occasionally, however, omitting the comma can cause confusion, and you will never be wrong if you include it.

▶ Diners had a choice of broccoli, green beans, peas**,** and carrots.

Without the comma after *peas,* you wouldn't know if there were three choices (the third being a *mixture* of peas and carrots) or four.

When the items in a series contain commas of their own or other punctuation, separate them with semicolons rather than commas.

Coordinate adjectives, those that relate equally to the noun they modify, should be separated by commas.

▶ **The long, twisting, muddy road led to a shack in the woods.**
          ^   ^

In a sentence like *The cracked bathroom mirror reflected his face,* however, *cracked* and *bathroom* are not coordinate because *bathroom mirror* is the equivalent of a single word, which is modified by *cracked.* Hence, they are *not* separated by commas.

You can usually determine whether adjectives are coordinate by inserting *and* between them. If the sentence makes sense with the *and,* the adjectives are coordinate and should be separated by commas.

▶ **They are sincere *and* talented *and* inquisitive researchers.**

The sentence makes sense with the *and*'s, so the adjectives *sincere, talented,* and *inquisitive* should be separated by commas.

▶ **Byron carried an elegant *and* gold *and* pocket watch.**

The sentence does not make sense with the *and*'s, so the adjectives *elegant, gold,* and *pocket* should not be separated by commas.

A Matter of Style: *Series Commas*

Comma conventions are quite often a matter of style—and of what is called, in the publishing industry, "house style." Many newspapers, for example, follow the style of omitting the comma after the next-to-last item in a series of three or more. Here is such an example from the *New York Times:*

> Current alternative rockers like Courtney Love, P. J. Harvey and Alanis Morisette owe Patti Smith no small debt.
> —JON PARELES, "Return of the Godmother of Punk"

You may be required (by an instructor or by your company's house style) to follow this convention. But, ordinarily, you will never be wrong if you put a comma after each item in a series except the last: *Current alternative rockers like Courtney Love, P. J. Harvey, and Alanis Morisette owe Patti Smith no small debt.*

38e Use commas to set off parenthetical and transitional expressions.

Parenthetical expressions add comments or information. Because they often interrupt the flow of a sentence or digress, they are usually set off with commas.

▶ Some studies, incidentally, have shown that chocolate, of all things, helps to prevent tooth decay.

▶ Roald Dahl's stories, it turns out, were often inspired by his own childhood.

Transitional expressions include conjunctive adverbs (words such as *however* and *furthermore*) and other words and phrases used to connect parts of sentences. They are usually set off with commas (24h, 31a).

▶ Ceiling fans are, moreover, less expensive than air conditioners.

▶ Ozone is a byproduct of dry cleaning, for example.

38f Use commas to set off contrasting elements, interjections, direct address, and tag questions.

CONTRASTING ELEMENTS

▶ On official business it was she, *not my father,* one would usually hear on the phone or in stores.
—RICHARD RODRIGUEZ, "Aria: A Memoir of a Bilingual Childhood"

INTERJECTIONS

▶ *My God,* who wouldn't want a wife?   —JUDY BRADY, "I Want a Wife"

DIRECT ADDRESS

▶ Remember, *sir,* that you are under oath.

TAG QUESTIONS

▶ The governor did not veto the unemployment bill, *did she?*

38g Use commas to set off parts of dates, addresses, titles, and numbers.

Dates

Use a comma between the day of the week and the month, between the day of the month and the year, and between the year and the rest of the sentence, if any.

▶ The war began on Thursday, January 17, 1991, with air strikes on Iraq.

Do not use commas with dates in inverted order or with dates consisting of only the month and the year.

▶ She dated the letter *26 August 2000.*
▶ Thousands of Germans swarmed over the wall in *November 1989.*

Addresses and place names

Use a comma after each part of an address or place name, including the state if there is no zip code. Do not precede a zip code with a comma.

▶ Forward my mail to the Department of English, The Ohio State University, Columbus, Ohio 43210.

▶ Portland, Oregon, is much larger than Portland, Maine.

Titles

Use commas to set off a title such as *M.D., Ph.D.,* and so on from the name preceding it and from the rest of the sentence.

▶ Oliver Sacks, M.D., has written about the way the mind works.

Numbers

In numerals of five digits or more, use a comma between each group of three, starting from the right.

▶ Danbury's population rose to *65,585* in the 1990 census.

The comma is optional within numerals of four digits but never occurs in four-digit dates, street addresses, or page numbers.

▶ The college had an enrollment of *1,789* [or *1789*] in the fall of 1999.
▶ My grandparents live at *2428* Loring Place.
▶ Turn to page *1566*.

38h Use commas to set off most quotations.

Commas set off a quotation from words used to introduce or identify the source of the quotation. A comma following a quotation goes *inside* the closing quotation mark.

▶ A German proverb warns, "Go to law for a sheep, and lose your cow."

▶ "All I know about grammar," said Joan Didion, "is its infinite power."

Do not use a comma after a question mark or exclamation point.

▶ "What's a thousand dollars?" asks Groucho Marx in *Cocoanuts.* "Mere chicken feed. A poultry matter."

▶ "Out, damned spot!" cries Lady Macbeth.

Do not use a comma when you introduce a quotation with *that.*

▶ The writer of Ecclesiastes concludes that "all is vanity."

Do not use a comma before an indirect quotation—one that does not use the speaker's exact words.

▶ Patrick Henry declared that he wanted either liberty or death.

38i   **Use commas to prevent confusion.**

Sometimes commas are necessary to make sentences easier to read or understand.

▶ The members of the dance troupe strutted in, in matching costumes.

▶ Before, I had planned to major in biology.

38j   **Eliminate unnecessary commas.**

Excessive use of commas can spoil an otherwise fine sentence.

Around restrictive elements

Do not use commas to set off restrictive elements—elements that limit, or define, the meaning of the words they modify or refer to (38c).

▶ I don't let my children watch TV shows/ that are violent.

  The *that* clause restricts the meaning of *TV shows,* so the comma should be omitted.

▶ A law/ requiring the use of seat belts/ was passed in 1987.

▶ My only defense/ against my allergies/ is to stay indoors.

▶ The actress/ Rosemary Harris/ has returned to Broadway.

Between subjects and verbs, verbs and objects or complements, and prepositions and objects

Do not use a comma between a subject and its verb, a verb and its object or complement, or a preposition and its object. This rule holds true even if the subject, object, or complement is a long phrase or clause.

▶ Watching movies late at night/ is a way for me to relax.

▶ Parents must decide/ how much TV their children may watch.

▶ The winner of͟/the trophy for community service stepped forward.

In compound constructions

In compound constructions (other than compound sentences), do not use a comma before or after a coordinating conjunction that joins the two parts (38b).

▶ **Improved health care͟/and more free trade were two goals of the Clinton administration.**

The *and* here joins parts of a compound subject, which should not be separated by a comma.

▶ **Mark Twain trained as a printer͟/and worked as a steamboat pilot.**

The *and* here joins parts of a compound predicate, which should not be separated by a comma.

Before the first or after the last item in a series

▶ The auction included͟/furniture, paintings, and china.

▶ The swimmer took slow, powerful͟/strokes.

39

Semicolons

If you've ever pored over the fine print at the bottom of an ad for a big sale, looking for the opening hours or the address of the store nearest you, then you've seen plenty of semicolons in action. Here's an example from a Bloomingdale's ad.

> Stores & Hours—
> *Short Hills:* SUN., 12–6; MON., 10–9:30; TUES., 10–5; WED. through FRI., 10–9:30; SAT., 10–8.

The semicolons separate the information for one day's hours from the next. Semicolons have the effect of creating a pause stronger than that of a comma but not as strong as the full pause of a period.

> *Editing for Semicolons*
> • Check to see whether you use any semicolons. If so, be sure they are used only between independent clauses—groups of words that can stand alone as sentences (39a, b)—or between items in a series. (39c)
> • If you find few or no semicolons in your writing, determine whether you should add some. Are there any closely related ideas in two sentences that might be better expressed in one sentence using a semicolon? (39a)

39a Use semicolons to link closely related independent clauses.

Though a comma and a coordinating conjunction often join independent clauses, semicolons provide writers with subtler ways of signaling closely related clauses. The clause following a semicolon often restates an idea expressed in the first clause, and it sometimes expands on or presents a contrast to the first.

▶ **Immigration acts were passed; newcomers had to prove, besides moral correctness and financial solvency, their ability to read.**
          —MARY GORDON, "More Than Just a Shrine"

   Gordon uses a semicolon to join the two clauses, giving the sentence an abrupt rhythm that suits the topic: laws that imposed strict requirements.

If two independent clauses joined by a coordinating conjunction contain commas, you may use a semicolon instead of a comma before the conjunction to make the sentence easier to read.

▶ **Every year, whether the Republican or the Democratic party is in office, more and more power drains away from the individual to feed vast reservoirs in far-off places; and we have less and less say about the shape of events which shape our future.**
          —WILLIAM F. BUCKLEY JR., "Why Don't We Complain?"

39b Use semicolons to link independent clauses joined by conjunctive adverbs or transitional phrases.

A semicolon should link independent clauses joined by conjunctive adverbs or transitional phrases.

▶ Every kid should have access to a computer/̣ furthermore, access to the
Internet should be free.

▶ The circus comes as close to being the world in microcosm as anything I
know; in a way, it puts all the rest of show business in the shade.
—E. B. WHITE, "The Ring of Time"

SOME CONJUNCTIVE ADVERBS

also	indeed	now
anyway	instead	otherwise
besides	likewise	similarly
certainly	meanwhile	still
finally	moreover	then
furthermore	namely	therefore
however	nevertheless	thus
incidentally	next	undoubtedly

SOME TRANSITIONAL PHRASES

as a result	granted that	in the meantime
as soon as	in addition	of course
even though	in conclusion	on the other hand
for example	in fact	on the whole
for instance	in other words	to summarize

When linking clauses with conjunctive adverbs or transitional phrases,
be careful not to write fused sentences or comma splices (30c).

39c Use semicolons to separate items in a series containing other punctuation.

Ordinarily, commas separate items in a series (38d). But when the items
themselves contain commas or other marks of punctuation, using semicolons to separate the items will make the sentence clearer and easier
to read.

▶ Anthropology encompasses archaeology, the study of ancient civilizations through artifacts⨯; linguistics, the study of the structure and development of language⨯; and cultural anthropology, the study of language, customs, and behavior.

39d Eliminate misused semicolons.

A comma, not a semicolon, should separate an independent clause from a dependent clause or phrase.

▶ The police found fingerprints⨯; which they used to identify the thief.

▶ The new system would encourage students to register for courses online⨯; thus streamlining registration.

A colon, not a semicolon, should introduce a series or list.

▶ The tour includes visits to the following art museums⨯; the Prado, in Madrid; the Louvre, in Paris; and the Van Gogh, in Amsterdam.

40

End Punctuation

Periods, question marks, and exclamation points often appear in advertising to create special effects or draw readers along from line to line. For example:

> The experts say America Online is a well-designed, easy-to-use service.
> So what are you waiting for?
> Get your hands on America Online today!

End punctuation tells us how to read each sentence—as a matter-of-fact statement, an ironic query, or an emphatic order. This chapter will guide you in using appropriate end punctuation in your own writing.

40a Periods

Use a period to close sentences that make statements, give mild commands, or make polite requests.

▶ **All books are either dreams or swords.**   —AMY LOWELL

▶ **Never use a foreign phrase, a scientific word or a jargon word if you can think of an everyday English equivalent.**
—GEORGE ORWELL, "Politics and the English Language"

▶ **Would you please close the door.**

A period also closes indirect questions, which report rather than ask questions.

▶ **I asked how old the child was.**

▶ **We all wonder who will win the election.**

In American English, periods are also used with most abbreviations. However, many abbreviations made up of capitalized letters may be written with or without periods.

Mr.	Dr.	BC (or B.C.)
Ms.	Ph.D.	BCE (or B.C.E.)
Mrs.	M.B.A.	AD (or A.D.)
Jr.	R.N.	a.m. (or AM)
ibid.	Sen.	p.m. (or PM)

Some abbreviations do not require periods. Among them are the postal abbreviations of state names, such as *FL* and *TN,* and most groups of initials (*GE, CIA, DOS, AIDS, YMCA, UNICEF*). If you are not sure whether a particular abbreviation should include periods, check a dictionary. (See Chapter 45 for more about abbreviations.)

Do not use an additional period when a sentence ends with an abbreviation that has its own period.

▶ **The social worker referred me to Evelyn Pintz, M.D.**

40b Question marks

Use question marks to close sentences that ask direct questions.

▶ **How is the human mind like a computer, and how is it different?**
   –Kathleen Stassen Berger and Ross A. Thompson,
   The Developing Person through Childhood and Adolescence

Question marks do not close *indirect* questions, which report rather than ask questions.

▶ **She asked whether I opposed his nomination.**

Do not use a comma or a period immediately after a question mark that ends a direct quotation.

▶ **"Am I my brother's keeper?" Cain asked.**

▶ **Cain asked, "Am I my brother's keeper?"**

Questions in a series may have question marks even when they are not separate sentences.

▶ **I often confront a difficult choice: should I go to practice? finish my homework? spend time with my friends?**

A question mark in parentheses indicates that a writer is unsure of a date, a figure, or a word.

▶ **Quintilian died in AD 96 (?).**

40c Exclamation points

Use an exclamation point to show surprise or strong emotion.

► **In those few moments of geologic time will be the story of all that has happened since we became a nation. And what a story it will be!**
   –JAMES RETTIE, "But a Watch in the Night"

Use exclamation points very sparingly, because they can distract your readers or suggest that you are exaggerating.

► **This university is so large, so varied, that attempting to tell someone everything about it would take three years~~!~~.**

Do not use a comma or a period immediately after an exclamation point that ends a direct quotation.

► **On my last visit, I looked out the sliding glass doors and ran breathlessly to Connor in the kitchen: "There's a *huge* black pig in the backyard!"~~.~~**   **–ELLEN ASHDOWN, "Living by the Dead"**

41

Apostrophes

The little apostrophe can sometimes make a big difference in meaning. One man found that out when he agreed to look after a neighbor's apartment for a few days. "I'll leave instructions on the kitchen counter," the neighbor said as she gave him her key. Here are the instructions he found: "The cat's food is on the counter. Once a day on the patio. Thanks. I'll see you Friday."

Because the note said *cat's*, the man expected one cat—and when he saw one, he put it and the food outside on the patio. When the neighbor returned, she found one healthy cat—and a second, very weak one that had hidden under the bed. The difference between *cat's* and *cats'* in this instance almost cost the neighbor a cat.

41a Use apostrophes to signal possessive case.

The possessive case denotes ownership or possession of one thing by another.

Singular nouns and indefinite pronouns

Add an apostrophe and -s to form the possessive of most singular nouns, including those that end in -s, and of indefinite pronouns. The possessive forms of personal pronouns do not take apostrophes: *yours, his, hers, its, ours, theirs.*

▶ The *bus's* fumes overpowered her.
▶ Katharine *Hepburn's* early movies are considered classics.
▶ *Anyone's* guess is as good as mine.

Plural nouns

To form the possessive case of plural nouns not ending in -s, add an apostrophe and -s.

▶ Robert Bly helped to popularize the *men's* movement.

For plural nouns ending in -s, add only the apostrophe.

▶ The *clowns'* costumes were bright green and orange.

Compound nouns

For compound nouns, make the last word in the group possessive.

▶ The *secretary of state's* speech was televised.
▶ Both her *daughters-in-law's* birthdays fall in July.
▶ My *in-laws'* disapproval dampened our enthusiasm for the new house.

Two or more nouns

To signal individual possession by two or more owners, make each noun possessive.

▶ Great differences exist between *Angela Bassett's* and *Oprah Winfrey's* films.

Bassett and Winfrey appeared in different films.

To signal joint possession, make only the last noun possessive.

▶ *MacNeil and Lehrer's* television program focused on current issues.

MacNeil and Lehrer participated in the same program.

41b Use apostrophes to signal contractions.

Contractions are two-word combinations formed by leaving out certain letters, which are indicated by an apostrophe.

it is, it has/it's	I would/I'd	will not/won't
was not/wasn't	he would/he'd	let us/let's
I am/I'm	would not/wouldn't	who is, who has/who's
he is, he has/he's	do not/don't	cannot/can't
you will/you'll	does not/doesn't	

Contractions such as the preceding ones are common in conversation and informal writing. Academic and professional work, however, often calls for greater formality.

Apostrophes signal omissions in some common phrases.

rock and roll   class of 1997
rock 'n' roll   class of '97

Distinguishing it's *and* its

Its is the possessive form of *it. It's* is a contraction for *it is* or *it has.*

▶ This disease is unusual; *its* symptoms vary from person to person.

▶ *It's* a difficult disease to diagnose.

41c **Use apostrophes to form the plurals of numbers, letters, symbols, and words used as terms.**

Use an apostrophe and *-s* to form the plural of numbers, letters, symbols, and words referred to as terms.

▶ The gymnasts need marks of 8's and 9's to qualify for the finals.

▶ The computer prints *e*'s whenever there is an error in the program.

▶ I marked special passages with a series of three **'s.

▶ The five *Shakespeare*'s in the essay were spelled five different ways.

As in the above examples, italicize numbers, letters, symbols, and words referred to as terms, but do not italicize the plural ending.

You can omit the apostrophe before the *s* for the plural of years (*2020s, fashion of the '80s*).

42

Quotation Marks

"Hilarious!" "A great family movie!" "A must see!" Claims of this kind leap out from most movie ads, always set off by quotation marks. In fact, the quotation marks are a key component of such statements, indicating that the praise comes from people other than the movie promoter. In other words, it is praise that we should believe. This chapter provides tips for using quotation marks for many purposes.

> **Editing Quotation Marks**
>
> • Use quotation marks around direct quotations and titles of short works. (42a, c)
> • Do not use quotation marks around set-off quotations of more than four lines of prose or more than three lines of poetry, or around titles of long works. (42b, c)
> • Check other punctuation used with closing quotation marks. (42e)
>   Periods and commas should be *inside* the quotation marks.
>   Colons, semicolons, and footnote numbers should be *outside*.
>   Question marks, exclamation points, and dashes should be *inside* if they are part of the quoted material, *outside* if they are not.
> • Never use quotation marks around indirect quotations. (42f)
>   ▶   Keith said that ⸍he was sorry.⸍
> • Do not rely on quotation marks to add emphasis to words. (42f)

42a   Use quotation marks to signal direct quotation.

▶ Jesse Jackson called for action to close the "digital divide" in Internet use.
▶ She smiled and said, "Son, this is one incident that I will never forget."

Use quotation marks to enclose the words of each speaker within running dialogue. Mark each shift in speaker with a new paragraph.

> "But I can see you're bound to come," said the father. "Only we ain't going to catch us no fish, because there ain't no water left to catch 'em in."
> "The river!"
> "All but dry." —EUDORA WELTY, "Ladies in Spring"

Single quotation marks

Single quotation marks enclose a quotation within a quotation. Open and close the quoted passage with double quotation marks, and change any quotation marks that appear *within* the quotation to single quotation marks.

▶ Baldwin says, "The title 'The Uses of the Blues' does not refer to music; I don't know anything about music."

> **For Multilingual Writers: *Quotation Marks***
>
> Remember that the way you mark quotations in English (" ") may not be the same as in other languages. In French, for example, quotations are marked with *guillemets* (« »), while in German, quotations take split-level marks („" or „").

42b Set off long quotations by indenting.

If the prose passage you wish to quote is more than four typed lines, set the quotation off by starting it on a new line and indenting it one inch (or ten spaces if you're using a typewriter) from the left margin. This format, known as block quotation, does not require quotation marks.

> In *Winged Words: American Indian Writers Speak,* Leslie Marmon Silko describes her early education, saying:
>> I learned to love reading, and love books, and the printed page, and therefore was motivated to learn to write. The best thing [. . .] you can have in life is to have someone tell you a story [. . .] but in lieu of that [. . .] I learned at an early age to find comfort in a book, that a book would talk to me when no one else would. (145)

The page number in parentheses at the end of the quotation is a citation following the Modern Language Association's (MLA) style. The American Psychological Association (APA) has different guidelines for setting off block quotations. (See Chapters 48 and 52.)

When quoting poetry, if the quotation is brief (fewer than four lines), include it within your text. Separate the lines of the poem with slashes, each preceded and followed by a space, in order to tell the reader where one line of the poem ends and the next begins.

> In one of his best-known poems, Robert Frost remarks, "Two roads diverged in a yellow wood, and I— / I took the one less traveled by / And that has made all the difference."

To quote more than three lines of poetry, indent each line one inch (or ten spaces if you're using a typewriter) from the left margin, and do not use quotation marks. When you quote poetry, take care to follow the indentation, spacing, capitalization, punctuation, and other features of the original passage.

The duke in Robert Browning's poem "My Last Duchess" is clearly a jealous, vain person, whose arrogance is illustrated through this statement:

> She thanked men,—good! but thanked
> Somehow—I know not how—as if she ranked
> My gift of a nine-hundred-years-old name
> With anybody's gift.

42c Use quotation marks around titles of short works.

Quotation marks enclose the titles of short poems, short stories, articles, essays, songs, sections of books, and episodes of television and radio programs.

- ▶ **"Dover Beach" moves from calmness to sadness.** [poem]
- ▶ **Alice Walker's "Everyday Use" is about more than just quilts.** [short story]
- ▶ **The *Atlantic* published an article entitled "Illiberal Education."** [article]
- ▶ **In "Photography," Susan Sontag considers the role of photography in our society.** [essay]
- ▶ **The *Nature* episode "Echo of the Elephants" portrays ivory hunters unfavorably.** [episode of a television program]

42d Use quotation marks around definitions.

- ▶ **In social science, the term *sample size* means "the number of individuals being studied in a research project."**
  —KATHLEEN STASSEN BERGER AND ROSS A. THOMPSON,
  The Developing Person through Childhood and Adolescence

42e Check other punctuation used with quotation marks.

Periods and commas go *inside* closing quotation marks.

- ▶ **"Don't compromise yourself," said Janis Joplin. "You are all you've got."**

Colons, semicolons, and footnote numbers go *outside* closing quotation marks.

▶ **I felt one emotion after finishing "Eveline": sorrow.**

▶ **Everything is dark, and "a visionary light settles in her eyes"; this vision, this light, is her salvation.**

▶ **Tragedy is defined by Aristotle as "an imitation of an action that is serious and of a certain magnitude."[1]**

Question marks, exclamation points, and dashes go *inside* if they are part of the quoted material, *outside* if they are not.

PART OF THE QUOTATION

▶ **Gently shake the injured person while asking, "Are you all right?"**

▶ **"Jump!" one of the firefighters shouted.**

NOT PART OF THE QUOTATION

▶ **What is the theme of "The Birth-Mark"?**

▶ **"Break a leg"—that phrase is supposed to bring good luck.**

A Matter of Style: *Direct Quotation*

As a way of bringing other people's words into our own, direct quotation can be a powerful writing tool. For example:

> Mrs. Macken urges parents to get books for their children, to read to them when they are "li'l," and when they start school to make certain they attend regularly. She holds herself up as an example of a "mill-hand's daughter who wanted to be a schoolteacher and did it through sheer hard work."   —SHIRLEY BRICE HEATH, *Ways with Words*

The writer could have paraphrased—and said, for example, that parents should read to their children when they are young. By quoting, however, she lets her subject speak for herself—and lets us as readers hear that person's voice. In fact, this writer is reporting from field research, which calls for the use of direct quotations. Thus the choice to quote directly is effective and appropriate to both the intended audience and the conventions of the field.

For information on using quotation marks with footnotes and in biblio-graphical references, see Chapters 49, 50, 52, 54, and 55.

42f Check for misused quotation marks.

Do not use quotation marks for indirect quotations—those that do not use someone's exact words.

▶ Mother smiled and said that "she would never forget the incident."

Do not use quotation marks just to add emphasis to particular words or phrases.

▶ Michael said that his views may not be "politically correct" but that he
  wasn't going to change them for anything.

▶ Much time was spent speculating about their "relationship."

Do not use quotation marks around slang or colloquial language; they create the impression that you are apologizing for using those words. If you have a good reason to use slang or a colloquial term, use it without quotation marks.

▶ After our twenty-mile hike, we were completely exhausted and ready to
  "turn in."

For Multilingual Writers: *Quoting in American English*

American English and British English offer opposite conventions for double and single quotation marks. Writers of British English use single quotation marks first and, when necessary, double quotation marks for quotations within quotations. If you have studied British English but are writing for an American audience, be careful to follow the U.S. con-ventions governing quotation marks: double quotation marks first and, when necessary, single quotation marks within double.

43

Other Punctuation

Parentheses, brackets, dashes, colons, slashes, and ellipses are all around us. Pick up the television listings, for instance, and you will find all these punctuation marks in abundance, helping viewers preview programs in the most clear and efficient way possible.

> P.O.V.: "A Litany for Survival—The Life and Work of Audre Lorde." 10 P.M. (13) An hour-long documentary about the poet who died of cancer in 1992 at 58. [Time approximate after pledge drive]

This chapter will guide you in deciding when you can use these marks of punctuation to signal relationships among sentence parts, to create particular rhythms, and to help readers follow your thoughts.

Editing for Effective Use of Punctuation

- Be sure that any material set off with dashes or enclosed in parentheses requires special treatment. Then check to see that the dashes or parentheses don't make the sentence difficult to follow. (43a, c)

- Decide whether the punctuation you have chosen creates the proper effect: parentheses tend to de-emphasize material they enclose; dashes add emphasis.

- Check to see that you use brackets to enclose parenthetical elements in material that is already within parentheses and to enclose words or comments inserted into a quotation. (43b)

- Check to see that you use colons to introduce explanations, series, lists, and quotations. Use dashes to mark off comments or to emphasize material at the end of a sentence. (43c, d)

- Check to be sure you've used slashes to mark line divisions in poetry quoted within text and to separate alternative terms. (43e)

- Make sure you've used ellipses (three equally spaced dots) enclosed in brackets to indicate omissions from quoted passages. (43f)

- If you are writing an online communication, check your use of asterisks to mark emphasis, underscore symbols before and after the titles of full-length works, and angle brackets to enclose email and World Wide Web addresses. Make sure you use emoticons sparingly. (43g)

43a Parentheses

Use parentheses to enclose material that is of minor or secondary importance in a sentence—material that supplements, clarifies, comments on, or illustrates what precedes or follows it.

▶ Inventors and men of genius have almost always been regarded as fools at the beginning (and very often at the end) of their careers.
—FYODOR DOSTOYEVSKY

▶ During my research, I found problems with the flat-rate income tax (a single-rate tax with no deductions).

Enclosing textual citations

▶ Freud and his followers have had a most significant impact on the ways abnormal functioning is understood and treated (Joseph, 1991).
—RONALD J. COMER, *Abnormal Psychology*

▶ Zamora notes that Kahlo referred to her first self-portrait, given to a close friend, as "your Botticelli" (110).

Enclosing numbers or letters in a list

▶ Five distinct styles can be distinguished: (1) Old New England, (2) Deep South, (3) Middle American, (4) Wild West, and (5) Far West or Californian.
—ALISON LURIE, *The Language of Clothes*

With other marks of punctuation

A period may be placed either inside or outside a closing parenthesis, depending on whether the parenthetical text is part of a larger sentence. A comma, if needed, is always placed *outside* a closing parenthesis (and never before an opening one).

▶ Gene Tunney's single defeat in an eleven-year career was to a flamboyant and dangerous fighter named Harry Greb ("The Human Windmill"), who seems to have been, judging from boxing literature, the dirtiest fighter in history.
—JOYCE CAROL OATES, "On Boxing"

Choosing among parentheses, commas, and dashes

In general, use commas when the material to be set off is least interruptive (38c, e, f), parentheses when it is more interruptive, and dashes when it is the most interruptive (43c).

43b Brackets

Use brackets to enclose parenthetical elements in material that is itself within parentheses. Also use brackets to enclose explanatory words, comments, or ellipses (43f) that you are inserting into a quotation.

Setting off material within parentheses

▶ **Eventually the investigation had to examine the major agencies (including the previously sacrosanct National Security Agency [NSA]) that were conducting covert operations.**

Inserting material within quotations

▶ **As Curtis argues, "He [Johnson] saw it [the war] as a game or wrestling match in which he would make Ho Chi Minh cry 'uncle.' "**

The bracketed words clarify the words *he* and *it* in the original quotation.

In the quotation in the following sentence, the artist Gauguin's name is misspelled. The bracketed word *sic,* which means "so," tells readers that the person being quoted—not the writer who has picked up the quotation—made the mistake.

▶ **One admirer wrote, "She was the most striking woman I'd ever seen— a sort of wonderful combination of Mia Farrow and one of Gaugin's [*sic*] Polynesian nymphs."**

See p. 347 for information on using angle brackets.

43c Dashes

Use dashes to insert a comment or to highlight material in a sentence. Dashes give more emphasis than parentheses to the material they enclose. On most typewriters and with some word-processing software, a dash is made with two hyphens (--) with no spaces before, between, or after. In some software, a solid dash can be typed as it is in this book (—). Many word-processing programs automatically convert two typed hyphens into a solid dash.

> ▶ The pleasures of reading itself—who doesn't remember?—were like those of Christmas cake, a sweet devouring.
> —EUDORA WELTY, "A Sweet Devouring"

> ▶ Mr. Angell is addicted to dashes and parentheses—small pauses or digressions in a narrative like those moments when the umpire dusts off home plate or a pitcher rubs up a new ball—that serve to slow an already deliberate movement almost to a standstill.
> —JOEL CONARROE, *New York Times Book Review*

Emphasizing material at the end of a sentence

> ▶ In the twentieth century it has become almost impossible to moralize about epidemics—except those which are transmitted sexually.
> —SUSAN SONTAG, *AIDS and Its Metaphors*

Marking a sudden change in tone

> ▶ New York is a catastrophe—but a magnificent catastrophe.
> —LE CORBUSIER

Indicating hesitation in speech

> ▶ As the officer approached his car, the driver stammered, "What—what have I done?"

Introducing a summary or explanation

> ▶ In walking, the average adult person employs a motor mechanism that weighs about eighty pounds—sixty pounds of muscle and twenty pounds of bone.   —EDWIN WAY TEALE

Use dashes carefully, not only because they are somewhat informal but also because they can cause an abrupt break in reading. Too many of them create a jerky, disconnected effect that can make it hard for readers to follow your thought.

43d Colons

Use a colon to introduce explanations or examples and to separate elements from one another.

Introducing an explanation, an example, or an appositive

▶ The men may also wear the getup known as Sun Belt Cool: a pale beige suit, open-collared shirt (often in a darker shade than the suit), cream-colored loafers and aviator sunglasses.
— ALISON LURIE, *The Language of Clothes*

Introducing a series, a list, or a quotation

▶ At the baby's one-month birthday party, Ah Po gave him the Four Valuable Things: ink, inkslab, paper, and brush.
— MAXINE HONG KINGSTON, *China Men*

▶ We began a series of workshops on nonviolence, and we repeatedly asked ourselves: "Are you able to accept blows without retaliation?"
— MARTIN LUTHER KING JR., "Letter from Birmingham Jail"

Separating elements

SALUTATIONS IN FORMAL LETTERS
▶ Dear Dr. Chapman:

HOURS, MINUTES, AND SECONDS
▶ 4:59 p.m.
▶ 2:15:06

RATIOS
▶ a ratio of 5:1

BIBLICAL CHAPTERS AND VERSES
▶ I Corinthians 3:3–5

TITLES AND SUBTITLES
▶ *The Joy of Insight: Passions of a Physicist*

CITIES AND PUBLISHERS IN BIBLIOGRAPHIC ENTRIES
▶ Boston: Bedford, 2001

Editing for colons

Do not put a colon between a verb and its object or complement—unless the object is a quotation.

▶ Some natural fibers are:/cotton, wool, silk, and linen.

Do not put a colon between a preposition and its object or after such expressions as *such as, especially,* and *including.*

▶ **In poetry, additional power may come from devices such as/ simile, metaphor, and alliteration.**

43e Slashes

Use slashes to mark line divisions between two or three lines of poetry quoted within text. When using a slash to separate lines of poetry, precede and follow it with a space (42b).

▶ **In Sonnet 29, the persona states, "For thy sweet love rememb'red such wealth brings / That then I scorn to change my state with kings."**

Use a slash to separate alternatives.

▶ **Then there was Daryl, the cabdriver/bartender.**
—JOHN L'HEUREUX, *The Handmaid of Desire*

43f Ellipses

Ellipses, or ellipsis points, are three equally spaced dots. Ellipses are usually used to indicate that something has been omitted from a quoted passage. Just as you should carefully use quotation marks around any material that you quote directly from a source, so you should carefully use ellipses to indicate that you have left out part of a quotation that otherwise appears to be a complete sentence. Ellipses have been used in the following example to indicate two omissions—one in the middle of the first sentence and one at the end of the second sentence. Note that MLA style calls for enclosing ellipsis points used to mark an omission in brackets [. . .] to let readers know that the ellipses are not part of the original passage.

ORIGINAL TEXT

Much male fear of feminism is the fear that, in becoming whole human beings, women will cease to mother men, to provide the breast, the lullaby, the continuous attention associated by the infant with the mother. Much male fear of feminism is infantilism—the longing to remain the mother's son, to possess a woman who exists purely for him.   —ADRIENNE RICH

WITH ELLIPSES

As Adrienne Rich argues, "Much male fear of feminism is the fear that [. . .] women will cease to mother men, to provide the breast, the lullaby, the continuous attention associated by the infant with the mother. Much male fear of feminism is infantilism—the longing to remain the mother's son [. . .]."

When you omit the last part of a quoted sentence, add a period after the ellipses—for a total of four dots. Be sure a complete sentence comes before and after the four points. If your shortened quotation ends with a source citation (such as a page number, a name, or a title), follow these steps:

1. Use three ellipsis points (enclosed in brackets) but no period after the quotation.
2. Add the closing quotation mark, closed up to the third ellipsis point.
3. Add the source of documentation in parentheses.
4. Use a period to indicate the end of the sentence.

▶ **Hawthorne writes, "My friend, whom I shall call Oberon—it was a name of fancy and friendship between him and me [. . .]" (575).**

You can also use ellipses to indicate a pause or a hesitation in speech in the same way that you can use a dash for that purpose (43c).

▶ **Then the voice, husky and familiar, came to wash over us—"The winnah, and still heavyweight champeen of the world . . . Joe Louis."**
   –MAYA ANGELOU, *I Know Why the Caged Bird Sings*

43g Online punctuation

If you participate in any computer bulletin boards, discussion groups, or other electronic communication, you are already familiar with some new uses of punctuation marks and other keyboard characters. These marks can add emphasis, set off the titles of works, and express something about the sender's mood. Limited by formatting constraints, online punctuation and mechanics reflect the informality of the Internet. (See Chapter 14.)

Emoticons, which are marks made with combinations of keyboard characters, commonly express humor or mood. Emoticons can show readers, for example, when you want your remarks to be considered humorous or ironic. (Look at them sideways.)

▶ **the smile: :-)**
▶ **the wink: ;-)**

When italics and underlining are unavailable, as they sometimes are in online communication, use asterisks to help create special emphasis.

▶ **Her homepage *must* be updated.**

Use the underscore symbol before and after the title of a full-length work.

▶ **Have you read Bill Gates's _The Road Ahead_?**

Use angle brackets to set off email addresses and addresses on the World Wide Web from the rest of your text (14g).

▶ **Visit us on the Web at <www.bedfordstmartins.com>.**

44

Capitalization

Capital letters are a key signal in everyday life. Look around any store to see their importance: you can shop for just Levi's or *any* blue jeans, for Coca-Cola or *any* cola, for Kleenex or *any* house brand. In each of these instances, the capital letter indicates a particular brand. This chapter will help you use capitals appropriately.

Editing for Capitalization

- Make sure to capitalize the first letter of each sentence. If you quote a poem, follow its original capitalization. (44a)
- Check to make sure you have appropriately capitalized proper nouns and proper adjectives. (44b)
- If you have used titles of people or of works, see that they are capitalized correctly. (44c, d)
- Double-check the capitalization of geographical directions (*north* or *North*?), family relationships (*dad* or *Dad*?), and seasons of the year (*spring*, never *Spring*). (44e, f, g)
- Check to make sure your word-processing program has not automatically capitalized words inappropriately. Many programs insert capitals after periods and other closing punctuation.

44a Capitalize the first word of a sentence.

The first word of a sentence is always capitalized. If you are quoting a full sentence, capitalize the first word of the quotation unless you are weaving the quotation into your sentence with *that.*

▶ **Getting everyone to the ceremony on time will present a challenge.**
▶ **I overheard Alex say, "Graduation will be traumatic."**
▶ **She said that graduation will be traumatic.**

Capitalization of a sentence following a colon is optional.

▶ **Gould cites the work of Darwin: The [*or* the] theory of natural selection incorporates the principle of evolutionary ties among all animals.**

Capitalize a sentence within parentheses unless the parenthetical sentence is inserted into another sentence.

▶ **Combining the best in Japanese engineering with the attitude of Evel Knievel (on a good day), the new MK9 is one bad hog. (It's also an ergonomically correct one.)**   **—*Wired*, July 1996**
▶ **Gould cites the work of Darwin (see page 150).**

When citing poetry, follow the capitalization of the original poem. Though most poets capitalize the first word of each line in a poem, some poets do not.

▶ **Morning sun heats up the young beech tree**
leaves and almost lights them into fireflies
    —JUNE JORDAN, "Aftermath"

44b Capitalize proper nouns and proper adjectives.

Capitalize proper nouns (those naming specific persons, places, and things) and most adjectives formed from proper nouns. All other nouns are common nouns and are not capitalized unless they are used as part of a proper noun: *a street,* but *Elm Street.*

PROPER	COMMON
Alfred Hitchcock, Hitchcockian	a director
Brazil, Brazilian	a nation
World Wide Web	a homepage, a site

Some commonly capitalized terms

GEOGRAPHICAL NAMES

Pacific Ocean	an ocean
the South	the southern part of the island
Africa, African sculpture	a beautiful sculpture

STRUCTURES AND MONUMENTS

Washington Monument	a monument

SHIPS, TRAINS, AIRCRAFT, AND SPACECRAFT

S.S. *Titanic*	a luxury liner
Challenger	a spaceship

ORGANIZATIONS, BUSINESSES, AND GOVERNMENT INSTITUTIONS

Library of Congress	a federal agency
General Motors Corporation	a blue-chip company

ACADEMIC INSTITUTIONS AND COURSES

University of California	a state university
Political Science 102	a political science course

HISTORICAL EVENTS AND ERAS

Shays's Rebellion	a rebellion
the Renaissance	a renaissance of sorts

RELIGIONS AND RELIGIOUS TERMS

God	a god
the Qur'an	a prayer book
Catholicism, Catholics	a religion

For Multilingual Writers: *Learning English Capitalization*

English capitalization may pose challenges for speakers of other languages because capitalization systems vary considerably among languages. Arabic, Chinese, and Hebrew, for example, do not use capital letters at all. English may be the only language to capitalize the first-person singular pronoun (*I*), but Dutch and German capitalize some forms of the second-person pronoun (*you*). German capitalizes all nouns; and, in fact, English used to capitalize more nouns than it does now.

ETHNIC GROUPS, NATIONALITIES, AND THEIR LANGUAGES

Russia, Russian	a language
African American	a group

TRADE NAMES

WordPerfect	word-processing software
Nike shoes	sneakers

For advice on using the unusually capitalized terms such as *QuickTime* and *AltaVista* often found online, see p. 143.

44c Capitalize titles before proper names.

When used alone or following a proper name, most titles are not capitalized. One common exception is the word *president*, which many writers capitalize when it refers to the President of the United States.

Justice O'Connor	Sandra Day O'Connor, the justice
Professor Lisa Ede	my history professor
Dr. R. Whisler	R. Whisler, our doctor

44d Capitalize titles of works.

Capitalize most words in titles of books, articles, speeches, stories, essays, plays, poems, documents, films, paintings, and musical compositions. Do not capitalize articles (*a, an, the*), short prepositions,

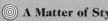

◎ **A Matter of Style:** *Shouting Online*

Some writers capitalize words or even passages to add special emphasis. Although you may see this use of capitals for emphasis in print, many listservs and newsgroups on the Internet ask participants to practice good netiquette by resisting the urge to use all capital letters, which can be irritating to readers who feel as if they are being SHOUTED AT. (Remember that using all lowercase letters can also be annoying.) Instead of uppercase letters, use asterisks to add emphasis: *Sorry for the abrupt response, but I am *very* busy.*

conjunctions, and the *to* in an infinitive unless they are the first or last words in a title or subtitle.

Walt Whitman: A Life	Declaration of Independence
"As Time Goes By"	*Sense and Sensibility*

44e **Capitalize compass directions only if the word designates a specific geographical region.**

▶ John Muir headed west, motivated by the desire to explore.

▶ Kobi divided the map into sections: the Northeast, the South, and the West.

44f **Capitalize family relationship words only when used as part of a name or when substituted for a name.**

▶ When she was a child, my mother shared a room with her aunt.

▶ I could always tell when Mother was annoyed with Aunt Rose.

44g **Do not capitalize seasons of the year or parts of the academic or financial year.**

spring	fall semester
winter	winter term
autumn	third-quarter earnings

45

Abbreviations and Numbers

Any time you open up a telephone book, you see an abundance of abbreviations and numbers, as in the following movie theater listing from the Berkeley telephone book:

Oaks Theater   1875 Solano Av   Brk

Abbreviations and numbers allow writers to present detailed information in a small amount of space. This chapter explains the conventions for using abbreviations and figures in academic and professional writing.

Editing Abbreviations and Numbers

- Make sure you use abbreviations and numbers according to the conventions of a specific field (see p. 354): 57% might be acceptable in a math paper, but *57 percent* may be more appropriate in a sociology essay.
- If you use an abbreviation readers might not understand, make sure you spell out the term the first time you use it and give the abbreviation in parentheses.
- If you use an abbreviation more than once, make sure you use it consistently.

45a Abbreviate titles used before and after proper names.

Ms. Susanna Moller	Henry Louis Gates Jr.
Mr. Aaron Oforlea	Karen Lancry, M.D.
Dr. Edward Davies	Samuel Cohen, Ph.D.

Other titles—including religious, academic, and government titles—should be spelled out in academic writing. In other writing, they can be abbreviated before a full name but should be written out when used with only a last name.

Rev. Fleming Rutledge Reverend Rutledge
Prof. Jaime Mejia   Professor Mejia
Gen. Colin Powell   General Powell

Do not use both a title and an academic degree with a person's name. Use one or the other. Instead of *Dr. Beverly Moss, Ph.D.*, write *Dr. Beverly Moss* or *Beverly Moss, Ph.D.*

45b Use abbreviations with years and hours.

399 BC ("before Christ")
AD 49 (*anno Domini,* Latin for "year of our Lord")
210 BCE ("before the common era")
11:15 a.m. (or AM)
9:00 p.m. (or PM)

BCE and CE ("common era") are becoming the preferred abbreviations with dates; both follow the year.

45c Use abbreviations for familiar business, government, and science terms.

As long as you can be sure your readers will understand them, use common abbreviations such as *PBS, NASA, DNA,* and *CIA.* If an abbreviation may be unfamiliar, however, spell out the full term the first time you use it, and give the abbreviation in parentheses. After that, you can use the abbreviation by itself.

▶ The Comprehensive Test Ban (CTB) Treaty was first proposed in the 1950s. For those nations signing it, the CTB would bring to a halt all nuclear weapons testing.

45d Use abbreviations in official company names.

Use such abbreviations as *Co., Inc., Corp.,* and *&* if they are part of a company's official name. Do not, however, use these abbreviations in most other contexts.

           corporation
▶ Sears, Roebuck & Co. was the only large ~~corp.~~ in town.

45e Use abbreviations in notes and source citations.

cf.	compare (*confer*)
e.g.	for example (*exempli gratia*)
et al.	and others (*et alia*)
etc.	and so forth (*et cetera*)
i.e.	that is (*id est*)
N.B.	note well (*nota bene*)

These abbreviations are not generally appropriate except in notes and citations in most academic and professional writing.

A Matter of Style: *Abbreviations and Numbers in Different Fields*

Use of abbreviations and numbers varies among different fields. See a typical example from a biochemistry textbook.

> The energy of a green photon . . . is 57 kilocalories per mole (kcal/mol). An alternative unit of energy is the joule (J), which is equal to 0.239 calorie; 1 kcal/mol is equal to 4.184 kJ/mol.
>
> —LUBERT STRYER, *Biochemistry*

These two sentences demonstrate how useful figures and abbreviations can be; just imagine how difficult trying to read the same sentences would be if the numbers and units of measurement were all written out.

You should become familiar with the conventions governing abbreviations and numbers in your field. The following reference books provide guidelines:

MLA Handbook for Writers of Research Papers
for literature and the humanities

Publication Manual of the American Psychological Association
for the social sciences

Scientific Style and Format: The CBE Manual for Authors, Editors, and Publishers
for the natural sciences

The Chicago Manual of Style
for the humanities

AIP Style Manual
for physics and the applied sciences

for example,
▶ Many firms have policies to help working parents—e.g., flexible hours,
   ^
parental leave, and day care.

▶ Before the conference began, Haivan unpacked the name tags, programs,
      and so forth.
pens, etc.
      ^

45f Abbreviate units of measurement, and use symbols in charts and graphs.

Symbols such as %, +, $, and = are acceptable in charts and graphs. Dollar signs are acceptable with figures: *$11* (but not with words: *eleven dollars*). Units of measurement can be abbreviated in charts and graphs (*4 in.*) but not in the body of a paper (*four inches*).

45g Use other abbreviations according to convention.

Some abbreviations required in notes and in source citations are not appropriate in the body of a paper.

CHAPTER AND PAGES	chapter, page, pages (*not* ch., p., pp.)
MONTHS	January, February (*not* Jan., Feb.)
STATES AND NATIONS	California, Mexico (*not* Calif., Mex.) Two exceptions are Washington, D.C., and U.S., which is acceptable as an adjective but not as a noun: *U.S. borders* but *in the United States* (not *in the U.S.*).

45h Spell out numbers expressed in one or two words.

If you can write out a number in one or two words, do so. Use figures for longer numbers.

         thirty-eight
▶ Her screams were heard by 38 people, none of whom called the police.
                           ^
         216
▶ A baseball is held together by ~~two hundred sixteen~~ red stitches.
                                 ^

If one of several numbers *of the same kind* in the same sentence requires a figure, you should use figures for all the numbers in that sentence.

$100
▶ An audio system can range in cost from ~~one hundred dollars~~ to $2,599.
                                         ^

45i   Spell out numbers that begin sentences.

When a sentence begins with a number, either spell out the number or rewrite the sentence.

One hundred nineteen
▶ ~~119~~ years of CIA labor cost taxpayers sixteen million dollars.
  ^

Most readers find it easier to read figures than three-word numbers; thus the best solution may be to rewrite this sentence: *Taxpayers spent sixteen million dollars for 119 years of CIA labor.*

45j   Use figures according to convention.

ADDRESSES	23 Main Street; 175 Fifth Avenue
DATES	September 17, 1951; 6 June 1983; 4 BCE; the 1860s
DECIMALS AND FRACTIONS	65.34; $8^{1/2}$
PERCENTAGES	77 percent (*or* 77%)
EXACT AMOUNTS OF MONEY	$7,348; $1.46 trillion; $2.50; thirty-five (*or* 35) cents
SCORES AND STATISTICS	an 8–3 Red Sox victory; a verbal score of 600; an average age of 22; a mean of 53
TIME OF DAY	6:00 a.m. (*or* AM)

For Multilingual Writers: *Use of* Hundred

The term *hundred* is used idiomatically in English. When it is linked with numbers like *two, eight,* and so on, the word *hundred* remains singular: *Eight hundred years have passed and still old animosities run deep.* Add the plural -s to *hundred* only when no number precedes the term: *Hundreds of priceless books were lost in the fire.*

46

Italics

The slanted type known as italics is more than just a pretty typeface. Indeed, italics give words special meaning or emphasis. In the sentence "Many people read *People* on the subway every day," the italics tell us that *People* is a publication. You may have a word processor that produces italic type; if not, underline words that you would otherwise italicize.

Editing for Italics

- Check that all titles of long works are italicized. (46a)
- If you use any words, letters, or numbers as terms, make sure they are in italics. (46b)
- Italicize any non-English words or phrases that are not in an English dictionary. (46c)
- When you use italics to emphasize words, check to be sure you use the italics sparingly. (46e)

46a Italicize titles of long works.

In general, use italics for titles of long works; use quotation marks for shorter works (42c).

BOOKS	*Paradise*
CHOREOGRAPHIC WORKS	Agnes de Mille's *Rodeo*
FILMS AND VIDEOS	*The Hurricane*
LONG MUSICAL WORKS	*Brandenburg Concertos*
LONG POEMS	*The Bhagavadgita*
MAGAZINES AND JOURNALS	*Ebony, New England Journal of Medicine*
NEWSPAPERS	the Cleveland *Plain Dealer*
PAINTINGS AND SCULPTURE	Georgia O'Keeffe's *Black Iris*
PAMPHLETS	Thomas Paine's *Common Sense*
PLAYS	*Rent*
RADIO SERIES	*All Things Considered*

RECORDINGS	*The Miseducation of Lauryn Hill*
SOFTWARE	*Quicken*
TELEVISION SERIES	*The Simpsons, Nightline*
WEB SITES	*Salon, Voice of the Shuttle*

Do not use italics for sacred books, such as the Bible and the Qur'an; for public documents, such as the Constitution and the Magna Carta; or for the titles of your own papers.

46b Italicize words, letters, and numbers used as terms.

▶ On the back of his jersey was the famous *24.*

▶ One characteristic of some New York speech is the absence of postvocalic *r*—for example, pronouncing the word *four* as "fouh."

46c Italicize non-English words and phrases.

Italicize words from other languages unless they have become part of English—like the French "bourgeois" or the Russian "samovar," for example. If a word is in an English dictionary, it does not need italics.

▶ At last one of the phantom sleighs gliding along the street would come to a stop, and with gawky haste Mr. Burness in his fox-furred *shapka* would make for our door.   —VLADIMIR NABOKOV, *Speak, Memory*

Always italicize Latin genus and species names.

▶ The caterpillars of *Hapalia,* when attacked by the wasp *Apanteles machaeralis,* drop suddenly from their leaves and suspend themselves in air by a silken thread.   —STEPHEN JAY GOULD, "Nonmoral Nature"

46d Italicize names of aircraft, spacecraft, ships, and trains.

Spirit of St. Louis	Amtrak's *Silver Star*
Discovery	U.S.S. *Iowa*

46e Use italics for emphasis.

Italics can help to create emphasis in writing, but use them sparingly for this purpose. It is usually better to create emphasis with sentence structure and word choice.

▶ **Great literature and a class of literate readers are nothing new in India. What is new is the emergence of a gifted generation of Indian writers** *working in English.* **–SALMAN RUSHDIE**

47
Hyphens

Hyphens show up every time you make a left-hand turn, wear a Chicago Bulls T-shirt, buy gasoline at a self-service station, visit a writing center for one-on-one tutoring, worry about a long-term relationship, listen to hip-hop, or eat Tex-Mex food. Sometimes the dictionary will tell you whether to hyphenate a word. Other times, you will have to apply some general rules, which you will find in this chapter.

Editing for Hyphens
- Check that a word that is broken at the end of a line is divided at an appropriate point. (47a)
- Double-check compound words to be sure they are properly closed up, separated, or hyphenated. If in doubt, consult a dictionary. (47b, c, d)
- Check all terms that have prefixes or suffixes to see whether you need hyphens. (47e)

47a Use a hyphen to divide a word at the end of a line.

Break words between syllables. The word *metaphor*, for instance, contains three syllables (*met-a-phor*), and you can break the word after either the *t* or the *a*. All dictionaries show syllable breaks, so the best advice for dividing words correctly is simply to look them up. In addition, you should follow certain other conventions.

- Never divide one-syllable words or abbreviations, contractions, or figures.
- Leave at least two letters on each line when dividing a word. Do not divide words such as *acorn* (*a-corn*) and *scratchy* (*scratch-y*) at all, and break a word such as *Americana* (*A-mer-i-can-a*) only after the *r* or the *i*.
- Divide compound words, such as *anklebone* or *mother-in-law*, only between their parts (*ankle-bone*) or after their hyphens.
- Divide words with prefixes or suffixes between the parts. Break the word *disappearance*, then, after its prefix (*dis-appearance*) or before its suffix (*disappear-ance*). Divide prefixed words that include a hyphen, such as *self-righteous*, only after the hyphen.

47b Check a dictionary to be certain when to use a hyphen with compound nouns and verbs.

Some compound nouns and verbs are one word, some are separate words, and some require hyphens. Consult a dictionary to be sure.

ONE WORD	rowboat, textbook, flowerpot, homepage
SEPARATE WORDS	high school, parking meter, shut up
WITH HYPHENS	city-state, sister-in-law, cross-fertilize

A Matter of Style: *When in Doubt, Close It Up*

New compound words associated with technology are quickly becoming part of our everyday language. What should you do when many of these words are not yet in dictionaries? Helpful advice comes from the editors of *Wired* magazine:

From computer commands like *whois* and onscreen nouns like *logon*, we have evolved this commandment: "When in doubt, close it up." Words spelled solid—like *startup* or *homepage* or *videogame*—may seem odd at first, but . . . we know from experience that new terms often start separated, then become hyphenated, and eventually end up as one word. Go there now.
     —*Wired Style*

47c Use a hyphen with compound adjectives before a noun.

Hyphenate most compound adjectives before a noun. Do not hyphenate compound adjectives that follow a noun.

a *well-liked* boss   Our boss is *well liked.*
a *six-foot* plank   The plank is *six feet* long.

In general, the reason for hyphenating compound adjectives is to facilitate reading.

▶ **Designers often use potted palms as living-room dividers.**
                                                        ^
Without the hyphen, *living* may seem to modify *room dividers.*

Never hyphenate an *-ly* adverb and an adjective.

▶ **They used a widely distributed mailing list.**

Use suspended hyphens in a series of compound adjectives.

▶ **Each student did the work him- or herself.**

47d Hyphenate fractions and compound numbers from *twenty-one* to *ninety-nine.*

two-sevenths   thirty-seven

47e Use a hyphen with some prefixes and suffixes.

Most words containing prefixes or suffixes are written without hyphens: *antiwar, gorillalike.* Here are some exceptions.

BEFORE CAPITALIZED WORDS	pro-Democratic, non-Catholic
WITH FIGURES	pre-1960, post-1945
WITH *ALL-*, *EX-*, AND *SELF-*	all-state, ex-partner, self-possessed
WITH *-ELECT*	mayor-elect
FOR CLARITY	re-cover, anti-inflation, troll-like

Re-cover means "cover again"; the hyphen distinguishes it from *recover,* meaning "get well." In *anti-inflation* and *troll-like,* the hyphens separate double and triple letters.

DIRECTORY TO MLA STYLE

MLA style for in-text citations (Chapter 48)

MLA style for a list of works cited (Chapter 50)

BOOKS

$\mathbf{T}$his part of *The Everyday Writer* discusses the basic format for the Modern Language Association (MLA) style and provides examples of various kinds of sources. MLA style is widely used to document sources in writing that deals with literature, languages, and other fields. For further reference, consult the *MLA Handbook for Writers of Research Papers*, fifth edition, 1999.

48

MLA Style for In-Text Citations

MLA style requires documentation in the text of an essay for every quotation, paraphrase, and summary as well as other material requiring documentation (12f). In-text citations document material from other sources with both signal phrases and parenthetical citations. Signal phrases introduce the material, often including the author's name. Keep your parenthetical citations short, but include the information your readers need to locate the full citation in the list of works cited at the end of the text.

Place a parenthetical citation as near the relevant material as possible without disrupting the flow of the sentence. Note in the following examples *where* punctuation is placed in relation to the parentheses.

1. AUTHOR NAMED IN A SIGNAL PHRASE

Ordinarily, you can use the author's name in a signal phrase—to introduce the material—and cite the page number(s) in parentheses.

```
Herrera indicates that Kahlo believed in a "vitalistic
form of pantheism" (328).
```

2. AUTHOR NAMED IN PARENTHESES

When you do not mention the author in a signal phrase, include the author's last name before the page number(s) in the parentheses. Use no punctuation between the author's name and the page number(s).

```
In places, de Beauvoir "sees Marxists as believing in
subjectivity" (Whitmarsh 63).
```

3. **TWO OR THREE AUTHORS**

Use all the authors' last names in a phrase or in parentheses.

```
Gortner, Hebrun, and Nicolson maintain that "opinion
leaders" influence other people in an organization
because they are respected, not because they hold high
positions (175).
```

4. **FOUR OR MORE AUTHORS**

Use the first author's name and *et al.* ("and others"), or name all the authors in a phrase or in parentheses.

```
Similarly, as Belenky, Clinchy, Goldberger, and Tarule
assert, examining the lives of women expands our
understanding of human development (7).
```

5. **ORGANIZATION AS AUTHOR**

Give the full name of a corporate author or a shortened form of it in a phrase or in parentheses.

```
Any study of social welfare involves a close analysis
of "the impacts, the benefits, and the costs" of its
policies (Social Research Corporation iii).
```

6. **UNKNOWN AUTHOR**

Use the full title, if it is brief, in your text—or a shortened version of the title in parentheses.

```
"Hype," by one analysis, is "an artificially
engendered atmosphere of hysteria" ("Today's
Marketplace" 51).
```

7. **AUTHOR OF TWO OR MORE WORKS**

If your list of works cited has more than one work by the same author, include a shortened version of the title of the work you are citing in a phrase or in parentheses.

Gardner shows readers their own silliness in his
description of a "pointless, ridiculous monster,
crouched in the shadows, stinking of dead men,
murdered children, and martyred cows" (<u>Grendel</u> 2).

8. TWO OR MORE AUTHORS WITH THE SAME LAST NAME

Always include the authors' first *and* last names in the signal phrases or in the parenthetical citations for their works.

Children will learn to write if they are allowed to
choose their own subjects, James Britton asserts,
citing the Schools Council study of the 1960s (37-42).

9. MULTIVOLUME WORK

In a parenthetical citation, note the volume number first and then the page number(s), with a colon and one space between them.

Modernist writers prized experimentation and gradually
even sought to blur the line between poetry and prose,
according to Forster (3: 150).

If you name only one volume of the work in your list of works cited, you need include only the page number in the parentheses.

10. LITERARY WORK

Because literary works are often available in many different editions, cite the page number(s) from the edition you used followed by a semicolon, and, in addition, give other identifying information that will lead readers to the passage in any edition—such as the act and/or scene in a play (37; sc. 1). For a novel, indicate the part or chapter (175; ch. 4).

In utter despair, Dostoyevsky's character Mitya
wonders aloud about the "terrible tragedies realism
inflicts on people" (376; bk. 8, ch. 2).

For poems, cite the part (if there is one) and line(s), separated by a period. If you are citing only line numbers, use the word *line(s)* in the first reference (lines 33–34).

> On dying, Whitman speculates, "All goes onward and
> outward, nothing collapses, / And to die is different
> from what anyone supposed, and luckier" (6.129-30).

For verse plays, give only the act, scene, and line numbers, separated by periods.

> As <u>Macbeth</u> begins, the witches greet Banquo as "Lesser
> than Macbeth, and greater" (1.3.65).

11. WORK IN AN ANTHOLOGY

For an essay, short story, or other piece of prose reprinted in an anthology, use the name of the author of the work, not the editor of the anthology, but use the page number(s) from the anthology.

> Narratives of captivity play a major role in early
> writing by women in the United States, as demonstrated
> by Silko (219).

12. BIBLE

Identify quotations by giving the title of the Bible, the book, and the chapter and verse separated by a period. In your text, spell out the names of books. In parenthetical citations, use abbreviations for books with names of five or more letters (*Gen.* for *Genesis*).

> He ignored the admonition "Pride goes before
> destruction, and a haughty spirit before a fall" (<u>New</u>
> <u>Oxford Annotated Bible</u>, Prov. 16.18).

13. INDIRECT SOURCE

Use the abbreviation *qtd. in* to indicate that you are quoting from someone else's report of a conversation, interview, letter, or the like.

As Arthur Miller says, "When somebody is destroyed
everybody finally contributes to it, but in Willy's
case, the end product would be virtually the same"
(qtd. in Martin and Meyer 375).

14. TWO OR MORE SOURCES IN THE SAME CITATION

Separate the information with semicolons.

Economists recommend that <u>employment</u> be redefined to
include unpaid domestic labor (Clark 148; Nevins 39).

15. ENTIRE WORK OR ONE-PAGE ARTICLE

Include the reference in the text without any page numbers or
parentheses.

Michael Ondaatje's poetic sensibility transfers
beautifully to prose in <u>The English Patient</u>.

16. WORK WITHOUT PAGE NUMBERS

If a work has no page numbers or is only one page long, you may
omit the page number. If a work uses paragraph numbers instead, use
the abbreviation *par(s)*.

Whitman considered their speech "a source of a native
grand opera," in the words of Ellison (par. 13).

17. ELECTRONIC OR NONPRINT SOURCE

Give enough information in a signal phrase or parenthetical citation
for readers to locate the source in the list of works cited. Usually give the
author or title under which you list the source. Specify a source's page,
section, paragraph, or screen numbers, if numbered, in parentheses.

Describing children's language acquisition, Pinker
explains that "what's innate about language is just a
way of paying attention to parental speech" (Johnson,
sec. 1).

49

MLA Style for Explanatory and Bibliographic Notes

MLA style allows explanatory notes for information or commentary that does not readily fit into your text but is needed for clarification or further explanation. In addition, MLA style permits bibliographic notes for citing several sources for one point and for offering thanks to, information about, or evaluation of a source. Use superscript numbers in the text to refer readers to the notes, which may appear as endnotes (typed under the heading *Notes* on a separate page after the text but before the list of works cited) or as footnotes at the bottom of the page.

1. SUPERSCRIPT NUMBER IN TEXT

Stewart emphasizes the existence of social contacts in Hawthorne's life so that the audience will accept a different Hawthorne, one more attuned to modern times than the figure in Woodberry.[3]

2. NOTE

[3] Woodberry does, however, show that Hawthorne was often an unsociable individual. He emphasizes the seclusion of Hawthorne's mother, who separated herself from her family after the death of her husband, often even taking meals alone (28). Woodberry seems to imply that Mrs. Hawthorne's isolation rubbed off onto her son.

50

MLA Style for a List of Works Cited

A list of works cited is an alphabetical list of the sources you have referred to in your essay. (If your instructor asks you to list everything you have read as background, call the list *Works Consulted*.) Here are some guidelines for preparing such a list.

- Start your list on a separate page after the text of your essay and any notes.
- Continue the consecutive numbering of pages.
- Type the heading *Works Cited*, not underlined, italicized, or in quotation marks, centered one inch from the top of the page.
- Start each entry flush with the left margin; indent subsequent lines one-half inch (or five spaces if you are using a typewriter). Double-space the entire list.
- List sources alphabetically by author's last name. If the author is unknown, alphabetize the source by the first major word of the title.

The sample works cited entries that follow observe MLA's advice to underline words that are often italicized in print. Although most computers can generate italics easily, the MLA recommends that "you can avoid ambiguity by using underlining" in your research essays. If you wish to use italics instead, first check with your instructor.

Books

The basic entry for a book includes the following elements:

- *Author.* List the author by last name first, followed by a comma and the first name. End with a period.
- *Title.* Underline or (if your instructor permits) italicize the title and subtitle; capitalize all major words. End with a period. (See 44d for more on capitalizing titles.)
- *Publication information.* Give the city of publication; then add a colon, a space, and a shortened version of the publisher's name (*Bedford* for *Bedford/St. Martin's; Harcourt* for *Harcourt Brace; Oxford UP* for *Oxford University Press*). End with a comma, the year of publication, and a period.

1. ONE AUTHOR

deCordova, Richard. <u>Picture Personalities: The
     Emergence of the Star System in America</u>. Urbana:
     U of Illinois P, 1990.

2. TWO OR THREE AUTHORS

Give the first author listed on the title page, last name first; then list the name(s) of the other author(s) in regular order, with a comma between authors and an *and* before the last one.

Appleby, Joyce, Lynn Hunt, and Margaret Jacob. <u>Telling
     the Truth about History</u>. New York: Norton, 1994.

3. FOUR OR MORE AUTHORS

Give the first author listed on the title page, last name first, followed by a comma and *et al.* ("and others"), or list all the names, since the use of *et al.* diminishes the importance of the other contributors.

Belenky, Mary Field, Blythe Clinchy, Jill Goldberger,
     and Nancy Tarule. <u>Women's Ways of Knowing</u>. New
     York: Basic, 1986.

4. ORGANIZATION AS AUTHOR

Give the name of the group listed on the title page as the author, even if the same group published the book.

American Chemical Society. <u>Handbook for Authors
     of Papers in the American Chemical Society
     Publications</u>. Washington: American Chemical Soc.,
     1978.

5. UNKNOWN AUTHOR

Begin the entry with the title, and list the work alphabetically by the first major word of the title after any initial *A, An,* or *The.*

<u>The New York Times Atlas of the World</u>. New York: New
     York Times Books, 1980.

6. TWO OR MORE BOOKS BY THE SAME AUTHOR(S)

Arrange the entries alphabetically by title. Include the name(s) of the author(s) in the first entry, but in subsequent entries, use three hyphens followed by a period.

```
Lorde, Audre. A Burst of Light. Ithaca: Firebrand,
    1988.
---. Sister Outsider. Trumansburg: Crossing, 1984.
```

If you cite a work by one author who is also listed as the first coauthor of another work you cite, list the single-author work first, and repeat the author's name in the entry for the coauthored work. Also repeat the author's name if you cite a work in which that author is listed as the first of a different set of coauthors. In other words, use three hyphens only when the work is by *exactly* the same author(s) as the previous entry.

7. EDITOR(S)

Treat an editor as an author, but add a comma and *ed.* (or *eds.*).

```
Wall, Cheryl A., ed. Changing Our Own Words: Essays
    on Criticism, Theory, and Writing by Black Women.
    New Brunswick: Rutgers UP, 1989.
```

8. AUTHOR AND EDITOR

If you have cited the body of the text, begin with the author's name. Then list the editor, introduced by *Ed.* ("Edited by"), after the title.

```
James, Henry. Portrait of a Lady. Ed. Leon Edel.
    Boston: Houghton, 1963.
```

If you have cited the editor's contribution, begin the entry with the editor's name followed by a comma and *ed.* Then list the author's name, introduced by *By*, after the title.

```
Edel, Leon, ed. Portrait of a Lady. By Henry James.
    Boston: Houghton, 1963.
```

9. WORK IN AN ANTHOLOGY OR CHAPTER IN A BOOK WITH AN EDITOR

List the author(s) of the selection or chapter; its title; the title of the book in which the selection or chapter appears; *Ed.* and the name(s) of the editor(s) in regular order; the publication information; and the inclusive page numbers of the selection.

> Gordon, Mary. "The Parable of the Cave." The Writer on
>   Her Work. Ed. Janet Sternburg. New York: Norton,
>   1980. 27-32.

If the selection was originally published in a periodical and you are asked to supply information for this original source, use the following format. *Rpt.* is the abbreviation for *Reprinted.*

> Didion, Joan. "Why I Write." New York Times Book
>   Review. 9 Dec. 1976: 22. Rpt. in The Writer on
>   Her Work. Ed. Janet Sternburg. New York: Norton,
>   1980. 3-16.

For inclusive page numbers up to 99, note all digits in the second number. For numbers above 99, note only the last two digits and any others that change in the second number (115–18, 1378–79, 296–301).

10. TWO OR MORE ITEMS FROM AN ANTHOLOGY

Include the anthology itself in your list of works cited.

> Donalson, Melvin, ed. Cornerstones: An Anthology
>   of African American Literature. New York:
>   St. Martin's, 1996.

Then list each selection separately by its author and title, followed by a cross-reference to the anthology.

> Baker, Houston A., Jr. "There Is No More Beautiful
>   Way." Donalson 856-63.
> Ellison, Ralph. "What America Would Be Like without
>   Blacks." Donalson 737-41.

11. TRANSLATION

Begin the entry with the author's name, and give the translator's name, preceded by *Trans.* ("Translated by"), after the title.

```
Zamora, Martha. Frida Kahlo: The Brush of Anguish.
     Trans. Marilyn Sode Smith. San Francisco:
     Chronicle, 1990.
```

12. EDITION OTHER THAN THE FIRST

Add the information, in abbreviated form, after the title.

```
Kelly, Alfred H., Winfred A. Harbison, and Herman
     Belz. The American Constitution: Its Origins and
     Development. 6th ed. New York: Norton, 1983.
```

13. ONE VOLUME OF A MULTIVOLUME WORK

Give the volume number after the title, and list the number of volumes in the complete work after the date, using the abbreviations *Vol.* and *vols.*

```
Foner, Philip S., and Ronald L. Lewis, eds. The Black
     Worker. Vol. 3. Philadelphia: Lippincott, 1980.
     8 vols.
```

14. TWO OR MORE VOLUMES OF A MULTIVOLUME WORK

If you cite two or more volumes of a multivolume work, give the number of volumes in the complete work after the title, using the abbreviation *vols.*

```
Foner, Philip S., and Ronald L. Lewis, eds. The Black
     Worker. 8 vols. Philadelphia: Lippincott, 1980.
```

15. PREFACE, FOREWORD, INTRODUCTION, OR AFTERWORD

List the author of the item, the item title, the title of the book, and author. List the inclusive page numbers at the end of the entry.

```
Schlesinger, Arthur M., Jr. Introduction. Pioneer
     Women: Voices from the Kansas Frontier. By
     Joanna L. Stratton. New York: Simon, 1981. 11-15.
```

16. ARTICLE IN A REFERENCE WORK

List the author of the article, if known. If no author is identified, begin with the title. For a well-known encyclopedia, just note the edition and date. If the entries in the reference work are in alphabetical order, you need not give volume or page numbers.

Johnson, Peder J. "Concept Learning." Encyclopedia of

Education. 1971.

"Traquair, Sir John Stewart." Encyclopaedia

Britannica. 11th ed. 1911.

17. BOOK THAT IS PART OF A SERIES

Cite the series name as it appears on the title page, followed by any series number.

Moss, Beverly J., ed. Literacy across Communities.

Written Language Series 2. Cresskill: Hampton,

1994.

18. REPUBLICATION

To cite a modern edition of an older book, add the original date, followed by a period, after the title.

Scott, Walter. Kenilworth. 1821. New York: Dodd, 1956.

19. GOVERNMENT DOCUMENT

Begin with the author, if identified. Otherwise, start with the name of the government, followed by the agency and any subdivision. Use abbreviations if they can be readily understood. Then give the title, and underline or italicize it. For congressional documents, cite the number, session, and house; the type *(Report, Resolution, Document)*, in abbreviated form; and the number of the material. If you cite the *Congressional Record*, give only the date and page number. Otherwise, end with publication information; the publisher is often the Government Printing Office *(GPO)*.

United States. Cong. House. Report of the Joint

Subcommittee on Reconstruction. 39th Cong., 1st

sess. H. Rept. 30. 1865. New York: Arno, 1969.

U.S. Bureau of the Census. <u>Historical Statistics of</u>
 <u>the United States, Colonial Times to 1870</u>.
 Washington: GPO, 1975.

20. PAMPHLET

Treat a pamphlet as you would a book.

<u>Why Is Central America a Conflict Area?</u> Opposing
 Viewpoints Pamphlets. St. Paul: Greenhaven, 1984.

21. PUBLISHED PROCEEDINGS OF A CONFERENCE

Treat proceedings as a book, adding any necessary information about the conference after the title.

Martin, John Steven, and Christine Mason Sutherland,
 eds. <u>Proceedings of the Canadian Society for the</u>
 <u>History of Rhetoric</u>. Calgary: Canadian Soc. for
 the History of Rhetoric, 1986.

22. PUBLISHER'S IMPRINT

If a book was published by a publisher's imprint (indicated on the title page), hyphenate the imprint and the publisher's name.

Rose, Phyllis. <u>Parallel Lives: Five Victorian</u>
 <u>Marriages</u>. New York: Vintage-Random, 1984.

23. TITLE WITHIN A TITLE

Do not underline or italicize the title of a book within the title of a book you are citing. Underline or italicize and enclose in quotation marks the title of a short work within a book title.

Gilbert, Stuart. <u>James Joyce's</u> Ulysses. New York:
 Vintage-Random, 1955.

Renza, Louis A. <u>"A White Heron" and the Question of a</u>
 <u>Minor Literature</u>. Madison: U of Wisconsin P,
 1984.

24. SACRED BOOK

To cite individual published editions of sacred books, begin the entry with the title, underlined or italicized. For versions of the Bible in which the version is not part of the title, list the version after the title. Otherwise, the Bible and other sacred writings should not appear in the works cited list.

<u>The Jerusalem Bible</u>. Garden City: Doubleday, 1966.

Periodicals

The basic entry for a periodical includes the following elements:

- *Author.* List the author's last name first, followed by a comma and the first name. End with a period.
- *Article title.* Enclose the complete title in quotation marks, and capitalize all major words. End with a period inside the closing quotation marks.
- *Publication information.* Give the periodical title (excluding any initial *A, An,* or *The*), underlined or italicized (if your instructor permits) and with all major words capitalized; the volume number and, if appropriate, issue number; and the date of publication. For journals, list the year in parentheses, followed by a colon, a space, and the inclusive page numbers. For magazines and newspapers, list the month (abbreviated, except for *May, June,* and *July*) or the day and month before the year, and do not use parentheses. For inclusive page numbers, note all digits for numbers 1 to 99, and note only the last two digits and any others that change for numbers above 99 (134–45, 198–201). End with a period.

25. ARTICLE IN A JOURNAL PAGINATED BY VOLUME

Follow the title of the publication with the volume number in arabic numerals.

Norris, Margot. "Narration under a Blindfold: Reading Joyce's 'Clay.'" <u>PMLA</u> 102 (1987): 206-15.

26. ARTICLE IN A JOURNAL PAGINATED BY ISSUE

Follow the volume number with a period and the issue number.

Lofty, John. "The Politics at Modernism's Funeral." <u>Canadian Journal of Political and Social Theory</u> 6.3 (1987): 89-96.

27. ARTICLE IN A MONTHLY MAGAZINE

Put the month (or months, hyphenated) before the year. Separate the date and page number(s) with a colon.

```
Weiss, Philip. "The Book Thief: A True Tale of
    Bibliomania." Harper's Jan. 1994: 37-56.
```

28. ARTICLE IN A WEEKLY MAGAZINE

Include the day, month, and year in that order, with no commas between them.

```
Van Biema, David. "Parodies Regained." Time 21 Mar.
    1994: 46.
```

29. ARTICLE IN A NEWSPAPER

After the author and title of the article, give the name of the newspaper, underlined or italicized, as it appears on the front page but without any initial *A, An,* or *The.* Add the city in brackets after the name if it is not part of the title. Then give the date and the edition if one is listed, and add a colon. Follow the colon with a space, the section number or letter (if given), and then the page number(s). If the article appears on discontinuous pages, give the first page followed by a plus sign.

```
Bruni, Frank, and B. Drummond Ayers, Jr. "Bush Moving
    toward Center." New York Times 8 Mar. 2000, natl.
    ed.: A1+.
Martin, Claire. "Primary Care System under Attack."
    Denver Post 3 Jan. 2000: F1+.
```

30. EDITORIAL OR LETTER TO THE EDITOR

Use the label *Editorial* or *Letter,* neither underlined nor in quotation marks, after the title or, if there is no title, after the author's name.

```
Magee, Doug. "Soldier's Home." Editorial. Nation 26
    Mar. 1988: 400-01.
```

31. UNSIGNED ARTICLE

Begin with the article title, alphabetizing the entry according to the first word after any initial *A, An,* or *The.*

```
"The Odds of March." Time 15 Apr. 1985: 20+.
```

32. REVIEW

List the reviewer's name and the title of the review, if any, followed by *Rev. of* and the title and author or director of the work reviewed. Then add the publication information for the periodical in which the review appears.

> Solinger, Rickie. "Unsafe for Women." Rev. of <u>Next</u>
>   <u>Time, She'll Be Dead: Battering and How to Stop</u>
>   <u>It</u>, by Ann Jones. <u>New York Times Book Review</u> 20
>   Mar. 1994: 16.

33. ARTICLE WITH A TITLE WITHIN THE TITLE

Enclose in single quotation marks the title of a short work within an article title. Underline or italicize the title of a book within an article title.

> Frey, Leonard H. "Irony and Point of View in 'That
>   Evening Sun.'" <u>Faulkner Studies</u> 2 (1953): 33-40.

Electronic sources

Electronic sources such as CD-ROMs, World Wide Web sites, and email differ from print sources in the ease with which they can be—and the frequency with which they are—changed, updated, or even eliminated. In addition, as the *MLA Handbook for Writers of Research Papers* notes, electronic media "so far lack agreed-on means of organizing works" so that it is often hard to identify information that can direct a reader to the source. In recommending the following guidelines for some of the most common kinds of electronic sources, the *Handbook* adds, "writers must often settle for citing whatever information is available to them." Further guidelines for citing electronic sources can be found in the *Handbook* and online at <http://www.mla.org>.

Note that MLA style requires that URLs in a Works Cited list be broken only after a slash.

34. CD-ROM, PERIODICALLY REVISED

Include the author's name; publication information for the print version, if any, of the text (including its title and date of publication); the title of the database, underlined or italicized; the medium (*CD-ROM*);

the name of the company producing it; and the electronic publication date (month and year, if possible).

> Natchez, Gladys. "Frida Kahlo and Diego Rivera: The
>
> Transformation of Catastrophe to Creativity."
>
> Psychotherapy-Patient 4.1 (1987): 153-74.
>
> PsycLIT. CD-ROM. SilverPlatter. Nov. 1994.

35. SINGLE-ISSUE CD-ROM, DISKETTE, OR MAGNETIC TAPE

Cite this kind of electronic source, which is *not* regularly updated, much like a book, but add the medium and, if appropriate, the number of the electronic edition, release, or version. If you are citing only a part of the source, end with the page, paragraph, screen, or other section numbers of the part if they are indicated in the source—either the range of numbers (*pp. 78–83*) or, if each section is numbered separately, the total number of sections in the part (*8 screens*).

> "Communion." The Oxford English Dictionary. 2nd ed.
>
> CD-ROM. Oxford: Oxford UP, 1992.

36. MULTIDISC CD-ROM

In citing a CD-ROM publication of more than one disc, include either the total number of discs or, if you use material from only one, the number of that disc.

> The 1998 Grolier Multimedia Encyclopedia. CD-ROM. 2
>
> discs. Danbury: Grolier Interactive, 1997.
>
> The 1998 Grolier Multimedia Encyclopedia. CD-ROM. Disc
>
> 2. Danbury: Grolier Interactive, 1997.

37. ONLINE SCHOLARLY PROJECT OR REFERENCE DATABASE

To cite an online scholarly project or reference database, begin with the title, underlined or italicized, then the name of the editor, if given. Include the electronic publication information, with version number, date of electronic publication or latest update, and name of the sponsoring organization. End with the date of access and URL, in angle brackets.

> The Orlando Project: An Integrated History of Women's
> 　　Writing in the British Isles. Ed. Paul Dyck and
> 　　Cathy Grant. 6 Apr. 2000. U of Alberta. 17 Apr.
> 　　2000 <http://www.ualberta.ca/ORLANDO/>.

To cite a poem, essay, or other short work within a scholarly project or database, begin with the author's name and the title of the work, in quotation marks, and give the URL of the short work rather than that of the project if they differ.

> Scott, Walter. "Remarks on Frankenstein, or the Modern
> 　　Prometheus: A Novel." Romantic Circles. Ed. Neil
> 　　Fraistat, Steven Jones, Donald Reiman, and Carl
> 　　Stahmer. 1996. 15 Apr. 1998 <http://www.udel.edu/
> 　　swilson/mws/bemrev.html>.

To cite an anonymous article from a reference database, begin with the article title, in quotation marks, and give the URL of the article rather than that of the database if they differ.

> "Sasquatch." The Encyclopedia Mythica. Ed. Micha F.
> 　　Lindemans. 1998. 31 Mar. 1998 <http://
> 　　www.pantheon.org/mythica/areas/folklore/>.

38. PROFESSIONAL OR PERSONAL WORLD WIDE WEB SITE

Give the author's name, if known, or start with the title of the site, underlined or italicized. Include the date of publication or the latest update, the name of any institution or organization associated with the site, the date of access, and the URL, in angle brackets.

> Bowman, Laurel. Classical Myth: The Ancient Sources.
> 　　24 June 1999. Dept. of Greek and Roman Studies,
> 　　U of Victoria. 7 Mar. 2000 <http://web.uvic.ca/
> 　　grs/bowman/myth>.

If no title exists, include a description such as *Homepage*.

> Kim, Angela. Homepage. 9 Oct. 1999 <http://www.
> 　　cohums.ohio-state.edu/english/people/kim.1/>.

39. ONLINE BOOK

Provide the author's name or, if only an editor, a compiler, or a translator is identified, the name of that person followed by a comma, and *ed., comp.,* or *trans.* Then give the title, underlined or italicized, and the name of any editor, compiler, or translator not listed earlier, preceded by *Ed., Comp.,* or *Trans.* Include the publication information (city, publisher, and year) for the print version, if given, or the date of electronic publication and the sponsoring organization if the work has not been published in print. End with the date of access and the URL, in angle brackets.

```
Riis, Jacob A. How the Other Half Lives: Studies among
    the Tenements of New York. Ed. David Phillips.
    New York: Scribner's, 1890. 26 Mar. 1998
    <http://www.cis.yale.edu/amstud/inforev/riis/
    title.html>.
```

If a book is part of a scholarly project, after the information about the print version give the information about the project (title, editor, date, and sponsor).

```
Burton, Annie L. Memories of Childhood's Slavery Days.
    Boston: Ross, 1909. Documenting the American
    South, or the Southern Experience in 19th-century
    America. Ed. Katharyn Graham. 1996. U of North
    Carolina, Chapel Hill. 31 Mar. 1998 <http://
    sunsite.unc.edu/docsouth/burton/burton.html>.
```

If you are citing a poem, essay, or other short work within a book, include its title, in quotation marks, after the author's name. Give the URL of the short work, not of the book, if they differ.

```
Dickinson, Emily. "The Grass." Poems: Emily Dickinson.
    Boston, 1891. Humanities Text Initiative American
    Verse Collection. Ed. Nancy Kushigian. 1995. U of
    Michigan. 9 Oct. 1997 <http://www.planet.net/
    pkrisxle/emily/poemsOnline.html>.
```

40. ARTICLE IN AN ONLINE PERIODICAL

To cite an article from an online journal, magazine, or newspaper, begin with the author's name, if known; the title of the work or material, in quotation marks; the name of the periodical, underlined or italicized; the volume or issue number, if any; the date of publication; and the page or paragraph numbers, if given. End with the date of access and the URL, in angle brackets.

```
Browning, Tonya. "Embedded Visuals: Student Design in
     Web Spaces." Kairos: A Journal for Teachers of
     Writing 2.1 (1997). 9 Oct. 1997 <http://
     english.ttu.edu/kairos/2.1/index_f.html>.
Gwande, Atul. "Drowsy Docs." Slate 9 Oct. 1997. 10
     Oct. 1997 <http://www.slate.com/MedicalExaminer/
     97-10-09/MedicalExaminer.asp>.
```

41. WORK FROM AN ONLINE SUBSCRIPTION SERVICE

To cite an article from an online service to which you subscribe personally, such as America Online, begin with the author's name, if known, and the title of the work, in quotation marks. Give the title of the online service, underlined or italicized, along with the date of access and the word *Keyword,* followed by the keyword used.

```
Weeks, W. William. "Beyond the Ark." Nature
     Conservancy Mar.-Apr. 1999. America Online.
     2 Apr. 1999. Keyword: Ecology.
```

For a work from an online service to which a library subscribes, list the information about the work, followed by the name of the service, the library, the date of access, and the URL of the service, in angle brackets.

```
"Breaking the Dieting Habit: Drug Therapy for Eating
     Disorders." Psychology Today Mar. 1995: 12+.
     Electric Lib. Main Lib., Columbus, OH. 31 Mar.
     1999 <http://www.elibrary.com/>.
```

42. POSTING TO A DISCUSSION GROUP

To cite a posting to an online discussion group such as a listserv or Usenet newsgroup, begin with the author's name; the title of the document, in quotation marks; the description *Online posting*; and the date of posting. For a listserv posting, then give the name of the listserv; the number of the posting, if any; the date of access; and the URL of the listserv or the email address of its moderator. For a newsgroup posting, end with the date of access and the name of the newsgroup, in angle brackets.

```
Martin, Jerry. "The IRA and Sinn Fein." Online
     posting. 31 Mar. 1998. 1 Apr. 1998
     <news:soc.culture.irish>.
```

You should always cite an archival version of a posting, if one is available.

```
Chagall, Nancy. "Web Publishing and Censorship." Online
     posting. 2 Feb. 1997. ACW: The Alliance for
     Computers and Writing Discussion List. 10 Oct.
     1997 <http://english.ttu.edu/acw-1/archive.htm>.
```

43. EMAIL MESSAGE

Include the writer's name; the subject line of the message, in quotation marks; a description of the message that mentions the recipient; and the date of the message.

```
Lunsford, Andrea A. "New Documentation Examples."
     Email to Kristin Bowen. 26 Jan. 1999.
```

44. SYNCHRONOUS COMMUNICATION (MUDs, MOOs)

In citing a posting in a forum such as a MUD, MOO, or IRC, include the name(s) of any specific speaker(s) you are citing; a description of the event; its date; the name of the forum; the date of access; and the URL. Always cite an archived version of the posting if one is available.

```
Patuto, Jeremy, Simon Fennel, and James Goss. The
     Mytilene Debate. 9 May 1996. MiamiMOO. 28 Mar.
     1998 <http://moo.cas.edu/cgi-bin/moo?look+4085>.
```

45. FTP (FILE TRANSFER PROTOCOL), TELNET, OR GOPHER SITE

Substitute *ftp, telnet,* or *gopher* for *http* at the beginning of the URL.

```
Korn, Peter. "How Much Does Breast Cancer Really
    Cost?" Self Oct. 1994. 5 May 1997 <gopher://
    nysernet.org:70/00/BCTC/Sources/SELF/94/how-much>.
```

46. OTHER ONLINE SOURCES

In citing other miscellaneous online sources, follow the guidelines given on pp. 389–390, but adapt them as necessary. Here are examples of citations for a work of art, a film clip, and an interview, accessed online.

```
Aleni, Guilio. K'un-yu t'u-shu. ca. 1620. Vatican,
    Rome. 28 Mar. 1998 <http://www.ncsa.uiuc.edu/SDG/
    Experimental/vatican.exhibit/exhibit/full-images/
    i_rome_to_china/china02.gif>.
Face/Off. Dir. John Woo. 1997. Hollywood.com. 8 Mar.
    2000 <http://www.hollywood.com/multimedia/movies/
    faceoff/trailer/mmindex.html>.
Dyson, Esther. Interview. Hotseat 23 May 1997 <http://
    www.hotwired.com/packet/hotseat/97/20/index4a.html>.
```

47. WORK IN AN INDETERMINATE ELECTRONIC MEDIUM

If you are not sure whether material accessed through a local network is stored on a central computer's hard drive, on a CD-ROM, or on the Web, use the label *Electronic.* Include any publication information that is available, the name of the network or of its sponsoring organization, and the date of access.

```
"Communion." The Oxford English Dictionary. 2nd ed.
    Oxford: Oxford UP, 1992. Electronic. OhioLink.
    Ohio State U Lib. 15 Apr. 1998.
```

Other sources

48. UNPUBLISHED DISSERTATION

Enclose the title in quotation marks. Add the identification *Diss.,* the name of the university or professional school, a comma, and the year the dissertation was accepted.

LeCourt, Donna. "The Self in Motion: The Status of the
    (Student) Subject in Composition Studies." Diss.
    Ohio State U, 1993.

49. PUBLISHED DISSERTATION

Cite a published dissertation as a book, adding the identification *Diss.* and the name of the university. If the dissertation was published by University Microfilms International, add *Ann Arbor: UMI* and the year, and list the UMI number at the end of the entry.

Botts, Roderic C. Influences in the Teaching of
    English, 1917-1935: An Illusion of Progress.
    Diss. Northeastern U, 1970. Ann Arbor: UMI, 1971.
    71-1799.

50. ARTICLE FROM A MICROFORM

Treat the article as a printed work, but add the name of the microform and information for locating it.

Sharpe, Lora. "A Quilter's Tribute." Boston Globe 25
    Mar. 1989. Newsbank: Social Relations 12 (1989):
    fiche 6, grids B4-6.

51. INTERVIEW

List the person interviewed and then the title of the interview, if any, in quotation marks (or underlined or italicized if the interview is a complete work). If the interview has no title, use the label *Interview* (not underlined, italicized, or in quotation marks), and identify the source. If you were the interviewer, use the label *Telephone interview, Personal interview,* or *Internet interview.* End with the date the interview took place.

Schorr, Daniel. Interview. Weekend Edition. Natl.
    Public Radio. WEVO, Concord. 26 Mar. 1988.
Beja, Morris. Personal interview. 2 Oct. 1997.

52. LETTER

If the letter was published, cite it as a selection in a book, noting the date and any identifying number after the title.

> Frost, Robert. "Letter to Editor of the Independent."
>   28 Mar. 1894. Selected Letters of Robert Frost.
>   Ed. Lawrance Thompson. New York: Holt, 1964. 19.

If the letter was sent to you, follow this form:

> Anzaldúa, Gloria. Letter to the author. 10 Sept. 1997.

53. FILM OR VIDEOCASSETTE

In general, start with the title, underlined or italicized; then name the director, the company distributing the film or videocassette, and the date of its release. Other contributors, such as writers or actors, may follow the director. If you cite a particular person's work, start the entry with that person's name. For a videocassette, include the original film release date (if relevant) and the label *Videocassette*.

> Face/Off. Dir. John Woo. Perf. John Travolta and
>   Nicholas Cage. Paramount, 1997.
> Weaver, Sigourney, perf. Aliens. Dir. James Cameron.
>   20th Century Fox, 1986.
> The Star. Dir. Lawrence Pitkethly. Videocassette.
>   CBS/Fox Video, 1995.

54. TELEVISION OR RADIO PROGRAM

In general, begin with the title of the program, underlined or italicized. Then list the narrator, writer, director, actors, or other contributors, as necessary; the network; the local station and city, if any; and the broadcast date. If you cite a particular person's work, begin the entry with that person's name. If you cite a particular episode, include any title, in quotation marks, before the program's title. If the program is part of a series, include the series title (not underlined, italicized, or in quotation marks) before the network.

> Box Office Bombshell: Marilyn Monroe. Narr. Peter
>   Graves. Writ. Andy Thomas, Jeff Schefel, and
>   Kevin Burns. Dir. Bill Harris. A&E Biography.
>   Arts and Entertainment Network. 23 Oct. 1997.

```
Watson, Emily, perf. The Mill on the Floss.
     Masterpiece Theatre. PBS. WNET, New York. 2 Jan.
     2000.
```

55. SOUND RECORDING

Begin with the name of the composer, performer, or conductor, depending on whose work you are citing. Next give the title of the recording, which is underlined or italicized, or the title of the composition, which is not. End with the manufacturer, a comma, and the year of issue. If you are not citing a compact disc, give the medium before the manufacturer. If you are citing a particular song, include its title, in quotation marks, before the title of the recording.

```
Grieg, Edvard. Concerto in A-minor, op. 16. Cond.
     Eugene Ormandy. Philadelphia Orch. LP. RCA, 1989.
Kilcher, Jewel. "Amen." Pieces of You. A&R, 1994.
```

56. WORK OF ART

List the artist; the work's title, underlined or italicized; the name of the museum or other location; and the city.

```
Kahlo, Frida. Self-Portrait with Cropped Hair. Museum
     of Modern Art, New York.
```

57. LECTURE OR SPEECH

List the speaker, the title in quotation marks, the name of the sponsoring institution or group, the place, and the date. If the speech is untitled, use a label such as *Lecture* or *Keynote speech.*

```
Lu, Min-Zhan. "The Politics of Listening." Conference
     on College Composition and Communication. Palmer
     House, Chicago. 3 Apr. 1998.
```

58. PERFORMANCE

List the title, other appropriate details (such as composer, writer, or director), the place, and the date. If you cite a particular person's work, begin the entry with that person's name.

<u>Frankie and Johnny in the Clair de Lune</u>. By Terrence
    McNally. Dir. Paul Benedict. Westside Arts
    Theater, New York. 18 Jan. 1988.

59. MAP OR CHART

Cite a map or chart as you would a book with an unknown author, adding the label *Map* or *Chart*.

<u>Pennsylvania</u>. Map. Chicago: Rand, 1985.

60. CARTOON

List the cartoonist's name, the title of the cartoon (if it has one), the word *Cartoon,* and the usual publication information.

Trudeau, Garry. "Doonesbury." Cartoon. <u>Philadelphia</u>
    <u>Inquirer</u> 9 Mar. 1988: 37.

61. ADVERTISEMENT

Name the item or organization being advertised, add the word *Advertisement,* and then supply the standard information about the source where the ad appears.

Dannon Yogurt Advertisement. <u>TV Guide</u> 4 Dec. 1999:
    A14.

51

A Sample Research Essay, MLA Style

Chapters 10–13 show the key parts of the research process. On the following pages, you will find the final research essay by Shannan Palma, an Ohio State student who followed the guidelines in those chapters. In preparing this essay, Palma followed the MLA guidelines described in the preceding chapters. Her name, course information, and the date appear as a heading at the top of the first page of her essay, preceding the title. Note that, to annotate this essay, we have reproduced it in a narrower format than you will have on a standard eight-and-a-half- by eleven-inch sheet of paper.

Palma 1

Shannan Palma

Professor Lunsford

English 167

18 November 2000

Title centered; announces topic, engages reader interest

Hollywood and the Hero:
Solving a Case of Mistaken Identity

Where are my angels?

Where's my golden one?

And where's my hope

now that my heroes

have gone?

Opening quotation appeals to readers and poses question that essay will answer

The song is "Amen" from Jewel Kilcher's best-selling album <u>Pieces of You</u>. The questions are ones worth asking. For the hero--what <u>The New Merriam-Webster Dictionary</u> defines as "a man admired for his achievements and qualities"--seems to have vanished from American culture. From Hercules to Robin Hood, from Joan of Arc to Scarlett O'Hara, male and female heroes alike have reflected the ideals and the most admired traits of their respective times: brute strength or sharply honed cunning, devotion to duty or desire for rebellion. Throughout history, and specifically U.S. history, the hero-ideal endured--until now. The twentieth century, which started off with the promising evolution of the hero

First paragraph of introduction provides background

Alphabetically organized reference book cited; page number not necessary

Palma 2

from figure of legend and literature to star
of the silver screen, seems to have ended
with the near death of the hero as ideal.

The eclipse of the hero is the result
of a case of what I will call "mistaken
identity," which has caused film heroes'
fates to become inextricably intertwined
with the fates of the actors who portray
them. In this research essay, I will explore
whether today's films truly signal the end
of the hero-ideal and preview a hero-less
future or whether they instead help the hero
evolve to a different, perhaps more
realistic, level. If the latter is true, the
question then becomes what form the new hero
will take on screen. In this essay, I argue
that recent films strongly suggest that the
hero of the twenty-first century will most
likely appear not as a Hollywood star or a
mythical manifestation but as a combination
of mortal and machine--in short, a cyborg.[1]

A brief look at Hollywood's
relationship with the hero may help answer
these questions. Our heroes once came
primarily from the fantasy of myth and the
remove of history and literature. King
Arthur, the Three Musketeers, Jo March of
Little Women, Annie Oakley--all have spent
time on the hero's pedestal. With the

Writer's last name and page number in upper right-hand corner

Second paragraph introduces major theme of "mistaken identity" and explains what writer will do in essay

Explicit thesis stated

Superscript refers to bibliographic note

Transition to first main idea: Hollywood studios transformed the hero

Palma 3

development of motion pictures in the early
twentieth century, many of these heroes
made the transition from legend to life,
or at least to life on the screen. Fans
began to identify a favorite hero character
with the particular actor who played him or
her, and this burgeoning case of mistaken
identity did not go unnoticed for long.
Film historian Morris Beja notes that
although the studios, then the most powerful
force in Hollywood, had originally hoped to
give actors as little influence as possible
over the studios' operations, it quickly
became obvious that "movie stars sold
tickets." Recognizing the huge financial
possibilities inherent in the mass
idolization of a commercialized hero,
the industry set out to manufacture this
product as efficiently as possible. As a
1995 video on the star system in Hollywood
explains:

> In the old days of the studio
> system there was a structure for
> developing stars. Players were
> owned body and soul, signed to
> long-term contracts. [. . .] The
> problem for the studio was to find
> the one persona out of many
> possible character roles that

First subordinate idea: fans confused characters with actors ("mistaken identity")

Quotation from interview

Second subordinate idea: heroes became products

Block quotation introduced by phrase with signal verb, indented and double-spaced as required by MLA style

would boost a character to
stardom. (The Star)

Studios found that manufacturing a
movie star was not easy. It required an
actor with just the right combination of
style, charisma, and talent, and it required
just the right roles and public persona to
make that actor a star. When the process
succeeded, however, the mistaken identity
was complete. The star became an icon--an
ideal--a hero. Many fictional hero types
(such as the romantic hero and the western
hero) carried over from the prefilm era; but
new kinds of heroes also emerged, identified
even more closely by the public with the
stars who originated them. Early examples
of the star-hero included silent film stars
Douglas Fairbanks and Mary Pickford.
"The swashbuckler was born with [. . .]
Fairbanks," according to Beja, who also sees
Pickford as the prototype of the brave or
"plucky" movie heroine. (See Fig. 1.) As
Richard deCordova notes in a memorable
phrase, the studios wanted to convince
millions of moviegoers that "the real hero
behave[d] just like the reel hero" (qtd. in
Gallagher, part 2). Therefore, the persona
that a studio developed to turn a working
actor into a star was the only public

Videocassette title cited in parentheses; for set-off quotation, parenthetical citation follows final punctuation

Examples of star-hero

Sentence combines quotation and paraphrase; bracketed ellipses indicate words omitted from quotation

Brackets enclose material altered so tense of quotation fits into sentence

Indirect online source without page numbers cited using *qtd. in* and part number

Palma 5

Fig. 1. Hollywood studios tried to stage-manage the images of stars such as Mary Pickford to create public illusions of heroic, almost mythological beings. Photofest, New York.

Caption relates figure to text

identity that actor would be allowed to have.

As long as the star-hero stayed separate from the public, buffered by studios in order to keep the image intact, his or her fictional self remained safe. But the strain of living up to a legend instead of living a life took a toll on the private, real selves. Brian Gallagher cites a remark by Cary Grant that sums up the strain many stars must have felt: "Everybody wants to be Cary Grant. Even I want to be Cary Grant" (part 3). As the studio system

Part number cited for online source without page numbers

Palma 6

Second main idea: the disintegration of the studio system revealed the problems with stardom

disintegrated in the 1950s and the 1960s, and stars lost the publicity shield the system had provided, the toll became obvious to an adoring public.

Subordinate idea: movie industry's self-awareness, with two examples

Films from this period show that the movie industry was self-mockingly aware of its pitfalls. Sunset Boulevard, released in 1950, showed what happened when a hero-image was no longer profitable and the system abandoned the star it had made. Gloria Swanson played the fictional silent film star Norma Desmond, once young and adored, now aging and forgotten, who tries in vain to recapture her lost glory and ends her quest in tragedy. A Star Is Born, remade in 1954 with Judy Garland in the lead role, chronicled the rise of a young woman from nobody to star, showing the reality of how the system created a perfect image and forced a human being to become it (Corey and Ochoa 353, 347). Yet, even though these films showed the artificiality and destructiveness of the star system, they also helped to perpetuate it. After all, the fictional star was played by a real-life one--and thus fiction and truth became even further intertwined.

Citation with two page references covers two preceding sentences; comma separates pages

Imperative sentence with film jargon introduces third main idea: a new form of mistaken identity and the continued decline of the hero

Fast forward from the fifties and sixties to the present: almost fifty years

Palma 7

later. A brief excerpt from the celebrity
gossip-fest Hollywood Confidential shows
that the last vestiges of the studio
system's image-projection and -protection
have vanished:

> Well into the throes of drug
> addiction by the time she was
> thirteen, Drew Barrymore attempted
> suicide by cutting her wrists with
> a kitchen knife.
>
> Rosemary Clooney was addicted
> to prescription drugs and, after
> two embattled marriages to José
> Ferrer, was admitted to a psych
> ward.
>
> Francis Ford Coppola takes
> lithium.
>
> Patty (Call Me Anna) Duke is a
> manic-depressive. (Amende 247)

No longer do stars try to hide their
personal lives from the public, and every
scandal, every lie is exposed. Thus today's
public holds very few illusions about the
lives of its star-heroes. Although stars are
still living heroes, the relationship
between the two terms has changed: rather
than admiring stars for their heroic
achievements and personal qualities, the
public simply envies them for their

Subordinate idea: disappearance of stars' image-protection

Set-off quotation from popular magazine cites author in parentheses rather than in signal phrase

Subordinate idea: stars are now envied rather than admired

Palma 8

Subordinate idea: current films reflect cynicism about hero-ideal and perpetuate a new form of mistaken identity

Extended example illustrates cynicism and reversal of mistaken identity

Neutral signal verb introduces description of film

Bracketed ellipses indicate omissions in quotation

Bracketed comment indicates underlining added by writer for emphasis

Author's name cited alone for one-page, one-paragraph source

lifestyle--their immense power, wealth, and fame. A profound cynicism exists toward the hero as ideal, and this cynicism is reflected in the portrayal of the fictional hero in current American films. It is a portrayal that perpetuates the problem of mistaken identity I identified earlier, but in reverse, with heroes being identified with the stars that portray them, rather than vice versa.

The 1994 film The Ref offers a striking example of this reversal and of the cynicism it both grows out of and feeds into. As a review on the ABC News Web site Mr. Showbiz notes:

> Judy Davis and Kevin Spacey are a married couple who for the life of them can't stop bickering. Denis Leary is the burglar who's taken them hostage on Christmas Eve. Writers Marie Weiss and Richard LaGravanese have built a [. . .] platform [. . .] from which Leary can freely launch himself into the mad stand-up monologues of outrage and spleen that are his trademark [emphasis mine]. (Feeney)

A closer look at this film tells us more. It takes place on Christmas Eve, a

Palma 9

traditional time of sharing and harmony
among loved ones, yet the couple in the
film and the relatives who descend upon them
for the holidays are all so bitter,
sarcastic, and self-absorbed that even a
hardened criminal is appalled by them. As
the set of values associated with Christmas
is turned on its ear, the criminal becomes ·········· Concept of antihero introduced
a sort of antihero: unlike his hostages, he
at least remembers how a family is supposed
to behave. The film's message is emphasized
by the casting of comedian Leary in the
title role, which capitalizes on his
reputation as a mouthpiece for American
cynicism in the nineties. Rather than the
hero creating the star, the star now forms
the hero.

   The disappearance of the hero-ideal as ·········· Transition to subordinate idea: absence of lasting audience empathy with most modern film heroes
a separate entity from, or as a model for,
the star has led to a second and perhaps
more complex problem: with most modern
films, there is a peculiar absence of
lasting empathy with the hero. Apart from
the rare phenomenon such as Luke Skywalker
in Star Wars (1977), not only do modern
movie heroes not exist apart from actors in
audiences' minds, but they do not stay in
their minds for long. Think of Sigourney ·········· Two examples cited
Weaver as Ripley, savior of humanity in

<u>Aliens</u> (1986), or Harrison Ford as president of the United States in <u>Air Force One</u> (1997). In fact, this wording reveals just how most moviegoers think of those heroes-- the roles are indistinguishable from the stars--and after audiences see a movie, they no longer associate the <u>character</u> and the film, but rather the <u>actor</u> and the film. The difference between the short shelf life of modern heroes and the staying power of their old-style predecessors is evident if we look at film remakes of novels like <u>Little Women</u> and <u>The Three Musketeers</u>, in which the characters supersede the actors in importance. But such films only cater to audience nostalgia. These classic heroes may endure in memory, but they will never again have the mythic power that they once did. To re-create that lasting empathy in a modern context, we need films that can overcome mistaken identity and that contain heroes who are believable and relevant to today's world. Fortunately, in 1997, such a film, and such a hero, came to the screen.

Think of the current film hero as, to borrow a term from <u>The Princess Bride</u> (1987), "mostly dead." Not having died, the hero needs not rebirth but revival or regeneration. To begin regenerating the

New films contrasted to remakes of novels

Transition to last main idea: remakes cater to nostalgia for old heroes, but we need new ones

Palma 11

hero, then, it is necessary to overcome (1) the audience's preconceptions about the stars' relationships to the characters they play and (2) the failure of recent hero-characters to invoke a lasting empathy in the public. The 1997 film Face/Off can serve as a prototype for overcoming both of these obstacles and thus for resolving the problem of mistaken identity.

First, the plot and characterization of this film prove that it is possible for a character to be identified apart from the star who plays him or her. During the course of the story, the two main characters, hero Sean Archer and villain Castor Troy, undergo surgery that exchanges their faces. The two stars of the film start off playing particular characters--John Travolta as Archer and Nicholas Cage as Troy--but approximately twenty minutes into the film, they switch roles. (See Fig. 2.) In an interview for a magazine article, Travolta described his take on imitating his costar:

> [I thought] maybe we could use that Nick Cage cadence for the bad guy's voice, too, and I could just adapt that. You know, the way Nick slows down and enunciates and

Parenthetical numbers used to define regeneration of the hero as a two-part challenge

Introduction of prototype for solution to problem: Face/Off

Subordinate idea: Face/Off turns mistaken identity against itself

Parenthetical reference directs readers to figure. (See p. 404.)

Bracketed words clarify beginning of quotation to fit writer's introduction

Palma 12

Parenthetical
citation indi-
cates indirect
source

pronunciates. He's almost poetic
in his talking. (qtd. in Daly 24)
Director John Woo and others involved in
the making of Face/Off seem to have used
audience preconceptions about actors'
idiosyncrasies being identical to
characters' idiosyncrasies--purposely
emphasized in the beginning of the film--to
make the switch of actors and roles more
shocking and real to the audience. They turn
mistaken identity against itself. This
disassociation of actor from character
negates the second obstacle to regeneration
of the hero as well. Without mistaken

Caption
relates figure
to text

Fig. 2. Nicholas Cage and John Travolta
switched roles partway through Face/Off, a
technique that helped audiences see their
characters as figures independent of the
actors portraying them. Photofest, New York.

Palma 13

identity to cloud the issue, Archer is able
to create a lasting empathy with the
audience. Even after the audience leaves the
darkness of the theater, his character
cannot be viewed on anything but its own
terms.

　　With the complex problem of mistaken
identity overcome, what remains is to create
a believable hero who is relevant to today's
world. In this context, the major challenge
is that the model for the hero, in Western
culture at least, is based on the view that
a human being is a unified organic whole
that can be labeled in some way: as epic
hero, romantic hero, tragic hero,
swashbuckling hero, western hero, detective
hero, and so on. In the contemporary world,
most moviegoers no longer believe in such a
one-dimensional being. In one of the essays
in her anthology Simians, Cyborgs, & Women,
historian of science Donna J. Haraway claims
that our dreams of organic unity and
coherence are futile. In their place, she
recommends the cyborg figure, which can give
us a new dream of ourselves as multiple,
surpassing either body or machine (181). In
fact, with computers, organ transplants, and
high-technology prostheses, humans in the
late twentieth century already live in a
world of cyborgs.

Transition to second subordinate idea: creating a believable contemporary hero is difficult

Paraphrase of source; signal verbs indicate disputable statements

Concept of cyborg introduced and explained

Palma 14

Cyborg concept applied to film heroes

Given Haraway's analysis, the reel hero can no longer exist as a contained organic whole in today's fractured, technology-driven society. The human aspect of the hero has been damaged by mistaken identity to the extent that moviegoers will no longer put

Earlier points summarized

faith in it. They no longer want the lie of static perfection betrayed by film stars of Marilyn Monroe's generation. Yet, within realistic heroes, people still want something untainted by human frailty. At just this moment, the cyborg hero has emerged in film.

Return to example of *Face/Off*

Again, Face/Off offers a useful demonstration. Archer, a tortured FBI agent who spends years tracking the criminal (Troy) who murdered his son, is not a hero in the classic sense, nor is he an antihero in the modern sense. Instead, he is a prototype for the emerging hero, a figure whose humanity is damaged beyond repair (like the American culture's belief in the hero-ideal). To defeat evil, Archer must use technology to become his enemy--to wear his face and take his place in the world. As

Introductory phrase calls attention to striking quotation and cites source title related to writer's point

Janice Rushing and Thomas Frentz put it in their book Projecting the Shadow: The Cyborg Hero in American Film, "To survive, a man must be technological, and to thrive, he

Palma 15

must be technologically adept" (147). The
new heroes cannot be sustained without
technology, which counteracts their human
weaknesses with cyborg prosthetics that give
them an inhuman capacity for human
salvation. Archer achieves this state and
triumphs--maybe not an angel, not a "golden ·············· Allusions to opening song quotation
one," but certainly a cause for hope.

    The emergence of cyborg figures in ····················· Conclusion cites additional examples of cyborgs in films and raises issue of cultural ambivalence toward them
films is not limited to Face/Off. Over the
past two decades, different facets of the
cyborg character have been explored in films
as diverse as Blade Runner (1982) and Star
Trek: First Contact (1996). These portrayals
reflect a deep ambivalence, since many in
our culture see the cyborg as a symbol not
of hope but of dehumanization. But these
films offer positive images of cyborgs as
well as negative ones, suggesting that their
future could go either way--or continue to
go both ways. Jewel asked the question: "And
where's my hope / now that my heroes / have ·············· Restatement of opening quotation/ question
gone?" Perhaps the 1991 film Terminator 2:
Judgment Day provides the answer, one that
speaks to the eventual triumph of the cyborg
as hero. Turning to human heroes Sarah
and John Connor, the cyborg Terminator
says simply, "Come with me if you want to ··········· Closing example suggests answer
live."

Palma 16

Notes

Heading centered

Indent one-half inch or five spaces to superscript number

[1] I want to thank those who have contributed to my thinking on this topic, including my professor and classmates, Professor Morris Beja, and two consultants from the Ohio State University Writing Center, Melissa Goldthwaite and Nels Highberg.

Bibliographic note acknowledges help

Palma 17

Works Cited ···········Heading centered

Amende, Coral. <u>Hollywood Confidential: An</u> ··········First line of each entry flush with left margin; subsequent lines indented one-half inch or five spaces
<u>Inside Look at the Public Careers and</u>
<u>Private Lives of Hollywood's Rich and</u>
<u>Famous</u>. New York: Penguin, 1997.

Beja, Morris. Personal interview. 2 Oct. ··········
2000. ···········Interview

<u>Blade Runner</u>. Dir. Ridley Scott. Warner ··········Film
Bros./Ladd, 1982.

Corey, Melinda, and George Ochoa. <u>The</u> ··········Book
<u>Dictionary of Film Quotations: 6,000</u>
<u>Provocative Movie Quotes from 1,000</u>
<u>Movies</u>. New York: Crown, 1995.

Daly, Steve. "Face to Face." <u>Entertainment</u> ··········Article in a weekly magazine
<u>Weekly</u> 20 June 1997: 20-24.

deCordova, Richard. <u>Picture Personalities:</u>
<u>The Emergence of the Star System in</u>
<u>America</u>. Urbana: U of Illinois P, 1990.

<u>Face/Off</u>. Dir. John Woo. Perf. John Travolta
and Nicholas Cage. Paramount, 1997.

Feeney, F. X. Rev. of <u>The Ref</u>, dir. Ted ··········Review from a Web site
Demme. <u>Mr. Showbiz: A World of</u>
<u>Entertainment from ABCNEWS.com</u>. 18 Oct.
2000 <http://www.mrshowbiz.com/reviews/
moviereviews/movies/TheRef_1994.html>.

Ford, Harrison, perf. <u>Air Force One</u>. Dir.
Wolfgang Petersen. Columbia, 1997.

Gallagher, Brian. "Some Historical ··········Article in an online journal
Reflections on the Paradoxes of Stardom
in the American Film Industry,

Palma 18

1910-1960." Images: A Journal of
Film and Popular Culture 3 (1997):
7 parts. Sept. 2000 <http://
www.imagesjournal.com/
issue03/infocus/stars1.htm>.

Essay in a collection · · · · · · Haraway, Donna J. "A Cyborg Manifesto:
Science, Technology, and Socialist
Feminism in the Late Twentieth
Century." Simians, Cyborgs, & Women.
New York: Routledge, 1991. 149-81.

Entry in a
well-known
reference · · · · · ·
work   "Hero." The New Merriam-Webster Dictionary.
1989.

Sound · · · · · · Kilcher, Jewel. "Amen." Pieces of You. A&R,
recording   1994.

Little Women. Dir. Gillian Armstrong.
Columbia Tri-Star, 1994.

Photograph · · · · · · Photograph of Mary Pickford. Undated.
obtained from
agency   Photofest, New York.

Photograph of Nicholas Cage and John
Travolta in Face/Off. Undated.
Photofest, New York.

The Princess Bride. Dir. Rob Reiner. 20th
Century Fox, 1987.

The Ref. Dir. Ted Demme. Perf. Denis Leary,
Judy Davis, and Kevin Spacey.
Touchstone, 1994.

Book with two · · · · · · Rushing, Janice Hocker, and Thomas S.
authors   Frentz. Projecting the Shadow: The
Cyborg Hero in American Film. Chicago:
U of Chicago P, 1995.

Palma 19

The Star. Dir. Lawrence Pitkethly. ·························· Videocassette
    Videocassette. CBS/FOX Video, 1995.
A Star Is Born. Dir. George Cukor. Perf.
    Judy Garland. Warner Bros., 1954.
Star Trek: First Contact. Dir. Jonathan
    Frakes. Paramount, 1996.
Star Wars. Dir. George Lucas. 20th Century
    Fox, 1977.
Sunset Boulevard. Dir. Billy Wilder. Perf.
    Gloria Swanson. Paramount, 1950.
Terminator 2: Judgment Day. Dir. James
    Cameron. Tri-Star, 1991.
The Three Musketeers. Dir. Stephen Herek.
    Disney, 1993.
Weaver, Sigourney, perf. Aliens. Dir. James ············ Performer in
    Cameron. 20th Century Fox, 1986.   a film

Chapters 52 and 53 discuss the basic formats prescribed by the American Psychological Association (APA), guidelines that are widely used in the social sciences. For further reference, consult the *Publication Manual of the American Psychological Association,* fifth edition. Chapter 54 deals with formats prescribed by the Council of Science Editors (formerly Council of Biology Editors, known as CBE), and Chapter 55 with formats from *The Chicago Manual of Style,* fourteenth edition, 1993.

DIRECTORY TO APA STYLE

APA style for in-text citations (52a)

APA style for a list of references (52c)

BOOKS

PERIODICALS

ELECTRONIC SOURCES

OTHER SOURCES

52a APA style for in-text citations

APA style requires parenthetical citations in the text to document quotations, paraphrases, summaries, and other material from a source (12f). These in-text citations correspond to full bibliographic entries in a list of references at the end of the text.

1. AUTHOR NAMED IN A SIGNAL PHRASE

Generally, use the author's name in a signal phrase to introduce the cited material, and place the date, in parentheses, immediately after the author's name. For a quotation, the page number, preceded by *p.*, appears in parentheses after the quotation.

```
Key (1983) has argued that the placement of women in
print advertisements is subliminally important.

As Briggs (1970) observed, parents play an important
role in building their children's self-esteem because
"children value themselves to the degree that they
have been valued" (p. 14).
```

Position the page reference in parentheses two spaces after the final punctuation of a long, set-off quotation. For electronic texts or other works without page numbers, paragraph numbers may be used instead, preceded by the ¶ symbol or the abbreviation *para.*

```
Denes (1980, ¶1) claimed that psychotherapy is an art
that is "volatile, unpredictable, standardless in its
outcome, subjective in its worth."
```

2. AUTHOR NAMED IN PARENTHESES

When you do not mention the author in a signal phrase in your text, give the name and the date, separated by a comma, in parentheses at the end of the cited material.

One study has found that only 68% of letters received by editors were actually published (Renfro, 1979).

3. TWO AUTHORS

Use both names in all citations. Use *and* in a signal phrase, but use an ampersand (&) in parentheses.

Murphy and Orkow (1985) reached somewhat different conclusions by designing a study that was less dependent on subjective judgment than were previous studies.

A recent study that was less dependent on subjective judgment resulted in conclusions somewhat different from those of previous studies (Murphy & Orkow, 1985).

4. THREE TO FIVE AUTHORS

List all the authors' names for the first reference.

Belenky, Clinchy, Goldberger, and Tarule (1986) have suggested that many women rely on observing and listening to others as ways of learning about themselves.

In subsequent references, use just the first author's name plus *et al.*

From this experience, observed Belenky et al. (1986), women learn to listen to themselves think, a step toward self-expression.

5. SIX OR MORE AUTHORS

Use only the first author's name and *et al.* in *every* citation.

As Mueller et al. (1980) demonstrated, television holds the potential for distorting and manipulating consumers as free-willed decision makers.

6. ORGANIZATION AS AUTHOR

If the name of an organization or a corporation is long, spell it out the first time, followed by an abbreviation in brackets. In later citations, use the abbreviation only.

FIRST CITATION (Centers for Disease Control [CDC], 1990)

LATER CITATION (CDC, 1990)

7. UNKNOWN AUTHOR

Use the title or its first few words in a signal phrase or in parentheses (in this example, a book's title is underlined.)

The school profiles for the county substantiated this trend (Guide to Secondary Schools, 1983).

8. TWO OR MORE AUTHORS WITH THE SAME LAST NAME

If your list of references includes works by different authors with the same last name, to avoid confusion, include the authors' initials in each citation.

G. Jones (1984) conducted the groundbreaking study of retroviruses.

9. TWO OR MORE SOURCES WITHIN THE SAME PARENTHESES

List sources by different authors in alphabetical order by author's last name, separated by semicolons: (Chodorow, 1978; Gilligan, 1982). List works by the same author in chronological order, separated by commas: (Gilligan, 1977, 1982).

10. SPECIFIC PARTS OF A SOURCE

Use abbreviations (*chap., p.,* and so on) in a parenthetical citation to name the part of a work you are citing.

Montgomery (1988, chap. 9) argued that his research yielded the opposite results.

11. EMAIL AND OTHER PERSONAL COMMUNICATION

Cite any personal letters, email, electronic bulletin-board correspondence, telephone conversations, or interviews with the person's initial(s) and last name, the identification *personal communication,* and the date. Note, however, that APA recommends not including personal communications in the reference list.

```
J. L. Morin (personal communication, October 14, 1999)
supported with new evidence the claims made in her
article.
```

12. WORLD WIDE WEB SITE

To cite an entire Web site, include its address in parentheses in your text (http://www.gallup.com); you do not need to include it in your list of references. To cite part of a text found on the Web, indicate the chapter or figure, as appropriate. To document a quotation, include the page or paragraph numbers, if available, or you may omit them if they are not available.

```
Shade argued the importance of "ensuring equitable
gender access to the Internet" (1993, p. 6).
```

52b   APA style for content notes

APA style allows you to use content notes to expand or supplement your text. Indicate such notes in your text by superscript numerals. Type the notes themselves on a separate page after the last page of the text, under the heading *Footnotes,* centered at the top of the page. Double-space all entries. Indent the first line of each note five spaces, but begin subsequent lines at the left margin.

SUPERSCRIPT NUMERAL IN TEXT

```
The age of the children involved was an important
factor in the selection of items for the questionnaire.[1]
```

FOOTNOTE

```
     [1] Marjorie Youngston Forman and William Cole of
the Child Study Team provided great assistance in
identifying appropriate items.
```

52c APA style for a list of references

The alphabetical list of the sources cited in your document is called *References*. (If your instructor asks that you list everything you have read as background—not just the sources you cite—call the list *Bibliography*.) Here are some guidelines for preparing such a list.

- Start your list on a separate page after the text of your document but before any appendices or notes.

- Type the heading *References,* neither underlined nor in quotation marks, centered one inch from the top of the page.

- Begin your first entry. Unless your instructor suggests otherwise, do not indent the first line of each entry, but indent subsequent lines one-half inch or five spaces. Double-space the entire list.

- List sources alphabetically by authors' last names. If the author of a source is unknown, alphabetize the source by the first major word of the title.

The APA style specifies the treatment and placement of four basic elements—author, publication date, title, and publication information.

- *Author.* List all authors last name first, and use only initials for first and middle names. Separate the names of multiple authors with commas, and use an ampersand before the last author's name.

- *Publication date.* Enclose the date in parentheses. Use only the year for books and journals; use the year, a comma, and the month or month and day for magazines; use the year, a comma, and the month and day for newspapers. Do not abbreviate.

- *Title.* Underline titles and subtitles of books and periodicals. Do not enclose titles of articles in quotation marks. For books and articles, capitalize only the first word of the title and subtitle and any proper nouns or proper adjectives. Capitalize all major words in a periodical title.

- *Publication information.* For a book, list the city of publication (and the country or postal abbreviation for the state if the city is unfamiliar), a colon, and the publisher's name, dropping *Inc., Co.,* or *Publishers.* For a periodical, follow the periodical title with a comma, the volume number (underlined), the issue number (if appropriate) in parentheses and followed by a comma, and the inclusive page numbers of the article. For newspapers and for articles or chapters in books, include the abbreviation *p.* ("page") or *pp.* ("pages").

The following sample entries are in a hanging indent format, in which the first line aligns on the left and the subsequent lines indent one-half inch or five spaces. This is the customary APA format for final copy, including student papers. Unless your instructor suggests otherwise, it is the format we recommend. Note, however, that for manuscripts submitted to journals, APA requires the reverse (first lines indented, subsequent lines flushed left), assuming that the citations will be converted by a typesetting system to a hanging indent. Similarly, APA allows for the substitution of italics for underlining in student papers; check which format your instructor prefers.

Books

1. ONE AUTHOR

Lightman, A. (1993). Einstein's dreams. New York:
Warner Books.

2. TWO OR MORE AUTHORS

Newcombe, F., & Ratcliffe, G. (1978). Defining
females: The nature of women in society. New
York: Wiley.

3. ORGANIZATION AS AUTHOR

Institute of Financial Education. (1983). Income
property lending. Homewood, IL: Dow Jones-Irwin.

Use the word *Author* as the publisher when the organization is both the author and the publisher.

American Chemical Society. (1978). Handbook for
authors of papers in American Chemical Society
publications. Washington, DC: Author.

4. UNKNOWN AUTHOR

National Geographic atlas of the world. (1988).
Washington, DC: National Geographic Society.

5. EDITOR

Hardy, H. H. (Ed.) (1998). The proper study of
mankind. New York: Farrar, Straus.

6. SELECTION IN A BOOK WITH AN EDITOR

West, C. (1992). The postmodern crisis of the black
    intellectuals. In L. Grossberg, C. Nelson, & P.
    Treichler (Eds.), Cultural studies (pp. 689-705).
    New York: Routledge.

7. TRANSLATION

Durkheim, E. (1957). Suicide (J. A. Spaulding &
    G. Simpson, Trans.). Glencoe, IL: Free Press of
    Glencoe.

8. EDITION OTHER THAN THE FIRST

Kohn, M. L. (1977). Class and conformity: A study in
    values (2nd ed.). Chicago: University of Chicago
    Press.

9. ONE VOLUME OF A MULTIVOLUME WORK

Baltes, P., & Brim, O. G. (Eds.). (1980). Life-span
    development and behavior (Vol. 3). New York:
    Basic Books.

10. ARTICLE IN A REFERENCE WORK

Ochs, E. (1989). Language acquisition. In
    International encyclopedia of communications
    (Vol. 2, pp. 390-393). New York: Oxford
    University Press.

If no author is listed, begin with the title.

11. REPUBLICATION

Piaget, J. (1952). The language and thought of the
    child. London: Routledge & Kegan Paul. (Original
    work published 1932)

12. GOVERNMENT DOCUMENT

U.S. Bureau of the Census. (1975). <u>Historical
    statistics of the United States, colonial times
    to 1870.</u> Washington, DC: U.S. Government Printing
    Office.

13. TWO OR MORE WORKS BY THE SAME AUTHOR(S)

List two or more works by the same author in chronological order.
Repeat the author's name in each entry.

Goodall, J. (1991). <u>Through a window.</u> Boston:
    Houghton-Mifflin.

Goodall, J. (1999). <u>Reason for hope: A spiritual
    journey.</u> New York: Warner Books.

Periodicals

14. ARTICLE IN A JOURNAL PAGINATED BY VOLUME

Shuy, R. (1981). A holistic view of language. <u>Research
    in the Teaching of English, 15,</u> 101-111.

15. ARTICLE IN A JOURNAL PAGINATED BY ISSUE

Maienza, J. G. (1986). The superintendency:
    Characteristics of access for men and women.
    <u>Educational Administration Quarterly, 22</u>(4),
    59-79.

16. ARTICLE IN A MAGAZINE

Gralla, P. (1994, April). How to enter cyberspace.
    <u>PC Computing,</u> 60-62.

17. ARTICLE IN A NEWSPAPER

Browne, M. W. (1988, April 26). Lasers for the
    battlefield raise concern for eyesight. <u>The New
    York Times,</u> pp. C1, C8.

18. EDITORIAL OR LETTER TO THE EDITOR

Russell, J. S. (1994, March 27). The language instinct [Letter to the editor]. The New York Times Book Review, 27.

19. UNSIGNED ARTICLE

What sort of person reads Creative Computing? (1985, August). Creative Computing, 8, 10.

20. REVIEW

Larmore, C. E. (1989). [Review of the book Patterns of moral complexity]. Ethics, 99, 423-426.

21. PUBLISHED INTERVIEW

McCarthy, E. (1968, December 24). [Interview with Boston Globe Washington staff]. Boston Globe, p. B27.

22. TWO OR MORE WORKS BY THE SAME AUTHOR IN THE SAME YEAR

List works alphabetically by title, and place lowercase letters (*a, b,* etc.) after the dates.

Murray, F. B. (1983a). Equilibration as cognitive conflict. Developmental Review, 3, 54-61.

Murray, F. B. (1983b). Learning and development through social interaction. In L. Liben (Ed.), Piaget and the foundations of knowledge (pp. 176-201). Hillsdale, NJ: Erlbaum.

Electronic sources

The APA's Web site, <http://www.apa.org/journals/webref.html>, includes current guidelines for citing some electronic sources, keeping up-to-date the information given in the *Publication Manual of the American Psychological Association.* However, with the exception of guidelines for citing email, Web sites, articles and abstracts from electronic databases, and software, the APA does not offer guidelines for citing some

common electronic sources. The following formats are based on the
APA Web site's January 2001 update. They also include additional elec-
tronic sources, adapted from APA style and based on guidelines from
Online! A Reference Guide for Using Internet Sources, 2000 edition, by
Andrew Harnack and Eugene Kleppinger.

The basic entry for most sources you access via the Internet should
include the following elements:

- *Author.* Give the author's name, if available.
- *Publication date.* Include the date of Internet publication or of the most
  recent update, if available.
- *Title.* List the title of the document or subject line of the message, neither
  underlined nor in quotation marks.
- *Publication information.* For documents from databases or other scholarly
  projects, give the city of the publisher or sponsoring organization, followed
  by the name. For articles from online journals or newspapers, follow the
  title with a comma, the volume number (underlined), the issue number (if
  appropriate) in parentheses and followed by a comma, and the inclusive
  page numbers of the article.
- *Retrieval information.* Type the word *Retrieved* followed by the date of access,
  followed by a comma, and the retrieval method (for example, *from the World
  Wide Web*), followed by a colon. End with the URL or other retrieval information and no period.

23. WORLD WIDE WEB SITE

To cite a whole site, give the address in a parenthetical citation
(p. 420).

To cite a document from a Web site, include information as you
would for a print document, followed by a note on its retrieval.

Mullins, B. (1995). Introduction to Robert Hass.
Readings in Contemporary Poetry at Dia Center for
the Arts. Retrieved April 24, 1997, from the World
Wide Web: http://www.diacenter.org/prg/poetry
/95_96/intrhass.html

Shade, L. R. (1993). Gender issues in computer
networking. Retrieved January 28, 2000, from the
World Wide Web: http://www0.delphi.com/woman
/text3.html

If no author is identified, give the title of the document followed by the date (if available), publication information, and retrieval statement.

```
DotComSense: Commonsense ways to protect your privacy

     and assess online mental health information.

     (2000, January). APA Monitor, 32. Retrieved

     January 25, 2001, from the World Wide Web:

     http://helping.apa.org/dotcomsense/
```

24. FTP (FILE TRANSFER PROTOCOL), TELNET, OR GOPHER SITE

After the retrieval statement, give the address (substituting *ftp, telnet,* or *gopher* for *http* at the beginning of the URL) or the path followed to access information, with slashes to indicate menu selections.

```
Korn, P. (October 1994). How much does breast cancer

     really cost? Self. Retrieved May 5, 1997:

     gopher://nysernet.org:70/00/BCIC/Sources/SELF

     /94/how-much
```

25. LISTSERV MESSAGE

Provide the author's name; the date of posting, in parentheses; the posting's subject line; the retrieval statement; and the listserv address.

```
Lackey, N. (1995, January 30). From Clare to here.

     Retrieved May 1, 1997, from the listserv:

     nanci@world.std.com
```

To cite a file that can be retrieved from a list's server or Web address, include the address or URL for the list's archive.

```
Lackey, N. (1995, January 30). From Clare to here.

     Retrieved May 1, 1997, from the listserv:

     http://www.rahul.net/frankf/Nancy/archives

     /95130.html
```

26. NEWSGROUP MESSAGE

Include the author's name and the date of posting, in parentheses. After the subject line from the posting, give a retrieval statement that ends with the name of the newsgroup.

Sand, P. (1996, April 20). Java disabled by default in
    Linux Netscape. Retrieved May 10, 1996, from the
    newsgroup: keokuk.unh.edu

27. EMAIL MESSAGE

The APA's *Publication Manual* discourages including email in a list
of references and suggests citing email only in text as personal communication (p. 419).

28. SYNCHRONOUS COMMUNICATION (MUDs, MOOs)

To cite postings in MUDs, MOOs, and IRCs, provide the speaker's
name, if known, or the name of the site; the date of the event, in parentheses; the title of the event, if appropriate; and the kind of communication (*Group discussion, Personal interview*) in square brackets if not
indicated elsewhere. Include a retrieval statement with the address
using a URL or other Internet address.

Cohen, S. (2000, March 15). Online Collaboration.
    [Group discussion]. Retrieved March 17, 2000,
    from the World Wide Web: http://moo.du.org:8000

29. MATERIAL FROM A CD-ROM DATABASE

Natchez, G. (1987). Frida Kahlo and Diego Rivera:
    The transformation of catastrophe to creativity
    [Abstract]. Psychotherapy-Patient, 8, 153-174.
    Retrieved from SilverPlatter database (PsycLIT,
    CD-ROM, 1999 release, Item 76-11344)

30. MATERIAL FROM AN INFORMATION SERVICE OR ONLINE DATABASE

Belenky, M. F. (1984). The role of deafness in the
    moral development of hearing impaired children.
    In A. Areson & J. De Caro (Eds.), Teaching,
    learning and development. Rochester, NY: National
    Institute for the Deaf. Retrieved January 20,
    2000, from ERIC online database (No. ED 248 646)

31. MATERIAL FROM A DATABASE ACCESSED VIA THE WEB

Pryor, T., & Wiederman, M. W. (1998). Personality
    features and expressed concerns of adolescents

with eating disorders. Adolescence, 33, 291-301.
Retrieved February 7, 2000, from Electric Library
database, on the World Wide Web: http://www
.elibrary.com

32. SOFTWARE OR COMPUTER PROGRAM

McAfee Office 2000. Version 2.0 [Computer software].
(1999). Santa Clara, CA: Network Associates.

Other sources

33. TECHNICAL OR RESEARCH REPORTS AND WORKING PAPERS

Wilson, K. S. (1986). Palenque: An interactive
multimedia optical disc prototype for children
(Working Paper No. 2). New York: Center for
Children and Technology, Bank Street College of
Education.

34. PAPER PRESENTED AT A MEETING OR SYMPOSIUM, UNPUBLISHED
Cite the month of the meeting if it is available.

Engelbart, D. C. (1970, April). Intellectual
implications of multi-access computing. Paper
presented at the meeting of the Interdisciplinary
Conference on Multi-Access Computer Networks,
Washington, DC.

35. DISSERTATION, UNPUBLISHED

Leverenz, C. A. (1994). Collaboration and difference
in the composition classroom. Unpublished
doctoral dissertation, Ohio State University,
Columbus.

36. POSTER SESSION

Ulman, H. L., & Walborn, E. (1993, March). Hypertext
in the composition classroom. Poster session

```
presented at the Annual Conference on College
Composition and Communication, San Diego.
```

37. FILM OR VIDEOTAPE

```
Hitchcock, A. (Producer & Director). (1954). Rear
     window [Film]. Los Angeles: MGM.
```

38. TELEVISION PROGRAM, SINGLE EPISODE

Begin with the names of the script writers, and give the name of the director, in parentheses, after the episode title.

```
Kuttner, P. K., Moran, C., & Scholl, E. (1994, July
     19). Passin' it on (W. Chamberlain, Executive
     Director). In D. Zaccardi (Executive Producer),
     P.O.V. New York: Public Broadcasting Service.
```

39. RECORDING

Begin with the name of the writer or composer, followed by the date of copyright. Give the recording date if it is different from the copyright date.

```
Colvin, S. (1991). I don't know why. [Recorded by
     A. Krauss and Union Station]. On Every time you
     say goodbye [Cassette]. Cambridge, MA: Rounder
     Records. (1992)
```

53

A Sample Research Essay, APA Style

An essay by Leah Clendening appears on the following pages. It follows the APA guidelines described in the preceding chapter.

In order to annotate this essay, we have reproduced it in a smaller space than you will have on a standard eight-and-a-half- by eleven-inch sheet of paper. The lines shown here are thus considerably shorter than the lines in your essay will be.

Content Analysis   1 ·········· Shortened
title and page
number
appear on
every page

A Content Analysis of ································· Heading
centered
Letters to the Editor   and double-
spaced in
Leah Clendening   upper- and
lowercase
Professor Garrett

Psychology 201

November 22, 1999

Abstract

This study analyzed the content of 624
letters to the editor in two newspapers--one
published in a city of over 500,000, the
other in a city of about 15,000--in order
to explore the relationship between
community size and subject matter of
letters. A researcher read all of the
letters printed in the newspapers on the
weekdays of three nonconsecutive months in
late 1987 and early 1988 and then classified
them according to whether they dealt with
local or national issues and recorded the
findings on a category sheet. Results
indicate a significant difference: letters
in the smaller community concentrated almost
entirely on local issues, whereas those in
the larger community concentrated more
frequently on national than on local issues.

No paragraph indent

Key words embedded in abstract to help readers identify the article

Content Analysis   3

A Content Analysis of Letters ·················· Title centered
to the Editor

Research has indicated that the average ·········· Paragraphs
indented five
person who writes letters to an American   spaces

newspaper tends to be a conservative, well-
·············· Double spac-
adjusted white male who is middle-aged or   ing used
throughout
older and a longtime resident of his

community (Singletary & Cowling, 1979). One

study concluded that 71.4% of the letters ·················· Previous
work
printed were written by people who wished to   surveyed

inform or persuade by writing their letters.
·········· Minimum of
Most of the remainder, 27%, wished only to   one-inch
margin on all
use the letter as a means of self-   sides

expression; the other 1.6% wished to arouse

readers to action (Lemert & Larkin, 1979).

Problem ······································· First-level
heading
But what are the major concerns of   centered

these letter writers? Are they more

concerned about events in their local

communities or about national issues? It is

said that papers in smaller communities

"tend to live by the mantra 'local, local,

local'" (Seaton, 1999). But does this

mandate actually reflect the interests of

small-town residents? Does the size of the ·············· Research
question
community have some influence on the   stated

subjects of letters its members write? These

questions led to the following hypothesis:

people living in a small community (with a ·············· Hypothesis
stated

Content Analysis   4

population of about 15,000) tend to be
concerned more with local than with national
issues. People living in a large community
(with a population over 500,000) show more
concern for national than for local issues.

Method

Newspapers

The two newspapers that served as data
sources, the Mount Vernon News and the
Cleveland Plain Dealer, were chosen mainly
for convenience and availability. Cleveland
has a population of 573,822 and a weekly
distribution of the Plain Dealer of 482,564.
Mount Vernon has a population of 14,380 and
a weekly distribution of the Mount Vernon
News of 10,936 (1985 IMS/Ayer Directory,
1985). Each newspaper's letters were read
for the weekdays of October 1987, December
1987, and February 1988. Sunday issues were
not taken into account.

A category sheet of possible subjects
for the letters to the editor was adapted
from the coding sheet of Donohew's study on
Medicare (Budd, Thorp, & Donohew, 1967,
p. 41). One column recorded national issues,
and a second, local issues. The sheet was
constructed with a space for the newspaper's
abbreviation, the date, and the letter
number(s). The Mount Vernon News was given

Content Analysis   5

the abbreviation MVN, and the Cleveland
<u>Plain Dealer</u>, the abbreviation CPD.

<u>Procedure</u>

    After the category sheet was finished
and approved, observation began. The letters
were read and marked for content in a
library setting. Each letter was then
classified on the category sheet that had
been titled with the proper abbreviations,
date, and letter number. As observation
progressed, constraints of time demanded a
change from filling out a separate sheet for
each letter to recording each day's letters
on the same category sheet. The space left
for recording the letter number was used to
record the total number of letters for each
particular day. After all observation was
finished, the counts for each of the
newspapers were totaled for each month and
overall.

Results

    During the three months, 60 letters
were read from the <u>Mount Vernon News</u>. Fifty-
three pertained to local issues, and seven
pertained to national issues. A Chi-square
test with an adjustment for continuity was
used on these data to find whether there
was a statistically significant difference
between concern with local issues and

Steps in carrying out research explained

Right margin not justified

Results from first newspaper analyzed statistically

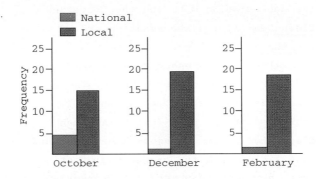

Figure 1. Frequency of national and local issues for the MVN

concern with national issues. Results showed an overwhelming difference between issues, even at the .01 probability level. A graph (Figure 1) was also constructed to show the number of national and local issues for each month for the MVN.

Of a total of 564 letters read from the Cleveland Plain Dealer, 248 pertained to local issues and 316 to national issues. A Chi-square test with an adjustment for continuity was also used on these data and, once again, showed a statistically significant difference. A graph (Figure 2) was constructed to show the frequency of

Content Analysis 7

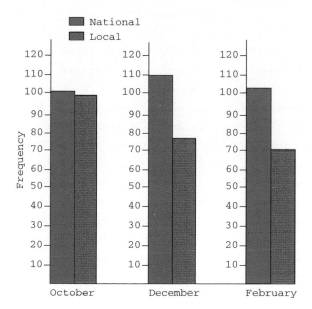

Figure 2. Frequency of national and local issues for the CPD

national and local issues for each month for the CPD.

One interesting side note is that 21.6% of the letters from the Plain Dealer expressed grievances or appreciation, compared with 36% of the letters from the Mount Vernon News. These findings differ considerably from those of Lister, who found that only 5% of letters to the editor were of this particular type (Lister, 1985).

Findings counter to previous research noted

Discussion

The findings of this study generally supported the hypothesis, especially in the smaller community, where letters concentrated overwhelmingly on local issues. Perhaps residents of such a community do not

Results interpreted

see themselves as strongly affected by national politics and events. For the larger community, the findings were not as clear; one possibility is that many of the letters were not from the larger community itself but from smaller communities surrounding it.

Biases and possible improvements in the study listed

If more time had been permitted, an entire year's letters could have been categorized, perhaps yielding more representative information. In addition, use of a second reader could have reduced bias on the part of a single reader in the categorization of letters. It was found as the study progressed that a few categories could have been added, such as religion and local and state elections; the lack of these categories, however, did not severely affect the study. Another bias that would be difficult to account for is editorial bias: one study has found that only 68% of letters received by editors were published (Renfro, 1979). The only way to eliminate this bias would be to read all the letters

received instead of only those that are
printed.

Conclusion

This study raises some interesting
questions that further study would probably
help to answer. Does gender or age influence
whether people are interested in local or
national issues? What is the causal
relationship between residence in small
towns and apparent greater interest in local
affairs? Future studies may answer such
questions, building on the information here.

Larger
questions
noted in
conclusion

Content Analysis   10

References

Budd, R. W., Thorp, K., & Donohew, L.
    (1967). Content analysis of
    communications. New York: Macmillan.

Lemert, J. B., & Larkin, J. P. (1979). Some
    reasons why mobilizing information
    fails to be in letters to the editor.
    Journalism Quarterly, 56, 504-512.

Lister, L. (1985). An analysis of letters to
    the editor. Social Work, 30, 77-78.

The 1985 IMS/Ayer Directory of Publications
    (117th ed.). (1985). Fort Washington,
    PA: IMS Press.

Renfro, P. C. (1979). Bias in selection of
    letters to the editor. Journalism
    Quarterly, 56, 822-826.

Seaton, E. L. (1999, February). Take a fresh
    look at international news: local
    ties. American Editor. Retrieved
    November 1, 1999, from the World Wide
    Web: http://www.asne.org/kiosk/editor/
    99.feb/seaton1.htm

Singletary, M. W., & Cowling, M. (1979).
    Letters to the editor of the non-daily
    press. Journalism Quarterly, 56, 165-
    168.

Heading centered on new page

Entries listed alphabetically by author, last names first; initials used for first and middle names

Title beginning with a number alphabetized as if the number were spelled out

First line of each entry flushes left with margin

Subsequent lines indent five spaces

54

CBE Style

Writers in the natural sciences, the physical sciences, and mathematics can find recommendations for documentation style in the manual of the Council of Science Editors (formerly the Council of Biology Editors, or CBE): *Scientific Style and Format: The CBE Manual for Authors, Editors, and Publishers*, sixth edition, 1994.

DIRECTORY TO CBE STYLE

CBE style for in-text citations (54a)

CBE style for a list of references (54b)

BOOKS

PERIODICALS

ELECTRONIC SOURCES

54a CBE style for in-text citations

In CBE style, citations within an essay follow one of two formats.

- The citation-sequence format calls for a superscript number ([1]) or a number in parentheses after any mention of a source.
- The name-year format calls for the last name of the author and the year of publication in parentheses after any mention of a source. If the last name appears in a signal phrase, the name-year format allows for giving only the year of publication in parentheses.

Dr. Edward Huth, chairperson of the Council of Science Editors Style Manual Committee, recommends using either the name-year or the superscript system rather than the number-in-parentheses system—and suggests that student writers check a current journal in the field or ask an instructor about the preferred style in a particular course or discipline.

1. IN-TEXT CITATION USING CITATION-SEQUENCE SUPERSCRIPT FORMAT

```
In his lengthy text, Gilman[1] provides the most
complete discussion of this phenomenon.
```

For the citation-sequence system, you would also use a superscript *1* ([1]) for each subsequent citation of this work by Gilman.

2. IN-TEXT CITATION USING NAME-YEAR FORMAT

```
In his lengthy text, Gilman provides the most complete
discussion of this phenomenon (1994).

Maxwell's two earlier studies of juvenile obesity
(1988, 1991) examined only children with diabetes.

The classic examples of such investigations (Morrow
1968; Bridger and others 1971; Franklin and Wayson
1972) still shape the assumptions of current studies.
```

54b CBE style for a list of references

The citations in the text of an essay correspond to items on a list called *References*.

- If you use the citation-sequence superscript format, number and list the references in the sequence in which the references are *first* cited in the text.
- If you use the name-year format, list the references, unnumbered, in alphabetical order.

In the following examples, you will see that the citation-sequence format calls for listing the date after the publisher's name in references for books and after the periodical name in references for articles. The name-year format calls for listing the date immediately after the author's name in any kind of reference. Notice also the absence of a comma after the author's last name, the absence of a period after an initial, and the absence of underlining in titles of books or journals.

Books

List the number of pages in a book.

1. ONE AUTHOR

CITATION-SEQUENCE SUPERSCRIPT

[1] Freidson E. Profession of medicine. New York: Dodd-Mead; 1972. 802 p.

NAME-YEAR

Freidson E. 1972. Profession of medicine. New York: Dodd-Mead. 802 p.

2. TWO OR MORE AUTHORS

CITATION-SEQUENCE SUPERSCRIPT

[2] Stalberg E, Trontelj JV. Single fiber electromyography: studies in healthy and diseased muscle. New York: Raven; 1994. 291 p.

NAME-YEAR

Stalberg E, Trontelj JV. 1994. Single fiber
    electromyography: studies in healthy and diseased
    muscle. New York: Raven. 291 p.

3. ORGANIZATION AS AUTHOR

Place any organization abbreviation at the beginning of the name-
year entry, and use it in the corresponding in-text citation.

CITATION-SEQUENCE SUPERSCRIPT

[3] World Health Organization. World health statistics
    annual: 1993. Geneva: World Health Organization;
    1994. 824 p.

NAME-YEAR

[WHO] World Health Organization. 1994. World health
    statistics annual: 1993. Geneva: WHO. 824 p.

4. BOOK PREPARED BY EDITOR(S)

CITATION-SEQUENCE SUPERSCRIPT

[4] Berge ZL, Collins MP, editors. Computer mediated
    communication and the online classroom.
    Cresskill, NJ: Hampton Pr; 1995. 230 p.

NAME-YEAR

Berge ZL, Collins MP, editors. 1995. Computer mediated
    communication and the online classroom.
    Cresskill, NJ: Hampton Pr. 230 p.

5. SECTION OF A BOOK WITH AN EDITOR

CITATION-SEQUENCE SUPERSCRIPT

[5] Adler M. Stroke. In: Dulbecco R, editor.
    Encyclopedia of human biology. San Diego:
    Academic; 1991. p 299-308.

NAME-YEAR

Adler M. 1991. Stroke. In: Dulbecco R, editor.
    Encyclopedia of human biology. San Diego:
    Academic. p 299-308.

6. CHAPTER OF A BOOK

CITATION-SEQUENCE SUPERSCRIPT

[6] Castro J. The American way of health: how medicine
    is changing and what it means to you. Boston:
    Little, Brown; 1994. Chapter 9, Why doctors,
    hospitals, and drugs cost so much; p 131-53.

NAME-YEAR

Castro J. 1994. The American way of health: how
    medicine is changing and what it means to
    you. Boston: Little, Brown. Chapter 9,
    Why doctors, hospitals, and drugs cost so
    much; p 131-53.

7. PUBLISHED PROCEEDINGS OF A CONFERENCE

CITATION-SEQUENCE SUPERSCRIPT

[7] [Anonymous]. International Conference on the Bus
    '86; 1986 Sep 9-10; London. [London]: Institution
    of Mechanical Engineers; 1986. 115 p.

The place of publication was not stated but inferred and placed in
brackets.

NAME-YEAR

[Anonymous]. 1986. International Conference on the Bus
    '86; 1986 Sep 9-10; London. [London]: Institution
    of Mechanical Engineers. 115 p.

Periodicals

For rules on abbreviating journal titles, consult the *CBE Manual,* or ask an instructor or librarian to refer you to other examples.

8. ARTICLE IN A JOURNAL PAGINATED BY VOLUME

CITATION-SEQUENCE SUPERSCRIPT

[8] Finkel MJ. Drugs of limited commercial value. New Engl J Med 1980;302:643-4.

NAME-YEAR

Finkel MJ. 1980. Drugs of limited commercial value. New Engl J Med 302:643-4.

9. ARTICLE IN A JOURNAL PAGINATED BY ISSUE

CITATION-SEQUENCE SUPERSCRIPT

[9] Fagan R. Characteristics of college student volunteering. J Vol Admin 1992;11(1):5-18.

NAME-YEAR

Fagan R. 1992. Characteristics of college student volunteering. J Vol Admin 11(1):5-18.

10. ARTICLE IN A WEEKLY JOURNAL

CITATION-SEQUENCE SUPERSCRIPT

[10] Kerr RA. How many more after Northridge? Science 1994 Jan 28;263(5146):460-1.

NAME-YEAR

Kerr RA. 1994 Jan 28. How many more after Northridge? Science 263(5146):460-1.

11. ARTICLE IN A MAGAZINE

CITATION-SEQUENCE SUPERSCRIPT

[11] Jackson R. Arachnomania. Natural History 1995
    Mar:28-31.

NAME-YEAR

Jackson R. 1995 Mar. Arachnomania. Natural
    History:28-31.

12. ARTICLE IN A NEWSPAPER

CITATION-SEQUENCE SUPERSCRIPT

[12] Christopher T. Grafting: playing Dr. Frankenstein in
    the garden. New York Times 1995 Feb 19;Sect Y:21
    (col 1).

NAME-YEAR

Christopher T. 1995 Feb 19. Grafting: playing Dr.
    Frankenstein in the garden. New York Times; Sect
    Y:21(col 1).

Electronic sources

Although the 1994 edition of *The CBE Manual* includes a few examples for citing electronic sources, the Council of Science Editors now recommends the guidelines provided at its Web site <http://www.councilscienceeditors.org/pubs_citing_internet.shtml>. The following formats are adapted from the advice on this site. To adapt these examples to the citation-sequence superscript system, simply add the superscripts, and reorder the entries.

The basic entry for most sources you access through the Internet should include the following elements:

- *Author.* Give the author's name, if available, last name first, followed by the initial(s) and a period.
- *Title.* For book, journal, and article titles, follow the style for print materials. For all other types of electronic material, reproduce the title as closely as possible to the wording that appears on the screen.

- *Content/medium.* Indicate, in brackets, that the source is not in print format by using designations such as *[Internet]* or *[database on the Internet]*.

- *Place of publication.* The city usually should be followed by the two-letter abbreviation for state. If the city is inferred, put the city and state in brackets, followed by a colon. If the city cannot be inferred, use the words *place unknown* in brackets, followed by a colon. Note that very well-known cities, such as New York or Chicago, may be listed without a state designation.

- *Publisher.* Include the individual or organization that produces or sponsors the site. It is often helpful to include a designation for country, in parentheses, after the publisher's name. If no publisher can be determined, use the words *publisher unknown* in brackets.

- *Dates.* Cite three important dates if possible: the date the publication was placed on the Internet or was copyrighted; the latest date of any update or revision; and the date the publication was accessed by you. Dates should be expressed in the format "year month day," and the date of copyright should be preceded by a *c* as in *c2000*. (Because several dates are preferred in citations from electronic sources, the following examples group all dates together after the publisher's name. Since this style is different from what is done with most print materials, check with your instructor to see if this style is acceptable.

- *Page, document, volume, and issue numbers.* When citing a portion of a larger work or site, list the inclusive page numbers or document numbers of the specific item being cited. For journals or journal articles, include volume and issue numbers.

- *Length.* The length may be shown as a total page count, such as *85p.* For much electronic material, length is approximate and is shown in square brackets, such as *[12 paragraphs]* or *[about 6 screens]*.

- *Address.* Include the URL or other electronic address; use the phrase *Available from:* to introduce the address.

13. ELECTRONIC JOURNAL ARTICLES

Include the authors' names; the title of the article; the title of the journal; the word *Internet* in brackets; as full a date of publication as possible; the date of access; the volume, issue, and page numbers (using designations such as *[16 paragraphs]* or *[5 screens]* if traditional page numbering is not available); and the URL.

```
Tong V, Abbott FS, Mbofana S, Walker MJ. In vitro
     investigation of the hepatic extraction of
     RSD1070, a novel antiarrhythmic compound.
```

J Pharm Pharm Sci [Internet]. 2001 [cited 2001
Oct 15];4(1):15-23. Available from: http://www
.ualberta.ca/~csps/JPPS4(1)/F.Abbott/RSD1070.pdf

14. ELECTRONIC BOOKS (MONOGRAPHS)

Johnson KA. (Harvard Medical School, Boston, MA.
keith@bwh.harvard.edu); Becker JA. (Massachusetts
Institute of Technology, Cambridge, MA.
jabecker@mit.edu). The whole brain atlas
[Internet]. Boston: Harvard Medical School;
c1995-99 [modified 1999 Jan 12; cited 2001
Mar 7]. Available from: http://www.med.harvard
.edu/AANLIB/home.html

15. WORLD WIDE WEB SITE

Include as many of the following dates as possible: the date of publication (or, if this is not available, the copyright date preceded by *c*); the date of the most recent revision; and the date of access.

Animal Welfare Information Center [Internet].
Beltsville (MD): National Agricultural Library
(US); [updated 2001 Oct 11; cited 2001 Oct 15].
Available from http://www.nal.usda.gov/awic
Hypertension, Dialysis & Clinical Nephrology
[Internet]. Hinsdale (IL): Medtext, Inc.;
c1995-2001 [cited 2001 Oct 15]. Available from:
http://www.medtext.com/hdcn.htm

16. EMAIL MESSAGE

Include the author's name; the subject line of the message; the word *Internet* in square brackets; the words *Message to:* followed by the addressee's name; information about when the message was sent and when it was cited; and the length of the message.

Voss, J. Questions about CBE style. [Internet].
    Message to: Stephanie Carpenter. 2002 Jan 29,
    3:34 pm [cited 2002 Jan 30]. [about 1 screen]

17. ELECTRONIC DISCUSSION LIST MESSAGE

Include as much of the following information as possible.

Rooyer, L. (State University of New York, Albany.
    lrooyer@suny.net. Routing BRM. IN: DOCLINE-L
    [Internet]. [Bethesda, MD]: National Library of
    Medicine (US); 2001 Apr 2, 21:17:35 [cited 2001
    Oct 15]. [about 2 paragraphs]. Available from:
    DOCLINE-L@LIST.NIH.GOV Archives available from:
    http://list.nih.gov/archives/docline-l.html

18. MATERIAL FROM AN ONLINE DATABASE

MEDLINE [Internet]. Bethesda (MD): National Library of
    Medicine (US). [cited 2001 Oct 15]. Available
    from: http://pubmed.gov
Ovid [Internet]. New York: Ovid Technologies, Inc.
    c2000-2001 - [cited 2001 May 3]. Available from:
    http://gateway.ovid.com/. Subscription required.

55
Chicago Style

The fourteenth edition of the style guide of the University of Chicago Press, published in 1993 and called *The Chicago Manual of Style,* provides a complete guide to Chicago style. For further reference, you can also consult the following much shorter volume intended for student writers:

Turabian, Kate L. *A Manual for Writers of Term Papers, Theses, and Dissertations.* 6th ed. Rev. John Grossman and Alice Bennett. Chicago: U of Chicago P, 1996.

In Chicago style, you use superscript numbers ([1]) to mark citations in the text. Number citations sequentially throughout the text. Make sure each citation corresponds to a note that contains either publication information about the sources cited or explanatory or supplemental material that you choose not to include in the main text. List sources in a bibliography at the end of the text.

DIRECTORY TO CHICAGO STYLE

Chicago style for in-text citations and notes (55a)

14. Listserv message 456
15. Newsgroup message 457
16. Synchronous communication (MUDs, MOOs) 457
17. FTP (file transfer protocol), telnet, or gopher site 457

SUBSEQUENT NOTES FOR PREVIOUSLY CITED SOURCES

Chicago style for bibliographic entries (55b)

BOOKS

1. One author 459
2. Two or three authors 459
3. Unknown author 459
4. Editor 459
5. Selection in an anthology, or chapter in a book, with an editor 459
6. Edition other than the first 460
7. Multivolume work 460

PERIODICALS

8. Article in a journal paginated by volume 460
9. Article in a journal paginated by issue 460
10. Article in a magazine 460
11. Article in a newspaper 460

INTERNET SOURCES

12. World Wide Web site 460
13. Email message 461
14. Listserv message 461
15. Newsgroup message 461
16. Synchronous communication (MUDs, MOOs) 461
17. FTP (file transfer protocol), telnet, or gopher site 461

55a Chicago style for in-text citations and notes

In the text, place the superscript number for each note near the cited material—at the end of the relevant quotation, sentence, clause, or phrase. Type the number after any punctuation mark except the dash; do not leave space between the superscript and the preceding letter or punctuation mark.

The notes themselves can be footnotes (each typed at the bottom of the page on which the citation for it appears in the text) or endnotes (all typed on a separate page at the end of the text under the heading "Notes"). Be sure to check your instructor's preference. The first line of each note is indented like a paragraph (five spaces or one-half inch) and begins with a number followed by a period and one space before the first word of the entry. All remaining lines of the entry are typed flush with the left margin. Type footnotes single-spaced with a double space between each note. Type all endnotes double-spaced.

IN THE TEXT

As Luftig notes, true friendship between the sexes may simply not be possible.[1]

IN THE NOTE

1. Victor Luftig. <u>Seeing Together: Friendship between the Sexes in English Writing</u> (Palo Alto, Calif.: Stanford University Press, 1993), 1.

The first note for any source gives full information about the source, whereas subsequent notes are shortened. Here are some guidelines for the format of notes in Chicago style.

Books

A note for a book typically includes four elements, separated by commas: the author's name, in normal order; the title and subtitle, underlined; the publication information, including the city of publication, the publisher's name, and the date, all enclosed in parentheses; and the page number(s) to which the note refers, followed by a period.

1. ONE AUTHOR

    1. Hayden Herrera, <u>Frida: A Biography of Frida Kahlo</u> (New York: Harper and Row, 1983), 356.

2. TWO OR THREE AUTHORS

    2. John T. McNeill and Helena M. Gamer, <u>Medieval Handbooks of Penance</u> (New York: Octagon Books, 1965), 139.

It is acceptable in Chicago style when there are more than three authors to give the first-listed author followed by *et al.* or *and others.* But since this practice doesn't acknowledge the contributions of all authors, we recommend listing *all* contributors' names.

3. UNKNOWN AUTHOR

    3. <u>The New York Times Atlas of the World</u> (New York: New York Times Books, 1980), 67.

4. EDITOR

    4. C. Vann Woodward, ed., <u>Mary Chesnut's Civil War</u> (New Haven, Conn.: Yale University Press, 1981), 214.

5. SELECTION IN AN ANTHOLOGY, OR CHAPTER IN A BOOK, WITH AN EDITOR

    5. Mary Gordon, "The Parable of the Cave," in <u>The Writer on Her Work</u>, ed. Janet Sternburg (New York: W. W. Norton, 1980), 30.

6. EDITION OTHER THAN THE FIRST

    6. Alfred H. Kelly, Winfred A. Harbison, and Herman Belz, <u>The American Constitution: Its Origins and Development</u>, 6th ed. (New York: W. W. Norton, 1983), 187.

7. MULTIVOLUME WORK

> 7. Philip S. Foner and Ronald L. Lewis, eds., The Black Worker, vol. 3 (Philadelphia: W. P. Lippincott, 1980), 134.

Periodicals

A note for a periodical typically includes the following elements, separated by commas: the author's name, in normal order; the article title, in quotation marks; and the periodical title, underlined. The format for the rest of the publication information, including the volume and issue numbers (if any), the date of publication, and the page number(s) to which the note refers, varies according to the type of periodical.

8. ARTICLE IN A JOURNAL PAGINATED BY VOLUME

> 8. Margot Norris, "Narration under a Blindfold: Reading Joyce's 'Clay,'" PMLA 102 (1987): 206.

9. ARTICLE IN A JOURNAL PAGINATED BY ISSUE

> 9. John Lofty, "The Politics at Modernism's Funeral," Canadian Journal of Political and Social Theory 6, no. 3 (1987): 89.

10. ARTICLE IN A MAGAZINE

> 10. Sarah Ferguson, "The Comfort of Being Sad: Kurt Cobain and the Politics of Suicide," Utne Reader, July-August 1994, 60.

11. ARTICLE IN A NEWSPAPER

> 11. Dennis Kelly, "A Financial Report Card for Colleges," USA Today, 5 July 1994, sec. D, p. 1.

Internet sources

The Chicago Manual does not include guidelines for citing Internet sources. The following formats, adapted from Chicago style, are from

Online! A Reference Guide to Using Internet Sources, by Andrew Harnack and Eugene Kleppinger.

The basic entry for most sources you access through the Internet should include the following elements:

- *Author.* Give the author's name, if available, in normal order, followed by a comma.
- *Title.* Give the title of the document or subject line of the message, enclosed in quotation marks and followed by a comma.
- *Publication date.* List the date of Internet publication or the most recent update, if available, followed by a comma. (If no date is available, use *n.d.*)
- *Address.* Include the URL, in angle brackets, or other retrieval information.
- *Date of access.* Enclose the date in parentheses, followed by a comma or by a period if it is the last item in the entry.
- *Text division.* List the page number or other internal division of the source, if applicable, followed by a period.

12. WORLD WIDE WEB SITE

After the document title, include the title of the complete work, if applicable, underlined.

> 12. Stephanie Brail, "Newsflash!" <u>Spider Woman:</u>
> <u>An Online Community & Resource for Women Web</u>
> <u>Designers</u>, n.d., <http://www.amazoncity.com/spiderwoman
> /web.html> (22 May 1997).

13. EMAIL MESSAGE

Include the author's email address, in angle brackets, after the author's name; include the type of communication (*Personal email, Distribution list*) after the subject line and the date composed.

> 13. Danielle Mitchell, <mitcheld@ucs.orst.edu>
> "PhD Decisions," 28 May 1997, Personal email (28 May
> 1997).

14. LISTSERV MESSAGE

Include the author's email address, in angle brackets, after the author's name, and the address of the listserv, in angle brackets, after the publication date.

```
    14. Ann Welpton Fisher-Wirth, <afwirth@sunset
.backbone.olemiss.edu> "Deserts," 27 May 1997,
<asle@unr.edu> (28 May 1997).
```

15. NEWSGROUP MESSAGE

Include the author's email address, in angle brackets, after (or instead of) the author's name, and the name of the newsgroup, in angle brackets, after the publication date.

```
    15. <kunk@astro.phys.unm.edu> "What Did the
Vandals Learn?" 30 May 1997, <soc.history.ancient>
(2 June 1997).
```

16. SYNCHRONOUS COMMUNICATION (MUDs, MOOs)

Cite the name of the speaker(s), if known, or the name of the site, followed by a comma; the title of the event, if appropriate, enclosed in quotation marks and followed by a comma; the date of the event, followed by a comma; the type of communication (*Group discussion, Personal interview*), if not indicated elsewhere in the entry, followed by a comma; the address, using either a URL or command-line directions; and the date of access, in parentheses, followed by a period.

```
    16. MediaMoo, "Netoric's Tuesday Cafe on Megabyte
University: A Look Back; a Look Ahead," 13 May 1997,
<telnet://purple-crayon.media.mit.edu:8888> (5 June
1997).
```

```
    17. Marcy Bauman, "Collaborative Software
Environments: What's on Your Wish List?" 15 April
1997, Group discussion, <telnet purple-crayon.media
.mit.edu/port=8888> (5 June 1997).
```

17. FTP (FILE TRANSFER PROTOCOL), TELNET, OR GOPHER SITE

After the document title, include the full title of the work, if applicable, underlined and followed by a comma. For a document obtained using gopher, include print publication information after the title of the document, if appropriate. Include the date of online publication, if available. For an FTP document, follow the online publication date with print publication information, if appropriate. Next, include *ftp, telnet,* or *gopher* followed by the address of the site, with no closing punctuation, and the full path to find the document, with no closing punctuation. Or you can use a URL in angle brackets instead.

```
    18. Zheng Wang, "EIP: The Extended Internet
Protocol: A Long-Term Solution to Internet Address
Exhaustion," June 1992, <ftp://munnari.OZ.AU
/big-internet/eip.txt> (5 June 1997).
```

Subsequent notes for previously cited sources

After giving a full citation the first time you refer to a work, for any additional reference to that work you need list only the author's name followed by a comma, a shortened version of the title, a comma, and the page number. If the reference is to the same source cited in the previous note, you can use the Latin abbreviation *Ibid.* instead of the name and title.

```
    19. Herrera, Frida, 32.

    20. Ibid., 33.

    21. Foner and Lewis, Black Worker, 138-39.

    22. Ferguson, "Comfort of Being Sad," 63.

    23. Martinots, "Spectors of Sartre."
```

55b Chicago style for bibliographic entries

An alphabetical list of sources in Chicago style is usually titled Bibliography. If *Sources Consulted, Works Cited,* or *Selected Bibliography* better describes your list, however, any of these titles is acceptable. Begin the list on a separate page following the main text and any endnotes. Continue the consecutive numbering of pages. Type the title (without underlining or quotation marks), and center it two inches below the top of the page. Begin each entry at the left margin. Indent the second and subsequent lines of each entry five spaces. Double-space the entire list.

List sources alphabetically by authors' last names (or by the first major word in the title if the author is unknown).

In the bibliographic entry for a source, include the same information as the first note for that source, except for the specific page reference. However, give the author's last name first; separate the main elements of the entry with periods rather than commas; and do not enclose the publication information for books and periodical articles in parentheses. The following examples demonstrate how to arrange the elements of bibliographic entries according to Chicago style.

Books

1. ONE AUTHOR

Herrera, Hayden. <u>Frida: A Biography of Frida Kahlo</u>.
    New York: Harper and Row, 1983.

2. TWO OR THREE AUTHORS

McNeill, John T., and Helena M. Gamer. <u>Medieval
    Handbooks of Penance</u>. New York: Octagon Books,
    1965.

It is acceptable in Chicago style when there are more than three authors to list all the authors or to give only the first followed by *et al.* or *and others*. Since this practice doesn't acknowledge the contributions of all authors, we recommend listing all authors' names.

3. UNKNOWN AUTHOR

<u>The New York Times Atlas of the World</u>. New York: New
    York Times Books, 1980.

4. EDITOR

Woodward, C. Vann, ed. <u>Mary Chesnut's Civil War</u>. New
    Haven, Conn.: Yale University Press, 1981.

5. SELECTION IN AN ANTHOLOGY, OR CHAPTER IN A BOOK, WITH AN EDITOR

Gordon, Mary. "The Parable of the Cave." In <u>The Writer
    on Her Work</u>, edited by Janet Sternburg, 30-45.
    New York: W. W. Norton, 1980.

6. EDITION OTHER THAN THE FIRST

Kelly, Alfred H., Winfred A. Harbison, and Herman
     Belz. The American Constitution: Its Origins and
     Development. 6th ed. New York: W. W. Norton,
     1983.

7. MULTIVOLUME WORK

Foner, Philip S., and Ronald L. Lewis, eds. The Black
     Worker. Vol. 3. Philadelphia: W. P. Lippincott,
     1980.

Periodicals

8. ARTICLE IN A JOURNAL PAGINATED BY VOLUME

Norris, Margot. "Narration under a Blindfold: Reading
     Joyce's 'Clay.'" PMLA 102 (1987): 206-15.

9. ARTICLE IN A JOURNAL PAGINATED BY ISSUE

Lofty, John. "The Politics at Modernism's Funeral."
     Canadian Journal of Political and Social Theory
     6, no. 3 (1987): 89-96.

10. ARTICLE IN A MAGAZINE

Ferguson, Sarah. "The Comfort of Being Sad: Kurt
     Cobain and the Politics of Suicide." Utne Reader,
     July-August 1994, 60-62.

11. ARTICLE IN A NEWSPAPER

Kelly, Dennis. "A Financial Report Card for Colleges."
     USA Today, 5 July 1994, sec. D, p. 1.

Internet sources

12. WORLD WIDE WEB SITE

Brail, Stephanie. "Newsflash!" Spider Woman: An Online
     Community & Resource for Women Web Designers.

n.d. <http://www.amazoncity.com/spiderwoman
/web.html> (22 May 1997).

13. EMAIL MESSAGE

Mitchell, Danielle. <mitcheld@ucs.orst.edu> "PhD
   Decisions." 28 May 1997. Personal email (28 May
   1997).

14. LISTSERV MESSAGE

Fisher-Wirth, Ann Welpton. <afwirth@sunset.backbone
   .olemiss.edu> "Deserts." 27 May 1997.
   <asle@unr.edu> (28 May 1997).

15. NEWSGROUP MESSAGE

<kunk@astro.phys.unm.edu> "What Did the Vandals
   Learn?" 30 May 1997. <soc.history.ancient>
   (2 June 1997).

16. SYNCHRONOUS COMMUNICATION (MUDs, MOOs)

MediaMoo. "Netoric's Tuesday Cafe on Megabyte
   University: A Look Back; a Look Ahead." 13 May
   1997. <telnet://purple-crayon.media.mit.edu:8888>
   (5 June 1997).

Bauman, Marcy. "Collaborative Software Environments:
   What's on Your Wish List?" 15 April 1997. Group
   discussion. telnet purple-crayon.media.mit.edu
   /port=8888 (5 June 1997).

17. FTP (FILE TRANSFER PROTOCOL), TELNET, OR GOPHER SITE

Wang, Zheng. "EIP: The Extended Internet Protocol:
   A Long-Term Solution to Internet Address
   Exhaustion." June 1992. <ftp://munnari.OZ.AU
   /big-internet/eip.txt> (5 June 1997).

56

Writing about Literature

Literature might be called the art of story, and story might in turn be called a universal language, for every culture we know of has a tradition of storytelling. No doubt stories have touched your life, too, from bedtime stories you may have heard as a child to news stories you see on TV or read in the newspaper. We might even say that a major goal of living is to create the story of our own lives, a story we hope to take pleasure and pride in telling. Thinking and writing about literature can give you insight into human motives, character, and potential—others' as well as your own.

56a Become a strong reader of literature.

As a reader of literature, you are not an empty cup into which the meaning of a literary work is poured. If such were the case, literary works would have exactly the same meanings for all of us, and reading would be a fairly boring affair. If you have ever gone to a movie with a friend and each come away with a completely different understanding or response, you already have ample evidence that literature never has just one meaning. The following guidelines will help you exercise your powers of interpretation and of making meaning.

Reading Literature

- *Read the work first for an overall impression.* How did the work make you feel? What about it is most remarkable? Are you confused about anything in it?
- *Reread the work, annotating* it in the margins to "talk back." Ask questions; point out anything that seems out of place, puzzling, or ineffective.
- *What is the genre*—gothic fiction? tragic drama? lyric poetry? creative nonfiction? What is noteworthy about the form of the work?
- *What is the point of view, and who is the narrator?* How reliable and convincing does the narrator seem? What in the work builds up or suspends your faith in the narrator's credibility?

(continues on next page)

- *What do you see as the major themes* of the work? How do plot, setting, character, point of view, imagery, and sound support the themes?
- *What may have led the author to address these themes?* Consider the time and place represented in the work as well as when and where the writer wrote the work. Also consider the social, political, or even personal forces that may have affected the writer.
- *Who are the readers the writer seems to address?* Do they include you? Do you sympathize with a particular character? Why?
- *Review your thoughts and any notes you have made.* What interests you most? Freewrite for fifteen minutes or so about your overall response to this work and about the key point you would like to make about it.

56b A glossary of literary terms

To analyze the sounds in a literary work, you might use the following terms:

alliteration the repetition of initial sounds to create special emphasis or rhythm, as in this sentence from Eudora Welty: "Monsieur Boule inserted a *del*icate *d*agger in Mademoiselle's left side and *d*eparted with a posed immediacy."

meter the rhythm of a line of verse, as determined by kind of foot—iambic, dactylic, and so on—and number of feet—pentameter, tetrameter—in a line. Iambic pentameter indicates five feet of iambs (two syllables, with the stress falling on the second of the two), as in the following line: *An aged man is but a paltry thing.* Blank verse refers to unrhymed iambic pentameter; free verse is the label for poetry without a fixed meter or rhyme scheme.

onomatopoeia the use of words whose sounds call up, or echo, their meaning: *hiss* or *sizzle,* for example.

rhyme scheme the pattern of end rhymes in a poem, usually designated by the letters *a, b, c.* A Shakespearean sonnet typically follows a rhyme scheme of *abab cdcd efef gg.*

rhythm in metrical poetry, the beat or pattern of stresses; in prose, the effect created by repetition, parallelism, and variation of sentence length and structure.

stanza a division of a poem: a four-line stanza is called a quatrain; a two-line stanza, a couplet.

Use the following terms to discuss imagery, the general label applied to vivid descriptions that evoke a picture or appeal to other senses:

allusion an indirect (that is, unacknowledged) reference in one work to another work or to a historical event, biblical passage, and so on.

analogy a comparison of two things that are alike in some respect, often to explain one of the things or to represent it more vividly by relating it to the second. A simile is an explicit analogy; a metaphor, an implied one.

figurative language hyperbole, metaphor, simile, personification, and other figures of speech that enrich description and create meaning (00).

symbolism the use of one thing to represent another thing or idea, as the flag symbolizes patriotism.

Helpful terms for analyzing the elements and structures of narrative include the following:

characters the people in a story, who may act, react, and change during the course of a story. In the essay on *The Third Life of Grange Copeland* (56d), Amy Dierst examines the characters in the novel in order to interpret its meaning.

dialogue the conversation among characters, which can show how they interact and suggest why they act as they do. Monologue is a speech by one character, spoken to himself or herself or aloud to another character.

heteroglossia a term referring to the many voices in a work. In Dickens's *Hard Times,* the voice of mass education speaks alongside the voices of fictional characters.

implied author the author that is inferred from or implied by the text, as distinct from the real person/author. In *The Adventures of Huckleberry Finn,* for example, the real author is the flesh-and-blood Samuel Clemens (or Mark Twain); the implied author is the author we imagine as Clemens presents himself in the text.

intertextuality the system of references in one text to other texts through quotations, allusions, parodies, or thematic references. Larson's *Far Side* Frankenstein cartoons refer intertextually to the original novel, *Frankenstein,* as well as to movie versions and to other works focusing on the delights—and limits—of science.

irony the suggestion of the opposite, or nearly the opposite, as in saying that being caught in a freezing downpour is "delightful."

narrator the person telling a story. In *The Adventures of Huckleberry Finn,* the narrator is Huck himself. In poetry, the narrator is known as the speaker. Both narrator and speaker can be referred to as the persona. See also *point of view.*

paradox a seemingly contradictory statement that may nonetheless be true. The ultimate Christian paradox is that in death one ultimately finds life.

parody an imitation intended for humorous effect, as in the takeoff on the magazine *Martha Stewart Living* entitled *Is Martha Stewart Living?*

plot   the events selected by the writer to reveal the conflicts, or struggles, among or within characters, often arranged chronologically but sometimes including flashbacks to past events. Traditionally, the plot begins with exposition, which presents background information; rises to a climax, the point of greatest tension; and ends with a resolution and dénouement, which contain the outcome.

point of view   the perspective from which the work is presented by a character in the work or by a narrator or speaker; terms relating to point of view include *omniscient narrator, limited third-person narrator, first-person narrator,* and *unreliable narrator.*

protagonist   the hero or main character, often opposed by an antagonist.

setting   the scene of the work, including time, physical location, and social situation.

style   the writer's choice of words and sentence structures.

theme   a major and often recurring idea; the larger meaning of a work, including any thoughts or insights about life or people in general.

tone   the writer's attitude, conveyed through specific word choices and structures.

Editing Your Writing about Literature

- What is your thesis, or central idea? (See Chapter 6.) How could it be stated more clearly?

- What support do you offer for your thesis? Check to be sure you include concrete instances drawn from the text you are writing about.

- How do you organize your essay? Do you move chronologically through the work of literature? Do you consider major elements such as images or characters one by one? If you cannot discern a clear relationship among your points, you may have to rearrange them, revise your materials, or substitute better evidence in support of your thesis.

- Check all quotations to make sure each supports your thesis and that you have properly used signal phrases, indentations (necessary for longer quotations), and citations in parentheses.

- If you quote, paraphrase, or summarize secondary sources, do you cite and document thoroughly and accurately following MLA guidelines? (See Chapters 48–51.)

- Be sure to use present-tense verbs when discussing literature: *Alice Walker's Grange Copeland displays his frustration through neglect.* Use past tense only to describe historical events: *Thus sharecropping, like slavery before it, contributed to the black man's feeling of powerlessness.* (See p. 470.)

56c Consider your assignment, purpose, and audience.

When you write about literature, you will often be responding to an assignment given by an instructor.

- Study the assignment carefully, noting any requirements about use of sources or overall length.
- Check the assignment for key words that specify a certain purpose. *Analyze*, for example, implies that you should look at one or more parts of the literary work and relate it to, say, a point or theme of the work.
- Consider the audience for your essay—your instructor, most likely, and perhaps others as well.

56d Select a critical stance.

Writers often adopt one of three stances in writing about literature:

- *a text-based stance,* which supports a thesis, or central idea, by focusing on specific features in the literary text in question
- *a context-based stance,* which supports a thesis by focusing on the context, or outside environment, in which the literary text exists
- *a reader-based stance,* which creates a thesis based on the response of a particular reader to the literary text and an interpretation that grows out of his or her personal response

The following essay, which is slightly abridged, demonstrates a text-based response to an assignment that asked students to "analyze some aspect of one of the works read" in an introductory literature class. Because the assignment called for an analysis of a work read by the entire class, the writer, Amy Dierst, could assume she need not review the plot. This was a fairly open-ended assignment, and so she checked with her instructor to make sure that her chosen focus, "the role of men," would qualify as an aspect of a work to be analyzed. Dierst makes a claim—her thesis—about the role of men in *The Third Life of Grange Copeland;* she then substantiates her thesis by citing passages from the primary source, the novel itself, as well as from secondary sources, other readers' interpretations of the novel. (See p. 393 for a full sample essay following MLA style.)

The Role of Men in
The Third Life of Grange Copeland

Many observers of American society charge that
it has created a distorted definition of manhood and
produced men who, in their need to assert control of
their lives, release their frustration at the expense
of women. In her novel The Third Life of Grange
Copeland, Alice Walker addresses this theme from the
point of view of black men and women, for whom racism
heightens the distortion and its consequences. She
suggests that by stifling black men's sense of freedom
and control, a racist society creates frustrations
that are released in family violence and inherited by
their children. Because his wife and children are the
only aspect of the black man's life that he can
control, they become the scapegoat upon which his
frustrations are released. As Walker's title suggests,
she sees redemption, or spiritual rebirth into a new
life, as the best defense against society's injustice.
Though Walker's male characters have been labeled by
some as either heartlessly cruel or pathetically weak
(Steinem 89), many of them, like Grange Copeland, do
change during the course of a work. Individual
transformation stimulates the potential for change in
the social system as a whole.

In this novel, Walker shows how the social and
economic system of the 1920s offered a futile
existence to southern black families. Grange Copeland,
like most southern black men of his era, lived and
worked on a farm owned and operated by a white man.
This system, called sharecropping, did not allow for
future planning or savings, for everything earned was
returned to the white man's pocket for rent. Thus
sharecropping, like slavery before it, contributed to

the black man's feelings of powerlessness. In his desperation and helplessness, Grange turns to exert power in the one place he is dominant, his home. He releases his frustration by abusing his family in a weekly cycle of cruelty:

> By Thursday, Grange's gloominess reached its peak and he grimaced respectfully, with veiled eyes, at the jokes told by the man who drove the truck [the white farm owner, Mr. Shipley]. On Thursday night, he stalked the house from room to room, pulled himself up and swung from the rafters. Late Saturday night Grange would come home lurching drunk, threatening to kill his wife and Brownfield [his son], stumbling and shooting his shotgun. (Walker 12)

At other times, Grange displays his frustration through neglect, a more psychologically disturbing device that later affects Brownfield's emotional stability. Grange's inability to rise above his own discontent with his life and express feeling toward his son becomes his most abusive act. Eventually, he abandons his family completely for a new life in the North. Even when he says good-bye, "even in private and in the dark and with his son, presumably asleep, Grange could not bear to touch his son with his hand" (Walker 121).

Brownfield picks up where Grange left off, giving his father's violent threats physical form by beating his own wife and children regularly. Although he, too, blames the whites for driving him to brutality, Walker suggests that his actions are not excusable on these grounds. By the time he reaches adulthood, sharecropping is not a black man's only option and cannot be used as a scapegoat. Nevertheless, he chooses to relinquish his freedom and work for Mr. Shipley.

By becoming the overseer on Mr. Shipley's plantation, Brownfield positions himself for the same failure that ruined his father. As Trudier Harris notes, over time Brownfield's loss of control of his life turns his feelings of depression and lost pride into anger, and his own destructive nature turns him toward violence and evil (240). Unable or unwilling to take responsibility for himself, Brownfield blames his own inadequacies on his wife, Mem, who bears the brunt of his anger:

> Brownfield beat his once lovely wife now,
> regularly, because it made him feel briefly
> good. Every Saturday night he beat her,
> trying to pin the blame for his failure on
> her by imprinting it on her face, and
> she [. . .] repaid him by becoming a
> haggard [. . .] witch. (Walker 55)

Brownfield demonstrates his power by stripping Mem, a former schoolteacher, of anything that would threaten his manhood. Reasoning that her knowledge is a power that he cannot have and therefore she does not deserve, he wants her to speak in her old dialect so that she will not appear to be more intelligent than he does. He also wants her to be ugly because her ugliness makes it easier for him to justify beating her. He wants her to reach a state of ultimate degradation where any strength of her character will be quickly extinguished by a blow to the face or a kick in the side. In fact, "he rather enjoyed her desolation because in it she had no hopes. She was totally weak, totally without view, without a sky"

(Walker 59). In a final attempt to release his
frustration, as Paul Theroux suggests, Brownfield
kills Mem, literally and symbolically obliterating the
remainder of her identity--her face (2).

But in the face of this brutality and
degradation, Walker raises the possibility of a
different fate for black men and women. While in the
North, Grange undergoes a spiritual rebirth and, as
Karen Gaston notes, comes to understand that white
injustice is not alone responsible for the cruelty of
black men toward their families (278). He also
realizes that to weaken and destroy a wife and family
is not a sign of manhood:

> You gits just as weak as water, no feeling
> of doing nothing yourself, you begins to
> destroy everybody around you, and you blame
> it on crackers [whites]. Nobody's as
> powerful as we make out to be, we got our
> own souls, don't we? (Walker 207)

Grange redeems his spirit in his "third life"
with his granddaughter, Ruth. His objective now is not
to destroy what he loves but to cherish it. . . .

Here is Amy Dierst's list of works cited in her essay.

Works Cited

Gaston, Karen C. "Women in the Lives of Grange
    Copeland." College Language Association Journal
    24 (1981): 276-86.

Harris, Trudier. "Violence in The Third Life of Grange
    Copeland." College Language Association Journal
    19 (1975): 238-47.

Steinem, Gloria. "Do You Know This Woman? She Knows
    You--A Profile on Alice Walker." Ms. June 1982:
    89-94.

Theroux, Paul. Rev. of <u>The Third Life of Grange</u>
<u>Copeland</u>, by Alice Walker. <u>Bookworld</u> 4 Sept.
1970: 2.

Walker, Alice. <u>The Third Life of Grange Copeland</u>. New
York: Harcourt, 1970.

57

Oral Presentations

When the Gallup Poll reports on what U.S. citizens say they fear most, the findings are always the same: public speaking is apparently more frightening to us than anything else, scarier even than an attack from outer space or nuclear holocaust. This chapter aims to allay any such fears *you* may have by offering guidelines that can help you prepare for and deliver successful oral presentations.

> ### *Editing Text for Oral Presentations*
> - How does your presentation fulfill your purpose? (57a)
> - How do you appeal to your audience's interests? (57a)
> - How does the introduction get the audience's attention? Does it provide necessary background information? (57b)
> - How do you guide listeners? Are your transitions explicit? Do you repeat key words or ideas? (57c)
> - Have you used straightforward sentences and concrete terms? (57c)
> - Have you marked your text for pauses and emphasis? (57d)
> - How, if at all, do you use visuals? Are they large enough to be seen? Would other visuals be helpful? (57e)

57a Consider your task, purpose, and audience.

Consider how much time you have to prepare, how long the presentation is to be, and whether visual aids, handouts, or other accompanying materials are called for. If you are making a group presentation, you will need time to divide duties and to practice with your colleagues.

Consider the purpose of your presentation. Are you to lead a discussion? present a proposal? teach a lesson? give a report? engage a group in an activity? And who will be the audience? Ask yourself what they know about your topic, what opinions they already hold about it, and what they need to know and understand to follow your presentation and accept your point of view.

57b Work on your introduction and conclusion.

Listeners tend to remember beginnings and endings most readily, so try to make these elements memorable. Consider, for example, using a startling statement, opinion, or question; a vivid anecdote; or a powerful quotation. (See 7f for examples.) Linking your subject to the experiences and interests of your listeners will help them remember you and your presentation.

57c Use explicit structure and signpost language.

Organize your presentation clearly and carefully, and, toward the beginning of your presentation, give an overview of your main points. (You may wish to recall these points again toward the end of the talk.) Throughout your presentation, pause between major points, and use signpost language to mark your movement from one idea to the next. Signpost language acts as an explicit transition in your talk: *The second crisis point in the breakup of the Soviet Union occurred hard on the heels of the first* instead of *Another thing about the breakup of the Soviet Union. . . .* (For a list of transitions, see p. 51.) Avoid long, complicated sentences, and remember that listeners can hold on to concrete verbs and nouns more easily than they can grasp abstractions. You may need to deal with abstract ideas, but try to provide concrete examples for each.

57d Prepare your text for ease of presentation.

Depending on the audience and your personal preferences, you may decide to prepare a full text of your presentation. If so, double- or triple-space it, and use fairly large print so that it will be easy to read. Try to end each page with the end of a sentence so that you won't have to pause while you turn a page. Or you may prefer to work from a detailed topic outline, from note cards, or from points on a transparency for an overhead projector. (See 58b for an example.) In any case—full text, outline, or notes—be sure to mark the places where you want to pause; in addition, highlight the words you want to emphasize.

Of the following paragraphs, the first is from an essay that is intended to be read by its audience. The second paragraph presents the same information but is intended for oral presentation. Note how the second text uses signpost language; repetition; vivid, concrete examples; and uncomplicated sentence structure to make it easy to follow by ear. Note also how the writer has marked her text for emphasis and pauses.

A PARAGRAPH FROM A WRITTEN ESSAY

The decision about a major or other course of study is crucial because it determines both what we study and how we come to think about the world. The philosopher Kenneth Burke explains that we are inevitably affected not only by our experiences but also by the terminologies through which our perceptions of those experiences are filtered. Burke calls these filters "terministic screens" and says that they affect our perception, highlighting some aspects of an experience while obscuring others. Thus the terminologies (or languages) we use influence how we see the world and how we think about what we see.

THE PARAGRAPH REVISED FOR ORAL PRESENTATION

Why is our decision about a major so crucial? I can give two important reasons. First, our major determines what we study. *Pause* Second, it determines how we come to think about the world. The philosopher Kenneth Burke explains these influences this way: our experiences, he says, influence what we think about ideas and the world. But those experiences are always filtered through <u>language</u>, through words and terminologies. Burke calls these terminologies "<u>terministic screens</u>," a complicated-sounding term for a pretty simple idea. Take, for example, the latest hike in

```
student fees on our campus. The Board of Trustees and
the administration use one set of terms to describe
the hike: "modest and reasonable," they call it. Stu-
dents I know use entirely different terms: "exorbitant
and unjust," they call it. Why the difference? Because
                                                  Pause
their terministic screens are entirely different.
                                                  ^
Burke says we all have such screens made up of lan-
guage, and these screens act to screen out some things
for us and to screen in, or highlight, others. Burke's
major point is this: the terms and screens we use have
a big influence on how we see the world and how we
think about what we see.
```

57e Use visuals.

Think of visuals—charts, graphs, photographs, summary statements, or lists—not as mere add-ons but as one of your major means of conveying information. Because of their importance, they must be large enough to be easily seen and read by your audience. Many speakers use Power-Point or overhead projections throughout a presentation to help keep themselves on track and to guide their audience. Posters, flip charts, and chalkboards can make strong visual statements as well. Be sure that the information on any visual is simple, clear, and easy to read and process. And remember not to turn your back on your audience while you refer to any of these visuals. (See more about visuals in Chapter 58.)

Most important, make sure that all visuals engage and help your listeners, rather than distract them from your message. Check the effectiveness of your visuals by trying them out on other people before you give your presentation.

You may also want to prepare handouts for your audience: pertinent bibliographies, for example, or text too extensive to be presented otherwise. Unless the handouts include material you want your audience to use while you speak, distribute them at the end of the presentation.

57f Practice your presentation.

Prepare a draft of your presentation, including all visuals, far enough in advance to allow for several run-throughs. Some speakers audiotape or videotape their rehearsals and then base their revisions on the tape-recorded performance. Others practice in front of a mirror or in front of colleagues or friends, getting comments on content and style.

Once you are comfortable giving the presentation, make sure you will stay within the allotted time. One good rule of thumb is to allow roughly two and a half minutes per double-spaced eight-and-a-half- by eleven-inch page of text (or one and a half minutes per five- by seven-inch card).

When the time comes to stand up before your real audience, pause before you begin to speak, concentrating on your opening lines. During your presentation, face the audience at all times, and make eye contact as often as possible. You may want to choose two or three people to look at and talk to, particularly if you are addressing a large group. Allow time for the audience to respond and to ask questions. Try to keep your answers short so that others may participate in the conversation. At the conclusion of your presentation, remember to thank your audience.

58
Multimedia Presentations

Thanks to computers, using multimedia—combining text, sound, graphics, video, and interactivity in a presentation—is now an every-day thing. Whether you're using PowerPoint for a sales presentation or creating a poster for a class project, you may find yourself drawing on a mix of oral, print, and electronic media to get your messages across. This chapter will help you to use PowerPoint, overhead transparencies, and posters to augment a presentation—to help guide you as you speak and to help your audience follow what you say.

58a PowerPoint or other presentation software

PowerPoint and similar presentation software allow you to prepare slides that you can project from a computer for all your audience to see—and even to enhance the images with sound. If you are using such a tool, keep some simple principles in mind:

- Use forty-four- to fifty-point type for titles and thirty- to thirty-four-point type for subpoints.

- Use bulleted or numbered lists rather than paragraphs. Be as concise as possible. Include only three to five points on each slide so that your audience doesn't have to look at one slide for too long.

- Consider using a wizard, a design template, that formats content automatically. Templates come in a variety of styles; choose one that conveys your message effectively without overwhelming your audience.

- Create a clear contrast between the text and the background. As a general rule, light backgrounds work better in a darkened room, dark backgrounds in a lighted one.

- Include only images—photographs, paintings, and so on—that will reproduce sharply, and make sure they are large enough to be clearly visible.

- If you are adding sound or video clips, make sure that they are clearly audible and that they relate clearly to the topic of the presentation. Especially if sound is to be used as background, make sure that it does not distract from or drown out what you are trying to say.

- PowerPoint files can be easily converted to HTML if you wish to post your presentation on the Web.

The first two slides of a PowerPoint presentation on world hunger appear on p. 480.

58b Overhead transparencies

Transparencies shown with an overhead projector can also present visual information as part of a presentation. As with PowerPoint (58a), transparencies need to be short and simple: a clear title and a few bulleted words or phrases, all big enough to be read when projected and in parallel grammatical form. An example of a transparency created for a presentation about the World Wide Web is shown on p. 481.

58c Poster presentations

Many college courses and conferences now call for poster presentations. In general, such presentations use a poster board, usually about forty- by fifty-inch, that displays major points, a model or diagram, or

POWERPOINT SLIDES

Appropriate image used to illustrate slide

Heading in large, easy-to-read type

Clear contrast between light-colored type and dark background

Design adapted from PowerPoint design template

Bulleted points kept brief; source of statistics included in oral presentation

Hunger Statistics

- 600 million people worldwide suffer from protein-energy malnutrition

- 35,000 people die every day from hunger and hunger-related diseases

- 1 out of 8 children go to bed hungry every night

Heading identifies worldwide charity organization and the topic

Map and side heading highlight specific geographic area for this portion of presentation

Dark background and light type are easy to read on screen in a well-lit room

Three bulleted points, each announcing a subtopic

World Vision Aid

- *Goal:* To help displaced people return to their homes after a violent political dispute

- *Funds Needed:* $128,630

- *Project Duration:* 1996-2000

SAMPLE TRANSPARENCY FOR A PRESENTATION

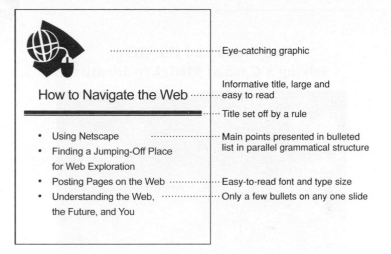

a drawing. During the class or conference session, the presenter uses this board as background while talking through the presentation and answering questions. If you are preparing a poster, keep these tips in mind:

- Be sure the poster can be read from at least three feet away.
- Include your name and other appropriate information: course title and number, instructor's name, conference title or session, and so on.
- Use bullets to identify your major points.
- Include an arresting image or an important table or figure if it illustrates your points in a clear and memorable way.
- Consider posing a provocative question toward the bottom of the poster to focus attention and anticipate your conclusion.
- Remember that simple, uncluttered posters are usually easier to follow and therefore more effective than very complex ones.

POSTER

Title set off by large font and color background

Photograph draws attention and adds emphasis

List of bulleted questions provides talking points to lead audience through presentation

White space is used effectively to highlight text and photo

Two hypotheses elaborated on in conclusion are highlighted as questions in colored ovals

Presenter, conference, place, and date are identified

- **What happened when heroes made the transition from literature and legend to movie screen?**

- **Why did audiences begin to mistake the movie actor for the hero--and with what effects?**

- **If the hero is not now dead, what will our future heroes be like?**

 **OR**

Shannan Palma
Twelfth National Conference
on Undergraduate Research

November 18, 2000
Salisbury State University
Salisbury, Maryland

59

Professional and Business Communication

From requesting a credit report to protesting a public official's stand on an issue to thanking a community group for help during a family emergency, much everyday business is conducted in writing. Professional and business communication takes various formats—proposals and reports, letters and memos, email, and faxes. This chapter provides information essential to using these formats effectively.

Editing Business and Professional Communication

- *Be clear.* Use simple words and straightforward sentences with active verbs. Use topic sentences to help readers follow your points.

- *Be concise.* Use the words you need to make your point but no more. Don't give readers information they don't need. Try to keep paragraphs short—in general, six lines or fewer.

- *Be courteous.* Write in a friendly, conversational tone. Imagine how you would respond if you were the reader.

- *Be correct.* Use a spell checker, and then proofread carefully.

- *Be consistent.* If you refer to someone as *Susan* in one sentence, don't switch to *Sue* in the next. If you use *kilograms* in one part of a letter, don't switch to *pounds* in another.

- *Be complete.* Include all the information readers need. You don't want them to have to call or write you for important, but missing, details.

59a Use a conventional format for memos.

Memos are a common form of printed correspondence sent *within* an organization. In established business or professional relationships, memos travel between organizations as well. Memos tend to be brief, often dealing with only one subject.

> ### *Guidelines for Writing Effective Memos*
> - State the date, the name of the recipient, your name, and the subject on separate lines at the top.
> - Begin with the most important information: get right to the point.
> - Try to involve readers in your opening paragraph, and attempt to build goodwill in your conclusion.
> - Focus each paragraph on one idea pertaining to the subject.
> - Emphasize specific action—exactly what you want readers to do, and when.
> - Initial your memo next to your name.

SAMPLE MEMO

Hand-written initials

Gets right to the point

Extra line of space between paragraphs

Specific action requested

Closing paragraph builds goodwill

```
Date:    December 10, 2000
To:      Members of the Shipping Department
From:    Willie Smith  WS
Subject: Scheduling holiday time

With orders running 25 percent higher than average
this season, I can give everyone an opportunity
to work overtime and still enjoy the company's
traditional half day off for holiday shopping.  I must
submit the schedule by tomorrow at 5:00 p.m., however;
so let me know your preferences right away.

Please fill out the attached form with the days and
hours you can work overtime and your first, second,
and third choices for time off.  Return it to me
before you leave today.

I will try to accommodate everybody's preferences,
relying on seniority in case of conflicts.  If we work
together, December should be good for all of
us--on and off the job.
```

59b Follow the conventions of email.

Email has revolutionized correspondence, causing us to send and receive more mail than ever before. Traveling instantaneously to individuals and groups anywhere in the world at any hour, email follows a format much like a memo, with lines for the sender, recipient, and subject. As with all writing, consider your rhetorical situation when you write email—your purpose, your audience, and so on (see Chapter 4).

Guidelines for writing effective email

- Use subject lines that state your purpose clearly and succinctly. The subject line *oops . . .* announces that you've made a mistake, but a much more helpful subject line would be *Sorry to miss the meeting 10/3/99.* When you use the "reply" or "forward" functions to send a message on a subject that is entirely different from the one stated in the original subject line, change the subject line to reflect your message's content (14a).

- Email to a friend or close associate is often informal, even conversational *(Hi Tamika, how're things?).* Contractions are generally fine—in fact, not using contractions may sound stiff.

- Use a more formal tone when you are writing to a supervisor or to someone you don't know, or to make clear you are taking a request seriously *(I am writing to respond to your request about the budget).* If in doubt, stick to the conventions of standard academic English.

- Use standard capitalization (14g). Capitalizing whole phrases for emphasis comes across as SHOUTING. Messages using all lowercase letters are similarly difficult to read and are too informal for most situations.

- Try to be brief. Because readers need to scroll to read email—and because yours may be one of many messages needing response—keep your email short and to the point.

- Use appropriate greetings and closings, especially when writing to someone you don't know. Because messages tend to be brief and direct, they can sometimes seem pointed and blunt. Use appropriate salutations and closings to convey respect and to set an appropriate tone with your reader (see p. 487).

- Long chunks of text are often difficult to read online; try to keep paragraphs brief. Break your text into block paragraphs, leaving an extra line of space between each one.

- Email is so fast and easy that some writers do not take time to proofread before they hit "send." If you want your message to be taken seriously, however, make sure it is clearly written and free of errors.

For further advice on the conventions of writing email, see 14a.

SAMPLE EMAIL

Subject line explicitly states the subject

Salutation

Message is as succinct and direct as possible

Double-space

Signature line with name and .sig file

```
To: techsoup@indirect.com
From: Andrea Lunsford <lunsford.2@osu.edu>
Subject: help finding a correct address

Dear Techsoup:

I am trying to send a message to Irene Whitney at
Pacific Synergies, which is headquartered in Whistler,
B.C. The email address she gave me is pacsyn@direct.net--
which is obviously not right since you returned it as
undeliverable. Perhaps I should have tried adding
"com" at the end? If you have an address for Pacific
Synergies, I would be very grateful to receive it.

Sincerely
Andrea Lunsford, Department of English
Ohio State University
164 W. 17th Street
Columbus, OH 43214
lunsford.2@osu.edu
(614) 292-6065 (o)
(614) 292-5824 (f)
```

www.bedfordstmartins.com/lunsford

◎ A Matter of Style: *Email Signatures*

Many writers conclude their online communications with a .sig file, a signature block that gives their name, title, address, phone and fax numbers, and so on. Signature blocks not only identify you but also establish your credentials and thus your authority. Keep your signature block concise:

Beverly Moss, Director   moss.1@osu.edu
University Writing Center   614-292-5607
Ohio State University   614-292-7816 (FAX)

Fancy formatting features may well be lost when readers open your message, so, in general, keep these .sig files simple.

Using an appropriate tone

Whether you are sending email to a friend or to someone you don't know well, you will want to adopt a tone or level of formality appropriate to your rhetorical situation. A student who interviewed at the retail store Abercrombie and Fitch for a summer position wrote a follow-up email message to thank the interviewer, Nikki Hamai. In the email below, note the ways in which the writer is very informal.

INFORMAL EMAIL

Hey Nikki:

Thanks so much for talking to me—I had a great time. A & F seems like a cool place to work. I especially love the idea of meeting lots of kids my age who want to look right out of *Teen*. And the salary is okay too. Give me a call.

Carlotta

This message assumes too much familiarity between the student and interviewer. In addition, it takes a chance by using overly informal syntax (the dash in sentence one) and colloquialisms like "Hey," "cool," and "okay." Finally, the student asks the interviewer to call but fails to provide a convenient telephone number. Revised, the message speaks more formally and effectively to the interviewer.

APPROPRIATELY FORMAL EMAIL

Dear Ms. Hamai:

Thank you very much for taking time to interview me yesterday. I enjoyed learning about Abercrombie and Fitch and believe I would work well with your other staff and customers. Thank you too for discussing details of salary and the work week. I hope to hear from you soon.

Sincerely yours,
Carlotta Martza
(917) 555-7106

59c Use a conventional format for letters.

When you send a business or professional letter, you are writing either as an individual or as a representative of an organization. In either case, and regardless of the purpose of the letter, it should follow certain conventions. Whenever possible, you should write to a specific person.

Many letters use the block format, in which all text aligns at the left margin. Some writers prefer a modified block format, aligning the return address, date, close, and signature on the right.

SAMPLE LETTER, MODIFIED BLOCK STYLE

Return address in modified block form (indented)

↓ *1"*

123 Main Street
Columbus, OH 43229
November 21, 2000

Recipient's address with full name and title

Ms. Leslie Austin
Personnel Director
Price Waterhouse
1900 Central Trust Center

1" margins

Cincinnati, OH 45202

Salutation (Ms. If you don't know the person's sex, use the full name— "Dear Leslie Austin")

Dear Ms. Austin:

Dr. John Smith, my accounting professor, advised me to contact you directly concerning a position that may be opening in the Accounting Department at Price Waterhouse. I expect to receive a Bachelor of Science in Business Administration, with a major in accounting, from the Ohio State University in June 2001.

As my enclosed résumé indicates, I have significant experience in customer relations, which is a must for the accounting field today. My work included determining customers' needs, getting efficient responses, and interacting regularly via computer with the home office.

Extra line of space between paragraphs

I am planning to visit Cincinnati for about five days in late January. If I do not hear from you by then, I will call your office before I arrive to arrange a convenient time for an interview. Please feel free to call me at (614) 471-5743 if an earlier appointment would be more convenient for you. I look forward to hearing from you.

Closing phrase

Sincerely yours,

Four line spaces for signature

Patricia I. Medley

Patricia I. Medley

Signals the enclosed résumé

Enclosure

> ***Guidelines for Writing Effective Letters***
> - Open cordially, and be polite—even if you have a complaint.
> - State the reason for your letter clearly. Include whatever details will help your reader see your point and respond.
> - If appropriate, make clear what you hope your reader will do.
> - Express appreciation for your reader's attention.
> - Make response simple by including your telephone or fax number or email address and, if appropriate, a self-addressed, stamped envelope.

59d Use a conventional format for résumés.

Often, a letter of application and a résumé travel together. A letter of application, or cover letter, emphasizes specific parts of the résumé, telling how your background is suited to a particular job. A résumé summarizes your experience and qualifications and provides support for your letter. An effective résumé is brief, usually one or two pages.

Research shows that employers usually spend less than a minute reading over a résumé. Remember that they are interested not in what they can do for you but what you can do for them. They expect a résumé to be typed or printed neatly on high-quality paper and to read easily, with clear headings, adequate spacing, and a conventional format. Such conventions may be hard to accept because you want your résumé to stand out, but a *well-written* résumé may be the best way to distinguish yourself.

Your résumé may be arranged chronologically (in reverse chronological order) or functionally (around skills or expertise). Either way, you will probably include the following:

1. *Name, address, phone and fax numbers, and email address,* usually centered at the top.
2. *Career objective(s).* List immediate or short-term goals and specific jobs for which you realistically qualify.
3. *Educational background.* Include degrees, diplomas, majors, and special programs or courses that pertain to your field of interest. List honors and scholarships and your grade-point average if it is high.
4. *Work experience.* Identify each job—whether a paying job, an internship, or military experience—with dates and names of organizations. Describe your duties by carefully selecting strong action verbs. Highlight any of your activities that improved business in any way.
5. *Skills, personal interests, activities, and awards.* Identify your technology skills. List hobbies, offices held, volunteer work, and awards.

6. *References.* List two or three people who know your work well, first asking their permission. Give their titles, addresses, and phone or fax numbers. Or simply say that your references are available on request.

Here are examples of a résumé, the second one formatted for scanning. Since many employers now enter résumés in databases to be searched and sorted, take careful note of how to prepare a scannable résumé.

SAMPLE RÉSUMÉ

Name in boldface and larger type size	**ANGELA SANTANA**

	CURRENT ADDRESS · · · · · · · · · · · · · PERMANENT ADDRESS
	75 West Fourth Avenue 549 Tyler Street
	Columbus, OH 43201 Anoka, MN 54268
	Phone: (614) 555-8926 Phone: (612) 555-1146
	Email: santana.324@osu.edu

Position being sought ···· CAREER OBJECTIVE Position on editorial staff of a journal or publishing firm

EDUCATION

Details of educational background B.A. in English, with Writing Emphasis, The Ohio State University, Columbus, Ohio, June 2000.
Senior thesis: "Literacy and Community Service"

Core courses: Literary Publishing, Poetry Writing Workshop, Writing and Learning Seminar, Rhetoric and Community Service, History and Theories of Writing

Significant academic information AWARDS Foster Award for Outstanding Undergraduate Essay, 1999

EXPERIENCE

1997 – 2000 *Mosaic: The Ohio State University Undergraduate Art and Literature Magazine*
Editor-in-Chief, 1999 – 2000

Work experience relevant to position being sought
• Oversaw work of editorial assistants; served as liaison to faculty advisor; drafted annual budget and grant proposals with business manager; used QuarkXPress, PageMaker, and ClarisWorks to design and assemble layout

Associate Literature Editor, 1997 – 1999
• Read submissions; selected poetry, fiction, and nonfiction; copy-edited manuscripts; solicited manuscripts

1999 Max M. Fisher College of Business
(The Ohio State University)
Summer Intern, Public Relations
• Designed and copy-edited brochures and promotional material; edited faculty biographies

Significant volunteer work LEADERSHIP AND VOLUNTEER ACTIVITIES

President, Alpha Chi Omega Sorority, 1998 – 2000
Workshop Organizer for Developmentally Disabled Children, The Ohio State University Hospitals, 1996 – present
Tutor, Godman Guild Literacy Center, 1996 – present

REFERENCES Available upon request

SAMPLE SCANNABLE RÉSUMÉ

Angela Santana

Current Address
75 West Fourth Avenue
Columbus, OH 43201
Phone: (614) 555-8926
Fax: (614) 555-1146
Email: santana.324@osu.edu

Permanent Address
549 Tyler Street
Anoka, MN 54268
(612) 555-1146

Keywords: literary journal editor; literary publishing; copy-editing; responsibility; leadership; editor-in-chief; editing experience; budget; grant-writing; promotional materials; treasurer, Phi Beta Kappa; QuarkXpress, PageMaker, ClarisWorks

Education
B.A. in English, with Writing Emphasis, June 2000, The Ohio State University, Columbus, Ohio
3.6/4.0 Grade Point Average
Senior thesis: "Literacy and Community Service"
Foster Award for Outstanding Undergraduate Essay, 1999

Core Courses
Literary Publishing
Poetry Writing Workshop
Writing and Learning Seminar
Rhetoric and Community Service
History and Theories of Writing

Additional Courses
Critical Writing
British Literature: Medieval to 1800
African American Literature
U.S. Literature: 1865 to the Present
Twentieth-Century Poetry

Experience
Mosaic: The Ohio State University Undergraduate Art and Literature Magazine
Editor-in-Chief, 1999–2000
Oversaw work of editorial assistants; served as liaison to faculty advisor; drafted annual budget and grant proposals with business manager; used QuarkXPress, PageMaker, and ClarisWorks to design and assemble layout

Associate Literature Editor, 1997–1999
Read submissions; selected poetry, fiction, and nonfiction; copy-edited manuscripts; solicited manuscripts.

Max M. Fisher College of Business (The Ohio State University)
Summer Intern, Public Relations
Designed and copy-edited brochures and promotional material; edited faculty biographies

Leadership and Volunteer Activities
President, Alpha Chi Omega Sorority, 1998–2000
Workshop Organizer for Developmentally Disabled Children, The Ohio State University Hospitals, 1996–present
Tutor, Godman Guild Literacy Center, 1996–present

Annotations (right margin):

- Text all flush left
- Each phone number on a separate line
- Standard sans serif typeface (Arial) and type size throughout
- Keywords listed for employers' computer searches
- No underlining, italics, boldface, boxes, lines, or columns
- White space used to mark off sections
- Keywords used in body of résumé wherever possible

60

Nouns and Noun Phrases

Everyday life is filled with nouns and noun phrases: orange juice, the morning news, a bus to work, meetings, pizza, email, Diet Coke, errands, dinner with friends, a chapter in a good book. No matter what your first language is, it includes nouns. This chapter will focus on some of the ways English nouns differ from those in some other languages.

60a Know how to use count and noncount nouns.

The nouns *tree* and *grass* differ both in meaning and in the way they are used in sentences.

> The hill was covered with trees.
> The hill was covered with grass.

Tree is a count noun, and *grass* a noncount noun. These terms do not mean that grass cannot be counted but only that English grammar requires that if we count grass, we express it indirectly: *one blade of grass, two blades of grass,* not *one grass, two grasses.*

Count nouns usually have singular and plural forms: *tree, trees.* Noncount nouns usually have only a singular form: *grass.*

Count nouns refer to distinct individuals or entities: *a doctor, a book, a tree; doctors, books, trees.* Noncount nouns refer to indeterminate masses or collections: *milk, ice, clay, blood, grass.*

COUNT	NONCOUNT
people (plural of *person*)	humanity
tables, chairs, beds	furniture
letters	mail
pebbles	gravel
beans	rice
facts	information
words	advice

Some words can be either count or noncount, depending on meaning.

COUNT	Before there were video games, children played with *marbles.*
NONCOUNT	The floor of the palace was made of *marble.*

When you learn a noun in English, you need to learn whether it is count, noncount, or both. Two dictionaries that supply this information are the *Oxford Advanced Learner's Dictionary* and the *Longman Dictionary of American English*.

60b State singular and plural forms explicitly.

Look at this sentence from a traffic report:

All four bridges into the city are crowded with cars right now.

This sentence has three count nouns; one is singular (*city*), and two are plural (*bridges, cars*). If you speak a language with nouns that generally have no distinct plural forms (for example, Chinese, Japanese, or Korean), you might argue that no information would be lost if the sentence were *All four bridge into the city are crowded with car right now.* After all, *four* indicates that *bridge* is plural, and obviously there would have to be more than one car if the bridges are crowded. But English requires that every time you use a count noun, you ask yourself whether you are talking about one item or more than one and that you choose a singular or a plural form accordingly.

Since noncount nouns have no plural forms, they can be quantified only with a preceding phrase: *one quart of milk, three pounds of rice, several bits of information.* The noun in question remains singular.

60c Use determiners appropriately.

A noun together with all its modifiers constitutes a noun phrase, and the noun around which the modifiers cluster is called the head. For example, in *My adventurous sister is leaving for New Zealand tomorrow,* the noun phrase *my adventurous sister* consists of two modifiers (*my* and *adventurous*) and the head *sister.*

Words like *my, our,* and *this* are determiners. They are common and important words in the English language. Determiners identify or quantify the noun head.

COMMON DETERMINERS

- the articles *a/an, the*
- *this, these, that, those*
- *my, our, your, his, her, its, their*
- possessive nouns and noun phrases (*Sheila's, my friend's*)

- *whose, which, what*
- *all, both, each, every, some, any, either, no, neither, many, much, (a) few, (a) little, several,* and *enough*
- the numerals *one, two,* etc.

Using determiners with singular count nouns

Every noun phrase with a singular count noun head must begin with a determiner.

▶ adventurous sister
  my

▶ big, bad wolf
  the

▶ old neighborhood
  that

If there is no reason to use a more specific determiner, use *a* or *an: a big, bad wolf; an old neighborhood.*

    Notice that every noun phrase need not begin with a determiner, only those whose head is a singular count noun. Noncount and plural count nouns sometimes have determiners, sometimes not: *This grass is green* and *Grass is green* are both acceptable, though different in meaning.

Remembering which determiners go with which types of noun

- *This* or *that* goes with singular count or noncount nouns: *this book, that milk.*
- *These, (a) few, many, both,* or *several* goes with plural count nouns: *these books, those plans, a few ideas, many students, both hands, several trees.*
- *(A) little* or *much* goes with noncount nouns: *a little milk, much affection.*
- *Some* or *enough* goes with noncount or plural count nouns: *some milk, some books; enough trouble, enough problems.*
- *A, an, every,* or *each* goes with singular count nouns: *a book, every child, each word.*

60d   Use *a, an,* or *the* to convey your intended meaning.

The articles *a, an,* and *the* can be challenging to multilingual speakers. Many languages have nothing directly comparable to them, and other languages that do have articles differ from English in the details of their use.

Using the

Use the definite article *the* with nouns whose identity is known or is about to be made known to readers. The necessary information for identification can come from the noun phrase itself, from elsewhere in the text, from context, from general knowledge, or from a superlative.

▶ Let's meet at *the* fountain in front of Dwinelle Hall.

The phrase *in front of Dwinelle Hall* identifies the specific fountain.

▶ Last Saturday, a fire that started in a restaurant spread to a neighboring dry-goods store. *The* Store was saved, although it suffered water damage.

The word *store* is preceded by *the,* which directs our attention to the information in the previous sentence, where the store is identified.

▶ Professor to student in her office: "Please shut *the* door when you leave."

The professor expects the student to understand that she is referring to the door in her office.

▶ ~~Pope~~ *The pope* is expected to visit Africa in October.

There is only one living pope, so his identity is clear.

▶ Willie is now *the* best singer in the choir.

The superlative *best* identifies the noun *singer.*

Using a *or* an

Use *a* before a consonant sound: *a car.* Use *an* before a vowel sound: *an uncle.* Pay attention to sounds rather than to spelling: *a house, an hour.*

A or *an* tells readers they do not have enough information to identify what the noun refers to. The writer may or may not have a particular thing in mind but in either case will use *a* or *an* if the reader lacks the information necessary for identification. Compare the following sentences:

▶ I need *a* new *parka* for the winter.
▶ I saw *a parka* that I liked at Dayton's, but it wasn't heavy enough.

The parka in the first sentence is hypothetical rather than actual. Since it is indefinite to the writer, it clearly is indefinite to the reader and is used with *a*, not *the*. The second sentence refers to a very specific actual parka, but, since the writer cannot expect the reader to know which one it is, it is used with *a* rather than *the*.

If you want to speak of an indefinite quantity, rather than just one indefinite thing, use *some* with a noncount noun or a plural count noun.

▶ This stew needs *some* more *salt*.
▶ I saw *some plates* that I liked at Gump's.

Zero article

If a noun appears without *the, a* or *an,* or any other determiner (even if it is preceded by other adjectives), it is said to have a zero article. The zero article is used with noncount and plural count nouns: *cheese, hot tea, crackers, ripe apples* (but not *cracker* or *ripe apple*). Use the zero article to make generalizations.

▶ In this world nothing is certain but death and taxes.
— BENJAMIN FRANKLIN

The zero article indicates that Franklin refers not to a particular death or specific taxes but to death and taxes in general.

Here English differs from many other languages—Greek or Spanish or German, for example—that would use the definite article to make generalizations. In English, a sentence like *The snakes are dangerous* can refer only to particular, identifiable snakes, not to snakes in general.

It is sometimes possible to make general statements with *the* or *a/an* and singular count nouns.

First-year college students are confronted with a wealth of new experiences.

A first-year student is confronted with a wealth of new experiences.

The first-year student is confronted with a wealth of new experiences.

These sentences all make the same general statement, but the last two are more vivid than the first. The second focuses on a hypothetical student taken at random, and the third sentence, which is characteristic of formal written style, projects the image of a typical student as representative of the whole class.

60e Arrange modifiers carefully.

Some modifiers can precede the noun head, and others can follow, and you need to learn both the obligatory and preferred positions for modifiers in order to know what can go where.

- Phrases or clauses follow the noun head: *the tiles on the wall, the tiles that we bought in Brazil.*
- Determiners go at the very beginning of the noun phrase: *these old-fashioned tiles.* *All* or *both* precedes any other determiners: *all these tiles.* Numbers follow any other determiners: *these six tiles.*
- Noun modifiers go directly before the noun head: *these kitchen tiles.*
- All other adjectives go between determiners and noun modifiers: *these old-fashioned kitchen tiles.* If there are two or more of these adjectives, their order is variable, but there are strong preferences, described below.
- Subjective adjectives (those that show the writer's attitude) go before objective adjectives (those that merely describe): *these beautiful old-fashioned kitchen tiles.*
- Adjectives of size generally come early: *these beautiful large old-fashioned kitchen tiles.*
- Adjectives of color generally come late: *these beautiful large old-fashioned blue kitchen tiles.*
- Adjectives derived from proper nouns or from nouns that refer to materials generally come after color terms and right before noun modifiers: *these beautiful large old-fashioned blue Portuguese ceramic kitchen tiles.*
- All other objective adjectives go in the middle, and adjectives for which a preferred order does not exist are separated by commas: *these beautiful large decorative, heat-resistant, old-fashioned blue Portuguese ceramic kitchen tiles.*

It goes without saying that the long noun phrase in the last bulleted item is a monstrosity that would be out of place in almost any conceivable kind of writing. You should always budget your use of adjectives.

61

Verbs and Verb Phrases

When there are things to do, verbs tell us what they are—from the street signs that say *stop* or *yield* to email commands such as *send* or *delete*. Verbs can be called the heartbeat of prose, especially in English. With rare exceptions, you cannot deprive an English sentence of its verb without killing it. If you speak Russian or Arabic, you might wonder what is wrong with the sentence *Where Main Street?* But unlike those and many other languages, English sentences must have a verb: *Where is Main Street?* This chapter will focus on some of the ways English verbs differ from verbs in other languages.

61a A review of verb phrases

Verb phrases can be built up out of a main verb (MV) and one or more auxiliaries (25b).

> My cat *drinks* milk.
>
> My cat *is drinking* milk.
>
> My cat *has been drinking* milk.
>
> My cat *may have been* drinking milk.

Verb phrases have strict rules of order. If you try to rearrange the words in any of these sentences, you will find that most alternatives are impossible. You cannot say *My cat drinking is milk* or *My cat have may been drinking* milk. The only permissible rearrangement is to move the first auxiliary to the beginning of the sentence in order to form a question: *Has my cat been drinking milk?*

Auxiliary and main verbs

In *My cat may have been drinking milk,* the main verb *drinking* is preceded by three auxiliaries: *may, have,* and *been.*

- *May* is a modal, which must be followed by a base form (*have*).
- *Have* indicates that the tense is perfect, and it must be followed by a past participle (*been*).
- *Been* (or any other form of *be*), when it is followed by a present participle (such as *drinking*), indicates that the tense is progressive.

- A form of *be* can also represent passive voice, but then the following verb form must be a past participle, as in *My cat may have been bitten by a dog.*

Auxiliaries must be in the following order: modal + perfect *have* + progressive *be* + passive *be*.

      PERF PASS   MV
▶ Sonya *has been invited* to stay with a family in Prague.

      PERF PROG   MV
▶ She *has been taking* an intensive course in Czech.

      MOD PROG MV
▶ She *must be looking* forward to her trip eagerly.

Only one modal is permitted in a verb phrase.

      MOD   MV
▶ Sonya *can speak* a little Czech already.

      MOD PROG MV
▶ She *will be studying* for three more months.

      will be able to speak
▶ She ~~will can speak~~ Czech much better soon.
      ^

Every time you use an auxiliary, you should be careful to put the next word in the appropriate form.

Modal + *base form*

Use the base form of the verb after *can, could, will, would, shall, should, may, might,* and *must.*

▶ Alice *can read* Latin.
▶ Paul *should have* studied.
▶ They *must be* going to a fine school.

In many other languages, modals like *can* or *must* are followed by the infinitive (*to* + base form). Do not substitute an infinitive for the base form in English.

▶ Alice can ~~to~~ read Latin.

Perfect have, has, *or* had + *past participle*

To form the perfect tenses, use *have, has,* or *had* with a past participle.

▶ Everyone *has gone* home.
▶ They *have been* working all day.

Progressive be + present participle

A progressive form of the verb is signaled by two elements, a form of the auxiliary *be* (*am, is, are, was, were, be,* or *been*) and the *-ing* form of the next word: *The children are studying.* Be sure to include both elements.

      are
▶ The children studying in school.
      ^

       studying
▶ The children are ~~study~~ in school.
        ^

Some verbs are rarely used in progressive forms. These are verbs that express unchanging conditions or mental states rather than deliberate actions: *believe, belong, cost, hate, have, know, like, love, mean, need, own, resemble, think, understand, weigh.*

Passive be + past participle

Use *am, is, are, was, were, being, be,* or *been* with a past participle to form the passive voice.

▶ Tagalog *is spoken* in the Philippines.

Notice that the difference between progressive *be* and passive *be* is that the following word ends in the *-ing* of the present participle with the progressive, but with the passive, the following word never ends in *-ing* and instead becomes the past participle.

▶ Meredith *is* studying music.
▶ Natasha *was* taught by a famous violinist.

If the first auxiliary in a verb phrase is *be* or *have,* it must show either present or past tense, and it must agree with the subject: *Meredith* <u>*has*</u> *played in an orchestra.*

    Notice that although a modal auxiliary may also show present or past tense (for example, *can* or *could*), it never changes form to agree with the subject.

      can
▶ Michiko ~~cans~~ play two instruments.
      ^

61b Use present and past tenses carefully.

Every English sentence must have at least one verb or verb phrase that is not an infinitive, a gerund, or a participle without any auxiliaries. Furthermore, every such verb or verb phrase must have a tense.

In some languages, such as Chinese and Vietnamese, the verb form never changes regardless of when the action of the verb takes place, and the time of the action is simply indicated by other expressions such as *yesterday, last year,* and *next week.* In English, the time of the action must be clearly indicated by the tense form of each and every verb, even if the time is obvious or indicated elsewhere in the sentence.

> During the Cultural Revolution, millions of young people ~~cannot~~ go to
>   *could not*^
>
>   *were*
> school and ~~are~~ sent to the countryside.
>   ^

In some languages (Spanish, for example), words end in either a vowel or a single consonant, not in one consonant followed by another. Remember to add the *-s* of the present-tense third-person singular and the *-ed* of the past tense.

>   *called*   *lives*
> Last night I ~~call~~ my aunt who ~~live~~ in Santo Domingo.
>   ^   ^

Using direct and indirect discourse

Changing direct quotations to indirect quotations can sometimes lead to inappropriate tense shifts. If the verb introducing the indirect discourse is in the present tense, the verb in the indirect discourse should also be in the present tense.

> DIRECT   She said, "My work *is* now complete."
>
> INDIRECT   She *tells* me that her work *is* now complete.

If the verb introducing the indirect discourse is in the past tense, stick with tenses that refer to past time in the indirect discourse.

> DIRECT   She said, "My exams *are* over and I have received the
>   highest score in my class."
>
> INDIRECT   She told me her exams *were* over and she *had received* the
>   highest score in her class.

If the introductory verb is in the past tense, but the information that follows holds true in the present, then shifting to a present tense verb is acceptable.

▶ She *told* me that her work *is* as exciting as ever.

61c Understand perfect and progressive verb phrases.

Distinguishing the simple present and the present perfect

▶ My sister *drives* a bus.

The simple present (*drives*) merely tells us about her current occupation. But if you want to add the phrase *for three years,* do not say *My sister drives a bus for three years.* You need to set up a time frame that encompasses the past and the present, and, therefore, you should use the present perfect or the present perfect progressive.

▶ My sister *has driven* a bus for three years.
▶ My sister *has been driving* a bus for three years.

Distinguishing the simple past and the present perfect

▶ Since she started working, she *has bought* a new car and a VCR.

The clause introduced by *since* sets up a time frame that runs from past to present, and requires the present perfect (*has bought*) in the subsequent clause. Furthermore, the sentence does not say exactly when she bought the car or the VCR, and that indefiniteness also calls for the perfect. It would be less correct to say *Since she started working, she bought a new car and a VCR.* But what if you should go on to say when she bought the car?

▶ She *bought* the car two years ago.

It would be incorrect to say *She has bought the car two years ago* because the perfect is incompatible with definite expressions of time. In this case, use the simple past (*bought*) rather than the present perfect (*has bought*).

Distinguishing the simple present and the present progressive

When an action is in progress at the present moment, use the present progressive. Use the simple present for actions that frequently occur during a period of time that might include the present moment (though such an assertion makes no claim that the action is taking place now).

▶ My sister *drives* a bus, but she *is taking* a vacation now.

▶ My sister *drives* a bus, but she *takes* a vacation every year.

Many languages, such as French and German, use the simple present (*drives, takes*) for both types of sentence. In English, it would be incorrect to say *but she takes a vacation now.*

Distinguishing the simple past and the past progressive

▶ Sally ~~was spending~~ the summer in Italy.
    spent

You might be tempted to use the past progressive (*was spending*) here instead of the simple past, since spending the summer involves a continuous stretch of time of some duration, and duration and continuousness are typically associated with the progressive. But English speakers use the past progressive infrequently and would be unlikely to use it in this case except to convey actions that are simultaneous with other past actions.

▶ Sally *was spending* the summer in Italy when she *met* her future husband.

Use the past progressive to focus on duration or continuousness and especially to call attention to past action that went on at the same time as something else.

61d Use modals appropriately.

Consider the following passage:

> College course work *will* call on you to do much reading, writing, research, talking, listening, and note-taking. And as you probably have already realized, you *will not*—or *need not*—always carry out all these activities in solitude. Far from it. Instead, you *can* be part of a broad conversation that includes all the texts you read.

This passage contains four modal auxiliaries: *will, will not, need not,* and *can.* These modals tell the reader what the writer judges to be the options available—in this case, in college work. The passage begins with *will,* which makes a firm prediction of what the reader is to expect.

It continues with a firm negative prediction (*will not*) but immediately revises it to a more tentative forecast (*need not*) and finally opens up a new vista of possibilities for the reader (*can*).

The nine basic modal auxiliaries are *can, could, will, would, shall, should, may, might,* and *must.* There are a few others as well, in particular *ought to,* which is close in meaning to *should.* Occasionally *need* can be a modal rather than a main verb.

The nine basic modals are the pairs *can/could, will/would, shall/should, may/might,* and the loner *must.* In earlier English, the second member of each pair was the past tense of the first. To a limited degree, the second form still functions as a past tense, especially in the case of *could.*

▶ Ingrid *can* ski.
▶ Ingrid *could* ski when she was five.

But for the most part, in present-day English, all nine modals typically refer to present or future time. When you want to use a modal to refer to the past, you follow the modal with a perfect auxiliary.

▶ If you have a fever, you *should* see a doctor.
▶ If you had a fever, you *should have seen* a doctor.

In the case of *must,* refer to the past by using *had to.*

▶ You *must* renew your visa by the end of this week.
▶ You *had to* renew your visa by the end of last week.

Using modals to make requests or to give instructions

The way modals contribute to human interaction is most evident in requests and instructions. Imagine making the following request of a flight attendant:

▶ *Will* you bring me a pillow?

You have expressed your request in a demanding manner, and the flight attendant might resent it.

▶ *Can* you bring me a pillow?

This question acknowledges that fulfilling the request may not be possible.

Another way of softening the request is to use the past form of *will,* and the most discreet choice is the past form of *can.*

▶ *Would* you bring me a pillow?

▶ *Could* you bring me a pillow?

Using the past of modals is considered more polite than using their present forms because it makes any statement or question less assertive.

Now consider each of the following instructions:

1. You *can* submit your report on disk.
2. You *may* submit your report on disk.
3. You *should* submit your report on disk.
4. You *must* submit your report on disk.
5. You *will* submit your report on disk.

Numbers 1 and 2 give permission to submit the paper on disk, but do not require it; of these, 2 is more formal. Number 3 adds a strong recommendation; 4 allows no alternative; and 5 implies, "Don't even think of doing otherwise."

Using modals to reveal doubt and certainty

Modals indicate how confident the writer is about the likelihood that what is being asserted is true. Look at the following set of examples, which starts with a tentative suggestion and ends with a logical assumption.

Please sit down; you *might be* tired.

Please sit down; you *may be* tired.

Please sit down; you *must be* tired.

61e Use participial adjectives appropriately.

Many verbs refer to feelings—for example, *bore, confuse, excite, fascinate, frighten, interest*. The present and past participles of such verbs (25a) can be used as ordinary adjectives. Use the past participle to describe a person having the feeling.

▶ The *frightened* boy started to cry.

Use the present participle to describe the thing (or person) causing the feeling.

▶ The *frightening* dinosaur display gave him nightmares.

Be careful not to confuse the two types of adjectives.

interested
▶ I am ~~interesting~~ in African literature.
　　　　　　　　　　　　　　　　interesting.
▶ African literature seems ~~interested.~~

62

Prepositions and Prepositional Phrases

If you were traveling by rail and asked for directions, it would not be helpful to be told to "take the Chicago train." You would need to know whether to take the train *to* Chicago or the one *from* Chicago. Words such as *to* and *from*, which show the relations between other words, are prepositions. Not all languages use prepositions to show such relations, and English differs from other languages in the way prepositions are used. This chapter provides guidelines for using prepositions in English.

62a Use prepositions idiomatically.

Even if you usually know where to use prepositions, you may have difficulty from time to time knowing which preposition to use. Each of the most common prepositions, whether in English or in other languages, has a wide range of different applications, and this range never coincides exactly from one language to another. See, for example, how English speakers use *in* and *on*.

The peaches are *in* the refrigerator.
The peaches are *on* the table.
Is that a diamond ring *on* your finger?

If you speak Spanish

Spanish uses one preposition (*en*) in all these sentences, a fact that might lead you astray in English.

on
▶ Is that a ruby ring ~~in~~ your finger?

There is no easy solution to the challenge of using English prepositions idiomatically, but the following strategies can make it less formidable.

Strategies for Using Prepositions Idiomatically

1. Keep in mind typical examples of each preposition.

   IN　　　　**The peaches are *in* the refrigerator.**

   　　　　　There are still some pickles *in* the jar.

   Here the object of the preposition *in* is a container that encloses something.

   ON　　　　**The peaches are *on* the table.**

   　　　　　The book you are looking for is *on* the top shelf.

   Here the object of the preposition *on* is a horizontal surface that supports something with which it is in direct contact.

2. Learn other examples that show some similarities and some differences in meaning.

   IN　　　　**You shouldn't drive *in* a snowstorm.**

   Here there is no container, but like a container, the falling snow surrounds and seems to enclose the driver.

   ON　　　　**Is that a diamond ring *on* your finger?**

   A finger is not a horizontal surface, but like such a surface it can support a ring with which it is in contact.

3. Use your imagination to create mental images that can help you remember figurative uses of prepositions.

   IN　　　　**Michael is *in* love.**

   Imagine a warm bath in which Michael is immersed (or a raging torrent, if you prefer to visualize love that way).

   ON　　　　**I've just read a book *on* computer science.**

   Imagine a shelf labeled *COMPUTER SCIENCE* on which the book you have read is located.

4. Try to learn prepositions not in isolation but as part of a system. For example, in identifying the location of a place or an event, the three prepositions *in, on,* and *at* can be used.

   　　At specifies the exact point in space or time.

   AT　　　　**There will be a meeting tomorrow *at* 9:30 a.m. *at*
   　　　　　160 Main Street.**

(continues on next page)

Expanses of space or time within which a place is located or an event takes place might be seen as containers and so require *in*.

IN   I arrived *in* **the United States** *in* **January.**

5. *On* must be used in two cases: with the names of streets (but not the exact address) and with days of the week or month.

ON   **The airline's office is** *on* **Fifth Avenue.**

        I'll be moving to my new apartment *on* **September 30.**

62b   Use two-word verbs idiomatically.

Some words that look like prepositions do not always function as prepositions. Consider the following two sentences.

▶ **The balloon rose** *off* **the ground.**

▶ **The plane took** *off* **without difficulty.**

In the first sentence, *off* is a preposition that introduces the prepositional phrase *off the ground.* In the second sentence, *off* neither functions as a preposition nor introduces a prepositional phrase. Instead, it combines with *took* to form a two-word verb with its own meaning. Such a verb is called a phrasal verb, and the word *off,* when used in this way, is called an adverbial particle. Many prepositions can function as particles to form phrasal verbs.

The verb + particle combination that makes up a phrasal verb is a tightly knit entity that usually cannot be torn apart.

                    off
▶ **The plane took without difficulty.** ~~off.~~
                  ^   ^

The exceptions are the many phrasal verbs that are transitive, meaning that they take a direct object (24k). Some transitive phrasal verbs have particles that may be separated from the verb by the object.

▶ I *picked up my baggage* **at the terminal.**

▶ I *picked my baggage up* **at the terminal.**

If a personal pronoun is used as the direct object, it must separate the verb from its particle.

▶ I *picked it up* **at the terminal.**

In some idiomatic two-word verbs, the second word is a preposition. With such verbs, the preposition can never be separated from the verb.

> *into*
> ▶ We ran our neighbor ~~into~~.
>   ^

Every comprehensive dictionary includes information about the various adverbial particles and prepositions that a verb can combine with, but only some dictionaries distinguish verb + particle from verb + preposition. The *Longman Dictionary of American English* is one that does.

63

Clauses and Sentences

Sound bites surround us, from Nike's "Just do it" to Avis's "We try harder." These short simple sentences may be memorable, but they don't tell us very much. Ordinarily, we need more complex sentences to convey meaning. The sentences of everyday discourse are not formed in the same way in every language. This chapter will focus on clauses and sentences in English.

63a Express subjects explicitly.

English sentences consist of a subject and a predicate. This simple statement defines a gulf separating English from many other languages, which leave out the subject when it can easily be inferred. Not English. With few exceptions, English demands that an explicit subject accompany an explicit predicate in every sentence. Though you might write *Went from Yokohama to Nagoya* on a postcard to a friend, in most varieties of spoken and written English, the extra effort of explicitly stating who went is not simply an option but an obligation.

In fact, every dependent clause must have an explicit subject.

> *it*
> ▶ They flew to London on the Concorde because was fast.
>   ^

English even requires a kind of dummy subject to fill the subject position in certain kinds of sentences. Consider the following sentences:

▶ *It* is raining on our wedding day.
▶ *There* is a strong wind in the park.

If you speak Spanish

Speakers of Spanish might be inclined to leave out dummy subjects. In English, however, *it* and *there* are indispensable.

It is
▶ ~~Is~~ raining on our wedding day.
^

There is
▶ ~~Has~~ a strong wind in the park.
^

63b Express objects explicitly.

Transitive verbs typically require that objects also be explicitly stated, and in some cases even other items of information as well (24k). For example, it is not enough to tell someone *Give!* even if it is clear what is to be given to whom. You must say *Give it to me* or *Give her the passport* or some other such sentence. Similarly, saying *Put!* or *Put it!* is insufficient when you mean *Put it on the table.*

63c Be careful of English word order.

You should not move subjects, verbs, or objects out of their normal positions in a sentence. In the following sentence, each element is in its appropriate place:

SUBJECT VERB OBJECT ADVERB
▶ **Omar reads books voraciously.**

Note, however, that this sentence would also be acceptable if written as *Omar voraciously reads books.*

If you speak Turkish, Korean, or Japanese

In these languages, the verb must come last. You may have to make a special effort never to write such a sentence as *Omar books voraciously reads,* which is not acceptable in English.

If you speak Russian

Russian permits a great deal of freedom in word order, but in English you must never interchange the position of subject and object (*Books reads Omar voraciously* is not acceptable). Also, avoid separating the verb from its object (*Omar reads voraciously books*). (See 24j and k for more on subjects and objects; see 28b for more on disruptive modifiers.)

63d Use noun clauses appropriately.

Examine the following sentence:

> In my last year in high school, my adviser urged that I apply to several colleges.

This is built up out of two sentences, one of them, (B), embedded in the other, (A):

> A. In my last year in high school, my adviser urged B.
> B. I (should) apply to several colleges.

When these are combined as in the first sentence above, sentence B becomes a noun clause introduced by *that* and takes on the role of object of the verb *urged* in sentence A. Now look at the following sentence:

> It made a big difference that she wrote a strong letter of recommendation.

Here the two component sentences are C and D:

> C. D made a big difference.
> D. She wrote a strong letter of recommendation.

In this case, the noun clause formed from sentence D functions as the subject of sentence C, so that the combination reads as follows:

> That she wrote a strong letter of recommendation made a big difference.

This is an acceptable sentence but somewhat top-heavy. Usually when a lengthy noun clause is the subject of the sentence, it is moved to the end. When that is done, the result is *Made a big difference that she wrote a strong letter of recommendation.* If you speak Italian or Spanish or Portuguese, you might see nothing wrong with such a sentence. In English, however, the subject must be stated. The dummy element *it* comes to the rescue and sets things right:

> It made
> ▶ ~~Made~~ a big difference that she wrote a strong letter of recommendation.
> ^

63e Know when to use infinitives and gerunds.

Knowing when to use infinitives or gerunds may be a challenge to multilingual writers. Though there is no simple explanation that will make it an easy task, here are some hints that will help you.

▶ My adviser urged me *to apply* to several colleges.

▶ Her *writing* a strong letter of recommendation made a big difference.

Why was an infinitive chosen for the first and a gerund for the second? In general, *infinitives* tend to represent intentions, desires, or expectations, while *gerunds* tend to represent facts. The gerund in the second sentence calls attention to the fact that a letter was actually written; the infinitive in the first sentence conveys the message that the act of applying was something desired, not an accomplished fact.

The distinction between fact and intention is not a rule but only a tendency, and it can be superseded by other rules. Use a gerund—never an infinitive—directly following a preposition.

▶ This fruit is all right for ~~to eat.~~ *eating.*

You can also get rid of the preposition and keep the infinitive.

▶ This fruit is all right ~~for~~ to eat.

▶ This fruit is all right *for us* to eat.

The association of fact with gerunds and of intention with infinitives can help you know in the majority of cases whether to use a gerund or an infinitive when another verb immediately precedes.

Gerunds

The following verbs can be followed only by gerunds, not by infinitives.

admit	discuss	finish	practice	resist
avoid	dislike	imagine	put off	risk
consider	enjoy	miss	quit	suggest
deny	escape	postpone	recall	tolerate

▶ Jerzy *enjoys going* to the theater.

▶ We *resumed working* after our coffee break.

▶ Kim *appreciated getting* candy from Sean.

In all of these cases, the second verb is a gerund, and the gerund indicates that the action or event that it expresses actually has happened. In fact, even when these verbs do not convey clear facts, the verb that comes second must still be a gerund.

▶ Kim *would appreciate getting* candy from Sean, but he hardly knows her.

Infinitives

▶ Kumar *expected to get* a good job after graduation.

▶ Last year, Fatima *decided to become* a math major.

▶ The strikers have *agreed to go* back to work.

Here it is irrelevant whether the actions or events referred to by the infinitives did or did not materialize; at the moment indicated by the verbs *expect, decide,* and *agree,* those actions or events were merely intentions. These three verbs, as well as many others that specify intentions (or negative intentions, like *refuse*), must always be followed by an infinitive, never by a gerund.

A few verbs can be followed by either an infinitive or a gerund. With some, such as *begin* or *continue,* the choice makes little difference in meaning. With others, however, the difference in meaning is striking.

Using an infinitive to state an intention

▶ Carlos was working as a medical technician, but he *stopped to study* English.

The infinitive indicates that Carlos intended to study English when he left his job. We are not told whether he actually did study English.

Using a gerund to state a fact

▶ Carlos *stopped studying* English when he left the United States.

The gerund indicates that Carlos actually did study English, but later stopped.

Checking when to use an infinitive or a gerund

A full list of verbs that can be followed by an infinitive and verbs that can be followed by a gerund can be found in the *Index to Modern English,* by Thomas Lee Crowell Jr. (McGraw-Hill, 1964).

63f Use adjective clauses carefully.

Adjective clauses can be a challenge. Look at the following sentence, and then see what can go wrong:

▶ The company *Yossi's uncle invested in* went bankrupt.

The subject is a noun phrase in which the noun *company* is modified by the article *the* and the adjective clause *Yossi's uncle invested in.* The sentence as a whole says that a certain company went bankrupt, and the adjective clause identifies the company more specifically by saying that Yossi's uncle had invested in it.

One way of seeing how the adjective clause fits into the sentence is to rewrite it like this: *The company (Yossi's uncle had invested in it) went bankrupt.* This is not a normal English sentence, but it helps to demonstrate a process which leads to the sentence we started with. Note the following steps:

1. Change the personal pronoun *it* to the relative pronoun *which: The company (Yossi's uncle had invested in which) went bankrupt.* That still is not acceptable English.
2. Move either the whole prepositional phrase *in which* to the beginning of the adjective clause, or just move the relative pronoun: *The company in which Yossi's uncle had invested went bankrupt* or *The company which Yossi's uncle had invested in went bankrupt.* Both of these are good English sentences, the former somewhat more formal than the latter.
3. If no preposition precedes, substitute *that* for *which* or leave out the relative pronoun entirely. *The company that Yossi's uncle had invested in went bankrupt* or *The company Yossi's uncle had invested in went bankrupt.* Both of these are good English sentences, not highly formal, but still acceptable in much formal writing.

Speakers of some languages find adjective clauses difficult in different ways. Following are some guidelines that might help:

If you speak Korean, Japanese, or Chinese

If you speak Korean, Japanese, or Chinese, the fact that the adjective clause does not precede the noun that it modifies may be disconcerting, both because that is the position of such clauses in the East Asian languages and because other modifiers, such as determiners and adjectives, do precede the noun in English.

If you speak Farsi, Arabic, or Hebrew

If you speak Farsi, Arabic, or Hebrew, you may expect the adjective clause to follow the noun as it does in English. However, remember to change the personal pronoun (*it*) to a relative pronoun (*which* or *that*) and then to move the relative pronoun to the beginning of the clause. You may then mistakenly put *that* at the beginning but keep the *it*, thus producing incorrect sentences such as *The company that Yossi's uncle invested in it went bankrupt.*

If you speak a European or Latin American language

If you are a speaker of some European or Latin American languages, you are probably acquainted with adjective clauses very much like those of English, but you may have difficulty accepting the possibility that a relative pronoun that is the object of a preposition can be moved to the beginning of the clause while leaving the preposition stranded. You might, therefore, move the preposition as well even when the relative pronoun is *that,* or you might drop the preposition altogether, generating such incorrect sentences as *The company in that Yossi's uncle invested went bankrupt* or *The company that Yossi's uncle invested went bankrupt.*

Finally, the fact that the relative pronoun can sometimes be omitted may lead to the mistaken notion that it can be omitted in all cases. Remember that you cannot omit a relative pronoun that is the subject of a verb.

who
▶ Everyone invested in that company lost a great deal.
⌃

63g Understand conditional sentences.

English pays special attention to whether or not something is a fact or to the degree of confidence we have in the truth or likelihood of an assertion. English distinguishes among many different types of conditional sentences, that is, sentences that focus on questions of truth and that are introduced by *if* or its equivalent. The following examples illustrate a range of different conditional sentences. Each of these sentences makes different assumptions about the likelihood that what is stated in the *if*-clause is true, and then draws the corresponding conclusion in the main clause.

If you *practice* (or *have practiced*) writing frequently, you *know* (or *have learned*) what your chief problems are.

This sentence assumes that what is stated in the *if*-clause may very well be true; the alternatives in parentheses indicate that any tense that is appropriate in a simple sentence may be used in both the *if*-clause and the main clause.

If you *practice* writing for the rest of this term, you *will* (or *may*) *get* a firmer grasp of the process.

This sentence makes a prediction about the future and again assumes that what is stated may very well turn out to be true. Only the main clause uses the future tense (*will get*) or some other modal that can indicate future time (*may get*). The *if*-clause must use the present tense, even though it too refers to the future.

If you *practiced* (or *were to practice*) writing every single day, it *would* eventually *seem* much easier to you.

This sentence casts some doubt on the likelihood that what is stated will be put into effect. In the *if*-clause, the verb is either past—actually, past subjunctive (25h)—or *were to* + the base form, though it refers to future time. The main clause contains *would* + the base form of the main verb.

If you *practiced* writing on Mars, you *would find* no one to read your work.

This sentence contemplates an impossibility at present or in the foreseeable future. As with the preceding sentence, the past subjunctive is used in the *if*-clause, although past time is not being referred to, and *would* + the base form is used in the main clause.

If you *had practiced* writing in ancient Egypt, you *would have used* hieroglyphics.

This sentence shifts the impossibility back to the past; obviously you are not going to find yourself in ancient Egypt. But, since past forms have already been used in the preceding two sentences, this one demands a form that is "more past": the past perfect in the *if*-clause, and *would* + the present perfect form of the main verb in the main clause.

A Writer's Almanac

General Information on the United States

U.S. Presidents

1. George Washington (1789–97)
2. John Adams (1797–1801)
3. Thomas Jefferson (1801–09)
4. James Madison (1809–17)
5. James Monroe (1817–25)
6. John Quincy Adams (1825–29)
7. Andrew Jackson (1829–37)
8. Martin Van Buren (1837–41)
9. William Henry Harrison (1841)
10. John Tyler (1841–45)
11. James K. Polk (1845–49)
12. Zachary Taylor (1849–50)
13. Millard Fillmore (1850–53)
14. Franklin Pierce (1853–57)
15. James Buchanan (1857–61)
16. Abraham Lincoln (1861–65)
17. Andrew Johnson (1865–69)
18. Ulysses S. Grant (1869–77)
19. Rutherford B. Hayes (1877–81)
20. James A. Garfield (1881)
21. Chester A. Arthur (1881–85)
22. Grover Cleveland (1885–89)
23. Benjamin Harrison (1889–93)
24. Grover Cleveland (1893–97)
25. William McKinley (1897–1901)
26. Theodore Roosevelt (1901–09)
27. William H. Taft (1909–13)
28. Woodrow Wilson (1913–21)
29. Warren G. Harding (1921–23)
30. Calvin Coolidge (1923–29)
31. Herbert Hoover (1929–33)
32. Franklin D. Roosevelt (1933–45)
33. Harry S Truman (1945–53)
34. Dwight D. Eisenhower (1953–61)
35. John F. Kennedy (1961–63)
36. Lyndon B. Johnson (1963–69)
37. Richard M. Nixon (1969–74)
38. Gerald R. Ford (1974–77)
39. Jimmy Carter (1977–81)
40. Ronald Reagan (1981–89)
41. George Bush (1989–93)
42. William J. Clinton (1993–2001)
43. George W. Bush (2001–   )

U.S. States and Territories: Postal Abbreviations, Capitals, Entry into Union, and Rank

NAME	POSTAL ABBREVIATION	CAPITAL	YEAR STATES ENTERED UNION	STATE'S RANK IN AREA	STATE'S RANK IN POPULATION[1]
Alabama	AL	Montgomery	1819	29	23
Alaska	AK	Juneau	1959	1	48

NAME	POSTAL ABBREVIATION	CAPITAL	YEAR STATES ENTERED UNION	STATE'S RANK IN AREA	STATE'S RANK IN POPULATION[1]
American Samoa	AS	Pago Pago			
Arizona	AZ	Phoenix	1912	6	20
Arkansas	AR	Little Rock	1836	27	33
California	CA	Sacramento	1850	3	1
Colorado	CO	Denver	1876	8	24
Connecticut	CT	Hartford	1788	48	29
Delaware	DE	Dover	1787	49	45
District of Columbia	DC				
Florida	FL	Tallahassee	1845	22	4
Georgia	GA	Atlanta	1788	21	10
Guam	GU	Agaña			
Hawaii	HI	Honolulu	1959	47	42
Idaho	ID	Boise	1890	13	40
Illinois	IL	Springfield	1818	24	5
Indiana	IN	Indianapolis	1816	38	14
Iowa	IA	Des Moines	1846	25	30
Kansas	KS	Topeka	1861	14	32
Kentucky	KY	Frankfort	1792	37	25
Louisiana	LA	Baton Rouge	1812	31	22
Maine	ME	Augusta	1820	39	39
Maryland	MD	Annapolis	1788	42	19
Massachusetts	MA	Boston	1788	45	13
Michigan	MI	Lansing	1837	23	8
Minnesota	MN	St. Paul	1858	12	21
Mississippi	MS	Jackson	1817	32	31
Missouri	MO	Jefferson City	1821	19	17
Montana	MT	Helena	1889	4	44
Nebraska	NE	Lincoln	1867	15	38
Nevada	NV	Carson City	1864	7	35
New Hampshire	NH	Concord	1788	44	41
New Jersey	NJ	Trenton	1787	46	9
New Mexico	NM	Santa Fe	1912	5	37
New York	NY	Albany	1788	30	3
North Carolina	NC	Raleigh	1789	28	11

NAME	POSTAL ABBREVIATION	CAPITAL	YEAR STATES ENTERED UNION	STATE'S RANK IN AREA	STATE'S RANK IN POPULATION[1]
North Dakota	ND	Bismarck	1889	17	47
Ohio	OH	Columbus	1803	35	7
Oklahoma	OK	Oklahoma City	1907	18	27
Oregon	OR	Salem	1859	10	28
Pennsylvania	PA	Harrisburg	1787	33	6
Puerto Rico	PR	San Juan			
Rhode Island	RI	Providence	1790	50	43
South Carolina	SC	Columbia	1788	40	26
South Dakota	SD	Pierre	1889	16	46
Tennessee	TN	Nashville	1796	34	16
Texas	TX	Austin	1845	2	2
Utah	UT	Salt Lake City	1896	11	34
Vermont	VT	Montpelier	1791	43	49
Virginia	VA	Richmond	1788	36	12
Virgin Islands	VI	Charlotte Amalie			
Washington	WA	Olympia	1889	20	15
West Virginia	WV	Charleston	1863	41	36
Wisconsin	WI	Madison	1848	26	18
Wyoming	WY	Cheyenne	1890	9	50

---

[1]Population rankings based on U.S. Census estimates for July 1999.

Branches of the Federal Government

EXECUTIVE BRANCH

President: elected to 4-year term, 2 terms maximum, annual salary (as of January 2001) $400,000

The Executive Office of the President, Cabinet (14 departments)
  <http://www.whitehouse.gov>

LEGISLATIVE BRANCH

Congress

House of Representatives (435 members): elected to 2-year terms, unlimited number of terms, annual salary for average members $141,300
<http://www.house.gov>

Senate (100 members): elected to 6-year terms, unlimited number of terms, annual salary $141,300 <http://www.senate.gov>

JUDICIAL BRANCH

U.S. Supreme Court: 9 members, lifetime appointments <http://www.supremecourtus.gov>

Chief Justice: annual salary $175,400

Associate justices: annual salary $167,900

Web Sites

FedStats <http://www.fedstats.gov>

FedWorld Information Network <http://www.fedworld.gov>

Internal Revenue Service <http://www.irs.gov>

Library of Congress <http://www.loc.gov>

National Archives <http://www.nara.gov>

Smithsonian <http://www.si.edu>

U.S. Postal Service <http://www.usps.gov>

Arts and Humanities

Major Art Museums

Art Institute of Chicago <http://www.artic.edu/>

Getty Museum, Los Angeles <http://www.getty.edu/museum>

Los Angeles County Museum of Art <http://www.lacma.org>

Metropolitan Museum, New York <http://www.metmuseum.org/>

Museum of Fine Arts, Boston <http://www.mfa.org/>

Museum of Modern Art, New York <http://www.moma.org>

National Gallery, Washington, DC <http://www.nga.gov/>

Common Musical Symbols, Notations, and Tempo Indications

o	whole note	♪	sixteenth note
♩	half note	▬	whole rest
♩	quarter note	—	half rest
♪	eighth note	‿	quarter rest

♪	eighth rest	*largo (grave)*	very slow
♬	sixteenth rest	*adagio*	slow
𝄞	treble (G) clef	*andante*	on the slow side
𝄢	bass (F) clef	*moderato*	moderate tempo
𝄡	viola (C) clef	*allegretto*	on the fast side
♯	sharp	*allegro*	fast
♭	flat	*molto allegro*	very fast
♮	natural	*presto*	very, very fast

Some Sacred Books

The Analects <http://www.powerup.com.au/~glt/library/confucius/framepage.htm>

The Avesta <http://www.avesta.org/avesta.html>

Bhagavad-Gita <http:www.bhagavadgita.org>

The Bible <http://www.bible.org>

The Book of Mormon <http://www.hti.umich.edu/relig/mormon>

The Dhammapada <http://www.ciolek.com/WWWVL-Buddhism.html>

The Holy Book of the Sikhs <http://www.sikhs.org/transl.htm>

Kitab-I-Aqdas <http://www.bahai.org>

The Qur'an <http://www.unn.ac.uk/socities/islamic/quran>

The Talmud (in Hebrew) <http://www.snunit.kiz.il/kodesh>
Another source on Judaism and Jewish resources: <http://shamash.org/trb/judaism.html#learning>

Tao Te Ching <http://www.human.toyogakuen-u.ac.jp/~acmuller/contao/laotzu.htm>

The Vedas <http://hindunet.org/scriptures>

Nobel Prize Winners in Literature since 1970 <www.nobel.se>

1970	Aleksandr I. Solzhenitsyn, U.S.S.R.
1971	Pablo Neruda, Chile
1972	Heinrich Böll, West Germany
1973	Patrick White, Australia
1974	Eyvind Johnson and Harry Edmund Martinson, Sweden
1975	Eugenio Montale, Italy
1976	Saul Bellow, United States
1977	Vicente Aleixandre, Spain

1978   Isaac Bashevis Singer, United States

1979   Odysseus Elytis, Greece

1980   Czeslaw Milosz, United States

1981   Elias Canetti, Bulgaria

1982   Gabriel García Márquez, Colombia

1983   William Golding, Britain

1984   Jaroslav Seifert, Czechoslovakia

1985   Claude Simon, France

1986   Wole Soyinka, Nigeria

1987   Joseph Brodsky, United States

1988   Naguib Mahfouz, Egypt

1989   Camilo José Cela, Spain

1990   Octavio Paz, Mexico

1991   Nadine Gordimer, South Africa

1992   Derek Walcott, Trinidad-Tobago

1993   Toni Morrison, United States

1994   Kenzaburo Oe, Japan

1995   Seamus Heaney, Ireland

1996   Wislawa Szymborska, Poland

1997   Dario Fo, Italy

1998   Jose Saramago, Portugal

1999   Günter Grass, Germany

Web Sites

ART

Art History Resources on the Net <http://witcombe.bcpw.sbc.edu /ARTHLinks.html>

History of Art Virtual Library <http://www.hart.bbk.ac/VirtualLibrary .html>

Virtual Library Museums Page <http://www.comlab.ox.ac.uk/archive /other/museums.html>

HISTORY

The History Net <http://www.theHistoryNet.com/>

History Sites by Time Period <http://www.tntech.edu/www/acad/hist /period.html>

History Sites by Subject <http://www.tntech.edu/www/acad/hist/subject.html>

World History Archives <http://www.hartford-hwp.com/archives/index.html>

LITERATURE

Literary Research Tools on the Net <http://andromeda.rutgers.edu/~jlynch/Lit/>

Literary Resources <http://www.lib.lsu.edu/hum/lit.html>

Resources in English Language and Literature <http://www.lib.cmich.edu/bibliographers/billmiles/english.htm>

The Voice of the Shuttle <http://vos.ucsd.edu>

LANGUAGES

French Resources <http://blair.library.rhodes.edu/ForLanghtmls/french.html>

German Resources <http://blair.library.rhodes.edu/ForLanghtmls/german.html>

Resources For Russian and Slavic Languages and Literature <http://www.library.vanderbilt.edu/central/russian.html#russia>

Romance Languages Resource Page <http://humanities.uchicago.edu/romance/resources/index.html>

MUSIC

Online Resources in Music <http://www.ruf.rice.edu/~brownlib/music/dbasesframes.html>

University of Maryland Music Resources <http://www.lib.umd.edu/UMCP/MUSIC/LINKS.HTM>

Worldwide Internet Music Resources <http://www.music.indiana.edu/music_resources>

Business and Finance

Index of Leading Economic Indicators

The index of leading economic indicators is a monthly composite, intended to predict future economic activity.

1. Average workweek of production workers in manufacturing
2. Average initial weekly claims for unemployment insurance
3. New orders for consumer goods and materials
4. Vendor performance

5. Contracts and orders for plant and equipment
6. New building permits issued
7. Change in manufacturers' unfilled orders
8. Change in sensitive materials prices
9. Index of stock prices
10. Money supply
11. Index of consumer expectations

Major American Stock Exchanges

AMEX (American Stock Exchange) <http://www.amex.com>

Nasdaq (National Association of Securities Dealers Automated Quotations) <http://www.nasdaq.com>

NYSE (New York Stock Exchange) <http://www.nyse.com>

Major Security Indexes

An index is a price-weighted average of selected securities.

Dow Jones Industrial Average (30 selected industrial firms) <http://averages.dowjones.com>

NASDAQ Composite <http://www.nasdaq.com>

NYSE Composite <http://stockcharts.com/education/glossary/NYSE Composite.html>

Standard & Poor's 500 (500 largest U.S. companies) <http://www.cftech .com/BrainBank/FINANCE/SandPIndexCalc.html>

Major Foreign Currencies

Argentina	peso	India	rupee (Re)
Britain	pound (£)	Italy	lira (L)
Canada	dollar ($)	Japan	yen (¥)
China	yuan	Mexico	peso ($)
European Community	euro (E)	Netherlands	guilder (Fl)
		Russia	ruble
France	franc (Fr)	South Africa	rand (R)
Germany	mark (DM)		

Web Sites

A Business Researcher's Interests <http://www.brint.com/interest.html>

Business Resource Center <http://www.morebusiness.com>

Campbell R. Harvey's Hypertextual Finance Glossary <http://www.duke.edu/~charvey/Classes/wpg/bfglosm.htm>

Federal Reserve Board <http://www.federalreserve.gov>

International Business Resources on the Net <http://ciber.bus.msu.edu>

SEC Edgar Database <http://www.sec.gov:80/edgarhp.html>

Webec <http://www.helsinki.fi/WebEc>

World Trade Organization <http://www.wto.org>

Mathematics/Weights and Measures

Common Symbols

π	pi (3.14159)	√	square root of
>	greater than	∪	union of two sets
<	less than	∩	intersection of two sets
≠	not equal to	∅	empty set
≈	approximately equal to	∞	infinity
∝	proportional to	∧	exponent
‖	parallel to	!	factorial
Σ	sum of	*f*	function
Δ	difference of	∫	integral

Useful Geometry Formulas

Circumference	$C = 2\pi r$
Area of a circle	$A = \pi r^2$
Area of a rectangle	$A = lw$
Area (surface) of a sphere	$A = 4\pi r^2$
Area of a square	$A = s^2$
Area of a triangle	$A = \frac{1}{2}bh$
Volume of a cone	$V = \pi r^2 h$
Volume of a cube	$V = s^3$
Volume of a cylinder	$V = \pi r^2 bh$
Volume of a pyramid	$V = hlw$
Volume of a sphere	$V = \left(\frac{4}{3}\right)\pi r^3$

VARIABLES

r	radius	*h*	height
s	side	*l*	length
b	base	*w*	width

Common Weights and Measures

LENGTH

English			Metric Equivalent	
		1 inch	=	2.54 centimeters
1 foot	=	12 inches	=	30.48 centimeters
1 yard	=	3 feet	=	.914 meter
1 fathom	=	6 feet		
1 rod	=	5.5 yards		
1 furlong	=	220 yards		
1 mile	=	1,760 yards	=	1.609 kilometers
1 nautical mile	=	1.152 miles		
1 league	=	3 miles		

AREA

English			Metric Equivalent	
		1 square inch	=	6.452 square centimeters
1 square foot	=	144 square inches	=	929.03 square centimeters
1 square yard	=	9 square feet	=	.836 square meter
1 square rod	=	30 square yards		
1 acre	=	160 square rods	=	.405 hectare
1 square mile	=	640 acres	=	2.59 square kilometers

WEIGHT

English			Metric Equivalent	
1 dram	=	27.344 grains		
1 ounce	=	16 drams	=	28.35 grams
1 pound	=	16 ounces	=	.4536 kilogram
1 ton	=	2,000 pounds	=	.907 metric ton
1 long ton	=	2,240 pounds		

VOLUME

English			Metric Equivalent	
		1 fluid ounce	=	29.574 milliliters
1 gill	=	4 fluid ounces		
1 liquid pint	=	16 fluid ounces	=	.473 liter
1 dry pint			=	.551 liter
1 liquid quart	=	2 liquid pints	=	.946 liter
1 gallon	=	4 liquid quarts	=	3.785 liters
1 dry quart	=	2 dry pints	=	1.101 liters
1 peck	=	8 dry quarts	=	8.810 liters
1 bushel	=	4 pecks	=	35.238 liters

◎ *Web Sites*

American Mathematical Society, Math on the Web <http://www.ams.org/mathweb/>

Math Archives Undergrads' Page <http://archives.math.utk.edu/undergraduates.html>

Mathematical Association of America <http://www.maa.org>

The Most Common Errors in Undergraduate Mathematics <http://math.vanderbilt.edu/~schectex/commerrs/>

NIST (National Institute of Standards and Technology) Virtual Library <http://nvl.nist.gov>

Science and Engineering

Common Units and Constants

NAME	SYMBOL	NAME	SYMBOL
ampere	A	kelvin	K
British thermal units	Btu	ohm	Ω
calorie	cal	unified mass unit	u
hertz	Hz	volt	V
joule	J	watt	W

Temperature Conversion — Celsius/Fahrenheit

$$°C = \frac{5}{9}\,(°F-32) \qquad °F = \frac{9°C}{5}+32$$

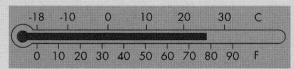

The freezing point of water is 0°C/32°F. The boiling point is 100°C/212°F.

Classifications of Organisms

	MODERN HUMANS
Kingdom	animals
Phylum	chordates
Class	mammals

MODERN HUMANS

Order	primates
Family	hominids
Genus	Homo
Species	sapiens

Earth's Geological Timeline

ERA	PERIOD	BEGAN (millions of years ago)
Cenozoic	Quaternary	1.6
(Age of Mammals)	Neogene	23.7
	Paleogene	66.4
Mesozoic	Cretaceous	144
(Age of Reptiles)	Jurassic	208
	Triassic	245
Paleozoic	Permian	286
	Carboniferous	360
	Devonian	408
	Silurian	438
	Ordovician	505
	Cambrian	570
Precambrian		~4600 (approximate formation of Earth)

Useful Astronomical Signs and Abbreviations

c	=	speed of light	=	186,282 miles/second
ly	=	light-year	=	5.88 trillion miles
pc	=	parsec	=	3.259 light-years
AU	=	astronomical unit (the mean distance between Earth and sun)	=	93 million miles
☌	=	conjunction (same longitude)		
□	=	quadrature (90° difference in longitude)		
△	=	trine (120° difference in longitude)		
☍	=	opposition (180° difference in longitude)		
☊	=	ascending node		
☋	=	descending node		

Planets and Solar System

Body (sign)	Average Diameter (miles)	Distance from Sun (AU)	Orbital Period (Earth years)	Surface Temperature (°F)
Sun (○)	865,120	—	—	+10,000
Mercury(☿)	3,030	0.387	0.241	+ 620
Venus(♀)	7,520	0.723	0.615	+ 900
Earth (⊕)	7,926	1.000	1.000	+ 70
Mars (♂)	4,217	1.524	1.881	− 67
Jupiter (♃)	88,724	5.203	11.86	− 166
Saturn (♄)	74,560	9.555	29.42	− 292
Uranus (♅)	31,600	19.22	83.75	− 360
Neptune (♆)	30,600	30.11	163.7	− 360
Pluto (♇)	1,860	39.54	248.0	− 369

◎ *Web Sites*

AIP Physics Information <http://www.aip.org>

Biochemnet <http://www.schmidel.com/bionet.htm>

Biosciences Index <http://mcb.harvard.edu/BioLinks.html>

CHEMINFO <http://www.indiana.edu/~cheminfo/cisindex.html>

Contemporary Physics Education Project <http://www.cpepweb.org>

ICE–Internet Connections for Engineering <http://www.englib.cornell.edu/ice/>

IEEE Spectrum <http://www.spectrum.ieee.org/>

National Institutes of Health <http://www.nih.gov/>

National Science Foundation: Biology <http://www.nsf.gov/home/bio/start.html>

Physics News <http://www.het.brown.edu/news/index.html>

Weill Cornell Medical Library <http://lib2.med.cornell.edu/>

WWW Virtual Library–Astronomy and Astrophysics <http://webhead.com/WWWVL/Astronomy>

WWW Virtual Library–Chemistry <http://www.chem.ucla.edu/chempointers.html>

WWW Virtual Library–Earth Science <http://vlib.org/EarthScience.html>

WWW Virtual Library–Engineering <http://www.eevl.ac.uk/wwwvl.html>

Social Sciences

Estimated U.S. population in April 2000: 274,667,839

Estimated population of the world in April 2000: 6,065,927,778

Gender percentages of U.S. population (projection for July 2001):
Female 51.1% (142,008,000); Male 48.8% (135,795,000)

Ten Largest American Cities

1998 population estimate, according to U.S. Census Bureau <http://www
.census.gov>

1.	New York	7,420,166
2.	Los Angeles	3,597,556
3.	Chicago	2,802,079
4.	Houston	1,786,691
5.	Philadelphia	1,436,287
6.	San Diego	1,220,666
7.	Phoenix	1,198,064
8.	San Antonio	1,114,130
9.	Dallas	1,075,894
10.	Detroit	970,196

Racial and Ethnic Makeup of the United States (projections for 2001)

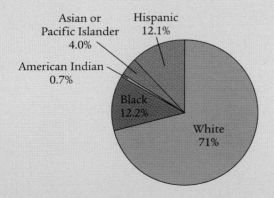

Asian or Pacific Islander 4.0%
Hispanic 12.1%
American Indian 0.7%
Black 12.2%
White 71%

(*Source:* U.S. Census Bureau)

◎ *Web Sites*

COMMUNICATION

Society of Professional Journalists <http://www.spj.org>

Links to Friendly Communications Homepages <http://www.csufresno .edu/speechcomm/wscalink.htm>

POLITICAL SCIENCE

Fedworld <http://www.fedworld.gov/>

Foreign Government Resources on the Web <http://www.lib.umich.edu /libhome/Documents.center/foreign.html>

The Gallup Organization <http://www.gallup.com>

Legal Information Institute <http://www.law.cornell.edu>

Political Science Virtual Library <http://spirit.lib.uconn.edu/PoliSci /polisci.htm>

Thomas: Legislative Information on the Internet <http://thomas.loc .gov>

UNESCO <http://www.unesco.org>

United Nations <http://www.un.org>

PSYCHOLOGY

American Psychological Association <http://www.apa.org/>

American Psychological Society <http://www.psychologicalscience .org>

Galaxy Psychology Page <http://galaxy.einet.net/galaxy/Social-Sciences /Psychology.html>

Internet Mental Health <http://www.mentalhealth.com/main.html>

SOCIOLOGY

Social Science Sites <http://www.tntech.edu/www/acad/hist/data.html>

A Sociological Tour through Cyberspace <http://www.trinity.edu /~mkearl/index.html>

The Socioweb <http://www.socioweb.com/~markbl/socioweb>

U.S. Census Bureau <www.census.gov>

Index

Acknowledgments

"College Binge Drinking" Web site. Courtesy Ohio State University students.

Emily Dickinson. Poems #435 and #1333. Reprinted by permission of the publishers and the Trustees of Amherst College from *The Poems of Emily Dickinson,* Ralph W. Franklin, ed., Cambridge, Mass.: The Belknap Press of Harvard University Press. Copyright © 1998 by the President and Fellows of Harvard College. Copyright © 1951, 1955, 1979 by the President and Fellows of Harvard College.

Dimensions Newsletter **front page.** Autumn Quarterly, 1999. Reprinted with permission from the African American Student Services.

"Eating Vegetarian" brochure. © ETR Associates. All Rights Reserved. Reprinted with permission from ETR Associates, Santa Cruz, CA. For information about this and other related materials, call 1-800-321-4407.

FACE/OFF movie still. With Nicholas Cage and John Travolta. Courtesy Photofest, Inc.

"film hero" as defined on the MLA International Bibliography online database. Reprinted by permission.

Robert Frost. Excerpt from "The Road Not Taken." From *The Poetry of Robert Frost.* © 1923, 1969 by Henry Holt & Company, Inc. Reprinted by permission of Henry Holt & Company, Inc.

D. Letticia Galindo. "Spanish-English Bilingualism and the Language Shift Process." (Figure 3) Originally titled "Bilingualism and Language Variation" by D. Letticia Galindo in *Language Variation in North American English.* Edited A. Wayne Glowka and Donald M. Lance. New York: MLA, 1993: 202. Reprinted by permission of the Modern Language Association of America.

June Jordan. Excerpt from "Aftermath" in *Naming Our Destiny.* Copyright © 1989 by June Jordan. Published by Thunder's Mouth Press. Reprinted by permission of the publisher.

Jewel Kilcher. Five lines from "Amen." © 1995 WB Music Corp. (ASCAP) & Wiggly Tooth Music (ASCAP). All Rights Administered by WB Music Corp. All Rights Reserved. Used by Permission. Warner Bros. Publications U.S. Inc., Miami, FL 33014.

Martin Luther King Jr. Excerpts from "Letter from Birmingham Jail" and "Our God Is Marching On." Reprinted by arrangement with The Heirs to the Estate of Martin Luther King Jr., c/o Writer's House, Inc. as agent for the proprietor. Copyright © 1963 by Martin Luther King Jr., copyright renewed 1991 by Coretta Scott King.

Michael I. Miller. "Word Choice by Race: Seesaw and Teeter-totter, Chicago 1986." (Table 1) Originally titled "How to Study Black Speech in Chicago" in *Language Variation in North American English,* edited by A. Wayne Glowka and Donald M. Lance. New York: MLA, 1993: 166. Reprinted by permission of the Modern Language Association of America.

Mary Pickford photo. Courtesy Photofest, Inc.

"Productivity and Wages-spiral spine" line graph. From *The New York Times,* January 2, 1996. Copyright © 1996 The New York Times. Reprinted by permission.

Bernard Weintraub. Quoting Steve Martin in "The Wiser Guy" article from *McCall's,* September 1999, p. 36. Reprinted with permission.

YAHOO! Screen shots. Reproduced with permission of Yahoo! Inc. © 1999 by Yahoo! Inc. YAHOO! and the YAHOO! Logo are trademarks of Yahoo! Inc.

Online Writing and Research Directory

For Multilingual Writers

Revision Symbols

abb	abbreviation *45a–g*		**//**	faulty parallelism *7e, 19*
ad	adjective/adverb *27*		**para**	paraphrase *12e, 12g, 13c*
agr	agreement *26, 29f*		**pass**	inappropriate passive *20c, 25g*
awk	awkward			
cap	capitalization *44*		**ref**	unclear pronoun reference *29g*
case	case *29a*			
cliché	cliché *8b, 35d*		**run-on**	run-on (fused) sentence *30*
co	coordination *18a*			
coh	coherence *7e, 21*		**sexist**	sexist language *29f, 33b*
com	incomplete comparison *17c*		**shift**	shift *20*
			slang	slang *35a*
concl	weak conclusion *7f, 13b*		**sp**	spelling *36*
cs	comma splice *30*		**sub**	subordination *18b*
d	diction *35*		**sum**	summarize *12e, 12g, 13c*
def	define *7c*		**t**	tone *8b, 12d, 35a, 35d*
dm	dangling modifier *28d*		**trans**	transition *7e, 23b*
doc	documentation *48–51, 52–53, 54, 55*		**u**	unity *7a, 21*
			vague	vague statement
emph	emphasis unclear *21*		**verb**	verb form *25a–d*
ex	example needed *7b–c*		**vt**	verb tense *25e–h*
frag	sentence fragment *31*		**wv**	weak verb *25*
fs	fused sentence *30*		**wrdy**	wordy *22*
hyph	hyphen *47*		**ww**	wrong word *8b, 35a–b*
inc	incomplete construction *17b–e*		**. ? !**	period, question mark, exclamation point *40*
intro	weak introduction *7e, 13b*		**,**	comma *38*
			;	semicolon *39*
it	italics (or underlining) *46*		**’**	apostrophe *41*
jarg	jargon *35a*		**“ ”**	quotation marks *42*
lc	lowercase letter *44*		**( ) [ ] —**	parentheses, brackets, dash *43a–c*
lv	language variety *34*			
mix	mixed construction *17a*		**: / …**	colon, slash, ellipsis *43d–f*
mm	misplaced modifier *28a*			
ms	manuscript form *15*		**∧**	insert
no ,	no comma *38j*		**∩**	transpose
num	number *45h–j*		**⌣**	close up
¶	paragraph *7*		**X**	obvious error

CONTENTS